# EVERYMAN'S LIBRARY
## EDITED BY ERNEST RHYS

## CLASSICAL

## THE DRAMAS OF SOPHOCLES IN ENGLISH VERSE. ❧ BY SIR GEORGE YOUNG, BART., M.A. LATE FELLOW TRINITY COLLEGE CAMBRIDGE

THE SAGES OF OLD LIVE AGAIN IN US

GLANVILL

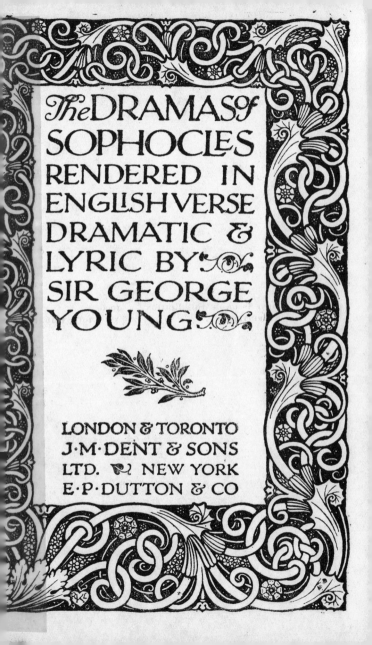

The DRAMAS of
SOPHOCLES
RENDERED IN
ENGLISH VERSE
DRAMATIC &
LYRIC BY
SIR GEORGE
YOUNG

LONDON & TORONTO
J·M·DENT & SONS
LTD. ❧ NEW YORK
E·P·DUTTON & CO

First Issue of this Edition . 1906
Reprinted . . . . . 1910, 1912, 1916, 1920

# CONTENTS

# INTRODUCTION

It is not proposed to detain the reader from Sophocles by any lengthened preface or criticism. It is assumed that those who desire to read or consult an English version of his plays will have had access to one or more of the many lives and introductions which have been produced by competent scholars. The scraps of incident recorded of his life, such as his leading the dance of triumph after Salamis, or his playing ball in the "Nausicaa," are of no more importance to the appreciation of his works than the parallel items in what is called the life of Shakspeare,—his holding horses at the theatre doors, or playing Adam in "As You Like It." If it is true that the Athenians appointed Sophocles with others a general of their army, to testify their admiration for his "Antigone," it gives us an idea—rather a poor one—of Athenian administration, but it does not tend to throw any fresh light upon the play. Much has been written, and well written, in English, of his philosophy and theodicy, of his moral and political views; but in such matters it ought rather to be the aim of a translator that the poet should be enabled to speak for himself.

A few remarks may be of service, to secure that the perusal of these pages shall not be approached with an eyesight, as it were, out of focus. Greek Drama, as Sophocles found it, was but emerging from a sort of chrysalis, a lyrical performance made up of song, ritual, and the dance; such as may be met with, to this day, by travellers, in remoter villages, among ruder races. The

Dionysiac Chorus, an ode or succession of odes, recited to measured steps, in figure, had somehow been brought to admit, with the progress of literary appreciation, the relief of personal human interest, in the form of speeches by way of interlude, in uniform metre and more or less in character, relating or representing some mythic incident. On such a tale the choric movements must have come to be strung, like beads upon a thread. A great step in advance must have been the introduction of dialogue; but in this, since no true dramatist had yet appeared to give life to the interchange of speech, a wrong course was unfortunately taken; the dull and irritating "stichomythia," or line and line alternation of remarks, survives as the most inartistic creation of all classic literature.

At the point at which it had now arrived the development of tragedy is illustrated by the appearance of a genius of the first order, the deep-thoughted Æschylus. The lapse of ages has not affected the interest with which readers have followed him in his broodings over the riddle of destiny, or diminished their appreciation of his sublimity as a lyric poet. Among playwrights he is the statuary in whose workshop are hewn out gods, Titans, and heroic men and women, effigies possessed of speech and almost of life, but practically incapable of action. After him the time was ripe for the consummate dramatic artist, who appears in Sophocles. His earliest innovations were revolutionary. The Chorus shrinks into an interlude; the recitative of Æschylus starts into life as drama; the Æschylean personages, with their sonorous ventriloquism, give place to flesh and blood. Sophocles is the inventor of plot; he is the first efficient organizer of dramatic action and incident; he is—last and greatest of his merits—the creator of character. To him first it was given to sound the depths and explore the shoals of human nature. His personages are real men and women, if on the heroic scale; the good are faulty, the bad are not without excuse; their acts are accounted for by adequate motives; they do their own talking. Sophocles may delight in the conflict of laws; he is powerfully attracted by the ironies of fortune; he revels in the half-sword parley of high hearts at variance; the forensic dialogue, if he cannot cure it of formality, he can at least modify and inspire with passion. Yet all these are but as the warp, on which his glancing shuttle weaves the web of portraiture. In this field he encounters no rivalry from Æschylus, and leaves Euripides behind.

Of his Choruses, forty-seven or forty-eight in all, about twenty are composite pieces, divided between the lyric and histrionic performers, and contributing, however slightly, to the action of the play. The remainder are self-contained poems, hardly any of them unworthy of inclusion in an anthology of the best Greek lyrics. Although in his highest flights as a lyrist he is surpassed by Æschylus, and perhaps equalled by Euripides, he holds his place among the greater singers, by virtue of his easy mastership in many moods, of his beautiful word-craft, and of his reverential access, as it were with unshod feet, to the deeper sources of emotion. The most noticeable blemish of his verse is an occasional tautology. His sparing use of adjectives is a feature in his diction which has not received adequate notice from commentators, and has been strangely disregarded by translators; he never indulges in an otiose epithet. His strophes and epodes are stanzas, not rhapsodies. In them, perhaps first of lyrics, is to be found the charm of melody as heightened by contrast. When rightly divided, the lines sing of themselves; their cadence is sufficient to shew, for the most part, how they must have been pronounced; their music, as it strikes the ear, puts to flight the horrid nightmares of the Byzantine accentuation, and of the Romaic etacism.

His backgrounds are the sunlight, the sea, the mountains, and the cultivated surface of the earth; he loved them well, and speaks of them nobly. His material is the Attic tongue at its climax of perfection, the most flexible and sonorous of languages. His style is such as it is difficult to qualify, except in a simile; it may be said to resemble Ionian drapery, faultless alike where it clothes, and where it reveals; but better suited to dignified movement than to violent action, and perhaps most beautiful in complete repose.

For the present version it may be claimed that it was first undertaken, now forty years ago, for pleasure, and has been executed with pains. The writer has been on his guard throughout against the common practice of making careful versions of favourite passages, and filling up the intervals with a hastily written sketch. Where the verse of Sophocles is least poetical, the purport is often dramatically most interesting. Where the dramatic interest begins to flag, the chances are that he supplies a new source of interest, in his rapid and glowing rhetoric. It is hard on the whole to say whether his more or his less obviously important passages demand the greater care in a translator, or better repay his labour. For this second issue of the work the whole has been once more thoroughly revised, in the light of various friendly criticisms which it received on its first appearance. As before, all the modern translations have been examined; but hardly anything has been borrowed from any of them. The hope of the writer is that at worst his version may be found more readable, while not less faithful to the original, than any other.

Questions of text are not often of importance to a translator. Accordingly that of Dindorf has been adopted (Oxford, 1st ed. 1847, 2nd ed. 1849, *Poetæ Scenici Græci*, 1851), as the text most widely circulated in England; the

places where a different reading has been preferred being
duly indicated in the notes, as also the very few passages
in which a suggestion is hazarded which has in it anything
of originality. The writer must disclaim, on his own
account, all title to sit as judge in matters of scholarship;
in cases of difficulty he takes shelter under authority; and
where authorities differ, he prefers to follow those considered
the highest, rather than to trust his own unaided sentiment.
In this connexion the recent edition of his friend and
correspondent, the late Sir Richard Jebb, must not pass
unmentioned. Appearing as it did after this version had
been completed, there is no debt to be acknowledged to it
for inspiration, but there is for correction. In the majority
of places where Jebb has given a new interpretation, or
advocated one different from that first followed, his rendering has now been adopted. His mastery of the language,
his unequalled power of exposition, his store of illustrative
learning, and his unfailing good sense, might well have
justified acceptance of his verdicts in the block; but there
are some places where between two courses it is open to
take either the one or the other, and a few in which liberty
has been claimed to differ from his conclusions.

In the work of translation the procedure followed has
been, first of all, to take into account the entire purport
and value of the passage in hand, including both sound
and sentiment, as well as the notions to be conveyed; and
next in order, to consider if there are any particular words
for which it is desirable to give a separate equivalent; in
the third place would stand to be considered the order of
the words, often of importance hardly inferior to that of the
words themselves; and in the last place, and first of all
to be sacrificed, where sacrifice is necessary, the syntax.
In laying down this last as a canon of translation, it
becomes necessary to guard against misunderstanding.
In arriving at a full comprehension of the original, the

writer claims to have paid as much attention as any to the niceties of grammatical construction. But he conceives it to be the duty of a verse-translator, when he comes to the stage of reproduction, to postpone grammatical form to expressional value, and to seek rather the best English rendering of the latter, than the English phrase most nearly correspondent to the former.

The verse translation so produced enters into no competition with the version in prose, frequently lapsing into verse, of Sir R. Jebb; which is unsurpassable for purposes of study side by side with the Greek, by those who are learning the language, but can hardly rank, and was never put forward by its author, as English literature. Neither, on the other hand, does it belong to that class of so-called translations, which are really re-writings of the original, not as the author wrote, but as the translator would have written. In Professor Gilbert Murray's preface to his brilliant Euripidean studies he has given an interesting account of the different procedure he followed. A less successful attempt of the same kind was made on Sophocles by Edward Fitzgerald. For himself the present writer much prefers Mr. Murray to Euripides, and Fitzgerald to all that he can gather (by means of a faithful translation) of Omar Khayyam. But Sophocles is not as Euripides, or as Omar; and he who would improve upon the diction of Sophocles should beware of Nemesis.

On some minor points a word of vindication seems called for, though not so urgently now as would have been the case twenty years ago, in view of certain fashions or fancies of the present day, or of yesterday. It may perhaps be taken for granted that, although the best of translations can hardly be mistaken for an English original, whether ancient or modern, yet none the less must every translation into English be recognizable above all things as English work. To this end, it is submitted, the classic forms of English literature should be observed. It is not for a translator to innovate in metre, either out of caprice, or with the vain idea of reproducing the lilt of the original. In this light English archaism is a dangerous indulgence; but the occasional use of "thou" for "you," and the corresponding verb-forms, may perhaps be excused in work which cannot but look for precedent to the Elizabethan dramatists. Proper names should surely be given in their English dresses; the Greek diphthongs, the *u* for *y*, the *k* for *c*, and the termination in -*os* being still as exotic in an English book as when they were first imported from Germany. Aias and Poluneikēs, in Roman type, are not so much Greek, as queer; while such fantastic combinations of letters as Klutaimnēstra and Oidipous and Laïos stand, if for anything, for sounds not so near to the most probable authentic pronunciation of the names as are the more popular forms in common use among ourselves. Latin correlatives have not been used for the designations of Greek deities; but English forms like "Proserpine," and "Jove" for the unmanageable "Zeus," have not been altogether excluded. The full liberty of a writer of English has been asserted in dealing with proper names, especially in throwing back the accent (as in Spérchius, Párnasus, etc.), thereby following the historical tradition of the English language. In all such matters English rather than Greek rule is to be observed. It is better to do as Shakspeare or Dryden did before us, than to disfigure our pages with exotic spelling, or to spoil our English accent out of deference to Greek quantity. Graecisms, and vulgarisms, and quaintnesses of all sorts, are alike condemnable; hard as it is to eliminate them altogether. Why, again, should a translator bind himself to render continuous verse into exactly the same number of lines as in the original? At least eleven English decasyllables, containing a smaller number of syllables than ten iambic trimeters, are generally

necessary to convey their purport, unless an undue number
of monosyllables is employed. Why should speeches in
English not begin or end in the middle of a line? The
Greek limitation in this respect was in part broken down
by Sophocles himself; it has no intrinsic beauty, and is
alien to the English metre. To break up the single-line
dialogue is often desirable; its stiffness, as above said, is a
blemish in the original, not a beauty; and Sophocles seems
to chafe at it, and to desire to vary it. Why then insist
superstitiously upon keeping it, at the cost of omissions,
harsh inversions, and a grammar that is crude, if not
canine?

Poetry should always be rendered by poetry; beauty
must be given to the transcript of a passage which in the
original produces the effect of beauty. Moreover, so far
as the forms of our language and the genius of our literature
will allow, this beauty must be, not a substitute, but the
same that was intended. Imagery and pathos must be
carefully treasured; the pace at which the original moves
must be observed; strong words, repetitions, and surprises
must be noted; a studied order in the sentence, or even
an intentional bathos in expression, if it have a dramatic
value, must on no account be ignored. That theory of
compensation, which prompts a translator to impart ornament either of his own invention, or inspired by modern
literature, to make up for beauty of the original which
has been missed, is to be utterly repudiated. There is
no play extant of Sophocles which has not its purple
passages, and many of the fragments are flawless gems.
On the other hand, there are a very few places in which
some softening of the literal expression is necessary, to
avoid offence.

If to be offensive is high treason in the translator, to be
prosy is petty treason. All the same, he should not be
scared out of fidelity by the fear of not being poetical

enough. He will find it impossible to satisfy the many, intoxicated with the beauties of romanticism, and accustomed to look for colour or other verbal decoration in every page, almost in every line of verse. Yet the truly Sophoclean beauties of English literature—Pericles mourning over Thaisa, Artevelde rebuking the Envoys—have not lost their charm. The closer he keeps to his text, the better the chance he will have of touching, here and there, one of those deeper notes which thrill the heart, as it were, with poetical magic.

For purposes of revision it has been found necessary that the manuscript should be put away for a time, and then taken up afresh. It would be possible, in the case of an author like Sophocles, to go on for a hundred years revising, say once in every ten years, and each time getting nearer to an adequate representation. But a day must come when the heap of filings is small, in comparison with the labour expended. It is then time either to publish the result, or to put it on the fire. There are those who advise, in all cases, the latter course, arguing that no poetic translation from the classics can as a literary work have any title to exist. Of this doctrine the achievements of both the greater and lesser masters in the art, of Pope and Shelley, as of Calverley and Conington, supply a sufficient refutation. In the same spirit did a great art critic once advise us to commit to the flames all our best line-engravings from the paintings of Rafaelle and Coreggio. These are rhetorical enhancements of a good argument, the argument that reproductive or imitative art has not the same value—has not even the same sort of value—as original work. The fallacy becomes obvious, if the argument is applied, as it should be in consistency, to the part of the performer in music, or of the actor in drama. Even in sculpture the last stage in the process of production is largely imitative.

Poetical translation, indeed, may be compared in many respects to the copying by a carver of an antique. Before him stands the immortal original, cast as it were in imperishable bronze; but the secret of the material is lost, and the mould is broken. The translator brings his modern language, exquisite in refinement, but deficient in plasticity. He places his marble by the side of the metal, and searches for the statue hidden in the stone. The earlier stages of his work are easy; freely he hews at the mass, guiding his chisel by the eye or pointer,—trusting to the mechanical accuracy of his scholarship, or to the first impressions of his poetic faculty. Many carry their work no further forward than this stage. Soon, however, the true craftsman is seen to hold his hand; he falls to comparing and measuring, to experimenting, and again correcting. Sometimes he cuts too deep—the result is bald and mean. Sometimes, in striving to be literal, he has lost the spirit,— he finds his material inadequate or traitorous, too scant of imminent shadow, or too absorbent of relieving light. Sometimes, again, he is tempted to chase, as it were, the drapery of his figure with modern ornament, beautiful, it may be, in itself, or acceptable for its association's sake; but on second thought to be discarded and condemned, as repugnant to the style and features of the model. The moments are rare when, in happier mood, he seems to attain to something of inspiration; when the verse becomes ductile, moulded to the shape and informed with the sentiment of the original; when he is able to say with confidence, "So might my author have expressed himself, if English, not Greek, had been his vehicle." When all is done there will remain only an outline, a faint adumbration, of what was embodied by the master. Yet in spite of shortcomings to the loyal workman there will come a conviction that his labour was not wasted. Through his means some home-keeping lovers of ideal beauty may discern, as Keats did, beyond the ages, those charmful graces which first prompted his endeavour. By the help of the copy which he places in their chamber some, whose ranging days are over, may be assisted to recall the lineaments of the masterpiece which they visited in youth across the sea.

# SELECT BIBLIOGRAPHY

## SOPHOCLES: GREEK TEXT.

Brunck, 1758, 1786, 1788, etc.; Erfurt, 1819, 1820, 1830; Hermann, 1823-1830; Elmsley, 1826; Dindorf, 1832, 1844, 1847, 1849, 1851, 1856; Mitchell, 1841-4; Wunder, 1841-6; Linwood, 1846, 1852, 1877; Blaydes and Paley, 1859, 1880; Campbell, 1871, 1881; R. C. Jebb, 1883-1896, 1897; Schneidewin (Nauck), 1880; Wecklein, 1875-1880; Facsimile of the Laurentian MSS., 1885.

## VERSE TRANSLATIONS.
### a. Complete.

T. Francklin, 1759, 1809, 1832, 1886 (H. Morley's ed.); Potter, 1788, 1808; Dale, 1824; Plumptre, 1865, 1867, 1902 (with select fragments); Whitelaw, 1883, 1897; Campbell, 1873-1883, 1896; Young, 1888 (with the fragments).

### b. Separate Plays.

"Antigone," Donaldson, 1848; Phillimore, 1902; Weld, 1905.

"Ajax," Theobald, 1714; Burges, 1849; D'Arcy Thompson (with select fragments), 1862.

"Electra," Wase, 1649; Theobald, 1714, 1780.

"Œdipus Tyrannus," Theobald, 1715; Maurice, 1779; Doyle, 1849; Kennedy, 1882; Morshead, 1885; Conybeare (with songs for Stanford's music by Verrall), 1887; Young, 1887; Phillimore, 1902.

"Œdipus Coloneus," Auchmuty, 1894; Pember, 1899; Phillimore, 1902.

\* \* \*

The separate issue of the prose translation, by Jebb, 1904, may also be mentioned.

Be his
My special thanks, whose even-balanced soul
From first youth tested up to extreme old age
Business could not make dull, nor passion wild;
Who saw life steadily, and saw it whole;
The mellow glory of the Attic stage,
Singer of sweet Colonos, and its child.

MATTHEW ARNOLD.

# SOPHOCLES

## ANTIGONE

### PERSONS REPRESENTED

ANTIGONE, } *daughters of Œdipus, late king of Thebes.*
ISMENE,

CREON, *brother to Jocasta, late queen of Thebes, Captain-general of the army, and successor to the throne.*

A *Sentinel.*

HÆMON, *son to Creon, betrothed to Antigone.*

TIRESIAS, *a seer.*

A *Messenger in attendance on Creon.*

EURYDICE, *wife to Creon.*

The CHORUS *is composed of Senators of Thebes.*

*Guards ; Attendants ; a Boy leading Tiresias.*

---

*Scene, before the Royal Palace at Thebes.   Time, early morning.   Enter* ANTIGONE *and* ISMENE.

*Antigone.*  Ismene, dear in very sisterhood,[1]
      Do you perceive how Heaven upon us two
      Means to fulfil, before we come to die,
      Out of all ills that grow from Œdipus—
      What not, indeed?[2] for there's no sorrow or harm,[3]
      No circumstance of scandal or of shame
      I have not seen, among your griefs, and mine.
      And now again, what is this word they say
      Our Captain-general proclaimed but now
      To the whole city?   Did you hear and heed?
      Or are you blind, while pains of enemies
      Are passing on your friends?

*Ismene.*                              Antigone,
      To me no tidings about friends are come,
      Pleasant or grievous, ever since we two

Of our two brothers were bereft, who died
Both in one day, each by the other's hand.
And since the Argive host in this same night
Took itself hence, I have heard nothing else,
To make me happier, or more miserable.

*Antigone.* I knew as much ; and for that reason made you
Go out of doors—to tell you privately.

*Ismene.* What is it ? I see you have some mystery.

*Antigone.* What ! has not Creon to the tomb preferred
One of our brothers, and with contumely
Withheld it from the other ? Eteocles [4]
Duly, they say, even as by law was due,
He hid beneath the earth, rendering him honour
Among the dead below; but the dead body
Of Polynices, miserably slain,
They say it has been given out publicly
None may bewail, none bury, all must leave
Unwept, unsepulchred, a dainty prize
For fowl that watch, gloating upon their prey !
This is the matter he has had proclaimed—
Excellent Creon ! [5] for your heed, they say,
And mine, I tell you—mine ! and he moves hither,
Meaning to announce it plainly in the ears
Of such as do not know it, and to declare
It is no matter of small moment ; he
Who does any of these things shall surely die ;
The citizens shall stone him in the streets.
So stands the case. Now you will quickly show
If you are worthy of your birth or no.

*Ismene.* But O rash heart, what good, if it be thus,
Could I effect, helping or hindering ?

*Antigone.* Look, will you join me ? will you work with me ?

*Ismene.* In what attempt ? What mean you ?

*Antigone.*                     Help me lift
The body up—

*Ismene.*            What, would you bury him ?
Against the proclamation ?

*Antigone.*            My own brother
And yours I will ! If you will not, I will ;
I shall not prove disloyal. [6]

*Ismene.*            You are mad !
When Creon has forbidden it ?

*Antigone.*                                  From mine own
    He has no right to stay me.

*Ismene.*                                    Alas, O sister,
    Think how our father perished! self-convict—
    Abhorred—dishonoured—blind—his eyes put out
    By his own hand! How she who was at once
    His wife and mother with a knotted noose
    Laid violent hands on her own life! And how
    Our two unhappy brothers in one day
    Each on his own head by the other's hand
    Wrought common ruin! We now left alone—
    Do but consider how most miserably
    We too shall perish, if despite of law
    We traverse the behest or power of kings.
    We must remember we are women born,
    Unapt to cope with men; and, being ruled
    By mightier than ourselves, we have to hear
    These things—and worse. For my part, I will ask
    Pardon of those beneath, for what perforce
    I needs must do, but yield obedience
    To them that walk in power; to exceed
    Is madness, and not wisdom.

*Antigone.*                                  Then in future
    I will not bid you help me; nor henceforth,
    Though you desire, shall you, with my good will,
    Share what I do. Be what seems right to you;
    Him will I bury. Death, so met, were honour;
    And for that capital crime of piety,
    Loving and loved, I will lie by his side.
    Far longer is there need I satisfy
    Those nether Powers, than powers on earth; for
       there
    For ever must I lie. You, if you will,
    Hold up to scorn what is approved of Heaven!

*Ismene.* I am not one to cover things with scorn;
    But I was born too feeble to contend
    Against the state.

*Antigone.*                         Yes, you can put that forward;
    But I will go and heap a burial mound
    Over my most dear brother.

*Ismene.*                                    My poor sister,
    How beyond measure do I fear for you!

*Antigone.* Do not spend fear on me.  Shape your own
          course.

*Ismene.* At least announce it, then, to nobody,
          But keep it close, as I will.

*Antigone.*                          Tell it, tell it!
          You'll cross me worse, by far, if you keep silence—
          Not publish it to all.

*Ismene.*                    Your heart beats hotly
          For chilling work!

*Antigone.*              I know that those approve
          Whom I most need to please.

*Ismene.*                        If you could do it!
          But you desire impossibilities.

*Antigone.* Well, when I find I have no power to stir,
          I will cease trying.

*Ismene.*                  But things impossible
          'Tis wrong to attempt at all.

*Antigone.*                      If you will say it,
          I shall detest you soon; and you will justly
          Incur the dead man's hatred.   Suffer me
          And my unwisdom to endure the weight
          Of what is threatened.   I shall meet with nothing
          More grievous, at the worst, than death, with honour.

*Ismene.* Then go, if you will have it : and take this with you,
          You go on a fool's errand !          [*Exit* ANTIGONE.
                              Lover true
          To your beloved, none the less, are you !          [*Exit*


          *Enter* THEBAN SENATORS, *as Chorus.*

                    CHORUS.

                    I. I.

          Sunbeam bright !   Thou fairest ray
            That ever dawned on Theban eyes
              Over the portals seven !
          O orb of aureate day,
            How glorious didst thou rise
              O'er Dirca's streams, shining from heaven,
          Him, the man with shield of white
          Who came from Argos [7] in armour dight
          Hurrying runagate o'er the plain,
          Jerking harder his bridle rein ;

Who by Polynices' quarrellous broil
Stirred up in arms to invade our soil
   With strident cries as an eagle flies
  Swooped down on the fields before him,
'Neath cover of eagle pinion white
As drifted snow, a buckler bright
    On many a breast, and a horsetail crest
From each helm floating o'er him.

### I. 2.

Yawning with many a blood-stained spear
   Around our seven-gated town
    High o'er the roofs he stood ;
Then, or ever a torch could sear
   With flames the rampart-crown—
    Or ever his jaws were filled with blood
Of us and ours, lo, he was fled !
Such clatter of war behind him spread,
Stress too sore for his utmost might
Matched with the Dragon in the fight ;[8]
For Zeus abhors tongue-glorious boasts ;
And straightway as he beheld their hosts,
Where on they rolled, covered with gold,
   Streaming in mighty eddy,
Scornfully with a missile flame
He struck down Capaneus,[9] as he came
Uplifting high his victory-cry
   At the topmost goal already.

### II. 1.

Tantalus-like[10] aloft he hung, then fell ;
   Earth at his fall resounded ;
Even as, maddened by the Bacchic spell,
   On with torch in hand he bounded,
    Breathing blasts of hate.
So the stroke was turned aside,
   Mighty Ares rudely dealing
Others elsewhere, far and wide,
   Like a right-hand courser wheeling
    Round the goals of fate.

For captains seven at portals seven
Found each his match in the combat even,

And left on the field both sword and shield
　　As a trophy to Zeus, who o'erthrew them;
Save the wretched twain, who against each other
Though born of one father, and one mother,
Laid lances at aim—to their own death came,
　　And the common fate that slew them.

### II. 2.

But now loud Victory returns at last
　　On Theban chariots smiling,
Let us begin oblivion of the past,
　　　Memories of the late war beguiling
　　　　Into slumber sound.
　　Seek we every holy shrine;
　　　There begin the night-long chorus;
　　Let the Theban Boy divine,
　　　Bacchus, lead the way before us,
　　　　Shaking all the ground.

Leave we the song: the King is here;
Creon, Menœceus' son, draws near;
To the function strange—like the heaven-sent change
　　Which has raised him newly to power:
What counsel urging—what ends of state,
That he summons us to deliberate,
The elders all, by his herald's call,
　　At a strange unwonted hour?

*Enter* CREON, *attended.*

*Creon.* Sirs, for the ship of state—-the Gods once more,
　　After much rocking on a stormy surge,
　　Set her on even keel.　Now therefore you,
　　You of all others, by my summoners
　　I bade come hither; having found you first
　　Right loyal ever to the kingly power
　　In Laius' time; and next, while Œdipus
　　Ordered the commonwealth; and since his fall,
　　With steadfast purposes abiding still,
　　Circling their progeny.　Now, since they perished,
　　Both on one day, slain by a two-edged fate,
　　Striking and stricken, sullied with a stain
　　Of mutual fratricide, I, as you know,

In right of kinship nearest to the dead,
Possess the throne and take the supreme power.
Howbeit it is impossible to know [11]
The spirit of any man, purpose or will,
Before it be displayed by exercise
In government and laws.   To me, I say,
Now as of old, that pilot of the state
Who sets no hand to the best policy,
But remains tongue-tied through some terror, seems
Vilest of men.   Him too, who sets a friend
Before his native land, I prize at nothing.
God, who seest all things always, witness it !
If I perceive, where safety should have been,
Mischief advancing toward my citizens,
I will not sit in silence ; nor account
As friend to me the country's enemy ;
But thus I deem : she is our ark of safety ;
And friends are made then only, when, embarked
Upon her deck, we ride the seas upright.
Such are the laws by which I mean to further
This city's welfare ; and akin to these
I have given orders to the citizens
Touching the sons of Œdipus.   Eteocles,
Who in this city's quarrel fought and fell,
The foremost of our champions in the fray,
They should entomb with the full sanctity
Of rites that solemnize the downward road
Of their dead greatest.   Him the while, his brother,
That Polynices who, returning home
A banished man, sought to lay waste with fire
His household Gods, his native country—sought
To glut himself with his own kindred's blood,
Or carry them away to slavery,
It has been promulgated to the city
No man shall bury, none should wail for him ;
Unsepulchred, shamed in the eyes of men,
His body shall be left to be devoured
By dogs and fowls of the air.   Such is my will.
Never with me shall wicked men usurp
The honours of the righteous ; but whoe'er
Is friendly to this city shall, by me,
Living or dead, be honoured equally.

1 *Senator.* Creon Menœceus' son, we hear your pleasure
    Both on this city's friend, and on her foe;
    It is your sovereignty's prerogative
    To pass with absolute freedom on the dead,
    And us, who have survived them.

*Creon.*          Please to see
    What has been said performed.

1 *Senator.*       That charge confer
    On some one who is younger.

*Creon.*         Of the body?
    Sentries are set, already.

1 *Senator.*       Then what else
    Is there, besides, which you would lay on us?

*Creon.* Not to connive at disobedience.

1 *Senator.* There's no such fool as to embrace his death.

*Creon.* Death is the penalty.   But men right often
    Are brought to ruin, through their dreams of gain.

*Enter a Sentinel.*

*Sentinel.* My lord, I will not say—" breathless with
    speed
    I come, plying a nimble foot;" for truly
    I had a many sticking-points of thought,
    Wheeling about to march upon my rear.
    For my heart whispered me all sorts of counsel;
    " Poor wretch, why go, to meet thy sentence?"—
      " Wretch,
    Tarrying again?   If [12] Creon hear the news
    From others' lips, how shalt thou then not rue it?"
    Out of this whirligig it came to pass
    I hastened[13]—at my leisure; a short road,
    Thus, becomes long.   Nevertheless at last
    It won the day to come hither, to your presence;
    And speak I will, though nothing have to say;
    For I come clinging[14] to the hope that I
    Can suffer nothing—save my destiny.

*Creon.* Well—and what caused you this disheartenment?

*Sentinel.* First let me tell you what concerns myself.
    I do protest, I neither did the deed,
    Nor saw it done, whoever 'twas who did it;
    Nor should I rightly come to any harm.

*Creon.* At all events you are a good tactician,

And fence the matter off all round. But clearly
You have some strange thing to tell?

*Sentinel.*                    Yes. Serious tidings
Induce much hesitation.

*Creon.*                  Once for all
Please to speak out, and make an end, and go.

*Sentinel.* Why, I am telling you. That body some one
Has just now buried—sprinkled thirsty dust
Over the form—added the proper rites,
And has gone off.

*Creon.*            What say you? What man dared
To do it?

*Sentinel.*        I know not. There was no dint there
Of any mattock, not a sod was turned;
Merely hard ground and bare, without a break,
Without a rut from wheels; it was some workman
Who left no mark. When the first day-sentry
Shewed what had happened, we were all dismayed.
The body had vanished; not indeed interred,
But a light dust lay on it, as if poured out
By one who shunned the curse; and there appeared
No trace that a wild beast, or any hound,
Had come, or torn the carcase. Angry words
Were bandied up and down, guard blaming guard,
And blows had like to end it, none being by
To hinder; for each one of us in turn
Stood culprit, none convicted, but the plea
"I know not"[15] passed. Ready were we to take
Hot iron in hand, or pass through fire, and call
The Gods to witness, that we neither did it,
Nor were accessory to any man
Who compassed it, or did it. So at last,
When all our searching proved to be in vain,
There speaks up one, who made us, every man,
Hang down our heads for fear, knowing no way
To say him nay, or without scathe comply,
His burden was, this business must be carried
To you, without reserve. That voice prevailed;
And me, poor wretch, the lot condemns to get
This piece of luck. I come a post unwilling,
I well believe it, to unwilling ears;
None love the messenger who brings bad news.

1 *Senator.*  My lord, my heart misgave me from the first
            This must be something more than natural.
*Creon.*  Truce to your speech, before I choke with rage,
        Lest you be found at once grey-beard and fool!
        To say that guardian deities would care
        For this dead body, is intolerable.
        Could they, by way of supereminent honour
        Paid to a benefactor, give him burial,
        Who came to fire their land, their pillared fanes
        And sacred treasures, and set laws at nought?
        Or do you see Gods honouring the bad?
        'Tis false.   These orders from the first some people
        Hardly accepted, murmuring at me,
        Shaking their heads in secret, stiffening
        Uneasy necks against this yoke of mine.
        They have suborned these sentinels to do it,
        I know that well.   No such ill currency
        Ever appeared, as money to mankind:
        This is it that sacks cities, this routs out
        Men from their homes, and trains and turns astray
        The minds of honest mortals, setting them
        Upon base actions; this made plain to men
        Habits of all misdoing, and cognizance
        Of every work of wickedness.   Howbeit
        Such hireling perpetrators, in the end,
        Have wrought so far, that they shall pay for it.
        So surely as I live to worship Jove,
        Know this for truth; I swear it in your ears;
        Except you find and bring before my face
        The real actor in this funeral,
        Death, by itself, shall not suffice for you,
        Before, hung up alive, you have revealed
        The secret of this outrage; that henceforth
        You may seek plunder—not without respect
        Of where your profit lies; and may be taught
        It is not good to covet all men's pay;
        For mark you! by corruption few men thrive,
        And many come to mischief.
*Sentinel.*                               Have I leave
        To say a word, or shall I turn and go?
*Creon.*  Cannot you see your prating tortures me?
*Sentinel.*  Pricks you how deep?   In the ears, or to the spleen?

*Creon.* Why do you gauge my chafing, where it lies?

*Sentinel.* Your heart-ache were the doer's, your ear-ache
        mine.

*Creon.* Out, what a bare-faced babbler [16] born art thou!

*Sentinel.* Never the actor in this business, though!

*Creon.* Yes, and for money you would sell your soul!

*Sentinel.* Plague on it! 'tis hard, a man should be suspicious,
    And with a false suspicion!

*Creon.*                Yes, suspicion;
    Mince it as best you may. Make me to know
    Whose are these doings, or you shall soon allow
    Left-handed gains work their own punishment.

                               [*Exit.*

*Sentinel.* I wish he may be found. Chance must decide.
    Whether or no, you will not, certainly,
    See me returning hither. Heaven be praised
    I am in safety, past all thought or dream!    [*Exit.*

## CHORUS.

### I. 1.

Much is there passing strange;
   Nothing surpassing mankind.
He it is loves to range
Over the ocean hoar,
Thorough the surges' roar,
   South winds raging behind;

Earth, too, wears he away,
   The Mother of Gods on high,
Tireless, free from decay;
With team he furrows the ground,
And the ploughs go round and round,
   As year on year goes by.

### I. 2.

The bird-tribes, light of mind,
   The races of beasts of prey,
And sea-fish after their kind,
Man, abounding in wiles,
Entangles in his toils
   And carries captive away.

The roamers over the hill,
　　The field-inhabiting deer,
By craft he conquers, at will;
He bends beneath his yoke
The neck of the steed unbroke,
　　And pride of the upland steer.

### II. 1.

He has gotten him speech, and fancy breeze-betost,
　　And for the state instinct of order meet;
He has found him shelter from the chilling frost
　　Of a clear sky, and from the arrowy sleet;
Illimitable in cunning, cunning-less
　　He meets no change of fortune that can come;
He has found escape from pain and helplessness;
　　Only he knows no refuge from the tomb.

### II. 2.

Now bends he to the good, now to the ill,
　　With craft of art, subtle past reach of sight;
Wresting his country's laws to his own will,
　　Spurning the sanctions of celestial right;
High in the city, he is made city-less,
　　Whoso is corrupt, for his impiety;
He that will work the works of wickedness,
　　Let him not house, let him not hold, with me!

At this monstrous vision I stand in
Doubt! How dare I say, well knowing her,
That this maid is not—Antigone!
　　Daughter of Œdipus!
Hapless child, of a hapless father!
Sure—ah surely they did not find thee
Madly defying our king's commandments,
　　And so prisoner bring thee here?

*Enter Sentinel with* ANTIGONE.

*Sentinel.* This is the woman who has done the deed.
　　We took her burying him. Where's Creon?
1 *Senator.* 　　　　　　　　　　　　　　　　Here
　　Comes he again, out of the house, at need.

*Enter* CREON.

*Creon.* What is it? In what fit season come I forth?

*Sentinel.* My lord, I see a man should never vow
He will not do a thing, for second thoughts
Bely the purpose. Truly I could have sworn
It would be long indeed ere I came hither
Under that hail of threats you rained on me.
But since an unforeseen happy surprise
Passes all other pleasing out of measure,
I come, though I forswore it mightily,
Bringing this maiden, who was caught in act
To set that bier in order. Here, my lord,
No lot was cast; this windfall is to me,
And to no other. Take her, now, yourself;
Examine and convict her, as you please;
I wash my hands of it, and ought, of right,
To be clean quit of the scrape, for good and all.

*Creon.* You seized—and bring—her! In what way, and
whence?

*Sentinel.* Burying that man, herself! You know the whole.

*Creon.* Are you in earnest? Do you understand
What you are saying?

*Sentinel.*                          Yes, that I saw this girl
Burying that body you forbade to bury.
Do I speak clear and plain?

*Creon.*                          How might this be,
That she was seen, and taken in the act?

*Sentinel.* Why thus it happened. When we reached the place,
Wrought on by those dread menacings from you,
We swept away all dust that covered up
The body, and laid the clammy limbs quite bare,
And windward from the summit of the hill,
Out of the tainted air that spread from him,
We sat us down, each, as it might be, rousing
His neighbour with a clamour of abuse,
Wakening him up, whenever any one
Seemed to be slack in watching. This went on,
Till in mid air the luminous orb of day
Stood, and the heat grew sultry. Suddenly
A violent eddy lifted from the ground
A hurricane, a trouble of the sky;

B

Ruffling all foliage of the woodland plain
It filled the horizon; the vast atmosphere
Thickened to meet it; we, closing our eyes,
Endured the Heaven-sent plague.　After a while,
When it had ceased, there stands this maiden in
　　　sight,
And wails aloud, shrill as the bitter note
Of the sad bird, when as she finds the couch
Of her void nest robbed of her young; so she,
Soon as she sees the body stripped and bare,
Bursts out in shrieks, and calls down curses dire
On their heads who had done it.　Straightway then
She gathers handfuls of dry dust, and brings them,
And from a shapely brazen cruse held high
She crowns the body with drink-offerings,
Once, twice, and thrice.　We at the sight rushed
　　　forward,
And trapped her, nothing daunted, on the spot;
And taxed her with the past offence, and this
The present.　Not one whit did she deny;
A pleasant though a pitiful sight to me;
For nothing's sweeter than to have got off
In person; but to bring into mischance
Our friends is pitiful.　And yet to pay
No more than this is cheap, to save one's life.

*Creon.*　Do you, I say—you, with your downcast brow—
　　　Own or deny that you have done this deed?

*Antigone.*　I say I did it; I deny it not.

*Creon.*　Take yourself hence, whither you will, sir knave;
　　　You are acquitted of a heavy charge.

　　　　　　　　　　　　　　　　[*Exit Sentinel.*

　　　Now tell me, not at length, but in brief space,
　　　Knew you the order not to do it?

*Antigone.*　　　　　　　　　　　　　Yes,
　　　I knew it; what should hinder?　It was plain.

*Creon.*　And you made free to overstep my law?

*Antigone.*　Because it was not Zeus who ordered it,
　　　Nor Justice, dweller with the Nether Gods,
　　　Gave such a law [17] to men; nor did I deem
　　　Your ordinance of so much binding force,
　　　As that a mortal man could overbear
　　　The unchangeable unwritten code of Heaven;

This is not of today and yesterday,
But lives for ever, having origin
Whence no man knows : whose sanctions I were loath
In Heaven's sight to provoke, fearing the will
Of any man.   I knew that I should die—
How otherwise? even although your voice
Had never so prescribed.   And that I die
Before my hour is due, that I count gain.
For one who lives in many ills, as I—
How should he fail to gain by dying?   Thus
To me the pain is light, to meet this fate ;
But had I borne to leave the body of him
My mother bare unburied, then, indeed,
I might feel pain ; but as it is, I cannot ;
And if my present action seems to you
Foolish—'tis like I am found guilty of folly
At a fool's mouth !

**1 Senator.**                     Lo you, the spirit stout
Of her stout father's child—unapt to bend
Beneath misfortune !

**Creon.**                     But be well assured,
Tempers too stubborn are the first to fail ;
The hardest iron from the furnace, forged
To stiffness, you may see most frequently
Shivered and broken ; and the chafing steeds
I have known governed with a slender curb.
It is unseemly that a household drudge
Should be misproud ; but she was conversant
With outrage, ever since she passed the bounds
Laid down by law ; then hard upon that deed
Comes this, the second outrage, to exult
And triumph in her deed.   Truly if here
She wield such powers uncensured, she is man,
I woman !   Be she of my sister born,
Or nearer to myself than the whole band
Of our domestic tutelary Jove,
She, and the sister—for her equally
I charge with compassing this funeral—
Shall not escape a most tremendous doom.
And call her ; for within the house but now
I saw her, frenzied and beside herself ;
And it is common for the moody sprite

         Of plotters in the dark to no good end
         To have been caught, planning its knavery,
         Before the deed is acted.    None the less
         I hate it, when one taken in misdoing
         Straight seeks to gloss the facts!

*Antigone.*                   Would you aught more
         Than take my life, whom you did catch? [18]

*Creon.*                          Not I;
         Take that, take all.

*Antigone.*             Then why do you delay?
         Since naught is pleasing of your words to me,
         Or, as I trust, can ever please, so mine
         Must needs be unacceptable to you.
         And yet from whence could I have gathered praise
         More worthily, than from depositing
         My own brother in a tomb?    These, all of them,
         Would utter one approval, did not fear
         Seal up their lips.    'Tis tyranny's privilege,
         And not the least—power to declare and do
         What it is minded.

*Creon.*                 You, of all this people,
         Are singular in your discernment.

*Antigone.*                Nay,
         They too discern; they but refrain their tongues
         At your behest.

*Creon.*               And you are not ashamed
         That you deem otherwise?

*Antigone.*              It is no shame
         To pay respect to our own flesh and blood.

*Creon.*  And his dead foeman, was not he your brother
         As well?

*Antigone.*      Yes, the same sire's and mother's son.

*Creon.*  Why pay, then, honours which are wrongs to
         him?

*Antigone.*  The dead clay makes no protest.

*Creon.*                     Not although
         His with a villain's share your reverence?

*Antigone.*  It was no bondman perished, but a brother.

*Creon.*  Spoiling, I say, this country; while his rival
         Stood for it.

*Antigone.*          All the same, these rites are due
         To the underworld.

*Creon.*                     But not in equal measure
Both for the good man and the bad.
*Antigone.*                              Who knows
This is not piety there ?
*Creon.*                          The enemy
Can never be a friend, even in death.
*Antigone.* Well, I was made for fellowship in love,
Not fellowship in hate.
*Creon.*                        Then get you down
Thither, and love, if you must love, the dead !
No woman, while I live, shall order me.

CHORUS.

See where out by the doors Ismene
Weeping drops of sisterly grieving
Comes ; and a cloud o'erhanging her eyebrows
Mars her dark-flushed cheek, and moistens
    Her fair face with pitiful tears.

*Enter Attendants with* ISMENE.

*Creon.* And you—who like a viper unawares
Have crept into my house, and sucked me bloodless,
While I unknowingly was fostering you,
Twin furies, to the upsetting of my throne—
Come, tell me, will you say you also shared
This burying, or protest your innocence ?
*Ismene.* Yes, I have done it—if Antigone
Says so—I join with her to share the blame.
*Antigone.* That justice will not suffer ; you refused,
And I—I had no partner.
*Ismene.*                       In your trouble
I do not blush to claim companionship
Of what you have to endure.
*Antigone.*                        Whose was the deed
Death and the spirits of the dead can tell !
A friend in words is not a friend for me.
*Ismene.* Shame me not, sister, by denying me
A death, for honouring the dead, with you !
*Antigone.* Mix not your death with mine.   Do not claim work
You did not touch.   I shall suffice to die.
*Ismene.* And what care I for life, if I lost you ?
*Antigone.* Ask Creon ; you are dutiful to him.

*Ismene.* Why do you cross me so, to no good purpose?
*Antigone.* Nay, I am sick at heart, if I do make
        My mock of you.
*Ismene.*                    Nay but what can I do,
        Now, even yet, to help you?
*Antigone.*                        Save yourself;
        I do not grudge you your escape.
*Ismene.*                                O me
        Unhappy! And must I miss to share your fate?
*Antigone.* You made your choice, to live; I mine, to die.
*Ismene.* Not if you count my words unsaid.[19]
*Antigone.*                            By some
        Your judgment is approved; by others mine.
*Ismene.* Then our delinquency is equal, too.
*Antigone.* Take courage, you are living; but my life
        Long since has died, so I might serve the dead.
*Creon.* Of these two girls I swear the one even now
        Has been proved witless; the other was so born.
*Ismene.* Ah sir, the wretched cannot keep the wit
        That they were born with, but it flits away.
*Creon.* Yours did so, when you chose to join ill-doers
        In their misdoing.
*Ismene.*                How could I live on
        Alone, without my sister?
*Creon.*                        Do not say
        "My sister"; for you have no sister more.
*Ismene.* What, will you put to death your own son's bride?
*Creon.* He may go further afield—
*Ismene.*                        Not as by troth
        Plighted to her by him.
*Creon.*                    Unworthy wives
        For sons of mine I hate.
*Antigone.*                    O dearest Hæmon,[20]
        How are you slighted by your father!
*Creon.*                                    I
        Am weary of your marriage, and of you.
*Ismene.* Your own son! will you tear her from his arms?
*Creon.* Death will prevent that bridal-rite, for me.
*1 Senator.* I see, the sentence of this maiden's death
        Has been determined.
*Creon.*                    Then we see the same.
        An end of trifling. Slaves, there, take them in!

As women, henceforth, must they live—not suffered
To gad abroad ; for even bold men flinch,
When they view Death hard by the verge of Life.
        [*Exeunt* ANTIGONE *and* ISMENE, *guarded.*

### CHORUS.

#### I. 1.

Happy the man whose cup of life is free
  From taste of evil !   If Heaven's influence shake them,
  No ill but follows, till it overtake them,
All generations of his family ;
    Like as when before the sweep
      Of the sea-borne Thracian blast
      The surge of ocean coursing past
    Above the cavern of the deep
    Rolls up from the region under
      All the blackness of the shore,
    And the beaten beaches thunder
      Answer to the roar.

#### I. 2.

Woes upon woes on Labdacus' race I see—
  Living or dead—inveterately descend ;
  And son with sire entangled, without end,
And by some God smitten without remedy ;
    For a light of late had spread[21]
      O'er the last surviving root
      In the house of Œdipus ;
    Now, the sickle murderous
    Of the Rulers of the dead,
    And wild words beyond control,
    And the frenzy of her own soul,
      Again mow down the shoot.

#### II. 1.

Thy power, O God, what pride of man **constraineth**,
Which neither sleep, that all things else enchaineth,[22]
  Nor even the tireless moons of Heaven **destroy?**
    Thy throne is founded fast,
  High on Olympus, in great brilliancy,
    Far beyond Time's annoy.

Through present and through future and through
    past
    Abideth one decree;
        Nought in excess[23]
Enters the life of man without unhappiness.

## II. 2.

For wandering Hope to many among mankind
Seems pleasurable; but to many a mind
    Proves but a mockery of its wild desires.
        They know not aught, nor fear,
    Till their feet feel the pathway strewn with fires.
        "If evil good appear,
    That soul to his ruin is divinely led"—
        (Wisely the word was said!)
            And short the hour
    He spends unscathed by the avenging power.

    Hæmon comes, thy last surviving
        Child.   Is he here to bewail, indignant,
    His lost bride, Antigone?   Grieves he
            For a vain promise—her marriage-bed?

### *Enter* HÆMON.

*Creon.*  We shall know soon, better than seers can tell us.
    Son, you are here in anger, are you not,
    Against your sire, hearing his final doom
    Upon your bride to be?   Or are we friends,
    Always, with you, whate'er our policy?
*Hæmon.*  Yours am I, father; and you guide my steps
    With your good counsels, which for my part I
    Will follow closely; for there is no marriage
    Shall occupy a larger place with me
    Than your direction, in the path of honour.
*Creon.*  So is it right, my son, to be disposed—
    In everything to back your father's quarrel.
    It is for this men pray to breed and rear
    In their homes dutiful offspring—to requite
    The foe with evil, and their father's friend
    Honour, as did their father.   Whoso gets
    Children unserviceable—what else could he
    Be said to breed, but troubles for himself,

And store of laughter for his enemies?
Nay, never fling away your wits, my son,
Through liking for a woman; recollect,
Cold are embracings, where the wife is naught,
Who shares your board and bed. And what worse
    sore
Can plague us, than a loved one's worthlessness?
Better to spurn this maiden as a foe!
Leave her to wed some bridegroom in the grave!
For, having caught her in the act, alone
Of the whole city disobeying me,
I will not publicly bely myself,
But kill her. Now let her go glorify
Her God of kindred! If I choose to cherish
My own born kinsfolk in rebelliousness,
Then verily I must count on strangers too.
For he alone who is a man of worth
In his own household will appear upright
In the state also; and whoe'er offends
Against the laws by violence, or thinks
To give commands to rulers—I deny
Favour to such. Obedience is due
To the state's officer in small and great,
Just and unjust commandments; he who pays it
I should be confident would govern well,
And cheerfully be governed, and abide
A true and trusty comrade at my back,
Firm in the ranks amid the storm of war.
There lives no greater fiend than Anarchy;
She ruins states, turns houses out of doors,
Breaks up in rout the embattled soldiery; [24]
While Discipline preserves the multitude
Of the ordered host alive. Therefore it is
We must assist the cause of order; this
Forbids concession to a feminine will;
Better be outcast, if we must, of men,
Than have it said a woman worsted us.

ι *Senator.* Unless old age have robbed me of myself,
    I think the tenor of your words is wise.
*Hæmon.* Father, the Gods plant reason in mankind,
    Of all good gifts the highest; and to say
    You speak not rightly in this, I lack the power;

Nor do I crave it. Still, another's thought
Might be of service; and it is for me,
Being your son, to mark the words, the deeds,
And the complaints, of all. To a private man
Your frown is dreadful, who has things to say
That will offend you; but I secretly
Can gather this; how the folk mourn this maid,
"Who of all women most unmeriting,
For noblest acts dies by the worst of deaths,
Who her own brother battle-slain—unburied—
Would not allow to perish in the fangs
Of carrion hounds or any bird of prey;
And" (so the whisper darkling passes round)
"Is she not worthy to be carved in gold?"
Father, beside your welfare there is nothing
More prized by me; for what more glorious crown
Can be to children, than their father's honour?
Or to a father, from his sons, than theirs?
Do not persist, then, to retain at heart
One sole idea, that the thing is right
Which your mouth utters, and nought else beside.
For all men who believe themselves alone
Wise, or that they possess a soul or speech
Such as none other, turn them inside out,
They are found empty; and though a man be wise,
It is no shame for him to live and learn,
And not to stretch a course too far. You see
How all the trees on winter torrent banks,
Yielding, preserve their sprays; those that would
    stem it
Break, roots and all; the shipman too, who keeps
The vessel's main-sheet taut, and will not slacken,
Goes cruising, in the end, keel uppermost:
Let thy wrath go! Be willing to relent!
For if some sense, even from a younger head,
Be mine to afford, I say it is far better
A man should be, for every accident,
Furnished with inbred skill; but what of that?
Since nature's bent will have it otherwise,
'Tis good to learn of those who counsel wisely.

1 *Senator.* Sir, you might learn, when he speaks seasonably;
And you, from him; for both have spoken well.

*Creon.* Men that we are, must we be sent to school
    To learn discretion of a boy like this?
*Hæmon.* None that's dishonest; and if I am young,
    It is not well to have regard to years
    Rather than services.
*Creon.*                Good service is it,
    To pay respect to rebels?
*Hæmon.*               To wrongdoers
    I would not even ask for reverence.
*Creon.* Was it not some such taint infected her?
*Hæmon.* So say not all this populace of Thebes.
*Creon.* The city to prescribe me my decrees!
*Hæmon.* Look, say you so, you are too young in this! 25
*Creon.* Am I to rule this land after some will
    Other than mine?
*Hæmon.*             A city is no city
    That is of one man only. 25
*Creon.*              Is not the city
    Held to be his who rules it?
*Hæmon.*              That were brave—
    You, a sole monarch of an empty land!
*Creon.* This fellow, it seems, fights on the woman's side.
*Hæmon.* An you be woman! My forethought is for you.
*Creon.* O villain—traversing thy father's rights!
*Hæmon.* Because I see you sinning against right.
*Creon.* Sin I, to cause my sway to be held sacred?
*Hæmon.* You desecrate, by trampling on Heaven's honour.
*Creon.* Foul spotted heart—a woman's follower!
*Hæmon.* You will not find me serving what is vile.
*Creon.* I say this talk of thine is all for her.
*Hæmon.* And you, and me, and for the Gods beneath!
*Creon.* Never shall she live on to marry thee!
*Hæmon.* Die as she may, she shall not die alone.
*Creon.* Art thou grown bold enough to threaten, too?
*Hæmon.* Where is the threat, to speak against vain counsel?
*Creon.* Vain boy, thyself shalt rue thy counselling.
*Hæmon.* I had called you erring, were you not my sire.
*Creon.* Thou woman's bondman, do not spaniel me!
*Hæmon.* Do you expect to speak, and not be answered?
*Creon.* Do I so? By Olympus over us,
    If thou revile me, and find fault with me,
    Never believe but it shall cost thee dear!

Bring out the wretch, that in his sight, at once,
Here, with her bridegroom by her, she may die!

*Hæmon.* Not in my sight, at least—not by my side,
Believe it, shall she perish! And for thee—
Storm at the friends who choose thy company!
My face thou never shalt behold again.    [*Exit.*

1 *Senator.* The man is gone, my lord, headlong with rage;
And wits so young, when galled, are full of danger.

*Creon.* Let be, let him imagine more, or do,
Than mortal may; yet he shall not redeem
From sentence those two maidens.

1 *Senator.*                              Both of them?
Is it your will to slay them both alike?

*Creon.* That is well said; not her who did not touch it.

1 *Senator.* And by what death mean you to kill the other?

*Creon.* Into some waste untrodden of mankind
She shall be drawn, and, in some rock-hewn cave,
With only food enough provided her
For expiation, so that all the city
Escape the guilt of blood, buried alive.
There, if she ask him, Hades, the one God
Whom she regards, may grant her not to perish;
Or there, at latest, she shall recognize
It is lost labour to revere the dead.      [*Exit.*


CHORUS.[26]

O Love, thou art victor in fight: thou mak'st all things afraid;
Thou couchest thee softly at night on the cheeks of a maid;
Thou passest the bounds of the sea, and the folds of the fields;
To thee the immortal, to thee the ephemeral yields;
Thou maddenest them that possess thee; thou turnest astray
The souls of the just, to oppress them, out of the way;
Thou hast kindled amongst us pride, and the quarrel of kin;
Thou art lord, by the eyes of a bride, and the love-light therein;
Thou sittest assessor with Right; [27] her kingdom is thine,
Who sports with invincible might, Aphrodita divine.

*Enter* ANTIGONE, *guarded.*

I too, myself, am carried as I look
Beyond the bounds of right;
Nor can I brook
The springing fountain of my tears, to see
My child, Antigone,
Pass to the chamber of universal night.

## I. 1.

*Antigone.*　Behold me, people of my native land :
I wend my latest way :
I gaze upon the latest light of day
That I shall ever see ;
Death, who lays all to rest, is leading me
To Acheron's far strand
Alive ; to me no bridal hymns belong,
For me no marriage song
Has yet been sung ; but Acheron instead
Is it, whom I must wed.

*Chorus.*　Nay but with praise and voicings of renown
Thou partest for that prison-house of the dead ;
Unsmitten by diseases that consume,
By sword unvisited,
Thou only of mortals freely shalt go down,
Alive, to the tomb.

## I. 2.

*Antigone.*　I have heard tell the sorrowful end of her,
That Phrygian sojourner
On Sipylus' peak, offspring of Tantalus ;
How stony shoots upgrown
Like ivy bands enclosed her in the stone ;
With snows continuous
And ceaseless rain her body melts away ;
Streams from her tear-flown head
Water her front ; likest to hers the bed
My fate prepares today.

*Chorus.*　She was of godlike nature, goddess-sprung,
And we are mortals, and of human race ;
And it were glorious odds

For maiden slain, among
The equals of the Gods
In life—and then in death—to gain a place.[28]

## II. 1.

*Antigone.* They mock me. Gods of Thebes! why scorn
  you me
Thus, to my face,
    Alive, not death-stricken yet?
O city, and you the city's large-dowered race,
    Ye streams from Dirca's source,
Ye woods that shadow Theba's chariot-course,
Listen and see,
    Let none of you forget,
How sacrificed, and for what laws offended,
By no tears friended,
    I to the prisoning mound
Of a strange grave am journeying under ground.
Ah me unhappy! [home is none for me;] [29]
Alike in life or death an exile must I be.

*Chorus.* Thou to the farthest verge forth-faring,
O my child, of daring,
Against the lofty threshold of the laws
Didst stumble and fall. The cause
Is some ancestral load, which thou art bearing.

## II. 2.

*Antigone.* There didst thou touch upon my bitterest bale—
A threefold tale—
    My father's piteous doom,
Doom of us all, scions of Labdacus.
    Woe for my mother's bed!
Woe for the ill-starred spouse, from her own
  womb
Untimely born!
    O what a father's-house
Was that from whence I drew my life forlorn!
To whom, unwed,
    Accursed, lo I come

To sojourn as a stranger in their home!
And thou too, ruined, my brother, in a wife,
Didst by thy death bring death upon thy sister's
life!

*Chorus.*   To pay due reverence is a duty, too:
And power—his power, whose empire is confest,
May no wise be transgressed;
But thee thine own infatuate mood o'er-threw.

*Antigone.*   Friendless, unwept, unwed,
I, sick at heart, am led
The way prepared for me;[30]
Day's hallowed orb on high
I may no longer see;
For me no tears are spent,
Nor any friends lament
The death I die.

### *Enter* CREON.

*Creon.* Think you that any one, if help might be
In wailing and lament before he died,
Would ever make an end?   Away with her!
Wall her up close in some deep catacomb,
As I have said; leave her alone, apart,
To perish, if she will; or if she live,
To make her tomb her tenement.   For us,
We will be guiltless of this maiden's blood;
But here on earth she shall abide no more.
*Antigone.* Thou Grave, my bridal chamber! dwelling-place
Hollowed in earth, the everlasting prison
Whither I bend my steps, to join the band
Of kindred, whose more numerous host already
Persephone hath counted with the dead;
Of whom I last and far most miserably
Descend, before my term of life is full;
I come, cherishing this hope especially,
To win approval in my father's sight,
Approval too, my mother, in thine, and thine
Dear brother! for that with these hands I paid
Unto you dead lavement and ordering

And sepulchre-libations; and that now,
Polynices, in the tendance of thy body
I meet with this reward. Yet to the wise
It was no crime, that I did honour thee.
For never had I, even had I been
Mother of children, or if spouse of mine
Lay dead and mouldering, in the state's despite
Taken this task upon me. Do you ask
What argument I follow here of law?[31]
One husband dead, another might be mine;
Sons by another, did I lose the first;
But, sire and mother buried in the grave,
A brother is a branch that grows no more.
Yet I, preferring by this argument
To honour thee to the end, in Creon's sight
Appear in that I did so to offend,
And dare to do things heinous, O my brother!
And for this cause he hath bid lay hands on me,
And leads me, not as wives or brides are led,
Unblest with any marriage, any care
Of children; destitute of friends, forlorn,
Yet living, to the chambers of the dead
See me descend. Yet what celestial right
Did I transgress? How should I any more
Look up to heaven, in my adversity?
Whom should I call to aid? Am I not come
Through piety to be held impious? If
This is approved in Heaven, why let me suffer,
And own that I have sinned; but if the sin
Belong to these—O may their punishment
Be measured by the wrongfulness of mine!

1 *Senator.* Still the same storms possess her, with the same
    Precipitance of spirit.

*Creon.*                Then for this
    Her guards shall rue their slowness.

*Antigone.*                   Woe for me!
    The word I hear comes hand in hand with death!

1 *Senator.* I may not say Be comforted, for this
    Shall not be so; I have no words of cheer.

*Antigone.* O City of Theba! O my country! Gods,
    The Fathers of my race! I am led hence—
    I linger now no more. Behold me, lords,

The last of your kings' house [28]—what doom is mine,
And at whose hands, and for what cause—that I
Duly performed the dues of piety!

[*Exeunt* ANTIGONE *and guards.*

CHORUS.

I. 1.

For a dungeon brazen-barred
    The body of Danae endured
        To exchange Heaven's daylight of old,
    In a tomb-like chamber immured,
Hid beneath fetter and guard;
And she was born, we are told,
    O child, my child, unto honour,
    And a son was begotten upon her
To Zeus in a shower of gold.
But the stress of a Fate is hard;
Nor wealth, nor warfare, nor ward,
    Nor black ships cleaving the sea
    Can resist her, or flee.

I. 2.

And the Thracians' king, Dryas' son, [32]
    The hasty of wrath, was bound
        For his words of mocking and pride;
    Dionysus closing him round,
Pent in a prison of stone;
Till, his madness casting aside
    Its flower and fury wild,
    He knew what God he reviled—
Whose power he had defied;
Restraining the Mænad choir,
Quenching the Evian fire,
    Enraging the Muses' throng,
    The lovers of song.

II. 1.

And by the twofold main [33]
    Of rocks Cyanean—there
        Lies the Bosporean strand,
And the lone Thracian plain
    Of Salmydessus, where

Is Ares' border-land:
Who saw the stab of pain
Dealt on the Phineid pair
At that fierce dame's command;
Blinding the orbits of their blasted sight,
Smitten, without spear to smite,
By a spindle's point made bare,
And by a bloody hand.

### II. 2.

They mourned their mother dead,
Their hearts with anguish wrung,
Wasting away, poor seed
Of her deserted bed;
Who, Boreas' daughter, sprung
From the old Erechtheid breed,
In remote caverns fed
Her native gales among,
Went swiftly as the steed,
Offspring of Heaven, over the steep-down wild;
Yet to her too, my child,
The Destinies, that lead
Lives of long ages, clung.

*Enter* TIRESIAS *led by a boy.*

*Tiresias.* Princes of Thebes, two fellow-travellers.
Debtors in common to the eyes of one,
We stand before you; for a blind man's path
Hangs on the guide who marshals him the way.
*Creon.* What would'st thou now, reverend Tiresias?
*Tiresias.* That will I tell. Do thou obey the seer.
*Creon.* I never have departed hitherto
From thy advice.
*Tiresias.*                    And therefore 'tis, thou steerest
The city's course straight forward.
*Creon.*                                        Thou hast done me
Good service, I can witness.
*Tiresias.*                              Now again
Think, thou dost walk on fortune's razor-edge.
*Creon.* What is it? I tremble but to see thee speak.
*Tiresias.* Listen to what my art foreshadoweth,
And thou shalt know. I lately, taking seat

On my accustomed bench of augury,
Whither all tribes of fowl after their kind
Alway resort, heard a strange noise of birds
Screaming with harsh and dissonant impetus;
And was aware how each the other tore
With murderous talons; for the whirr of wings
Rose manifest. Then feared I, and straight made trial
Of sacrifices on the altar-hearths
All blazing; but, out of the offerings,
There sprang no flame; only upon embers charred
Thick droppings melted off the thigh-pieces,
And heaved and sputtered, and the gall-bladders
Burst, and were lost, while from the folds of fat
The loosened thigh-bones fell. Such auguries,
Failing of presage through the unseemliness
Of holy rites, I gather from this lad,
Who is to me, as I to others, guide.
And this state-sickness comes by thy self-will;
For all our hearths and altars are defiled
With prey of dogs and fowl, who have devoured
The dead unhappy son of Œdipus.
Therefore the Gods accept not of us now
Solemn peace-offering or burnt sacrifice,
Nor bird trills out a happy-boding note,
Gorged with the fatness of a slain man's blood.
This, then, my son, consider; that to err
From the right path is common to mankind;
But having erred, that mortal is no more
Losel or fool, who medicines the ill
Wherein he fell, and stands not obstinate.
Conceit of will savours of emptiness.
Give place, then, in the presence of the dead.
Wound not the life that's perished. Where's thy valour
In slaying o'er the slain? Well I advise,
Meaning thee well; 'tis pleasantest to learn
Of good advisers, when their words bring gain.

*Creon.* Old man, ye all, like archers at a mark,
Are loosing shafts at me; I am not spared
Even your soothsayers' practice; by whose tribe
Long since have I been made as merchandize,
And bought, and sold. Gather your gains at will!
Market your Sardian silver, Indian gold!

That man ye shall not cover with a tomb;
Not though the eagle ministers of Jove
To Jove's own throne should bear their prey of him,
Not even for horror at such sacrilege
Will I permit his burial.   This I know;
There is no power in any man to touch
The Gods with sacrilege; but foul the falls
Which men right cunning fall, Tiresias—
Old man, I say—when for the sake of gain
They speak foul treason with a fair outside

*Tiresias.* Alas, does no man know, does no man think—
*Creon.* What should one think?   What common saw is this?
*Tiresias.* How far good counsel passes all things good?
*Creon.* So far, I think, folly's the worst of harm!
*Tiresias.* That is the infirmity that fills thy nature.
*Creon.* I care not to retort upon thee, seer.
*Tiresias.* Thou dost, thou say'st my oracles are false.
*Creon.* All the prophetic tribe are covetous.
*Tiresias.* And that of kings fond of disgraceful gain.
*Creon.* Know'st thou of whom thou speak'st? I am thy lord.
*Tiresias.* Yea, thou hast saved the state; I gave it thee.
*Creon.* Thou art a wise seer, but in love with wrong.
*Tiresias.* Thou wilt impel me to give utterance
  To my still dormant prescience.
*Creon.*                              Say on;
  Only beware thou do not speak for gain.
*Tiresias.* For gain of thine, methinks, I do not speak.
*Creon.* Thou shalt not trade upon my wits, be sure.
*Tiresias.* And be thou sure of this; thou shalt not tell
  Many more turns [34] of the sun's chariot-wheel,
  Ere thou shalt render satisfaction, one
  From thy own loins in payment, dead for dead,
  For that thou hast made Life join hands with Death,
  And sent a living soul unworthily
  To dwell within a tomb, and keep'st a corpse
  Here, from the presence of the Powers beneath,
  Not for thy rights or any God's above,
  But lawlessly in their despite usurped,
  Unhallowed, disappointed, uninterred; [25]
  Wherefore the late-avenging punishers,
  Furies, from Death and Heaven, lay wait for thee,
  To take thee in the evil of thine own hands.

Look to it, whether I be bribed who speak;
For as to that, with no great wear of time,
Men's, women's wails to thine own house shall answer.
Also all cities rise in enmity,
To the strown relics of whose citizens
None pays due hallowing, save beasts of prey,
Dogs, or some fowl, whose pinions to their gates—
Yea, to each hearth—bear taint defiling them. [28]
Such bolts, in wrath, since thou dar'st anger me,
I loosen at thy bosom, archer-like,
Sure-aimed, whose burning smart thou shalt not shun.
Lead me away, boy, to my own home again;
And let him vent his spleen on younger men,
And learn to keep a tongue more gentle, and
A brain more sober, than he carries now.

[*Exeunt* TIRESIAS *and Boy.*

1 *Senator.* The seer is gone, my lord, denouncing woe;
  And from the day my old hairs began to indue
  Their white for black, we have known him for a
    watch
  Who never barked to warn the state in vain.
*Creon.* I know it too; and I am ill at ease;
  'Tis bitter to submit; but Até's hand [35]
  Smites bitterly on the spirit that abides her.
1 *Senator.* Creon Menœceus' son, be wise at need!
*Creon.* What should I do? speak, I will hearken.
1 *Senator.*                                        Go,
  Set free the maiden from the vault, and build
  A tomb for that dead outcast.
*Creon.*                        You approve it?
  You deem that I should yield?
1 *Senator.*                        Sir, with all speed.
  Swift-footed come calamities from Heaven
  To cut off the perverse.
*Creon.*                    O God, 'tis hard!
  But I quit heart, and yield; I cannot fight
  At odds with destiny.
1 *Senator.*                Up then, to work!
  Commit it not to others!
*Creon.*                    I am gone
  Upon the instant. Quickly, quickly men,

You and your fellows, get you, axe in hand,
Up to the place, there, yonder ; and because
I am thus minded, other than before,
I who did bind her will be there to loose ;
For it misgives me it is best to keep
The old appointed laws, all our life long.

[*Exeunt* CREON *and Attendants.*

CHORUS.

I. 1.

Thou by many names addrest,
Child of Zeus loud-thundering,
Glory of a Theban maid,
Who unbidden wanderest
    Fair Italia's King,
And art lord in each deep glade
Whither all men seek to her,
Eleusinian Demeter ;
Bacchus, who by soft-flowing waters
Of Ismenus habitest
Theba, mother of Bacchant daughters,
With the savage Dragon's stock,

I. 2.

Thee the lurid wild-fire meets
O'er the double-crested rock,
Where Corycian Nymphs arow
Bacchic-wise ascending go,
    Thee Castalia's rill ;
Thee the ivy-covered capes
Usher forth of Nysa's hill,
And the shore with green of grapes
Clustering, where the hymn to thee
Rises up immortally,
Visitant in Theban Streets,
"Evoe, O Evoe !"

II. 1.

Wherefore, seeing thy City thus—
City far above all other

Dear to thee, and her, thy mother
Lightning-slain—by sickness grievous
Holden fast in all her gates,
Come with quickness to relieve us,
By the slopes of Parnasus,
   Or the roaring straits.

## II. 2.

Hail to thee, the first advancing
In the stars' fire-breathing chorus!
Leader of the nightly strain,
Boy and son of Zeus and King! [36]
Manifest thyself before us
With thy frenzied Thyiad train,
Who their lord Iacchus dancing
   Praise, and all night sing.

*Enter a* MESSENGER.

*Messenger.* You citizens who dwell beside the roof
Of Cadmus and Amphion, there is no sort
Of human life that I could ever praise,
Or could dispraise, as constant; Fortune still
Raising and Fortune overthrowing still
The happy and the unhappy; and none can read
What is set down for mortals. Creon, methought
Was enviable erewhile, when he preserved
This land of Cadmus from its enemies,
And took the country's absolute monarchy,
And ruled it, flourishing with a noble growth
From his own seed; and now, he has lost all.
For when men forfeit all their joys in life,
One in that case I do not count alive,
But deem of him as of some animate corse.
Pile now great riches, if thou wilt, at home;
Wear thou the living semblance of a king;
An if delight be lacking, all the rest
I would not purchase, as compared with joy,
From any, for the shadow of a shade.

**1** *Senator.* What new affliction to the royal stock
   Com'st thou to tell?

*Messenger.*               Death is upon them—death
   Caused by the living.

1 *Senator.*              And who is the slayer?
       Speak! who the victim?
*Messenger.*             Hæmon is no more;
       His life-blood spilt, and by no stranger's hand.
1 *Senator.* What, by his father's, or his own?
*Messenger.*               Self-slaughtered;
       Wroth with his father for the maiden slain.
1 *Senator.* Prophet! how strictly is thy word come true!
*Messenger.* Look to the future, for these things are so.
1 *Senator.* And I behold the poor Eurydice
       Come to us from the palace, Creon's wife;
       Either of chance, or hearing her son's name.

*Enter* EURYDICE.

*Eurydice.* O all you citizens, I heard the sound
       Of your discourse, as I approached the gates,
       Meaning to bring my prayers before the face
       Of Pallas; even as I undid the bolts,
       And set the door ajar, a voice of woe
       To my own household pierces through my ears;
       And I sink backward on my handmaidens
       Afaint for terror; but whate'er the tale,
       Tell it again; I am no novice, I,
       In misery, that hearken.
*Messenger.*            Dear my mistress,
       I saw, and I will speak, and will let slip
       No syllable of the truth. Why should we soothe
       Your ears with stories, only to appear
       Liars thereafter? Truth is alway right.
       —I followed in attendance on your lord,
       To the flat hill-top, where despitefully
       Was lying yet, harried by dogs, the body
       Of Polynices. Pluto's name, and hers,
       The wayside goddess, we invoked, to stay
       Their anger and be favourable; and him
       We washed with pure lustration, and consumed
       On fresh-lopped branches the remains of him,
       And piled a monument of natal earth
       High over all; thence to the maiden's cell,
       Chamber of death, with bridal couch of stone,
       We made as if to enter. But afar
       One fellow hears a loud uplifted wail

Fill all the unhallowed precinct; comes, and tells
His master, Creon; the uncertain sound
Of piteous crying, as he draws more nigh,
Comes round him, and he utters, groaning loud
A lamentable plaint; "Me miserable!
Was I a prophet? Is this path I tread
The unhappiest of all ways I ever went?
My son's voice thrills my ear. What ho, my guard!
Run quickly thither to the tomb where stones
Have been dragged down to make an opening,
Go in and look, whether I really hear
The voice of Hæmon, or am duped by Heaven."
Quickly, at our distracted lord's command,
We looked: and in the tomb's inmost recess
Found we her, as she had been hanged by the neck,[37]
Fast in a strip-like loop of linen; and him
Laid by her, clasping her about the waist,
Mourning his wedlock severed in the grave,
And his sire's deeds, and his ill-fated bride.
He, when he sees them, with a terrible cry
Goes in towards him, calling out aloud
"Ah miserable, what hast thou done? what mind
Hadst thou? by what misfortune art thou crazed?
Come out, my son,—suppliant I ask of thee!"
But with fierce aspect the youth glared at him;
Spat in his face; answered him not a word;
Grasped at the crossed hilts of his sword and drew it,
And—for the father started forth in flight—
Missed him! then, angered with himself, poor fool,
There as he stood he flung himself along
Upon the sword-point firmly planted in [38]
The middle of his breast, and, conscious yet,
Clings to the maid, clasped in his failing arms,
And gasping, sends forth on the pallid cheek
Fast welling drops of blood: So lies he, dead,
With his arms round the dead; there, in the grave
His bridal rite is full; his misery
Is witness to mankind what worst of woe
The lack of counsel brings a man to know!
[*Exit* EURYDICE.

1 *Senator.* What do you make of this? The woman's gone
Back, and without one word, of good or bad!

*Messenger.*   I marvel too ; and yet I am in hope
      She would not choose, hearing her son's sad fate,
      In public to begin her keening-cry ;
      But rather to her handmaids in the house
      Dictate the mourning for a private pain.
      She is not ignorant of self-control,
      That she should err.

I *Senator.*             I know not ; but on me
      Weigh heavily both silence over-much,
      And loud complaint in vain.

*Messenger.*             Well, we shall know it,
      If she hide aught within a troubled heart
      Even to suppression of its utterance,
      If we approach the house.   Yes, you say truly,
      It does weigh heavy, silence over-much.

                                  [*Exit.*

CHORUS.

      Lo now, Creon himself draws near us,
      Clasping a record
      Manifest, if we sin not, saying it,
      Of ruin unwrought by the hands of others,
        But fore-caused by his own self-will.

*Enter* CREON, *attended, with the body of* HÆMON.

I. I.

*Creon.*       O sins of a mind
         That is minded to stray !
      Mighty to bind
         And almighty to slay !
Behold us, kin slayers and slain, O ye who stand by
      the way !

         Ah, newness of death !
           O my fruitless design !
         New to life's breath,
           O son that wert mine,
Ah, ah, thou art dead, thou art sped, for a fault that was
      mine, not thine !

1 *Senator.* Ah, how thou seem'st to see the truth, too late!
*Creon.* Ah yes, I have learnt, I know my wretchedness!

## II. 1.

Heaviness hath o'ertaken me
And mine head the rod;
The roughness hath shaken me
Of the paths I trod;
Woe is me! my delight is brought low, cast under the
feet of a God!

Woe for man's labours that are profitless!

*Re-enter the* MESSENGER.

*Messenger.* O master, now thou hast and hast in store
Of sorrows; one thou bearest in thine arms,
And one at home thou seemest to be come
Merely to witness.
*Creon.* And what more of sorrow,
Or what more sorrowful, is yet behind? [39]
*Messenger.* Thy wife, the mother—mother of the dead—
Is, by a blow just fallen, haplessly slain.

## I. 2.

*Creon.* O hard to appease thee,
Haven of Death,
How should it please thee
To end this breath?
O herald of heavy news, what is this thy mouth uttereth?

O man, why slayest thou
A man that is slain?
Alas, how sayest thou
Anew and again
That the slaying of a woman is added to slaying—a pain to
a pain?

*Messenger.* See for thyself; the palace doors unclose.

*The Altar is disclosed, with the dead body of Eurydice.*
*Creon.* Woe is me again, for this new sorrow I see.

### II. 2.

What deed is not done?
What tale is not told?
Thy body, O son,
These arms enfold—
Dead—wretch that I am! Dead, too, is the face these eyes behold.

Ah, child, for thy poor mother! ah for thee!

*Messenger.* She with a sharp-edged dagger in her heart [40]
Lies at the altar; and her darkened lids
Close on her wailing for the glorious lot
Of Megareus, who died before, and next
For his, and last, upon her summoning
Evil to fall on thee, the child-slayer!

### III. 1.

*Creon.*       Alas, I faint for dread!
Is there none will deal
A thrust that shall lay me dead
With the two-edged steel?
Ah woe is me!
I am all whelmed in utter misery!

*Messenger.* It may be so; thou art arraigned of her
Who here lies dead, for the occasion thou
Hast wrought for Destiny on her, and him.
1 *Senator.* In what way did she slay herself and die?
*Messenger.* Soon as she heard the raising of the wail
For her son's death, she stabbed herself to the heart.

### IV. 1.

*Creon.*       Woe is me! to none else can they lay it,
This guilt, but to me!
I, I was the slayer, I say it,
Unhappy, of thee!
O bear me, haste ye, spare not,
To the ends of earth,
More nothing than they who were not
In the hour of birth!

1 *Senator.* Thou counsellest well—if anything be well
    To follow, in calamity; the ills
    Lying in our path, soonest o'erpast, were best.

### III. 2.

*Creon.*　　　Come, thou most welcome Fate,
　　　　　Appear, O come;
　　　　Bring my days' final date,
　　　　　Fill up their sum!
　　　Come quick, I pray;
　　　Let me not look upon another day!

1 *Senator.* This for to-morrow; we must take some thought
    On that which lies before us; for these griefs,
    They are their care on whom the care has fallen.
*Creon.* I did but join your prayer for our desire. [41]
1 *Senator.* Pray thou for nothing more; there is no respite
    To mortals from the ills of destiny.

### IV. 2.

*Creon.*　　　Lead me forth, cast me out, no other
　　　　　Than a man undone;
　　　　Who did slay, unwitting, thy mother
　　　　　And thee, my son!
　　　I turn me I know not where
　　　　For my plans ill-sped,
　　　And a doom that is heavy to bear
　　　　Is come down on my head.
　　　　　　　　　[*Exit* CREON, *attended.*

### CHORUS.

Wisdom first for a man's well-being
Maketh, of all things.　Heaven's insistence
Nothing allows of man's irreverence;
And great blows great speeches avenging,
　Dealt on a boaster,
Teach men wisdom in age, at last.
　　　　　　　　　[*Exeunt omnes.*

# AJAX

## PERSONS REPRESENTED

*The Goddess* ATHENA.

ULYSSES, *son of Lartius (or as some said of Sisyphus,) King of Ithaca.*

AJAX, *son of Telamon and Eribœa, leader of the forces of Salamis.*

TECMESSA, *daughter of Teuthras or Teleutas, King of Phrygia, the captive-wife of Ajax.*

EURYSACES, *a child, son of Ajax by Tecmessa.*

TEUCER, *son of Telamon by his captive-wife Hesione.*

MENELAUS, *King of Sparta, brother to Agamemnon.*

AGAMEMNON, *King of Argos, General-in-chief of the Greeks.*

*A* Messenger, *a soldier in the Salaminian forces.*

*The* CHORUS *is composed of Mariners of the Salaminian squadron.*

*Servants to Ajax.*

---

*Scene, the sea-shore of Troia, before the quarters of Ajax.*

### *Enter* ULYSSES, *and* ATHENA *above.*

*Athena.* Ever I find you, son of Lartius,
　　　　Hunting to achieve some venture on a foe;
　　　　And I behold you now at Ajax' tent,
　　　　Where he lies quartered, farthest of the fleet,
　　　　This long time dogging him, and measuring
　　　　The newly-printed footmarks he has made,
　　　　That you may learn if he is within, or no.
　　　　And keen the scent, as of a Spartan hound,
　　　　That carries you right bravely o'er the ground;
　　　　For so it is, he is but now come in,
　　　　Dripping with sweat, both from his countenance
　　　　And his hands armed for slaughter. So no longer
　　　　Need you be peering here inside the wicket;
　　　　Rather be telling why you set yourself
　　　　This task, that you may learn from me, who know.

# Ajax

**43**

*Ulysses.* O accents of the friendliest Power to me
      Of all the Gods—Athena—with what clearness,
      Although thou art remote from my regard,
      As of some brazen-mouthed Etrurian horn,
      I hear and recognize the voice of thee !
      Rightly didst thou discern my prowling round
      After a foe—Ajax the Shield-bearer ;
      He and no other is it whom I am tracking.
      He has committed against us, last night,
      An unaccountable act ; if he has done it ;
      For we know nothing sure ; we are astray.
      I volunteered to undertake this labour ;
      For, we discover, all the herds, our spoil,
      Have been destroyed, slaughtered by violence,
      Together with the herdsmen ; and the deed
      Every man lays to him.   One scout, who saw him
      Alone, with reeking sword, bounding along,
      Spake and informed me ; and immediately
      I started on the trail ; and of some footprints
      I am assured ; others have baffled me ;
      And whose they are I know not.   In good time
      Art thou come hither ; for in all things, past
      And present, I am governed by thy hand.
*Athena.* I knew it, Ulysses ; and went forth betimes,
      Ready to guard your hunting.
*Ulysses.*                     Do I toil,
      Dear mistress, to good purpose ?
*Athena.*                   Yes, so far,
      That it was he who did it.
*Ulysses.*                And how came he
      To set a hand to such extravagance ?
*Athena.* Mastered by fury about Achilles' arms.
*Ulysses.* Why does he make this onslaught upon cattle ?
*Athena.* He thought to imbrue his hands in your hearts'
         blood.
*Ulysses.* What, did he mean to fall on Argives ?
*Athena.*                     Yes,
      And would have done it, had I suffered him.
*Ulysses.* How did he dare or hope to compass it ?
*Athena.* At night, by stealth, singly he came on you—
*Ulysses.* What, did he reach us and attain his goal ?
*Athena.* Yes, he was just at the two Captains' doors.

*Ulysses.* What made him hold his hand, raging for blood?
*Athena.* I kept him off; I cast upon his eyes
    Grievous conceits of his infatuate glee,[1]
    And turned him toward the flocks and common herd
    Of captured cattle in the herdmen's charge,
    Yet undivided.   There he fell on them,
    And slashed about the horned carcases,
    Cleaving their chines; and he supposed himself
    Sometimes to seize and slay with his own hand
    The two Atridæ, and sometimes to fall
    Upon some other of the generals.
    I, as he raged in his delirium-fit,
    Urged him—impelled him deeper in the toils.
    Next, when he rested from this work, he tied
    The oxen that survived, and all the sheep,
    Together, deeming them no horned spoil,
    But men, and drave them home; and now within
    Bound to each other he is torturing them.
    Here—I will shew you his sheer lunacy;
    That you yourself may see it, and report
    To all the Argives.   Stand courageously!
    Do not imagine he is dangerous;
    For I will turn and keep away his eyes
    From looking on your presence.—Ho Sir, you,
    Tying your prisoners' hands behind their backs—
    Ajax, I say!   Come forth, out from the palace!
*Ulysses.* What dost thou, Athena?   Call him out by no
    means!
*Athena.* Will you be silent, and not play the coward?
*Ulysses.* Do not, for Heaven's sake, do it!   Be content,
    And let him keep within.
*Athena.*                            For fear of what?
    Was he not, all along, a man?[2]
*Ulysses.*                                   To me
    A foeman; and he is so, even now.
*Athena.* And is not mocking sweetest, when you make
    Your mock of enemies?
*Ulysses.*                            I am content
    He should remain within.
*Athena.*                                 Are you afraid
    To view a man, because he is stark mad?
*Ulysses.* If he were sane, I had not budged for fear.

*Athena.* But now he shall not see that you are by.
*Ulysses.* How can that be, unless his eyes are blind?
*Athena.* I will bedarken even eyes that see.
*Ulysses.* Well, anything may happen, if a God
    Take it in hand to do!
*Athena.*                 Now, hold your peace;
    Remain where you are standing.
*Ulysses.*               So I will;
    But I could wish that I were out of it.
*Athena.* Ho, Ajax, once again I summon you!
    Why do you heed so little your ally?

*Enter* AJAX, *with a scourge.*

*Ajax.* Welcome, Athena! Welcome, Child of Jove!
    Well art thou come! and I will honour thee
    With golden trophies for this prize of mine!
*Athena.* That was well said; but did you—tell me now—
    Wash well your spear among the Argive host?
*Ajax.* So I may boast, and I will not deny it!
*Athena.* Did you lift hand against the Atridæ, too?
*Ajax.* So, that they never shall flout Ajax more!
*Athena.* The men are dead—so I conceive you mean?
*Ajax.* Dead. Let them rob me of my armour, now!
*Athena.* Well, what about the son of Lartius?
    How has he fared? Has he eluded you?
*Ajax.* Where that confounded fox is, asked you me?
*Athena.* I did—Ulysses, your competitor.
*Ajax.* He sits within, a most sweet prisoner;
    I do not mean to kill him yet, my queen.
*Athena.* Till you have done—or got—what further?
*Ajax.*                         Till
    Bound to a pillar of the court inside—
*Athena.* What mischief will you do to him, poor wretch?
*Ajax.* Score his back purple, and so finish him.
*Athena.* Nay, torture not the wretched creature so!
*Ajax.* Athena, to the rest I make thee welcome;
    But he shall suffer this, and this alone.
*Athena.* Well, well, if it would give you so much pleasure,
    Lay on, spare nought of what you think to do.
*Ajax.* I go to work. This I commit to thee;
    Stand by me, ever, such a friend as now.     [*Exit.*

c

*Athena.* Seest thou how great, Ulysses, is the might
      Of Deities? Whom could you have found more
        prudent,
      Or abler to perform his part, than he?
*Ulysses.* I know of none; and I commiserate him—
      Wretch—notwithstanding that he is my foe,
      Bound hand and foot with dire calamity;
      Pondering his case no deeper than my own,
      Seeing in us all, as many as are alive,
      Nothing but phantoms or a fleeting shade.
*Athena.* Thou therefore, looking on such sights as this,
      Speak before Heaven no overweening word,
      Nor e'er presume, though thou at all prevail
      In weight of hand or plenteousness of wealth.
      A day can prostrate and upraise again
      All that is human; but the temperate
      Heaven favours, and abominates the froward.

*Exeunt severally. Enter Mariners of Salamis, as Chorus.*

### CHORUS.

      Son of Telamon, who dost keep
      Seat where wave-girt Salamis
      Borders on the ocean-deep,
      I am joyful in thy bliss;
      But if stroke from Jove on high,
      Or ungentle calumny
      From the Danaans light on thee,
      Straight I fear exceedingly,
      And am daunted, like the eye
      Of some fluttering dove. And thus,
      In the night just faded now,
      Noisy rumours saddle us
      With dishonour, how that thou
      Did'st to the meadow take thy way
      Where our steeds run wild, and slay
      All the Danaans' flocks and herds—
      All the leavings of their spears,
        With thy gleaming blade.
      In such form his whispered words
      Ulysses pours in all men's ears,
        And can well persuade.

For he tells a tale of thee
Credible ; and each who hears
Sends it on with greater glee,
In thy sorrows triumphing.
Aim thy darts at greater hearts,
Thou canst not miss ;[3] against the king
Envy creeps ; while one who jeered
Thus at me would ill be heard.
Yet, without the great, the small
Make the tower but feeble wall ;
And happiest ordered were that state
Where small are companied with great.
    Where strong are propped by weak.
But with precepts of this lore
Vain the effort o'er and o'er
Foolish men to indoctrinate ;
And such are they who at thee rail ;
And we without thee nought avail
    In thy defence to speak.
While they escape thine eye, my king,
    Like birds on wing
    They chatter loud and shrill ;
But if thou wert to appear,
Quickly would they cower, in fear
Of the mighty vulture, and be still.

## I.

Did Artemis divine,
Jove's Taurian daughter—ah that I should name
The loud-voiced rumour, mother of my shame—
    Send thee against the common herds of kine ?
Was't for some unrequited victory ?
    Was she defrauded of some trophied gear ?
Or of some gift withheld unthankfully
    In huntings of the deer ?
Did mail-clad Ares, to avenge some slight
    Of his auxiliar spear,
Punish the affront in stratagems of night ?

## II.

For ne'er can'st thou have gone
Of set intention, son of Telamon,

So far astray, as upon creatures dumb
  To make assault.   True, plagues from Heaven must
      come ;
But Zeus and Phœbus keep us from the ill
  Men rumour !   While the kings illustrious—
While any abandoned son of Sisyphus
      Insinuates calumny,
Raise not, my liege, raise not reproach for me,
      By thus regarding still
Nothing, beyond thy chamber by the sea !

Up and leave thy seat, wherever thou art rooted
  In this age-long ceasing from the fight,
Kindling wrath in heaven !   The scoffs of foes are bruited
  In the wind-swept glens, without affright ;
And by all men thou art babbled at and hooted,
  And to me comes nothing but despite.

*Enter* TECMESSA.

*Tecmessa.*  Mariners of Ajax' fleet,
      Of Erectheus' earth-born stock,
      Lamentable is our case
      Who in this far distant place
      Love the house of Telamon ;
      Now our rugged mighty one,
      Dreaded Ajax, is down-beat
      By a wildering tempest-shock !

*Chorus.*  And by what so heavy chance
      Has the night's tranquillity [4]
      Been broken, say ? since Ajax great
      Loves and sets thee by his side—
      Thee, Teleutas' daughter, thee
      Phrygian-born, a spear-won bride ;
      Therefore not in ignorance
      Need'st thou answer.
*Tecmessa.*                  How should I
      Things unspeakable relate ?
      You shall hear of misery
      Deep as death ; for in the night,
      In one frenzy-fit, is gone
      All our Ajax' old renown ;
      Such blood-boltered butcheries

In the hut await your sight,
Victims of no hand but his.

*Chorus.* What story, impossible to blink or bear,
    Dost thou relate, of one as fierce as flame,
By the great Danaans rumoured everywhere,
    And waxing with the loudness of its fame?
Ah woe is me, I fear the fate that comes!
    In all men s eyes the man will yield his breath,
    For that his frenzied hand brought common death,
Under the sword's dark edge, on herds and herdmen-grooms.

*Tecmessa.*             Thence, alas!
            Thence it was
            That with wonder
            We saw him come,
            With the sheep, all bound;
            And slaughter some
            Within, on the ground;
            And cleave asunder
            The ribs of others;
            And seizing upon
            Two white-hoofed brothers,
            The severed tongue
            And head of the one
            On the earth he flung;
            And the second tied
            By a post upright;
            And snatching a thong
            Of harness-leather,
            Fiercely he plied
            The whistling bight
            On the poor wether,
Uttering the while reproaches many and dire,
Such as some power scarce human might inspire.

*Chorus.* High time it were to cover up the face,
    Take to our feet, and vanish stealthily;
Or seat us at the oar, each in his place,
    To get the vessel under weigh for sea.
With such loud menaces the Atridæ twain
    Ply oar against us; I am sore afraid
    The folk will stone us—his companions made
In suffering—whom so sore a fate has overta'en.

*Tecmessa.*     No, no more ;
                His frenzy is o'er ;
                Keen was the gale ;
                It rose full fast ;
                But the lightnings fail,
                And the storm is past.
                And now, though sane,
                He endures fresh pain ;
For to behold harms of our own hands' doing,
Where none beside us wrought, causes sharp ruing.


*1 Mariner.* But I suppose that all may yet be well,
            If they have ceased ; for lesser is the count
            Of ill that's past already.
*Tecmessa.*                          Would you choose,
            If choice were free, to have delights yourself,
            Vexing your friends, or in their company
            To share the anguish equally with them ?
*1 Mariner.* The twofold evil is the greater, lady.
*Tecmessa.* We are the worse, then, for recovering !
*1 Mariner.* How say you so ?   I know not what you say.
*Tecmessa.* The man we speak of, when he was diseased,
            Himself had pleasure from his malady,
            Whilst we, in our right minds, were pained for him ;
            Now, since he rose and breathed, freed from his
                madness,
            He has been all distracted with sore grief,
            And we are left no lighter than before.
            Is not this trouble doubly multiplied ?
*1 Mariner.* I am of your opinion ; and I fear
            Some heaven-sent stroke may have come on him.
                How else,
            If, being made whole, he is no more at ease
            Than when he was in sickness ?
*Tecmessa.*                              Thus it is,
            You may be well assured.
*1 Mariner.*                      How did the evil
            First light upon him ?   Tell us what has happened ;
            We grieve with you.
*Tecmessa.*                  You shall hear all that passed,
            Being sharers in the event.   At dead of night,
            When the evening camp-fires now no longer blazed,

He grasped his two-edged weapon, and seemed bent
To sally upon some errand, objectless.
I, in surprise, said to him "What dost thou, Ajax?
Why thus unsummoned either by the voice
Of messengers, or any trumpet-call,
Goest thou forth? Now the whole host is sleeping!"
But briefly he replied and in cant phrase;
"Woman, a woman should be seen, not heard."[5]
I held my tongue, and he rushed forth alone.
What there befell him truly I cannot say;
But he came in and brought, bound all together,
Bulls, herdmen's dogs and fleecy spoil of sheep.[6]
Some he beheaded; of some, their heads bent upward,
He cut the throats and clave the chines in twain,
And some he bound and tortured, as if human,
(Though it was cattle he fell on;) and at last
Rushing out through the door he hurled up words
To a phantom, some against the Atridæ, some
About Ulysses, laughing loud and long
At all the outrage he had wreaked on them;
Then darting back into the hut, once more
Hardly and by degrees he comes to reason;
When looking on the chamber filled with havock
He shrieked, and smote his head. Then he sat down,
Flinging himself among the weltering wrack
Of sheep that he had butchered, and clutched hold
Upon his hair with his clenched fists. Since then,
Most of the time he sat, uttering no sound;
After, he threatened me—'twas terrible!
If I disclosed not all that had befallen,
And questioned me, what could have come to him.
O friends, in fear, I told him the whole story,
So far as I well knew it. Instantly
He burst out crying lamentably—cries
Such as I never heard from him before.
For clamour of the kind, he ever taught,
Belonged to base and pusillanimous spirits;
Rather, suppressing all shrill outcries, he
Would groan, low, like the rumbling of a bull.
Now, prostrate under such adversity,
He, without meat or drink, sits on the ground
Among the beasts his edge has dealt on, dumb.

And plain it is he meditates no good ;
That way, at least, his words and wailings tend.
But O dear friends—for therefore was my errand—
Come in and help us, if by any means
You have the power ; for such men as he
Are conquered by the counsels of a friend.

1 *Mariner.* Tecmessa—daughter of Teleutas—this
Is evil news you bring us—that your lord
Has been driven quite beside himself with trouble !

*Ajax* (*within*). Woe, woe is me !

*Tecmessa.* It seems the trouble will be worse anon.
Did you not hear the voice of Ajax crying ?

*Ajax* (*within*). Woe, woe is me !

1 *Mariner.* The man seems either to be mad, or grieved
By presence of his former madness.

*Ajax* (*within*).               Here,
My boy, my boy !

*Tecmessa.* Me miserable ! Eurysaces, 'tis thee
He calls for ! What is in his mind ? Where art thou ?
Unhappy that I am !

*Ajax* (*within*).              Teucer I want !
Where's Teucer ? Will he never have done foraying ?
And I—am perishing !

1 *Mariner.*            The man appears
To be of sound mind. Open, there ! Perhaps
He may be moved, even at the sight of me.

*Tecmessa.* Here, I will open. You can see his work ;
And in what present plight he finds himself.

*The Scene opens, and discovers* AJAX *among the slain animals.*

*Ajax.*     O friends, O sailors good,
Faithful alone among the faithless found,
Behold me, by what storm-driven surge of blood
I am encompassed round !

1 *Mariner.* It seems, alas, your words are all too true.
How mad the work, it may itself shew clearly.

*Ajax.*     O comrades, who with me
Plied the oar-blade, your mariner's craft, o'er sea,
You, you alone stand by me in my pain !
Come, slay me—as these are slain !

**1 Mariner.** Speak not so rashly.   Do not make the pain
Worse, of the mischief, adding ill to ill
By way of remedy.

*Ajax.*                 Dost thou behold
How I, stout heart and bold,
I, the undaunted once in open battle,
Lay violent hands on unsuspecting cattle?
Alas for scorn!   How am I put to shame!

*Tecmessa.* Pray, my lord Ajax, do not say these things!
*Ajax.* Away, take yourself hence!   Alas, alas!
*Tecmessa.* O, in Heaven's name, yield to me and be wise!

*Ajax.*                 Woe, woe is me,
That let slip through my hands the slaves of destiny,
And falling among horned kine, and goat-flocks good,
Let out their turbid blood!

**1 Mariner.** Why will you grieve over what's past and done?
It cannot now be altered, not to be.

*Ajax.*                 Ah Lartius' son!
Ah thou all-spying one!
Thou of all ills the ever-willing tool!
Thou most foul knave, making the host thy fool,
I warrant thou art laughing loud for joy.

**1 Mariner.** As the God wills, every man laughs, and mourns.
*Ajax.* Wreck as I am, would that I could but see him!
O woe is me.
**1 Mariner.** Speak mildly.   See you not your evil case?

*Ajax.*                 O Zeus most high,
Forefather of my forefathers, would that, having slain
That wiliest hateful villain, and those monarchs twain,
Myself might lastly die!

*Tecmessa.* When you pray that, pray that I too may perish;
For why should I be living, and you dead?

*Ajax.*                 O darkness, now my light,
O gloom to me most bright,

Take me, yea take me for your habitant:
    Take me! for I can brook
    No longer now to look
Either to God or mortal, in my want.
     Nay, rather upon me
     The strong divinity,
Daughter of Jove, destructive torment sends;
    Then what escape is best?
    Where should I turn for rest,
Now that my former fame is fading, friends,
And retribution follows instantly,
    And here I sit, with my ridiculous prey,
And the whole host will aim a dart at me,
    Once and again, to slay?

*Tecmessa.* O misery, that a man so good should speak
    Thus—as he never would have deigned, before!

*Ajax.*         Ye ways where surges roar,
     Sea caves and green-clad shore,
Ye kept me for a long long time indeed
     Lying Troy's walls beneath;
     But now—no more in breath;
No more; a riddle that the wise may read.
     O streams that take your course
     Down from Scamander's source
You kindly neighbours to the Argive host,
     Through all futurity
     You ne'er again shall see
The face of one, who utters now this boast,
That of all those from Grecian soil who came
    Troy saw no other soldier such as I,
Who notwithstanding, put to open shame,
    Upon the ground here lie!

1 *Mariner.* I have no voice to stay you, or bid you speak,
    When woes so grievous have befallen you.
*Ajax.* Ah, who would have supposed it possible
    The name I bear should ever be attuned
    To these misfortunes!   Doubly, trebly now
    May I lament; so sore bested am I;
    Whose father in Ida bore the palm once
    From the whole host, and went, all-honoured, home;
    While I, his son, who with no meaner power

Invaded this same tract of Troy, nor less
Myself exhibited of prowess, thus,
Being dishonoured by the Argives, perish!
And yet this much, truly, I think I know;
That if Achilles were alive, to choose
For his own arms, to whom the prize was due,
No other would have snatched it, over me.
But now the Atridæ have by practice wrought
For an unscrupled villain, and passed over
The might of this right hand.   Had but mine
        eyesight—
Had but my counsels swerved not from their aim,
Never another cause were theirs to judge
As they judged mine!   'Twas the unmastered Power,
Jove's grim-eyed daughter, that illuded me,
There as I stood, raising my hand to smite them,
Casting upon me a sick frenzy-fit,
So that my hands were reddened with the blood
Of these poor cattle!   And they laugh at me;
Having escaped—not as I meant for them.
Yes; if some deity must interfere,
The bad will scape the better.   As things are,
What must I do?  whom plainly the Gods hate,
Whom the Hellenian host abominate,
Whom all Troy loathes, ay and this soil of it!
Am I to quit the staith, where lies the fleet,
Leave the Atridæ in the lurch, and pass
Homeward, across the Ægean?   And what visage
Shall I display, when I appear before
My father, Telamon?   How will he endure
To look upon me in his presence, bare,
Denied the honours that became to him
A crown of glory?   That may never be.
Then shall I march against the fence of Troy,
Fall singly on the foe, on the foe only,
Do some good service, and so lastly die?
That is the way to please the Atridæ, though
It is impossible.   Some enterprise
Must be sought out, by which to manifest
To my old father that, in heart at least,
Not wholly nerveless I descend from him.
It is a shame to crave long life, when troubles

Allow a man no respite.   What delight
Bring days, one with another, setting us
Forward or backward on our path to death?
I would not take the fellow at a gift
Who warms himself with unsubstantial hopes;
But bravely to live on, or bravely end,
Is due to gentle breeding.   I have said.

1 *Mariner.* That not heart-felt, but feigning, are the words
Which you have spoken, Ajax, none will say.
Still, pause an instant; let these fancies be,
And suffer friends to master your resolve.

*Tecmessa.* O my lord Ajax, in the ills of men
There is none sorer than Necessity.
I was the offspring of a sire free-born,
Strong in his wealth, no Phrygian more than he;
And now, I am a slave.   So the Gods willed it,
And thy right hand determined.   Coming thus
Unto thy bed, I am on thy side, now.
And I beseech thee by our household Jove,
And by thy couch, which thou didst share with me,
Leave me not open to contemptuous talk
From thy foes' tongues, bequeathing me to be
Handmaid to some one!   For the very day
Thou diest, and dying puttest me away,
Think how the Argives will lay violent hands
On me who, with thy son, must thenceforth eat
The bread of bondage!   And some master then,
In bitter language aiming taunts at me,
Will word me—"Look at Ajax' concubine!
His, who was once the mightiest of the host;
What servitude, after such envied state,
Is come on her!"   Such things will some one say,
And I shall be the sport of destiny,
But thee and thine these sayings will bring to shame.
O tremble, ere in sorrowful old age
Thou leav'st thy father—leav'st thy mother, too,
Who has seen so many years, and oft to Heaven
Is praying for thy return in safety home!
And pity, O king, thy son—if he, bereft
Of childish nurture, must survive alone,
Under unfriendly guardians—what sore trouble
Is this which, by thy death, thou wilt impart

To him and me? For I no longer know
To whom to look, save thee; my native land
Thy spear destroyed; and yet another stroke
Brought low my mother and my sire, to be
Inhabitants of Hades with the dead.
What home, then, could supply thy place to me?
What wealth? All my existence is in thee.
Have thou some care for me. Some mindfulness
A man should surely keep, of any thing
That pleased him once. Kindness is kindness'
    mother;
Nor can we count him gentle any more,
Whose memory fails him of a benefit.

1 *Mariner.* Ajax, I wish that you felt pity at heart
    As I do; then you would approve her words.

*Ajax.* Approval she shall have from me —at least
    If she resolves to do my bidding well.

*Tecmessa.* O my dear Ajax, wholly I obey.

*Ajax.* Bring me my son, that I may see him, now.

*Tecmessa.* I was afraid, and let him go away.

*Ajax.* During these troubles, was it? Or what mean you?

*Tecmessa.* Lest he should meet you and be killed, poor
    child!

*Ajax.* Truly it would have matched my fortunes well!

*Tecmessa.* Oh but I watched well, and prevented it.

*Ajax.* Praised be the work, and your good providence!

*Tecmessa.* How can I be of service to you now?

*Ajax.* Give me a sight of and a word with him.

*Tecmessa.* Yes. He is in the servants' charge, hard by.

*Ajax.* Why is he not yet here, though?

*Tecmessa.*               Here, my boy,
    Your father calls you. Bring him hither, you,
    Whichever of the men is minding him.

*Ajax.* Lags he behind, or comes he at your call?

*Tecmessa.* Oh yes, the servant here is bringing him.

*Enter Servant with* EURYSACES.

*Ajax.* Lift him up, lift him hither; he will not quail
    To gaze upon this slaughter freshly wrought,
    If he be mine of right paternity.
    He must begin, now, to be broken in
    To the rough fashions of his father's way,

And grow the same in nature.   O my son,
May you be luckier than your father ! else
As good as he was ; and you will do bravely.
Ay, and already I could well envy you,
Because you have no inkling of these ills ;
The happiest life consists in ignorance,[7]
Before you learn to grieve and to rejoice ;
But, when you come to it, it will be for you
To approve, upon your father's enemies,
Your birth and breeding.   Gentle airs, meanwhile,
Give thee repast ; dally with infancy,
And be thy mother's darling !   Well I know
There is no Greek will try to injure thee
With foul reproach, though thou be fatherless ;
So watchful is the guardian I shall leave
About thee—Teucer—tireless in thy care,
Albeit now, chasing the common foe,
He wanders far.   Seamen and shield-bearers !
To you as well do I commit this charge,
And tell him my behest ; to take this boy
Home, and present him there to Telamon,
And Eribœa my mother ; let him be
The unremitting solace of their age.[7]
And for my arms—they shall not be a stake
Set for the Argives, by some arbiter—
By him, my bane !   Eurysaces, my son—
Take it—the broad impenetrable shield
Of seven-fold hide, from which thou hast thy name,
And in the knotted cordage of the loop
Entwine thy grasp.   The rest shall share my grave.
—Now take the boy away immediately ;
Make the house fast, and raise no noise of crying
At the tent door.   'Tis a most piteous thing,
Truly—a woman !   Quicker, fasten it !
He's but a sorry leech, who mutters spells
Over a sore that must be cut away ![8]

1 *Mariner.* I do not like the tone of this resolve.
　　It is no pleasure that your tongue is keen.
*Tecmessa.* O my lord Ajax, what is thine intent ?
*Ajax.* Ask not : enquire not.   Self-restraint is good.
*Tecmessa.* O how my spirit sinks !   In thy child's name
　　And Heaven's, I supplicate, betray us not !

*Ajax.* Thou art too troublesome.   Art ignorant
That, once for all, I have cleared scores with
    Heaven?
*Tecmessa.* Speak not so rashly!
*Ajax.*                     Talk to those who listen!
*Tecmessa.* Wilt not thou hearken?
*Ajax.*                     Far too much already
Hast thou complained.
*Tecmessa.*                 Because I fear, my king.
*Ajax.* Take her and shut her up immediately.
*Tecmessa.* Relent, for Heaven's sake!
*Ajax.*                     I must think thee fool,
To deem that thou canst school my temper, now.

*The Scene closes on* AJAX, TECMESSA, EURYSACES *and the servant.*

CHORUS.[9]

I. 1.

Fair Salamis, where sea-waves roar
    Thou dwell'st, methinks, at peace;
And ever glorious is thy shore
    Among the sons of Greece;
Poor I, for many a weary day,
Tarry, each night, on Ida's grass,[10]
Watching the countless seasons pass,
    Worn by the long delay;
Comfortless—reckless—hopeless, save
In the drear prospect of the looming Grave.

I. 2.

And Ajax, deaf to all relief,
    A frenzy-haunted man,
Stands by to renovate my grief;[11]
    Whom, when the war began,
    Thou didst send forth, a prince in fight;
But now he broods in heart, alone,
A deep affliction to his own;
    The triumphs of his might
Seem hostile all to hostile eyes;
The sons of Atreus see them, and despise.

## II. 1.

Surely the mother, in her close of day,
She that did rear him, aged now, and grey,
When she shall hear his madness whispered nigh,
    "Woe woe!" will be her cry!
No plaintive murmur of the nightingale,
        No querulous bird-like wail,
But piercing notes will echo through the air,
Loud beatings of her breast, and rendings of her hoary hair.

## II. 2.

Better in Hades, hidden from the day,
Were he, the man whose wits are far astray,
Who by ancestral lineage towering most
        O'er the whole toil-worn host,
No longer in his moods remains unchanged,
        But walks as one estranged.
Unhappy sire! what ruin of thine own son
Awaits thine ear! save him, to thee and thy whole race
unknown.

*Enter* AJAX, *with a drawn sword.*

*Ajax.* All things obscure the slow uncounted hours
    Bring forth to light, and cover all things plain;
    And nothing is so strange it may not be,
    But the stern oath—ay, and the stubborn mind
    Yield.   Even I, that was so stout of late—
    Yea, hard as tempered steel, before yon woman
    Felt my keen edge of resolution turned
    To feminine softness; and it pities me
    To leave her widow and my child fatherless
    Among their foes.   But I will take my way
    Down to the meadows by the shore, and bathe,
    So I may cleanse my soilure, and escape
    The heavy wrath of Her, the Deity;
    And passing onward till I reach some spot
    Untrodden, I will bury this my sword—
    Weapon most hostile—digging in the earth
    Where none shall see; let Night and Hades there
    Keep it, below!   For from the hour I gat
    This gift from Hector, my arch-enemy,
    Never one boon, from Argives, did I gather:

But that is a true proverb which men use,
" A foe's gifts are no gifts," and profit not.
—Wherefore in future we must learn to bend
Before the Gods, and try to reverence
The sons of Atreus.  They are lords of us,
And we must needs give way to them.   How else?
For even things terrible and exceeding strong
Do homage to the worthier; thus is it
Snow-laden winters pass away before
Fair-fruited summer-time; Night's gloomy round
Gives place anon to the white steeds of Day
To blaze with lustre; the fell blast of winds
Can make cessation in the roaring main;[12]
And Sleep, the universal vanquisher,
Sets free the captives he enchained, at last.
And who are we, that we should not learn wisdom?
I for my own part, having learnt of late
Those hateful to us we are not to hate
As though they might not soon be friends again,
Intend to measure, now, the services
I render to my friend, as if not so
To abide for ever; for of mortals most
Find friendship an unstable anchorage.
But as to these things all shall now be well;
Only do thou, woman, betake thee in,
And pray the Gods fully to grant fulfilment
Of what my heart desires; and you, my comrades,
Grant me the self-same favour equally,
And signify to Teucer, if he come,
To care for us, and to be good to you.
For I am going thither, where I must go;
But do ye as I bid you, and perchance
Ye may soon hear that I have gained, in spite
Of present evil, safe deliverance.

[*Exit.*

CHORUS.

I.

I flutter in transport, I thrill with delight!
    Pan, what ho!—Pan, what ho!
Hither from the rocky height
    Cyllenian, beat by snow,

O Pan, sea-faring Pan,
     Appear, appear !
   King of Gods who lead the measure,
     Be present here !
    Begin the round that winds at pleasure,
Nysian or Cnosian ;
     For now would I be dancing;
And across the Icarian sea
     Let the Delos-born, advancing,
King Apollo, visibly
Stand by me, and in all things favour me !

## II.

Lo, Ares disperses a gloom from our eyes !
     Now again—now again
Cause the sun-light to arise,
    And white days, free from pain,
O'er the swift careering fleet,
     O Zeus most high !
   Now that Ajax, his distresses
     Anew laid by,
   All worship to the Gods addresses,
Honouring them, as is most meet.
     'Tis a long road knows no turning, [5]
And there's nothing may not be,
     Now, from choler and heart-burning
Huge, against the Atreïdæ,
Ajax relents so unexpectedly.

*Enter a Messenger.*

*Messenger.* Friends, I would first announce—Teucer is here,
Come from the Mysian heights ; and entering in
To the assembly, is being set upon
By all the Greeks at once.  Being ware of him,
They ringed him round as he drew near, and straight
Assailed him with reproaches, right and left,
Not one of them excepted ; styling him
" Kin to the madman, the conspirator
" Against the host, he should not come off clear,
Short of being stoned to death ! "  It went so far,
Swords leaped to hands, drawn from their sheaths,
     already,

When the dispute, though it had run past bounds,
Ended, at instance of the seniors.
But where is Ajax, to receive my story?
One must report things to one's officers. [13]

1 *Mariner.* He is not within; he has fitted his changed will
To a changed way, and is but now gone forth.

*Messenger.* Heigh ho!
Either my sender on this errand, then,
Sent me too late, or I am proved a laggard!

1 *Mariner.* Why, what is lacking to this urgency?

*Messenger.* Teucer enjoined he should by no means pass
Forth of the hut, before himself was present.

1 *Mariner.* He is gone, I tell you; his intention turned
To the best of ends, that he may be relieved
From the Gods' wrath.

*Messenger.* These words are full of folly,
If Calchas justly can at all divine.

1 *Mariner.* To what effect? What does he know of it?

*Messenger.* This much I know, for I was present there.
Out from the council and the circle of kings
Calchas apart from the Atridæ drew,
Put hand in Teucer's in a friendly way,
And spake, and charged him by all means to keep
Ajax for this day present, that now is,
Within his tents—not let him go abroad,
If he would ever look on him alive.
For till this day is done—such was his rede—
The wrath of great Athena strikes at him.
"For lives presumptuous and unprofitable
Fail beneath sore misfortunes wrought by Heaven,"
The seer declared, "whenever seed of man
Ceases to think as fits humanity.
Now he, the moment he set out from home,
In answer to his father's good advice
Proved himself void of sense; for he said to him,
'Son, at the spear's point seek thou victory;
'But seek it, always, with the blessing of God.'
But he replied vainly and vauntingly;
'My father, backed by Gods, a man worth nothing
'Might win the day; but by the hair I trust
'To pluck this glory, though they stand aloof.'
So high he boasted; then again, in answer

To great Athena, when she cheered him on,
Saying 'Turn thy hand upon the foe, and slay,'
Straight he returned her back a perilous word,
Unmeet for utterance : 'Queen, stand thou behind
'The other Argives ; where we keep the ring,
'The battle never shall break out of it!' [14]
He by such words earned of the Goddess wrath
Implacable, at his more than human pride ;
But if he is alive this day, perhaps—
God willing—we may be his saviours."
So far the seer ; and Teucer sent me on
To bring you note of this, for your good heed,
Straight from the assembly. But if I come too late,
And Calchas dote not, Ajax lives no more.

1 *Mariner.* O miserable Tecmessa ! Come and see—
Poor child !—what news this fellow is telling us !
It will go hard but this will cause some sorrow.

### Enter TECMESSA.

*Tecmessa.* Why do you rouse me from my seat again,
Weary, just eased from my persistent griefs ?

1 *Mariner.* Hearken to this man, how he brings with him
News about Ajax which distresses me.

*Tecmessa.* O sir, what say you ? Are we clean undone ?

*Messenger.* I know not your condition ; but of Ajax—
If now abroad, I am not sure of him.

*Tecmessa.* He is abroad ; and I—in agony
To hear you !

*Messenger.*      Teucer bids us keep the man
Within the tent, not let him forth alone.

*Tecmessa.* And where is Teucer, and what makes him say it?

*Messenger.* He is just arrived ; and he suspects, if Ajax
Go forth just now, 'twill be the death of him.

*Tecmessa.* Me miserable ! Who could have told him so ?

*Messenger.* The soothsayer, Thestor's son, who for this day
Makes prophecy of life or death to him.

*Tecmessa.* Alas, O friends, stand between me and ruin !
And hurry, some, for Teucer to come quickly,
And some the western, some the eastward bays
Seek, and search out the unlucky track of him.
For now I see my lord has cheated me,
And from his old affection cast me out.

O me, what shall I do, child? not stand idle!
Follow I will, wherever I am able.
Let us begone, let us be busy; this
Is no time to sit still, when we are trying
To save a man who is rushing on his death.[15]

1 *Mariner.* I am off, and not in word alone; I'll shew it;
For speed of act, and of feet too, shall follow.

[*Exeunt.*

*The scene changes to a lonely part of the sea-shore.   Enter*
AJAX, *who fixes his sword in the ground.*

*Ajax.* Now he stands fast, my executioner;
Most trenchant so—if there were leisure left
To reason about it; being, first, Hector's gift,
The most unwelcome foeman to my sight
And worse detested; he is fixed, besides,
In hostile soil, the Troad; newly edged
Upon the whetting-stone that feeds on steel;
And I myself fixed him, and set him well,
Of my quick death the officious instrument!
So we are ready; and in due course thou first,
Zeus, as is right, befriend me!   I shall demand
No mighty boon of thee; send us some herald
To carry the ill news to Teucer's ear,
That he may raise me first, where I have fallen
Upon this sword, while my blood reeks on it,
Lest I be seen first by some enemy,
And be cast out, a prey for dogs and fowl,
Headlong.   So much, Zeus, I implore of thee
Hermes, our convoy to the under-world,
Alike I summon; when upon this blade
With no distracted or irresolute leap
I force a mortal passage through my side,
Give me good rest!   And to my aid I call
The dread Erinyes, with no lagging stride
Pursuing, virgin ever, evermore
Noting whate'er mankind endure, to mark
How I by the Atridæ's malice perish!
Whom let them seize on most perniciously,
Pernicious and abandoned utterly,
Even as they see me abandoned.[16]   Up,
You swift avenging Furies, glut yourselves,

Spare nothing, on the general host!—Thou too,
Driving thy chariot up the steep of heaven,
When thou revisitest my native land,
Sun, draw thy gilded rein, and tell of me,
My woes and ruin, to the old man my sire,
And that unhappy dame who nurtured me.
How will that sad one utter loud laments
To the whole city, when she hears this tale!
But idle wailings are of no use now;
I must to work, and briskly.   O Death, Death,
Come, look me in the face!   And yet with thee
I can hold converse when I meet thee, there;
But you, the instant beams of shining day
And the careering Sun, once more I name,
And ye shall never hear my voice again.
O Light!   O sacred soil of Salamis
My native land!   O altar of my home!
Thou glorious Athens, and thy sons, my playmates,
You springs, you rivers here, and plains of Troy—
You I address—Comrades of mine, farewell!
This his last word Ajax bestows on you;
The next is greeting to the Shades below.

> [*Falls on his sword and dies.*

*Enter the first Semi-Chorus.*

1 *Mariner.*          Every pother
                        Brings another
Following hard upon its brother.
              For where, where,
              Did I not fare?
And never a spot can show
What I would know.

Hilloa! I hear a noise, once more.

*Enter the second Semi-Chorus.*

2 *Mariner.*                              Hilloa!
Only ourselves, your shipmates.
1 *Mariner.*                        Well, what cheer?
2 *Mariner.* West of the fleet we have scoured the country-
                        side.
1 *Mariner.* And have you found?

**2 *Mariner*.**                                    Plenty of trouble, truly ;
And nothing more to see.
**1 *Mariner*.**                                Nor eastward, neither,
In any quarter, is the man in sight.

*Chorus*.     Is there no fisher bent on toil,
Busied all night in quest of some sea-spoil,
Is there no Goddess from the Olympian hill,
No Nymph of any Bosporus-feeding rill,
To tell if they have seen our rude-souled king
             Anywhere wandering ?
             'Tis hard for me,
Roving about so long and painfully,
Never to hail him with a favouring breeze,
Nor even sight the madman, where on earth he is !

*Tecmessa (behind)*.  O me unhappy !
**1 *Mariner*.**                      Hark ! whose cry was that
Came from the grove close to us ?
*Tecmessa (behind)*.                            Woe is me !
**1 *Mariner*.** 'Tis the ill-fated captive bride, I see,
Tecmessa, overwhelmed in sorrow, there !
*Tecmessa*. I faint, I die ! Friends, I am all undone !
**1 *Mariner*.** What is it ?
*Tecmessa*.                    Here is Ajax newly slain,
Lying in a heap, with a sword under him.

*Chorus*.    O my far home, I may not see again !
Oh, thou didst kill, my chief,
Me, O rash heart, thy comrade on the main !
O woman full of grief !

*Tecmessa*. Yes, here he lies ; and we may wail for him.
**1 *Mariner*.** By whose hand could he do it, hapless one ?
*Tecmessa*. By his own, clearly ; planted in the ground
This sword on which he lies accuses him.

*Chorus*.    O my hard luck ! Why shed thy life-blood thus,
Devoid of help from us ?
And I the utter dullard, utter dunce,
Never guessed once !—
Where lies our Ajax ? where
The man of boding name, immitigable by prayer ?

*Tecmessa*. He is not for your sight. Rather, I will shroud him,
From head to foot, in this enfolding robe ;

For nobody that loved him could endure
To look upon him, spouting livid blood
Out at his nostrils, and from the red wound
Of his self-ministered murder.—O my heart!
What shall I do?—Who, of all friends, shall raise
thee?—
Where's Teucer? Ah how timely, if he came,
Would he arrive now, to compose the limbs
Of this his brother who has perished! O
Unhappy Ajax! Whither, from what state,
Art thou now fallen! how worthy to receive
Tribute of mourning even from enemies!

*Chorus.* Was this thy meaning, this—
At last—rashly obdurate—to fulfil
An evil doom of infinite miseries?
For this, all night, and in the daylight, still,
O ruthless heart, didst thou send out thy groans,
Defying Atreus' sons
In thy despair?
Truly that hour was author large of woes,
When for the arms [Achilles used to wear][17]
Strife of the bravest hearts and foremost hands arose!

*Tecmessa.* Ah, woe for me!
1 *Mariner.* Sorrow so notable
Goes to the heart, I know.
*Tecmessa.* Woe, woe for me!
1 *Mariner.* I well believe you might cry woe twice over,
Lady, being just bereft of such a lover!
*Tecmessa.* It is for you to think, for me to feel.
1 *Mariner.* I own it.
*Tecmessa.* Ah my child, under what yoke
Of bondage—to what taskmasters we go!

*Chorus.* Oh, thou art prophesying of distress
Nameless—in this lament;
Work of the twins of Atreus, pitiless!
Which may some God prevent!

*Tecmessa.* But for the Gods it had not happened thus.
1 *Mariner.* They wrought a sorrow far too sore to bear.
*Tecmessa.* Jove's awful daughter, Pallas, brings to pass,
To please Ulysses, all this misery.

*Chorus.* Now he exults in his black-visaged mood,
  The man of patient blood,
 And laughs loud laughter at these frenzied griefs;
  And with him the high chiefs—
   Woe, woe is me!
 Are laughing as they hear, the twin Atreïdæ.

*Tecmessa.* So let them laugh, and glory in this man's ruin.
 Perhaps, though living they would none of him,[18]
 In the spear's press they may bewail him, dead.
 Men of perverse opinion do not know
 The excellence of what is in their hands,
 Till some one dash it from them.   Sweet to them,
 Bitter it is to me, that he is dead;[19]
 While for himself 'tis pleasant.   For of that
 Which he desired, he did possess himself,
 Death, as he willed it.   Therefore over him
 Why should they triumph?   He by Heaven's hand
  has fallen,
 Not by theirs, never!   Let Ulysses, then,
 Vainly exult; for Ajax is no more
 Under their power, but is past beyond them—
 Leaving me anguish, and laments for him.

*Teucer* (*within*). Woe, woe for me!
1 *Mariner.*      Peace! for I seem to hear
 The voice of Teucer crying in a strain
 Not dissonant with this calamity.

     *Enter* Teucer.

*Teucer.* O dearest Ajax, O my kinsman true,
 And hast thou fared [20] as the report prevails?
1 *Mariner.* Of that be sure, Teucer; the man is dead.
*Teucer.* Alack therefore, for my so heavy chance!
1 *Mariner.* Since it is so—
*Teucer.*     Alas, alas for me
1 *Mariner.* There's room to groan.
*Teucer.*     O overhasty blow!
1 *Mariner.* Too hasty, Teucer.
*Teucer.*    Out, alas—Ay surely,
 What of his child?   Where, in all Troia, is he?
1 *Mariner.* Alone, by the tents.
*Teucer.*    Will you not fetch him, then,
 With all speed hither, lest some enemy

Should snatch him up, like whelp of lioness
Reft of her mate?  Go, hurry, lend a hand;
All use to insult over the prostrate dead.

1 *Mariner.*  Ay, Teucer; and indeed before he died
Our master left the charge to you, to watch
Over his offspring, which you now perform.

*Teucer.*  O of all sights that ever I beheld
Most grievous!  O of all my journeyings
The journey most afflicting to my breast,
On which I came but now, soon as I heard
Thy fate, O dearest Ajax—following thee,
And tracking out thy steps!  For a swift rumour,
(As from some God) of thee, how thou hadst perished,
Went throughout all the Achaians; hearing it,
I, miserable, was groaning to myself
Yet being afar; now seeing, I am undone.
O woe is me!  Go and uncover him,
That I may view the whole calamity.
O sight of horror and fell hardihood,
What sorrows has thy withering sown for me?
For whither—to what people—can I go,
Who never in thy troubles succoured thee?
Will Telamon, mine and thy father too,
As mildly, as benignly, welcome me,
Returning without thee?  Much chance he will;
Whose wont it is not even when prosperous
Ever to smile at all more graciously.
What will he spare to utter?  What reproach
Will he not lay on me—the bastard—me—
Child of the war-spear, who betrayed, through baseness,
Thee, dearest Ajax—yea through cowardice,
Or of design, that after thou wert dead
I might obtain thy lordship, and thy hall?
A man of choleric mood, sullen with age,
Will say such things, working himself up to quarrel
At nothing!  And in the end, a banished man,
Bondman, for free, proclaimed, I shall be cast
Out of the land.  So shall I fare at home;
And here in Troia many enemies
And scanty aids have I.  And from thy death
I reap all this!  Ah me, what shall I do?

How shall I drag thee off, O hapless one,
From this cruel gleaming point, by dint of which
Thou didst expire?   Sawest thou how at last
Hector though slain would be the death of thee?
In heaven's name, note the fortune of this pair!
Hector, to whom by this man it was given,
Pinned by a girdle to the chariot rings,
Was torn along, till he breathed out his life;
While Ajax, who accepted this from him,
By it has perished, falling on it, and dying.
Was not Erinys forger of the blade,
And Hades of that girdle, craftsman dire?
These accidents, and everything beside,
Are snares, I would aver, Gods lay for men;
Let him in whose opinion this sounds strangely
Keep of the other counsel: I keep mine.

*1 Mariner.* Do not discourse at length; only take thought
How you will get this body under ground,
And what you have to plead; for I behold
An adversary coming; one full likely
To triumph, like a caitiff, in mishap.
*Teucer.* Which of the captains is it you espy?
*1 Mariner.* Menelaus; he on whose account we sailed.
*Teucer.* I see him; near, he is not hard to know.

*Enter* MENELAUS, *attended.*

*Menelaus.* Fellow, I forbid thee to lend hand to bear
That corpse out for the interring; let it lie.
*Teucer.* What moves you to the expense of so much breath?
*Menelaus.* My pleasure; his too, who commands the host.
*Teucer.* Please you to say what reason is alleged?
*Menelaus.* Because we meant to bring him to the field
A friend and aider to the Achaian side,
And found him worse than Phrygian in the trial;
Who could contrive to murder the whole host,
And sally at night to put them to the sword;
And had not some God quenched his enterprise,
Ours had the lot been, which has fallen to him,
Now to lie dead, by a most shameful fate,
While he lived on.   But as it is, a God
Turned the encounter of his violence
On sheep and cattle.   Wherefore, as for him,

There is no man possessed of so much power
As to entomb his body in a grave;
But cast out prone upon the yellow sands
To the sea-birds he shall become a prey.
—Never uprear your crest and threaten me!
Even if we failed to govern him in life,
Our hands, at least, shall, though you like it not,
Rule and control him dead.   Troth, while he lived
He would not listen to one word from me!
Yet is it factious, when a common man
Turns a deaf ear to those set over him.
For never in a city can the laws
Be well sustained, where reverence is impaired,
Nor can an army be discreetly ruled,
Having no bulwark of respect or shame.
No; though he swell his body to a size,
It is becoming to a man, to think
How by a little evil he may fall.
He who is modest—ay, and reverent—
Be well assured—is in security;
But where excess and license range unstayed—
Deem of that city that, with all sails set,
It must at some time founder.   Let me keep
Seasonable fear; and let us not suppose
That, doing merely what will give us pleasure,
We shall not pay by troubles in full measure.[21]
These things wag on by turns.   This man was once
A glorious braggart; it is my day now;
And I prohibit you to bury him,
Lest in so doing you dig yourself a grave.

1 *Mariner.* O Menelaus, do not you lay down
     Maxims of wisdom, and become yourself
     A scorner of the dead!

*Teucer.*                 Sirs, for the future
I should not be surprised at any man
Who, being naught by birth, behaves amiss,
When those who seem to be of noble race
Offend so widely in their oratory.
Come now, repeat that preface; sayest thou
Thou didst find him, and bring him as ally
To the Achaians hither?   Sailed he not
Forth of himself, in his own mastery?

When wert thou made a captain over him?
Where lies thy title to command the folk
He led to fight? As Sparta's king thou camest,
Not as our master. There's no room to say
It was laid down in any rule of state
That thou shouldst order him, more than he thee.
Another's officer thou sailedst hither,
Not in command of the whole host, that thou
Shouldst ever be to Ajax general.
Rule those thou rulest, and find fault with them
In good set terms; but this man, whether thou
Or the other general prohibit it,
I will deposit duly in the tomb,
Unfrighted by your clamours. He, I tell you,
Not for your wife's sake ever went to war,
Like some poor hind, laden with drudgery,
But for the oath's that bound him : not at all
For you ; mere ciphers he regarded not!
Now fetch more heralds, fetch your general,
And then come on! For all your blustering,
You being but what you are, I shall not waver.

1 *Mariner.* I do not love such talk at all the more
  Amid misfortunes; hard words carry a sting,
  Though they be more than just.

*Menelaus.*       The bowman seems
  To be—not humble.

*Teucer.*       Yes, the art I practise
  Is no mechanic art.

*Menelaus.*      Get you a shield,
  And we shall see big boasting.

*Teucer.*       Lightly armed
  I were a match for you in panoply.

*Menelaus.* How fierce the spirit is, which is in your tongue!

*Teucer.* Oh, with the right, high mettle is not amiss.

*Menelaus.* Right is it, he, my murderer, should find favour?

*Teucer.* Your murderer! that is strange indeed, that you
  Should be alive, when murdered!

*Menelaus.*       Yes, a God
  Keeps me in life. But dead I were, for him.

*Teucer.* Then don't dishonour Gods—if Gods have kept you.

*Menelaus.* Is it I, who quarrel with Heaven's ordinance?

*Teucer.* Yes, if you come and hinder burials.

*Menelaus.* Only of my own foes, I ; for that's disgraceful.

*Teucer.* Did Ajax ever rank among your foes ?

*Menelaus.* He hated me, and I him ; and that you knew.

*Teucer.* I know you cozened him, through bribery.

*Menelaus.* The judges cast him in the suit, not I.

*Teucer.* Your cozenage may have covered much foul play
In secret, with fair seeming.

*Menelaus.* After that,
Some one shall dearly rue !

*Teucer.* No more, I fancy,
Than we shall furnish cause for penitence.

*Menelaus.* Look, in one word, he is not to be buried.

*Teucer.* I say, he shall be buried instantly !

*Menelaus.* Once I beheld a man in language brave
Who egged on seamen in a storm to sail,
Who had no power of utterance left in him,
When he was caught in the storm's violence ;
But crept under a blanket, and gave leave
To any of the crew to trample on him.
And so thee also, and thy brawling tongue,
From a small cloud out-blowing, some great storm
May come to quell, for all thy clamorousness.

*Teucer.* So too have I set eyes upon a man
So full of folly, that he made a mock
Of troubles of his neighbours ; and then one
Answering to me, and like me in his mood,
Looking upon him, said a word like this ;
" Sir, do not wrong the dead ; for if you do,
You certainly will have to pay for it ! "
In such wise did he caution, to his face,
A man misguided. And that man I see ;
And 'tis no other, as appears to me,
Than thou thyself. Is not my riddle easy ?

*Menelaus.* I am going. It is disgraceful to be heard
Chiding with words, when it is in one's power
To use compulsion.

*Teucer.* Go thy ways. To me
It is the worst disgrace to have to hear
A shallow man, prating sheer foolishness.

*Chorus.* This great strife approaches an issue.
Only, O Teucer, with all speed hasten

Some deep hollow to find, where Ajax
    May in his grave have rest—by mortals
      Unforgotten—his mouldering grave.

TECMESSA *comes forward with* EURYSACES.

*Teucer.* And in good time here are his wife and child,
    Waiting to deck a tomb for the poor corpse.
    Come hither, boy; stand near, and put thy hand
    On the sire's form who gat thee, suppliant-wise,
    And seat thee as in sanctuary, and hold
    Locks of her hair, and mine, and of thine own,
    For votive offerings.   And if by force
    Any of the host should tear thee from this body,
    Evil, in evil, may he be cast out
    And find no burial, utterly cut off
    Down to the root of his whole family,
    Even as I shear this curl.   Here, take it, boy;
    And keep it, and let no man make thee stir;
    Kneel there; hold fast!  And do not you stand round,
    Like women, and not men; but second us,
    Till I take order for his funeral—
    Though nobody permit me—and return.    [*Exit.*

## CHORUS.

### I. 1.

When, ah when will come relief?
    When will end
All the tale of tortured years—
    Years that send
Over me their waves of doom
    Without cease,
Labours, brandishing of spears,
    As I roam
Over Troy's wide plain, the grief
    And shame of Greece?

### I. 2.

O that into the dim vast
    Of the wind,
Or the common gulf of life,
    He had past

Long before, the Greek who first
    Openly
Taught the art of arms accurst—
    Public strife—
Toils on toils, alas! for he
    Hath ruined mankind!

## II. 1.

He made me to be a stranger to the pleasures
    Of the flower-coronal, of the wine-cup deep;
He robbed me cruelly of the sweet flute-measures,
    And barred me from the nightly joys of sleep;
Yea from love too, from love he severed me;
    And all uncared for, here I lie—my hair
Steeped in thick-falling dews continually—
    Bethinking me of Troy, the causer of my care.

## II. 2.

And Ajax' arm hitherto shielded me
    From hostile weapons, and the fears of night;
But yields him now to a dark destiny;
    And what is left—what, that can give delight?
O that I stood where sea-washed promontories
    O'erhang the deep, beneath the upland plain
Of Sunium's wood, so I might hail Her glories,
    And greet the sacred soil of ATHENS once again!

*Enter* TEUCER.

*Teucer.* I came with haste, seeing the general,
    Agamemnon, hurrying thither: it is plain,
    Sinister threats he means to launch at us.

*Enter* AGAMEMNON.

*Agamemnon.* Is it you, they tell me, with impunity
    Venture to snarl in this fierce fashion at me,
    You, I repeat, the captive woman's child?
    Had but your mother been well-born, methinks
    You would have boasted loftily indeed,
    And gone your gates on tiptoe, when, being nothing
    You stand against me on behalf of one
    Who is as nothing; swearing that I came
    Neither as general nor admiral

To you or the Achaians, but, you tell me,
Himself being in command Ajax set sail!
Is not this monstrous for a serf to say?
What was the man, of whom you have croaked out
Such insolence? On what service did he go,
What post did he maintain, where I was missing?
Are there no men among the Greeks but he?
To our cost, seemingly, did we proclaim
Contests to the Argives for Achilles' arms,
If, come what will, Teucer is to call us villains,
And even when beaten you will never deign
To accept the general judgment of the Court,
But either go on pelting with abuse,
Or slyly trying to stab us, when you lose!
With such behaviour there can never be
Establishing of any ordinance,
If we must thrust out those who rightly win
To bring the hindmost forward. But all this
Must be kept under; for the trustiest men
Are not the broad of breast and shoulder-blade;
But the well-judging everywhere prevail;
And underneath the lash, light though it be,
The big-ribbed ox plods straight along the way.
Which same corrective shortly, I perceive,
Except you pick up some sagacity,
Will visit you; who for a man that now
No longer is, but is become a shade,
Swagger your fill and spit out insolence!
Will you not be discreet? Will you not mind
Your own extraction, and—bring in with you
Some other man, free born, to say your say
Before us, in your stead? Since, when you talk,
I cannot comprehend you; in a word,
I have not learnt the outlandish dialect!

1 *Mariner.* Would that you both had wit to be discreet—
Since better may not be to say to you.

*Teucer.* Alas, how quick the gratitude in men
Fades and is found a traitor to the dead,
If this man, here, not even in small measure,
Ajax, retains a memory of thee,
For whom thou hast done good service in the fight
Often, and to the spear proffered thy life!

Truly all these things are past and thrown aside.
—Thou prater of unprofitable talk,
Dost thou no longer recollect the time
When, shut up close behind your battlements,
Just in extremity of overthrow,
Ajax, unaided, came and rescued you,
The fire already blazing all about
The topmost rowers' benches of the fleet,
And Hector in mid leap upon the hulls
Over your trenches?   Who averted that?
Was it not Ajax did it, who, thou sayest,
Nowhere so much as stirred one step to aid?
Do you confess he did his duty there?
And when again he singly, in single fight,
Chosen by lot, and of his own free will,
Entered the lists with Hector,—when the lot
He cast into the midst no skulker proved,
No lump of sodden soil, but such as promised
Lightly to leap first from the crested helm—
'Twas he that did it!   And I too was there,
The serf, the foreign mother's progeny—
Wretch, with what forehead dar'st thou mutter it?
Hast thou forgot thy grandsire's parentage,
Old Pelops, a barbarian Phrygian born?
Or Atreus, who begat thee—how he served
His brother a most execrable meal
Of his own children?   Thou thyself wert born
Son of a Cretan mother, whose father found
A strange lover in her arms, and packed her off,
Food for the fishes!   And dost thou, being such,
Taunt with his origin a man like me,
Sprung on the father's side from Telamon,
Who, being foremost of the army, won
And took my mother to his bed, by birth
A princess, daughter of Laomedon,
Whom as a guerdon set apart for him
Alcmena's offspring gave him?   And shall I,
Born of two noble parents, and in this
Myself most noble, shame my own kith and kin,
Whom when laid low by such a load of cares
Thou dost thrust out unburied, and not blush
To avow the deed?   Be well assured of it,

If you do cast him out, us three, besides,
You will cast out lying dead along with him !
It would become me better to be slain
Fighting for him before the eyes of men,
Than for your wife—or rather, brother's wife ;
Wherefore look to it ; not my case, but your own ;
Since, if you injure me in anything,
The time will come, you will be glad to choose
To play the recreant, before braving me.

*Enter* ULYSSES.

1 *Mariner.* My lord Ulysses, I would have you know
   You have come in season, if you come to help
   In setting straight, not in embroiling us.
*Ulysses.* What is it, sirs ? I heard a long way off
   The Atridæ, loud, over our mighty dead.
*Agamemnon.* And have not we, from this man, heard but now
   Words, lord Ulysses, the most scandalous ?
*Ulysses.* How so ? for I can hardly blame a man
   Who, being reviled, joins railing issue.
*Agamemnon.*           Scandals
   He heard ; for he was acting such to me.
*Ulysses.* What did he to you that could injure you ?
*Agamemnon.* He swears he will not suffer that this corpse
   Should lack a tomb, but in my teeth will bury it.
*Ulysses.* Then—may a friend speak truth, and yet keep stroke
   As well as ever in the boat with you ?
*Agamemnon.* Speak ; I were foolish else ; for I account
   Of all the Argives you my greatest friend.
*Ulysses.* Then, hear me. Do not, in the name of Heaven,
   Harden your heart, thus cruelly to expose
   Ajax unburied ; nor let violence
   Drive you, by any means, to hate so deeply
   As to tread justice under. Why, to me
   This man was once of the whole host worst foe,
   After I won Achilles' arms ; and yet,
   Being such to me, I would not so far wrong him,
   As not to say that I beheld in him
   The foremost of the Argives—of us all,
   Saving Achilles, who came here to Troy.
   Not justly, then, would you dishonour him ;

For against him your trespass would not be,
But against Heaven's decrees.  The man of merit,[22]
Once he be dead, it is ill done to harm,
However you may hate him.

*Agamemnon.*               Is it you
Thus fight for him, Ulysses, against me?

*Ulysses.* Yes; but remember that I hated him,
While I could hate with honour.

*Agamemnon.*             Is it wrong, then,
You should go on, and trample on him dead?

*Ulysses.* Do not exult, Atrides, in advantage,
That brings dishonour.

*Agamemnon.*           It is difficult
For monarchs to avoid all sacrilege.

*Ulysses.* But easy to defer to friends' good counsel.

*Agamemnon.* Your "man of merit"[22] should obey, by right,
Those in command.

*Ulysses.*            Peace! you command then truly
When you surrender to your friends.

*Agamemnon.*           Remember
To what a man you shew this favour.

*Ulysses.*             Yes,
He was a foeman, but magnanimous.

*Agamemnon.* What are you doing, reverencing thus
The body of an enemy?

*Ulysses.*          With me
The valour far outweighs the enmity.

*Agamemnon.* Men of your sort the world calls feather-
headed!

*Ulysses.* Well, many are first friends, then bitter to us.

*Agamemnon.* And do you like to have such friends as that?

*Ulysses.* A flinty heart I do not use to like.

*Agamemnon.* You will have us to appear afraid this day.

*Ulysses.* Rather, just men; as all the Greeks will say.

*Agamemnon.* And do you bid me let them bury the dead?

*Ulysses.* Yes, for I too must lie on that same bed.

*Agamemnon.* All are alike; all toil for their own profit.

*Ulysses.* And for whom should I toil, before myself?

*Agamemnon.* It shall be known, then, as your doing, not
mine.

*Ulysses.* So that you will but do it, anyhow,
You will do worthily.

*Agamemnon.*                    O, be sure of it,
To you I would concede even more than this;
But this man, dead or living equally,
Shall have my utmost hatred.   As for you—
Do what you please.                    [*Exit.*

1 *Mariner.*                    Ulysses! He who says
That you are not born wise, being what we see
          you,
He is a fool!

*Ulysses.*                    And for the future now
To Teucer here do I declare myself
As much a friend, as I was once a foe.
And I would join in burying this your dead,
And aid you in your charge, failing in nought
That men should render to their worthiest.

*Teucer.* Worthiest Ulysses, I can praise you, wholly,
In what I say.   You disappointed, much,
My expectation; for, of all the Greeks
You, being Ajax' greatest enemy,
Alone, in act, stood by him; and in this presence
Had not the heart to do foul ignominy,
The living to the dead; as he has done—
This general, this infatuate fool, who comes—
He and his brother—and would cast Ajax out
Injuriously, robbed of his burial.
Wherefore may the elder Father of high Heaven,
Erinys, with unfading memory,
And end-accomplishing Justice, wither them,
Evil, with evil, even as they sought
To cast out Ajax with unmerited shame!
—And now I hesitate to suffer you,
O son of old Laertes, to set hand
To this interment, lest I do a thing
Displeasing to the dead; in all, save this,
Help us and welcome—and that you desire
To follow any soldier to the grave,
To us shall be no grievance.[23]   For the rest
I will provide; and be assured, we deem you
A "man of merit."[22]

*Ulysses.*                    Well, it was my wish.
But if you do not choose that I should do it,
I bow to your decision, and will go.        [*Exit.*

*Teucer.*　　Enough; for time and to spare
　　　　　　Already has been spun out.
　　　　　　Now hurry, you to prepare
　　　　　　A deep-dug hollow, and you
　　　　　　To set up, ready to hand,
　　　　　　A tripod, girded about
　　　　　　With fire, on high in the field,
　　　　　　For the laving rites that are due.
　　　　　　Then fetch from the tent, one band,
　　　　　　The harness, all but the shield.
　　　　　　But do thou, boy, lovingly
　　　　　　Lay hold along with me
　　　　　　Of thy dead father's side,
　　　　　　And lift him, with all thy pains;
　　　　　　For still the dark black tide
　　　　　　Wells up from the warm veins.
　　　　　　Come, all you that assume
　　　　　　To attend as friends; come, pay
　　　　　　Service here to the one
　　　　　　At all points worthy; than whom—
　　　　　　Than Ajax—while living, I say,[24]
　　　　　　In the whole world better was none!

### CHORUS.

Full many a thing mortals may know, who see;
　　But ere they see them, none
　　Is able to look on
Into the future, what his lot shall be.

*[Exeunt omnes.*

# ELECTRA

---

### PERSONS REPRESENTED

ORESTES, *son of Agamemnon, the late king of Argos and Mycenæ, and of Clytæmnestra.*

PYLADES, *friend to Orestes.*

*An old Attendant, Guardian to Orestes.*

ELECTRA,
CHRYSOTHEMIS, } *daughters of Agamemnon and Clytæmnestra.*

CLYTÆMNESTRA, *queen of Argos and Mycenæ.*

ÆGISTHUS, *cousin to Agamemnon, and in his lifetime the paramour of Clytæmnestra.*

*The Chorus is composed of Ladies of Mycenæ, friends to Electra. Attendants on Clytæmnestra.*

---

*Scene, before the Palace at Mycenæ.*

*Enter* ORESTES, PYLADES *and Guardian.*

*Guardian.* Son of our Captain in the wars of Troy,
Great Agamemnon, it is given thee now
With thine own eyes, Orestes, to behold
Those scenes thou hast ever longed for.   Here it lies,
Argos, the ancient land of thy desire;
The sacred glade of her the gadfly drave,
Inachus' daughter; that's the Agora
They call Lycean, from the wolf-slaying God;
This, on the left, Hera's renowned fane;
And from the point we are reaching you can swear
You see Mycenæ's Golden City, and this,
The death-fraught house of Pelops' family;
Whence I received you at your sister's hands,
And saved you from the slaughter of your sire,
And carried you away, and fostered you
So far toward manhood, ready to revenge
A father's blood.   Wherefore, Orestes, now—
And Pylades, thou dearest of allies—

Take we brief counsel what is right to do;
For see, already the bright gleam of day
Calls up the birds to sing their matins clear
Above us, and the sable star-lit night
Has passed away.   Now, before any man
Comes forth abroad, join you in conference;
For where we stand,[1] it is no season more
To hesitate; the hour is come for action.

*Orestes.* My faithfullest of followers, what clear signs
You manifest of your good will to us!
For as a generous steed, though he be old,
Beset with difficulties, pricks his ears
And bates not of his courage, you impart
Spirit to us, and lag no whit behind.
As you desire, I will unfold my scheme;
Do you the while mark my words heedfully,
And if I miss the target, mend my aim.
Late, when I sought the Pythian oracle,
To learn how I might execute revenge
Upon my father's murderers, Phœbus gave me
Answer in this sort; I will tell it you;
*I by myself unarmed with shields and martial bands*
*By craft held condign slaughter hidden in my hands.*
Well, with this answer sounding in our ears,
Go you, as opportunity may lead,
Into the house, and gather all that passes,
And bring us word of all; for in old age,
And so long after, they will never know
Now, nor suspect you, frosted thus by time.
Tell your tale thus; you are a citizen
Of Phocis, and you come from Phanoteus,
Who is their best ally; tell them (and swear it)
Orestes has been killed by accident,
By a fall from his chariot, at the Pythian games;
Let it stand so.   We, as He bade, the while,
First with libations and shorn curls of hair
Will deck my father's grave; then back again
Return, carrying an urn of beaten brass,
(The same, you know, that in the brake lies hidden,)
That in feigned words we may convey to them
Glad tidings—how my body is destroyed,
Burnt up already and made embers of!

For where's the harm to be called dead, when really
I am alive, and gather praise thereby?
No word that profits us can hurt, I fancy.
Why, I have seen men often, who were wise,
Falsely pretending death; then, when again
They came back home, they have been more prized
        than ever;
So I expect yet, out of this report,
To blaze forth, star-like, living, on my foes.
But O my native land! Gods of the soil!
Welcome me with good fortune in these ways;
And thou, paternal Home! for I thy cleanser
Come here of right, the ambassador of Heaven;
Send me not with dishonour from this land,
But grant me to inherit and set up
The old estate.—I have spoken. Now, old friend,
Be it your care to guard your post; go forward;
And let us forth. It is the season; this,
In every action, is men's best ally.

*Electra (within).* Ah woe is me!

*Guardian.* Hark!
    I thought I heard some handmaiden cry faintly
    Inside the doors, my son!

*Orestes.*                Is it perhaps
    The wronged Electra? Shall we stay awhile
    And listen to her sorrowing?

*Guardian.*              By no means.
    Do nothing ere performing what is bidden
    Of Loxias, and initiate all from thence,
    Pouring lustrations on your father's grave.
    This wafts us victory, and nerves our doings.
                                *[Exeunt.*

*Enter* ELECTRA.

*Electra.*     Holy Light, with Earth, and Sky,
    Whom thou fillest equally,[2]
    Ah how many a note of woe,
    Many a self-inflicted blow
    On my scarred breast might'st thou mark,
    Ever as recedes the dark;
    Known, too, all my nightlong cheer
    To bitter bed and chamber drear,
    How I mourn my father lost,

Whom on no barbarian coast
   Did red Ares greet amain,
But as woodmen cleave an oak
My mother's axe dealt murderous stroke,
Backed by the partner of her bed,
Fell Ægisthus, on his head;
Whence no pity, save from me,
O my father, flows for thee,
   So falsely, foully slain.
Yet I will not cease from sighing,
Cease to pour my bitter crying,
While I see this light of day,
Or the stars' resplendent play,
Uttering forth a sound of wail,
Like the child-slayer,[3] the nightingale,
Here before my father's door
Crying to all men evermore.
O Furies dark, of birth divine!
O Hades wide, and Proserpine!
   Thou nether Hermes! Ara great!
Ye who regard the untimely dead,
The dupes of an adulterous bed,[4]
Come ye, help me, and require
The foul murder of our sire;
And send my brother back again;
Else I may no more sustain
   Grief's overmastering weight.

*Enter Chorus of Ladies of Mycenæ.*

*Chorus.*    O child, Electra, child
Of one too fatally bold,
How sighest thou, unsatisfied yet,
Evermore wasting away,
For him, Agamemnon, beguiled
By thy crafty mother of old,
Spite of all Gods, in her net,
To base hands given for a prey?
Accurst be the author of this!
   If I pray not amiss.

*Electra.*    O women of noble strain,
Ye are come to solace my pain;

I know it, I well perceive ;
It escapes me not at all ;
Howbeit I will not leave
To lament my father's fall.
Ye my love who repay
With all love ever gave,
Ah let me be, I pray,
    Leave me to rave.

*Chorus.*

But not from Hades below,
Not from the all-welcoming shore,
Even with strong crying and prayer
Canst thou raise thy father again.
Past all measure in woe
Thou art perishing evermore,
Sinking deep in despair,
Where no release is from pain ;
Ah why so bent upon grief,
    Too sore for relief ?

*Electra.*

None but fools could forget
Their fathers' wrongs, who are gone.
But on her my fancy is set,
The bird, Heaven's messenger,
Wildly bemoaning her
For Itys, Itys alone !
O forlorn Niobe,
As one godlike I deem of thee,
Alas ! that abidest, weeping,
    In a rock-tomb's keeping !

*Chorus.*

Not first of mortals with thee,
Daughter, did sorrow begin ;
Whereas thou passest the rest,
Thy kith and kindred within,
The life Chrysothemis lives,
And Iphianassa, and he
In the flower of his youth who grieves,
Hid, but not all unblest,
Whom the land, Mycenæ fair,
Will receive, her princes' heir,
When he, Orestes, shall come
    By Heaven's guidance home.

*Electra.*

Whom I wait for, and go
Ceaselessly wet with tears,
Unespoused, childless, forlorn,
Bearing still, as I must,
The unending burden of woe;
But he forgets with the years
All he has heard and borne;
For what message comes I can trust?
Ever he longs to be here—
    He will not appear!

*Chorus.*

Nay cheer thee, cheer thee, my child;
God in the Heavens is yet great,
Who surveys all else and commands.
Leave thou then in his hands
Anger—the excess of regret,
Nor chide overmuch—nor forget
Those whom thou needs must hate.
For Time is a God right mild;
Nor can Agamemnon's son
By Crisa's pastoral shore,
Nor the monarch of Acheron,
    Be deaf evermore.

*Electra.*

But already most of my day,
Hopeless, has faded away;
I can do no longer withal;
Without parents to cherish me I waste,
Without husband's love, to defend;
Yea alien-like, disgraced,
I inhabit my father's hall,
And in this guise attend
At a board with no feast laid,
    Uncomely arrayed.

*Chorus.*

At his return arose
A burden of woes—of woes
To thy father's resting-place,
What time was darted a thrust,
From fangs all brass, at his face.
Fraud was deviser—Lust
Was slayer—embodying the shade
Of a fell deed foully planned,

Yea, whether by heavenly aid
Or a mortal's hand.

*Electra.*  O day that far beyond all
Dawned most hateful to see !
O night—O sorrows abhorred
Of that ghastly festival—
Murder done villainously
On my sire, by the hands of twain
Who took my life as a prey,
Who annihilated me !
Whom may God with rightful reward,
The Olympian Power, again
For their deeds amply repay,
Nor let them compass their bliss
By an act like this !

*Chorus.*  Take heed ; say no more.
Hast thou no consciousness
Out of what wealth before
Thou fall'st thus miserably
Into ills that abide with thee ?
Thou hast wrought thee woes in excess,
Bringing forth strife on strife
To the heaviness of thy life ;
And is it so easy a thing
To contend with a king ?

*Electra.*  Hard is my fate, full hard ;
I know it ; I am mad, I confess ;
Yet not for the fates that oppress
Will I keep this wrath under guard,
The while my life shall endure !
For from whom, companions dear,
Should I submissively hear
Reason, or from whom, that is wise,
Counsel, fit for mine ear ?
Let me be ; cease to advise ;
All this must pass without cure ;
I shall never be free from distress,
And laments numberless.

*Chorus.*  Yet I bid thee, faithful still,
As a mother, and in good will,
Do not add new ill unto ill.

*Electra.*   And where should a limit be set
                    For evil to spread?
            Or how is it well, to forget
                    The cause of the dead?
            In what man's heart
                    Could a plant like this find place?
            Be mine no part
                    In such men's favour or grace!
            Nor, if with any good things
                    My fortune is blent,
            Be it mine to rest in content,
                    And fetter the wings
            Of piercing cries, or tire,
                    Praising my sire.
            For if in the earth, as nought,[5]
                    The dead must lie,
            And these, in return, who ought,
                    The slayers, not die,
            Then farewell honour, and fall
                    Men's reverence, all!

1 *Lady.*   I came, my daughter, zealous for your good
            As for my own; but if I say not well,
            Have it your way; for we will follow you.
*Electra.*  I am ashamed, dear ladies, if to you
            Through frequent lamentations I appear
            Too sorely oppressed; but, for necessity
            Obliges me to do so, pardon me.
            For how should any woman gently born,
            Viewing the sorrows of her father's house,
            Do otherwise than I, who witness them
            For ever day by day and night by night
            Rather increase than lessen? to whom, first,
            The mother's face who bare me has become
            Most hostile; next, I must be companied
            In my own home with my sire's murderers,
            By them be ruled, take at their hands, or else
            At their hands hunger!   Then, what sort of days
            Do you suppose I lead, when I behold
            Ægisthus seated on my father's throne,
            Wearing the selfsame garments which he wore,
            And pouring out libations on the hearth

By which he slew him?  When I witness, too,
The consummation of their impudence,
The homicide lying in my father's bed
With that abandoned mother—if it be right
To call her mother, who consorts with him!
And she—so profligate that she lives on
With her blood-guilty mate—fearing no vengeance—
Rather, as if exulting in her doings—
Looks out the day on which by cunning erst
She slew my father, and each month on it
Sets dances going, and sacrifices sheep
In offering to her guardian deities!
I see it, I, ill-fated one!  At home
I weep and waste and sorrow as I survey
The unblest feast that bears my father's name,
In private; for I cannot even weep
So freely as my heart would have me do;
For this tongue-valiant woman with vile words
Upbraids me, crying "Thou God-forsaken thing,
Has no man's father died, save only thine?
Is nobody in mourning, except thee?
Ill death betide thee, and the nether Gods
Give thee no end to these thy sorrowings!"
So she reviles; save when she hears it said
Orestes is at hand; then instantly
She is possest, and comes and screams at me—
"Is it not you who are the cause of this?
Pray is not this your doing, who stole Orestes
Out of my hands, and conjured him away?
But mind you, you shall pay me well for it!"
So snarling, there joins with her and stands by
And hounds her forward her illustrious groom,
The all unmanly, all injurious pest,
Who fights no battles without women!  I,
Waiting and waiting, till Orestes come
And end it, miserably daily die.
For always meaning, never doing, he
Has utterly confounded all my hopes
Remote or present.  Friends, in such a case,
There is no room—no, not for soberness
Or piety; but, beneath injuries,
There is deep need we prove injurious, too!

1 *Lady*. Stay, tell me, is it with Ægisthus near
          You talk thus to us, or is he gone from home?
*Electra*. That is he.   Never think, if he were by,
          I could roam forth; but he is abroad just now.
1 *Lady*. Then I might come with better confidence
          To speech of you, that being so.
*Electra*.                              Oh, ask freely;
          He is not here.   What do you want to know?
1 *Lady*. And so I will.   What of your brother say you?
          I would fain know, will he come soon, or tarry?
*Electra*. He says he will.   He does not keep his word.
1 *Lady*. A man is backward, when on some great exploit.
*Electra*. I was not backward, when I rescued him!
1 *Lady*. Take courage, he is of a worthy stock;
          He will not fail his friends.
*Electra*.                              I trust so.   Else
          I never should have been alive so long.
1 *Lady*. Hush, say no more just now; for I perceive
          Chrysothemis your sister, who was born
          Of the same mother and same sire as you.
          Come from the palace, carrying in her hands
          Oblations customary to the dead.


                    *Enter* CHRYSOTHEMIS

*Chrysothemis*. Sister, what talk is this, you come and cry
          Aloud, abroad, before the outer gate,
          Nor will not learn, taught by long years, to cease
          Vainly indulging unavailing rage?
          I for myself can say as much as this—
          I chafe at those I live with, in such fashion
          As, if I could get power, I would make plain
          The sort of temper that I bear towards them;
          But in these dangers it seems good to sail
          Close-reefed, and not pretend to be at work,
          But effect nothing harmful; and I wish
          You too would do the like; and yet, the right
          Is not as I declare, but as you judge it;
          Still, if I am to live at liberty,
          I must in all things heed my governors.
*Electra*. Well, it is strange that you, being his child
          Who was your sire, should have regard for her.

Your mother, and have quite forgotten him!
All this good counsel you bestow on me
Is of her teaching; and of your own self
You can say nothing.   Therefore take your choice;
Either to be of evil mind, or else
Well minded to forget those dear to you;
Who said but now, if you could get the power,
You would shew plain the hate you have for them;
And yet, while I am doing everything
To avenge our father, do not take your part,
And seek to turn me from it, who take mine!
Danger!   Is there not cowardice as well?
Come, answer me, what should it profit me
To cease my mourning?   Or else hear me speak;
Do I not live? unprosperously I know,
But well enough for me; to them, the while,
I am a torment, and so render honour
To him that's gone, if there be service there!
You—madam hatress—you pretend you hate,
But really take your father's murderers' side!
For my part, I will never bend to them;
Not though a man should come and offer me
These gauds of yours, in which you glory now!
Yours be the full-spread board, the cup o'erflowing;
For me—be it my only sustenance
Not to offend against my conscience.   Thus,
I do not ask to share your dignities,
And were you well-advised, no more would you!
But now, though it be in your power to be called
Your father's child—the foremost of mankind,
Be called—your mother's!   So you shall appear
In most men's eyes unmeritoriously,
False to your friends, and to your father's shade.

1 *Lady.* Now in Heaven's name, no chiding!   There is
  good
    In what you both have said, if you would learn
    Something from her, and she, in turn, from you.

*Chrysothemis.*  Oh, I am quite accustomed to her talk;
    Nor, ladies, had I ever said one word,
    Had I not heard a very great mishap
    Was coming on her, which will make her cease
    From her long sorrowing.

*Electra.*                    Come, your bug-bear, tell it!
              If you can mention any greater grief
              Than these I have, I will reply no more.
*Chrysothemis.* Well, I will tell you everything I know.
              They are going, if you will not cease this mourning,
              To send you where you will not any more
              See daylight, but sing sorrow underground,
              Buried alive, out of this territory.
              Wherefore take heed, or by and by, in trouble
              Never blame me.   Prudence is easy, now.
*Electra.* Ay? have they purposed to do so to me?
*Chrysothemis.* Most surely, when Ægisthus shall come home.
*Electra.* Why as for that, let him come speedily!
*Chrysothemis.* What was it that you prayed for, silly one?
*Electra.* For him to come; if he is that way minded.
*Chrysothemis.* So you may get—what treatment?   Are you
              mad?
*Electra.* So I may get—farthest away from you!
*Chrysothemis.* And of life present have you no regard?
*Electra.* Living like mine is choice, to marvel at!
*Chrysothemis.* It might be, had you sense to be discreet.
*Electra.* Do not instruct me to be treacherous.
*Chrysothemis.* I do not; but to yield to those who govern.
*Electra.* Well, gloze it so; you do not speak my language.
*Chrysothemis.* Yet it were well not to be ruined through
              folly.
*Electra.* Come ruin, if needful, in a father's quarrel!
*Chrysothemis.* I am sure our father pardons us for this.
*Electra.* That is the speech a villain might approve.
*Chrysothemis.* You will not hearken and agree with me?
*Electra.* I trust I am not yet so senseless.   No!
*Chrysothemis.* Then I will go on whither I was sent.
*Electra.* Where are you going?   To whom bear you these
              offerings?
*Chrysothemis.* My mother sends me, to strew my father's
              grave.
*Electra.* How say you?   To the most detested foe—
*Chrysothemis.* Yes—"whom she murdered!"   That is what
              you mean?
*Electra.* By whom, of all friends, bidden?   At whose desire?
*Chrysothemis.* Through some nocturnal panic, to my thinking.
*Electra.* God of my fathers, only aid me now!

*Chrysothemis.* Do you gain any courage from her scare?

*Electra.* Tell me about the dream, and I could say.

*Chrysothemis.* Only I do not know it; except just
    In brief, the story.

*Electra.*             Well, but tell me that;
    Brief words ere now have often led astray—
    And righted mortals.

*Chrysothemis.*          It is said she saw
    An apparition of your sire and mine
    Come back again to daylight; and he took
    The sceptre which he sometime bore himself,
    But now Ægisthus bears, and planted it
    Upon the hearth, and out of it a shoot
    Budded and grew, till all Mycenæ's land
    Was covered with its shadow. So I heard
    Related by a fellow who was by,
    While to the Sun-God she disclosed her dream.
    But more than this I know not; only that
    She sends me on account of this alarm.
    Now I beseech you, by our country's Gods,
    Listen to me, and be not ruined by folly;
    For though you should repulse me, by and by
    In trouble you will turn to me again.

*Electra.* Nay but let nothing of your fardel, dear,
    Light on the tomb! for it were shame—were sin
    From an abominable spouse to bring
    Lustrations near, or perform obsequies
    To a sire's shade. Let the winds have them, rather!
    Or hide them deep in dust, where none of them
    Shall ever touch our father's resting-place;
    Let them be kept, stored underground, for her
    When she is dead! Why, if she were not grown
    The most abandoned of all womankind,
    She never would have dreamt of smothering
    With her unfriendly strewments him she murdered!
    Why look you, think you the entombed dead
    Will take these gifts in kindness, at her hands
    Who slew him foully, like an enemy,
    Lopped of the extremities, the stains of blood
    Smeared off, for lustral washings, on his head!
    Do you imagine what you bear can purge
    Her from her murder? Never! Let it be!

Cut from your head the longest locks of hair—
And mine, unhappy—small the gift, indeed,
But what I have—and give it him, this hair
Untended, and my girdle, unadorned
With broiderings!  Fall upon your knees, **and pray**
     him
In favour come and help us, from the earth,
Against our enemies ; and that his boy
Orestes may set foot, before he die,
Superior, on the bodies of his foes,
That we may crown him afterward with hands
Larger in gift than we can proffer now!
Yea I believe, I do believe, that he
Had part in sending her this ugly dream ;
But still, sister, do this, for your own good,
And mine, and his, the man of all mankind
Dearest, our sire, who in the grave lies dead.

1 *Lady.*  The princess speaks religiously, my friend ;
    And you, if you are wise, will heed her.

*Chrysothemis.*               Yes.
It stands to reason, not that two should quarrel
Over their duty, but be quick and do it.
Only while I essay this business, friends,
Do you keep secret, in the name of Heaven !
For if my mother hears it, to my cost,
Methinks, I shall attempt this venture, yet.

                     [*Exit* CHRYSOTHEMIS.

### CHORUS.

#### I.

If I be seer
Not wholly erring and unpolicied,
Self-prophesying Justice means to appear,
Bringing large succour to the righteous side,
And following on, my child, with no long waiting-tide.
Courage springs up within me, as I hear
The voice of dreams, breathing sweet music near ;
He who begat thee, the Hellenian King,
Forgets not ever ; nor that Ancient Thing,
The two-edged brazen fang, by which he foully died.

## 2.

Lo, this is she,
Erinys, hiding her dread ambushed bands,
Sandalled with brass, with myriad feet and hands.
Yea time hath been, when they who should not, plied
A blood-stained spousal-work, unmeet for bed or bride.
Whence it comes o'er me, I shall never see
On doer and accomplice harmlessly
This portent fall ; and nothing future can
By good or ill dream be revealed to man,
If this night-vision speed not, landward, on the tide.

O chariot-race weary
Of Pelops of old,
How fateful, how dreary,
Thou hast proved to this land !
For since Myrtilus slumbered,
From the chariot, all gold,
Torn, silenced for ever,
Flung far from the strand,
From thenceforth never
The weary disgrace
Of troubles unnumbered
Hath passed from the race.

*Enter* CLYTÆMNESTRA, *attended.*

*Clytæmnestra.* You gad abroad, then, masterless again,
Ægisthus absent ; who did hinder you
From bringing scandal on your family
By brawling at the doors !  Now he is gone,
You pay no heed to me ; though many a time,
In many people's ears, you have proclaimed—
I, without shame or warrant, violate
Your rights and honours !  I meanwhile commit
No violence ; I but repay with scorn
The scorn you heap on me.  Your father, though—
This and no other—is your pretext still,
How by my hand he died !  By mine ; I know it ;
There's no denial of the deed in me.
But Justice slew him ; I was not alone ;
And had you sense, you ought to take her side ;
Since he, this father whom you still bewail,

Alone of all the Argives had the heart
To offer to the Gods your sister's life—
Whose pains in her begetting equalled not
My travail-pangs, who bare her !   Be it so ;
Now tell me for what cause, and for whose sake,
He offered her ?   For the Argives, will you say ?
They had no right to kill a child of mine !
If for his brother Menelaus' sake
He slew my daughter, was not he to pay
Forfeit for that ?   Were there not children twain
Born to that father, who, had right been done,
Ought rather to have died, whose sire and dam
Themselves had caused that voyage ?   Had the **Grave**
Some fancy for my offspring, for its feast,
Rather than hers ?   Or had all natural love
Expired in that pernicious father's heart
For children born of me, but not for children
Of Menelaus ?   Was it not the act
Of a perverse insensate sire ?   I think it,
Though you deny ; and so would that dead girl
Say, could she speak.   For what my hands have done
I do not feel remorse ; but if to you
I seem of evil mind, censure your folk,
When you yourself are just ! [6]

*Electra.*                   You cannot say
Now, that I crossed you and you answered me !
Yet if you gave me scope, I would speak fairly
For him that's dead, and for my sister too.

*Clytæmnestra.* I give it you !   If you addressed me thus
Always, it would not chafe me so to hear.

*Electra.* Then listen !   You avow my father's death ;
What could more ill become your mouth than this,
Whether he were unjustly slain or no ?
But let me tell you that you slew him not
For Justice, but perverted by the lure
Of a base wretch, who is your consort now.
What !   Question of the Huntress Artemis
On whose account she held the various winds
Spell-bound in Aulis !   Rather, I will tell ;
For 'tis not given you to learn of her.
My father once, as I have heard the tale,
While sporting in a sacred wood of hers,

Roused as he went a dappled antlered roe,
And with some careless vaunt of slaughtering it
Shoots at and hits it; wherefore Leto's maid,
Wrathful at this, kept back the Achaian host,
Till he should render up for sacrifice,
In payment for the beast, his daughter dear—
And therefore was she offered; since escape
There was none other for the armament,
Either toward Ilium, or backward home.
Whence much enforced, and much resisting it,
Not for the sake of Menelaus, he
Unwillingly gave her to the knife at last.
But what an if (for I will take your story)
He did it through benevolence for him?
Was it thereafter just that he should perish,
And at your hand? Under what law? Beware
You do not, while you set this law to others,
Lay up repentance for yourself, and pain.
If we begin to exchange life for life,
You should die next, if you received your due.
But look you do not proffer for excuse
That which is not; for tell me, if you will,
Why you are now doing things most execrable,
Consorting with the branded murderer
By whose connivance erst you slew my sire,
And bearing children, to the extrusion of
Your honest first-born, born in honesty?
How should I pardon this? Or will you claim
In this, too, to be trying to avenge
Your daughter? It sounds vilely, if you do;
For 'twere unseemly in a daughter's quarrel
To couple with an enemy! Ay truly,
It's an offence even to admonish you,
Who let your tongue run freely, when you say
That I speak evil of my mother! I
A slave-mistress account you, over us,
As much as mother; for a servile life
Is that I lead, compassed with many griefs,
Wrought by yourself and by your paramour.
And poor Orestes is an exile, too,
Hardly delivered from your violence,
And living on in wretchedness—the same

You have so oft charged me with nurturing
To take revenge on you; and so I would—
Never doubt that—if I were strong enough.
Now, for that treason, publish me to all
Shameless—perverse—abusive—what you will;
And if I be an adept in the same,
I do bare justice to your blood in me!

1 *Lady.* I see her breathing fury! Right or wrong,
  Now, 'tis all one, for any thought she gives it!

*Clytæmnestra.* What sort of thought, then, must I give to her,
  Who in this fashion dares insult her mother,
  And at her years? Do you suppose she means
  To exceed all measure in her shamelessness?

*Electra.* Now understand, I do feel shame at this,
  Although to you I may not seem to feel it.
  I do perceive that I am doing things
  Unseasonable, and unbefitting me.
  Only your acts and your hostility
  Force me to this behaviour. Infamy
  Is got by contact with the infamous.

*Clytæmnestra.* Insolent creature! I, my words and acts,
  Make you so loudly over-eloquent?

*Electra.* It is your fault, not mine; you are the doer,
  And deeds find names.

*Clytæmnestra.*                Now not by Artemis,
  Who is my mistress, when Ægisthus comes
  Shall you escape, for this audacity!

*Electra.* See, now you fly into a frenzy! First
  You let me speak my mind—then, you'll not listen!

*Clytæmnestra.* Will you not let me sacrifice, without
  Words of ill omen, after suffering you
  To say all that you can?

*Electra.*                Go, sacrifice!
  I let you! Nay, I bid you! Censure not
  My mouth again, for I shall say no more.

*Clytæmnestra.* Take up the offerings, you that wait on me,
  The fruits of earth, that unto this my Lord
  I may prefer petitions for release
  Out of my present terrors.—Hear thou now,
  Protector Phœbus, my unuttered vow!
  For what I say I say not among friends,
  Nor is it meet to uncover all my ends

Here, in her presence, to the open sky,
Lest she with malice and loud clamorous cry
Scatter vain babblings to the city round;
But softly list, and soft my words shall sound.
The ambiguous visions, whose dim shadowing
Last night I witnessed, O Lycean King,
If they portended good, give them like close;
If evil, turn them backward on my foes.
And do not thou, if any would by stealth,
Let them disturb me from my present wealth;
Let me live on securely, as to-day,
Holding the Atridæ's palace, and their sway,
Abiding with the friends I bide withal
Now, in good case; and with my children, all
Through whom no bitter pang is made to strike
Their mother's heart, nor shudder of dislike.
Hear, great Apollo, what I pray for thus,
And, as we ask, in grace give all of us.
—The rest, I think, thou, being divine, perceiv'st,
Though I be silent; for it cannot be
But all is open to the sons of Jove.

*Enter Guardian.*

*Guardian.* Ladies, to whom I am a foreigner,
    Pray how might I discover if this palace
    Be that of King Ægisthus?

1 *Lady.*                Sir, it is;
    Your guess is right.

*Guardian.*           And am I further right
    In guessing that this lady is his wife?
    She bears a queenly presence.

1 *Lady.*              Certainly:
    You see her there before you.

*Guardian.*           Madam, hail!
    I bring you pleasant tidings from a friend;
    You, and Ægisthus also.

*Clytæmnestra.*        They are welcome.
    But I would hear first, who he was that sent you.

*Guardian.* Phanoteus of Phocis, with a weighty charge.

*Clytæmnestra.* Of what sort, stranger, say? for I am sure,
    Being from a friend, that you will speak us friendly.

*Guardian.* Briefly I speak. Orestes is no more.

*Electra.* O I am lost, unhappy!

*Clytæmnestra.*　　　　　　　What sir, what?
　　Never mind her!

*Guardian.*　　　　　　I say as I have said.
　　Orestes is dead.

*Electra.*　　　　　　O me, I am undone!
　　Now I am nothing!

*Clytæmnestra.*　　　　　　Yea, see thou to that.
　　How came he by his death, sir? Tell me truly.

*Guardian.* I will tell all; for to that end I came.
　　The man had gone to the great festival—
　　The glory of Hellas—for the Delphian games;
　　And when he heard the shouting of the crier
　　Calling the foot-race, which is first adjudged,
　　He entered for it, comely to behold,
　　The worship of the eyes of all men there;
　　And having reached the limit of the course
　　Whence they were started, he came out of it
　　With the all-honoured prize of victory.
　　To say but little out of much I might,
　　I never saw before the acts and prowess
　　Of such a man as he; but take one statement;
　　In every heat for which the judges set
　　The customary courses, [7] out and home,
　　He brought off all the honours of the day,
　　And was congratulated, and proclaimed
　　"An Argive, named Orestes"—and "the son
　　Of Agamemnon," him who mustered once
　　The illustrious host of Hellas.　So far well.
　　But if some Deity is bent on harm,
　　It is not even a strong man can escape.
　　For he, another day at sunrise, when
　　Owners of horses met to try their speed,
　　With many other charioteers, went in.
　　One was Achaian, one from Sparta, two
　　Libyans, skilled masters of the yoke and car;
　　He among these, with mares of Thessaly,
　　Came fifth; the sixth was from Ætolia,
　　With bright bay colts; the seventh Magnesian;
　　The eighth of Ænian birth, his horses white;
　　The ninth from Athens the divinely builded;
　　Last, a Bœotian's car made up the ten.

These, stationed where the judges of the course
Cast each his lot, and ranked his driving-board,
Forth started at the brazen bugle's note,
And cheering to their horses all at once
Shook the grasped reins; then the whole course was
    filled
With rattle of the chariot metal-work;
The dust rose high; crowded together, all
Spared not the goad—so might some one of them
Fore-reach on snorting steed and axle-tree;
While evermore alike on back and wheel,
Foaming and quick, the coursers' panting came.
But he kept close under the endmost mark,
Sweeping his axle round continuously,
And, giving rein to the right-handmost steed,
Pulled back the inner goer.   And at first
The driving-boards all held themselves upright;
But afterwards the Ænian's hard-mouthed colts
Bolt violently; and coming from the turn,
After the sixth, just in the seventh round,
Dash all their fronts against the Barca car;
Then, in an instant, from one accident,
Car upon car began to crash and fall,
And the whole plain of Crisa became filled
With wreck of steeds and tackling.   At the sight
That crafty driver, he from Athens, draws
Out of the way, and slackens, passing by
The surge of chariots eddying in the midst.
Last came Orestes, trusting to the close,[8]
Keeping his fillies back; but seeing him
Left in alone, he launches a shrill whoop
Through his fleet coursers' ears, and races him,
And yoke and yoke the couple drove along,
Now one and now the other shewing head
Out in the front, over their carriages.
Well, all his rounds, poor fellow, till the last,
He stood up straight, and kept his chariot straight,
And drove straight through; then, slackening the
    left rein
As his horse turns, he struck unwittingly
The corner of the mark, and snapped the nave
Short from the axle, and slipped instantly

Over the rail, and in the cloven reins [9]
Was tangled; as upon the plain he fell,
His steeds into the middle of the course
Ran all astray. Then the whole host, that saw him
Precipitated from the driving-board,
Lifted their voices to bewail the youth
Who did such feats, and met with such hard fate,
Now dashed upon the ground, now seen with limbs
All upward flung to heaven; till chariot-men
Hardly restrained the steeds in their career,
And loosed him, bathed in blood, so that no friend,
Seeing the poor body, could have known 'twas he.
Then certain Phocians, ordered for the task,
Straightway consumed it on a funeral pile,
And hither in a little urn they bring
That mighty stature, in poor embers now,
To win a tomb in his own fathers' land.
Such is my tale; right piteous in the telling;
But in the sight of us, who witnessed it,
The saddest thing of all I ever saw.

1 *Lady.* Alack, the lineage of our lords of old
     Is all, too plainly, ruined from the root.

*Clytæmnestra.* O God, this fortune—shall I call it fair,
     Or black, though profitable? yet is it hard
     That I should save my own life, through misfortunes
     Which are my own!

*Guardian.*             Why thus regretful, lady,
     At what I have just told you?

*Clytæmnestra.*           It is strange—
     This motherhood; for sons of one's own bearing,
     However ill entreated at their hands,
     One cannot muster hatred.

*Guardian.*            I am come,
     It seems, in vain.

*Clytæmnestra.*        Nay indeed, not in vain.
     Why should you say in vain? if you are come
     With a sure token that the man is dead,
     Who was indeed the offspring of my being,
     But from this bosom and maternal care
     Revolted, and became as one estranged,
     An exile; never, from the day he left
     This country, saw me more; but, laying to me

His father's death, was ever threatening me,
So that sweet sleep by neither night nor day
Would cover me, but the impending hour
Held me continually in fear of death;
While now, since I am this day freed from terror
Of him, and of her too—for she dwelt with me
A far worse canker, ever draining deep
My very life-blood—now, for all her menaces,
I shall dwell tranquil!

*Electra.*                    O me miserable!
Why now, Orestes, there is room enough
To groan for thy misfortune, when, being thus,
Thou art scorned by this thy mother! Is it well?

*Clytæmnestra.* Not thou—but he being as he is, is well.

*Electra.* Hear, Nemesis of him who is no more!

*Clytæmnestra.* Those she should hear Nemesis did hear, and well
Did she perform!

*Electra.*                    Triumph! you are happy now.

*Clytæmnestra.* You and Orestes cannot hinder me.

*Electra.* 'Tis we are hindered; far from hindering you.

*Clytæmnestra.* I were beholden to your coming, friend,
If you could hinder her from her loud clamour.

*Guardian.* Well then, I will be going—if all is well.

*Clytæmnestra.* Nay, for it were unworthy both of me
And of the friend who sent you, did you meet
Such entertainment. Please you enter in?
Leave her alone, to sorrow out of doors
For her dear friends' misfortunes, and her own.

                    [*Exeunt* CLYTÆMNESTRA *and Guardian.*

*Electra.* Seems it to you as if, in grief and pain,
She was lamenting, weeping sore—the wretch!
Over her son, thus lost? She is gone smiling!
O me unhappy! Orestes, O my darling,
How has thy death undone me! Parting thus,
Thou tearest all the hopes out of my heart—
All I had left—that thou would'st come, some day,
Living, avenger of thy father's death,
And of my wrongs. Now, whither should I turn?
I am alone; I have no father; now
I have not thee. Must I be slave once more
Among the most detested of mankind,

My father's murderers? Is it well with me?
Nay, for the future never more at all
Shall one roof hold us; rather, on this door-stone, friendless
I will sink down and wear away and die!
For this if any of the tribe within
Is angered, let him kill me; death were welcome;
Life is but pain, and I am sick of it.[10]

### I. 1.

*1 Lady.* Where be Jove's thunders, where the flaming Day,
  If, seeing these things, they hide them, and are still?
*Electra.* Ah, welaway!
*1 Lady.*                My child, why weepest thou?
*Electra.* Fie then—
*1 Lady.*        Speak gently.
*Electra.*                Thou wilt slay me.
*1 Lady.*                                How?
*Electra.* Yea, in my wasting, thou wilt trample more
  Upon me, if thou wilt suggest a hope
  For those who manifestly are dead and gone.

### I. 2.

*1 Lady.* I know that women's gold-bound toils ensnared
  The king Amphiaraus; and now beneath—
*Electra.* Ah well a day!
*1 Lady.*                He reigns, with all his powers.
*Electra.* Ah, woe!
*1 Lady.*        Woe, for the murderess—
*Electra.*                        Slain?
*1 Lady.*                                Ay, slain.
*Electra.* I know it, I know it; a champion was revealed
  For him, in trouble; none is left, for me;
  He who yet was is taken from me, and gone.

### II. 1.

*1 Lady.* Thou art meet for pity; piteous is thy lot.
*Electra.* That know I well, too well; my life is full
  With month on month, with surge on surge of woes,
  Hateful and fearful.
*1 Lady.*                All thy groans we know.
*Electra.* Therefore no more dissuade me, since not one—

*1 Lady.* How say'st thou?

*Electra.* Is left of all my hopes of aid,
From him, the heir, born of one birth with me.

## II. 2.

*1 Lady.* All have their fate.

*Electra.* Meet all such fate as his,
Dragged in a cleft of the reins,[9] poor hapless one,
Among fleet emulous hoofs?[11]

*1 Lady.* Strange, the mishap!

*Electra.* How otherwise, when without care of mine,
A stranger—

*1 Lady.* Out, alas!

*Electra.* He passed away,
Meeting no burial, no lament, from me.

*Enter* CHRYSOTHEMIS.

*Chrysothemis.* My dearest, I am driven, for delight,
To throw decorum to the winds, and run!
For I bring pleasure, and an end of ills
You suffered from before, and sorrowed for.

*Electra.* Whence would you fetch assistance for my woes,
Whereof all healing is impossible?

*Chrysothemis.* Orestes is at hand! I tell you so!
He's here, in sight, plainly as you see me!

*Electra.* Fie, are you frantic, wretch, and do you jest
At your own sorrows, and at mine?

*Chrysothemis.* Not I,
By the house-altar! I do not say this
For wantonness; but he is come, indeed![12]

*Electra.* O wretched that I am! and from whose mouth
Did you receive this tale, that you believe
So over fondly?

*Chrysothemis.* It is proved to me
By my own eyes, none other; for I see
Clear evidence.

*Electra.* See proof? O wretch, what proof?
What did you see, to inflame you all at once
With this mad fever?

*Chrysothemis.* Listen, in Heaven's name,
That you may learn; and call me, afterwards,
Crazed, if you like, or sober.

*Electra.*                         Say your say,
　　If it affords you any pleasure.
*Chrysothemis.*                    I
　　Am telling you exactly what I saw.
　　As I approached our sire's ancestral grave,
　　I observed streams upon the pillar's top
　　Of milk fresh-running, and the sepulchre
　　Circled with garlands of all flowers in bloom.
　　I was surprised to see it, and looked round,
　　To see that no one near laid hand on me.
　　But when I found all quiet about the place,
　　I crept up to the tombstone, and perceived,
　　Upon the very corner of the pile,
　　A severed ringlet of a young man's hair.
　　No sooner did I see it, than there darts
　　Into my heart an image—ah! well known,
　　This that I was beholding was the token
　　Of my most dear Orestes!  No light word
　　I uttered; but I took it in my hands,
　　And my eyes filled with tears at once, for joy.
　　And well I know, and well I knew it then,
　　How from no other came that ornament.
　　For whose work should it be, save yours or mine?
　　And I at least, I am certain, did it not,
　　Nor yet did you; how could you? when you know
　　You cannot even with impunity
　　Go out of doors to worship at a shrine;
　　Nor can it be our mother who would care
　　To do it, or have done it unperceived.
　　No, 'twas Orestes made those offerings.
　　But O dear heart, take courage!  The same Power
　　Succours not always the same side alike;
　　And on us twain it has frowned hitherto;
　　But none the less, this morning shall be fraught
　　With many things for good.
*Electra.*                         Alack the while!
　　How I pity you for your folly!
*Chrysothemis.*                    But what is it?
　　Do I not speak to please you now?
*Electra.*                         You know no[t]
　　Whither you are borne—how far you are astray!
*Chrysothemis.*  But how can I not know, what I saw plainly

*Electra.* O wretched girl, he's dead! his saving us
    Is done and ended; never look to him!
*Chrysothemis.* Alas for pity! Who was it told you so?
*Electra.* One that was present with him, when he perished.
*Chrysothemis.* 'Tis very strange. Where is he?
*Electra.*                   In the house;
    Welcome, not odious, in our mother's eyes.
*Chrysothemis.* Alas for pity! But from whom, then, came
    All those oblations to our father's grave?
*Electra.* I think most likely some one put them there
    In memory of Orestes, who was dead.
*Chrysothemis.* O miserable! and I was hastening hither,
    Joyful to have such tidings, unaware
    What mischief was upon us! Now, arrived,
    I find the old sorrows still, with others new.
*Electra.* 'Tis so indeed; but if you list to me,
    You can relieve the burden of the woe
    Weighing on us now.
*Chrysothemis.*            What, can I raise the dead?
*Electra.* That is not what I said; I am not so senseless!
*Chrysothemis.* What do you bid me, that is in my power?
*Electra.* Dare to do that which I shall urge on you!
*Chrysothemis.* If it will aid us, I shall not refuse.
*Electra.* Look, without effort nothing thrives.
*Chrysothemis.*                  I know it.
    All I have strength for I will help to bear.
*Electra.* Hear, then, the course I am resolved upon.
    Friends to stand by us even you must know
    That none are left us; but the Grave has taken
    And reft them; and we two remain alone.
    I, while I heard my brother was alive
    And well, had hopes that he would come, one day,
    To the requiting of his father's death;
    But since he is no more, to you I look
    Not to refuse, with me, your sister here,
    To slay the author of that father's murder,
    Ægisthus; (we need have no secrets, now.)
    For whither—to what still surviving hope
    Do you yet look, and suffer patiently?
    Who for the loss of your ancestral wealth
    Have cause for grieving, and have cause for pain
    At all the time that passes over you,

Growing so old, a maiden and unwed.
And these delights no longer hope to gain
At any time; Ægisthus is too prudent
To suffer that your progeny or mine
Should see the light, to his own clear undoing!
While, if you will be guided by my counsels,
First, you shall have the praise of piety
From your dead sire and brother in the grave,
Next, shall be called hereafter, as at first,
Free, and obtain a marriage worthy of you
For all men pay regard to honesty.

And as for glory—see you not what glory
You will confer upon yourself and me,
If you should heed me?   For what citizen
Or stranger, who beholds us, will not greet
Our passing steps with praises such as these:
"Friends, look at those two sisters, who redeemed
Their fathers' house; who, prodigal of life,
Were ministers of slaughter to their foes
Who prospered well before; to them be worship,
To them the love of all men; at high feasts,
In general concourse, for their fortitude,
That pair let all men honour."   Of us two
Such are the things that every man will say,
So that our glory shall not cease from us,
Living or dead.   O, be persuaded, dear!
Succour your father's, aid your brother's cause,
Liberate me from evils, and yourself,
Remembering this, that a dishonoured life
Is shame to those who have been born in honour.

1 *Lady.* In work like this forethought is serviceable
     Both to the speaker and the listener.
*Chrysothemis.* And if she were not mentally perverse,
     She would have had some thought of prudence, ladies,
     Before she ever spake—which now she has not.
     Why, in what prospect do you arm yourself
     With such a valour, and call me to aid?
     Can you not see, you are not man, but woman?
     Your hand is weaker than your enemies'.
     Heaven sends good fortune daily upon them,
     Which runs from us, and comes to nothingness.
     Who, then, that schemed the death of one so mighty,

Could scape uninjured by calamity?
Look that we do not happen on worse ills,
Ill as we fare, if some one hears these sayings.
Death, with disgrace, though we obtain some credit,
Is no advantage and no help to us;
For death is not the worst; rather, in vain
To wish for death, and not to compass it
But I beseech you, ere we are destroyed
With a complete destruction utterly,
Ere you abolish our whole family,
Set bounds on passion! What you said just now
I will keep close, unspoken, unensued;
Only be wise enough to yield at length
To stronger power, having yourself no strength.

1 *Lady.* Let her persuade you; there is no good thing
    Better than foresight and sobriety.

*Electra.* You have said nought I did not look for. Well
    I knew, you would reject my instances.
    Yes, I must do it by myself alone;
    At least, without one blow, we will not leave it.

*Chrysothemis.* Ah, would you had been so minded, when
      our sire
    Was murdered! Then you would have ended all!

*Electra.* I was, in temper; I lacked wisdom then.

*Chrysothemis.* Try and remain as wise for evermore!

*Electra.* Now that you preach, I know you will not help me!

*Chrysothemis.* And any man would come to harm who did!

*Electra.* I envy you your prudence; for your cowardice,
    I hate you!

*Chrysothemis.*       I will bear it, when you praise.

*Electra.* Only you never will get praise of me!

*Chrysothemis.* It will be long, yet, before that is settled.

*Electra.* There is no service in you; get you gone.

*Chrysothemis.* There is! With you there is no towardness.

*Electra.* Go to your mother; tell it all to her.

*Chrysothemis.* Nay, I am not so much your enemy.

*Electra.* Do not forget, though, to what shame you drag me.

*Chrysothemis.* Shame not at all; but forethought for your
      good.

*Electra.* So I must follow what you think is just?

*Chrysothemis.* When you are prudent, you shall guide us
    both.

*Electra.* Pity that you should speak so well, and miss it!

*Chrysothemis.* You have named right the fault on your own
        side.

*Electra.* How can that be? Do you deny the justice
        Of what I say?

*Chrysothemis.*       Justice sometimes brings damage.

*Electra.* Under those laws I do not choose to live

*Chrysothemis.* Well, you will find me right, if you will do it.

*Electra.* Ay and I will! You cannot frighten me.

*Chrysothemis.* Is't really so? Will you not change your
        mind?

*Electra.* Nothing's more odious than an evil mind.

*Chrysothemis.* You seem to care for nothing I can say.

*Electra.* I have resolved to do it of old time,
        Not newly.

*Chrysothemis.*       I am going. Neither you
        Deign to approve my words, nor I your ways.

*Electra.* Go in, then! I shall never follow you;
        Not though you come to wish it earnestly;
        There were small sense in running after—folly!

*Chrysothemis.* And if you think that reason is with you,
        So reason still! for, when your footsteps light
        In evil ways, then you will find me right.

                        [*Exit* CHRYSOTHEMIS.

CHORUS.

I. 1.

We that regard
The excellent wisdom of the birds of air,
    Who for the nurture care
Of those they spring from—those who gave them food,
        Why is it hard
For us, like them, to render good for good?
But, by the thunderbolt of sovereign Jove,
      And Themis, throned above,
        We scape not long!
Thou, who to mortals in the realms of death
Passest through earth, send forth thy voice, O Fame,
With piteous cry, to Atreus' sons beneath,
      Bearing thy tale of shame
        Unmeet for song

# Electra

### I. 2.

How first of all
Corruption dwells within their palace hall,
        And, with their children, strife ;
The dissonant watchword harmonized no more
            Now, as before,
By sweet endearments of their household life.
Electra, left alone, by rude waves tossed,
        Mourns for her father lost [12]
            With ceaseless wail,
Even as the ever-sorrowing nightingale,
Careless for death, so she might end them too,
The accursed pair—yea, ready for the gloom ;
        What woman lives as true
            This side the tomb ?

### II. 1.

For none among the great
        Would court oblivion,
Darkening his honour by a life of pain,
        As thou, my child, hast done,
        Choosing to share a fate
Full of all tears, not caring to obtain
At once, in the same breath, the twofold prize
Of daughter perfect, and of maiden wise. [13]

### II. 2.

Live thou—in wealth and force
        Above thy foes as far
As now thou dwellest underneath their might !
        For under no good star
        Have I beheld the course
Lying, of thy life ; yet in the paths of Right
Most sovereign—thou, I say, in these hast trod
The foremost, through thy piety to God.

*Enter* ORESTES *and* PYLADES, *with an urn.*

*Orestes.* Were we told right, and are we tending right,
        As we desire, fair ladies ?
1 *Lady.*                    And what seek you ?
        What are you here for ?

*Orestes.* I was asking where
Ægisthus lodged.

1 *Lady.* Then you are well arrived,
And your informant blameless.

*Orestes.* Which of you
Would kindly carry word to those within
Of the long-looked-for presence of us twain?

1 *Lady.* If the most near ought to announce it, she
will.

*Orestes.* Lady, go in and tell them certain Phocians
Seek for Ægisthus.

*Electra.* O me miserable!
Are you not bringing tokens to confirm
The tale we heard?

*Orestes.* I do not know your story;
But my old master, Strophius, gave me charge
To tell about Orestes.

*Electra.* O sir, what?
How terror creeps upon me!

*Orestes.* We bring home
Poor relics of him, in a narrow urn,
Dead, as you see.

*Electra.* Unhappy that I am!
Here is the thing already evident.
I see your burden, I suppose, at hand.

*Orestes.* If you are grieving for Orestes' ills,
Know, that this vessel holds the dust of him.

*Electra.* O sir, in Heaven's name give it—if this urn
Hides him indeed—into my hands, to hold,
That I may weep and mourn to the uttermost
For my own self, and my whole race, at once,
Over these ashes!

*Orestes.* Bring it here, and give her,
Whoever she may be; for I am sure
She does not ask it out of enmity,
But as some friend, or blood-relation born.

*Electra.* Ah thou memorial of my best-beloved,
All that is left me of Orestes, how
Do I receive thee back—not as I hoped,
When I first sped thee on thy way! For now
I bear thee in my hands, and thou art nothing;
But O my child, I sent thee forth from home

Glorious with life! Would that I first had died,
Before I sent thee to a foreign land,
Stolen by these hands and out of slaughter
 saved;
So had that day beheld thee lying dead,
Partaking with me in thy father's grave.
But now thou hast perished—perished miserably,
An exile in a strange land, far from home,
Far from thy sister; nor with loving hands
Bathed I thy body, and laid it out—woe's me!
Nor, as was fitting, from the blazing pyre
Took up the poor remains. But cared for—ah,
By unfamiliar hands thou art come hither,
A little burden, in a little urn.
Ah me unhappy for my ancient care
Made fruitless, for the pleasing toil I spent,
Often, on thee! for not at any time
Wert thou thy mother's darling, more than mine;
I was thy nurse; no houselings fostered thee;
I was thy "sister," ever, too, by name.
But now all this has vanished in a day,
Even with thy death. For thou hast gathered all
Together, like a whirlwind, and art gone;
My father is no more; I too am dead
In thee; thyself art dead, and gone from me;
And our foes laugh; and that disnatured mother,
Of whom thou hast often sent word privily
Thou would'st thyself appear to punish her,
Raves with delight! This the ill Destiny
Of thee and me wrested away; who sent thee
On to me thus—not the dear form I loved,
But embers, and an unavailing shade.
—Woe's me! O piteous sight! Alas, alas,
A terrible journey hast thou gone, my dear; [14]
Woe's me! and without thee I am undone;
I am undone without thee, O my brother!
Receive me then into this house of thine,
Nought unto nought, to dwell with thee below
For evermore. For when thou wast on earth,
All that I had on earth I shared with thee;
And—for I see no grieving in the dead—
I would die now, so I might share thy tomb.

1 *Lady.* Your sire, Electra, was a mortal man ;
So was Orestes ; wherefore do not grieve
Beyond all bounds ; we all owe Heaven a death.

*Orestes.* O Heavens, what shall I say ? whither shall I turn
For lack of words ? for I have lost the power
Of speech !

*Electra.* What ails you ? Wherefore do you say it ?

*Orestes.* Is this the illustrious Electra—you ?

*Electra.* That is it, and in case right miserable.

*Orestes.* Alack therefore, for this thy wretched lot !

*Electra.* Sir, you are not lamenting thus for me ?

*Orestes.* O beauty foully—impiously destroyed !

*Electra.* The wretch you speak of is no other, sir,
Than I.

*Orestes.* Alas for thy estate, unwed,
Unfortunate !

*Electra.* Why do you groan, sir, thus,
Gazing on me !

*Orestes.* How did I nothing know
Of my own woes !

*Electra.* By what, that has been said,
Did you discover that ?

*Orestes.* By seeing you,
Preëminent in multitude of griefs.

*Electra.* And yet you see but little of my woes.

*Orestes.* How could there be worse things than these to
see ?

*Electra.* That I am sorted with the murderers.

*Orestes.* Whose murderers ? Whence is this hint of crime ?

*Electra.* My father's. Next, I am perforce their slave.

*Orestes.* Who is it bends you to this exigence ?

*Electra.* My mother—in name—but nothing mother-like.

*Orestes.* And how ? by force, or wearing injury ?

*Electra.* By force, by wearing, and all ills that be.

*Orestes.* And was none by to help or hinder it ?

*Electra.* No ; him I had you have brought here in ashes.

*Orestes.* Ill-fated one, how has the sight of you
Moved my compassion !

*Electra.* Know, you are the first
Who ever had compassion upon me.

*Orestes.* Because I am the first to come, who feel
With your misfortunes.

*Electra.* It can never be
        You are some kinsman, who have come—whence
        could you?

*Orestes.* If these are friends about us, I will tell.

*Electra.* Yes, they are friends; you parley to safe ears.

*Orestes.* Put down this vessel, now, and learn the whole.

*Electra.* Ah sir, for Heaven's sake urge not this on
        me!

*Orestes.* Do as I tell you, and you shall not err.

*Electra.* Now, I adjure you, do not take away
        My greatest treasure!

*Orestes.* I will not let you hold it.

*Electra.* O my Orestes! Woe is me for thee,
        If I must be deprived of burying thee!

*Orestes.* Do not speak rashly. You do wrong to mourn.

*Electra.* How wrong, in mourning for my brother dead?

*Orestes.* It is not meet that you should call him so.

*Electra.* Am I then so disdained of him that's dead?

*Orestes.* Disdained of none; but you have no part here.

*Electra.* Not when I bear Orestes' ashes?

*Orestes.* Not
        Orestes' ashes; only his in feigning.

*Electra.* Then where is that poor body's sepulchre?

*Orestes.* No where. The living have no sepulchre!

*Electra.* What say you, fellow?

*Orestes.* What I say is true.

*Electra.* Is he alive?

*Orestes.* Yes, unless I am dead!

*Electra.* What, are you he?

*Orestes.* See here, my father's seal!
        Look at it well, and learn if I speak truly.

*Electra.* O happy day!

*Orestes.* Most happy; even so.

*Electra.* O art thou come, dear voice?

*Orestes.* No more to sound
        From alien lips.

*Electra.* What, have I got you?

*Orestes.* Yes,
        For you to keep, in future, evermore.

*Electra.* O dearest friends! O ladies, neighbours! Look,
        Here is Orestes, only dead in craft,
        And by that craft alive and safe at home!

1 *Lady.* Daughter, we see it; and the tears of joy
  Steal from our eyes, at what has come to pass.

*Electra.*   O son, dear seed
   Of one most dear to me!
   And art thou come indeed?
  Thou hast found—hast come, hast seen those thou
   didst seek to see!

*Orestes.* Yes, I am here; but hush, keep silence.
*Electra.*           Why?
*Orestes.* Best to keep close, lest some one hear indoors.

*Electra.* Nay but, by the ever-virgin Artemis,
  I never think to quail again at this,
  The cumbering plague of numbers feminine,
   That ever swarm within!

*Orestes.* O but remember that in women too
  There lives a spirit of war; and thou hast proved it.

*Electra.*   Ah well a day!
  Thou makest the memory plain—
   That will not pass away—
  That cannot be forgotten—of my pain.

*Orestes.* Sister, I know it; but, when occasion speaks,
  Then is it we should call to mind these doings.

*Electra.*   All day, all night,
  Were not too much for me
   To speak of them aright;
  Now that my lips at last are set at liberty.

*Orestes.* I say not nay; therefore take heed.
*Electra.*         Of what?
*Orestes.* Now 'tis no time for talk, be sparing of it.

*Electra.* Who, after thy appearing, would exchange
  Language for silence?   That were dearly bought,
  Now I have found thee, in a manner strange
   Beyond all hope or thought!

*Orestes.* You saw me then, when the Gods urged my
  coming.

*Electra.*   O grace, far more
  Than that thou first didst tell!
   If to thy kinsmen's door
  God sent thee safe, that count I miracle!

*Orestes.* I am unwilling to restrain your joy,
    But fear you are too much overcome with rapture.

*Electra.*    Oh, if after years of waiting
    I have found thee condescending
    By a way full fraught with blessing
      Here before me to appear,
    Seeing me so full of troubles,
    Spare, O spare—

*Orestes.*              What should I spare thee?

*Electra.*    Be not thou so much my wronger
    As to make me lose the pleasure
    Of thy presence!

*Orestes.*           Nay,
    I should be very wroth with other men
    If I beheld them—
*Electra.*        Do you say so?
*Orestes.*                How
    Could I forbear?

*Electra.*  Hark, the voice, women dear,
    I had never hoped to hear!
    Listening, how could I have heard,
    And held my peace, without one word,
    Sorrowing?[15]  But I have thee, now!
    With most sweet face there standest thou,
    Face, that even in misery
    Could not pass away from me.

*Orestes.* Pass what need not be said; spare me the telling
    How base our mother; how Ægisthus drains
    The family substance, giving largess here,
    There scattering without purpose; for the tale
    Would keep you from the occasion time has given.
    But what will fit the present urgency,
    Where, either visible or from ambushment,
    We may give pause in this day's enterprise
    To foes who mock, explain; be careful, too,
    That as we enter at the palace door
    Your mother do not spy your secret out
    In your glad aspect; but be sighing, still,
    As at that fiction of calamity;

For when we are successful, we shall be
Free to rejoice and laugh ungrudgingly.

*Electra.* Well, brother, as it pleases you in this,
So too shall be my pleasure; for from you
I have derived the blessings I enjoy—
Blessings not mine; and I could never bear,
By causing you annoy, ever so brief,
To reap great gain myself; for ill should I
So minister to the Providence at hand.
You know, no doubt, all that is passing here;
You heard Ægisthus was away from home,
My mother in the palace; and for her,
Fear not she will perceive my countenance
Radiant with smiles; for my long-standing hate
Is well worn in; and, having seen thy face,
I shall not leave off weeping now, for joy.
How should I leave it? who in this day's work
Saw thee first dead, then living! Yea, thou hast
    wrought
Very strangely with me; so that if my sire
Were to come here in life, I should not now
Deem it a marvel, but believe I saw him.
Since then by such a road thou art come hither
Lead on, as thou art minded; for alone
One of two things I had not failed to achieve—
Bravely to right myself, or bravely perish.

1 *Lady.* Peace, I advise you; for of those within
I hear one coming outward.

*Electra.*                         Enter, sirs;
The rather that you bring—what none would drive
Far from their doors—or willingly receive!

*Enter Guardian.*

*Guardian.* O most unwise and impotent of mind,
Have you no longer any care to live,
Or is no natural prudence bred in you,
When in the very midst of ills most great,
Not on their verge, you stand, and do not see it?
If I had not been keeping, all along,
Watch at the door-posts, all your business here
Would have forestalled your presence in the house;
But as it is, I took good heed of that.

    Now make an end of your long conference,
    And this insatiate crying out for joy,
    And pass within; for in such work as this
    Delay is loss, and it is time to finish.

*Orestes.* What will the issue be, if I go in?

*Guardian.* All's well so far, that you are quite unknown.

*Orestes.* You told them, I suppose, that I was dead?

*Guardian.* You'd think you were in Hades, though alive,
    To hear them talk!

*Orestes.*               Do they rejoice at that?
    What are they saying?

*Guardian.*               When the time is ripe
    I will inform you; but as things are now,
    All they are doing, however ill, goes well.

*Electra.* Brother, who is this man? For Heaven's sake, tell
    me!

*Orestes.* Do you not know him?

*Electra.*               I cannot even guess.

*Orestes.* Not him, to whom you once delivered me?

*Electra.* What man? what do you mean?

*Orestes.*               Him, in whose hands
    I was made off with to the Phocians' land
    By your providing?

*Electra.*             What, is this the man
    Whom only I found faithful out of many
    When our sire perished?

*Orestes.*              Once for all, 'tis he.

*Electra.* O happy day![16] O only saviour
    Of Agamemnon's house! How art thou come
        hither!
    Art thou the man who out of many woes
    Didst save both him and me? O hands most
        dear!
    O feet, most grateful for your ministry!
    How could'st thou so long hide thee in my presence
    And kill me with false words, and shew me not,
    Knowing all the while, the sweet reality?
    O welcome, father! in thee I seem to see
    A father! Welcome! Surely of all men thee
    Within one day I have hated most—and love!

*Guardian.* Enough, I say; the story of all since then
    Many revolving nights and days as many

Shall make to pass before Electra's eyes.—
But now I warn you both, you who stand by,
This is the time to act ; now Clytæmnestra
Is left alone ; now no one of the men
Is within doors ; but if you will delay,
Consider, you will have to cope with these,
And more besides, and of more wit, than they.

*Orestes.* This need not be a matter to us now
For any long discoursing, Pylades !
Rather, first worshipping the ancestral shrines
Of all the Gods who keep this vestibule,
As quickly as we may, let us pass in.

[*Exeunt* ORESTES, PYLADES *and Guardian.*

*Electra.* O King Apollo, hear them graciously,
And me as well ; me, who have come to thee
Right often, with persistent hand, that gave
Of all I had ; so now with all I have,
Apollo, King Lycean, I implore,
I supplicate, I pray thee—go before,
And help us to our ends ; and make mankind confess
How the Gods quit them, for their wickedness !

[*Retires.*

CHORUS.

1.

Behold where Ares, breathing forth the breath
    Of strife and carnage, paces—paces on.
The inevitable hounds of death,
    Hunters upon the track of guilt, are gone.
They stand the roof beneath ;
And now not long the vision of my prayer
Shall tarry, floating in the fields of air.

2.

For now within these walls, with stealthy pace,
    The aider of the kingdoms of the dead
To his ancestral dwelling-place,
    Bearing keen slaughter in his hands, is led.
Hermes, of Maia's race,
Hiding his toils in darkness, leads the way
Straight to the goal, and makes no more delay.

*Electra (advancing).* O dearest women, 'tis the moment, now,
    For them to do the deed; but hush, keep still.

1 *Lady.* How then? What are they doing?

*Electra.*                       She is dressing
    The urn for burial; and the Pair stand by.

1 *Lady.* And what did you rush out for?

*Electra.*                      To take care
    Ægisthus come not in without our knowing.

*Clytæmnestra (within).* Woe's me! Alack, the house—
    Empty of friends, and filled with murderers!

*Electra.* A cry within! O friends, do not you hear it?

1 *Lady.* I heard, unhappy, sounds I might not hear;
    And I am chill with horror.

*Clytæmnestra (within).*               Woe is me!
    Ægisthus, O where are you?

1 *Lady.*                  Hark again,
    Some one is shrieking loud.

*Clytæmnestra (within).*          O child, my child,
    Have mercy on your mother!

*Electra.*                  Thou hadst none
    On him, or on his father who begat him.

### CHORUS.

    O city, O race ill-starred!
    The curse is ever on thee, day by day,
    To fade, and fade![17]

*Clytæmnestra (within).* O, I am smitten!

*Electra.*                If thou beëst a man,
    Strike twice!

*Clytæmnestra (within).* Again!

*Electra.*               O for Ægisthus too!

### CHORUS.

    The curse is fulfilled.
    They live, who lie in the grave.
    Slain long since, they drink, at last,
    The blood of their slayers, in turn.

1 *Lady.* See, they come forth! Their fingers drip with
    gore
    Poured out on Ares' altar. I am dumb.

*Enter* ORESTES *and* PYLADES.

*Electra.* How is it with you, Orestes?
*Orestes.*                                    In the house
    Well; if Apollo's oracle be well.
*Electra.* Is the wretch dead?
*Orestes.*                                    No longer be afraid
    Thy mother's pride shall trample on thee more.
1 *Lady.* Cease, for I see Ægisthus full in view!
*Electra.* Back, boys!
*Orestes.*                    Where do you see the man?
*Electra.*                                              He comes
    Towards us from the precincts, gay at heart.


CHORUS.

    Make for the entrance, quick!
    Now, as ye have well achieved the former task,
    Finish this too!

*Orestes.* Be easy; we will do it.
*Electra.*                         Go your ways.
*Orestes.* I am gone.
*Electra.*                    I will provide for matters here.
                [*Exeunt* ORESTES *and* PYLADES.


CHORUS.

    'Twere well to pronounce
    Brief words in this man's ear,
    Mildly couched, that he may rush
    On the hidden struggle of doom.


*Enter* ÆGISTHUS.

*Ægisthus.* Which of you knows, where are those Phocian
      strangers
    They say have brought us tidings that Orestes
    Has lost his life, by shipwreck of his team?
    You there, my question is of you, yes, you
    That used before to be so malapert;
    For it concerns you most, I think, to know,
    And more than all, it is for you to say.

*Electra.* I know. How could I help it? Otherwise
    I should be ignorant of calamity
    Nearest to me—of mine.
*Ægisthus.*                 And where may be
    The strangers? tell me, pray.
*Electra.*               They are within.
    They—fell on a kind hostess !
*Ægisthus.*              Did they say
    That he is dead in very earnest?
*Electra.*              Nay,
    They brought and shewed it us—no merely told us.
*Ægisthus.* Is it hard by, that I may see, and know?
*Electra.* You may, indeed—a very sorry sight.
*Ægisthus.* Your words have pleased me much; which is
    not usual.
*Electra.* If they can give you pleasure, pray be pleased.
*Ægisthus.* Now hold your peace, and open wide the gates,
    For Myceneans, Argives—all to see,
    So that, if any of them heretofore
    Were buoyed by empty hopes of such an one,
    Seeing him now dead, they may accept my curb,
    And, having me for chastener, may not need
    To be compelled to bring forth fruits of wisdom !
*Electra.* It is all done, on my part ; for at last
    I have the wit to choose the stronger side.

*The scene opens, disclosing the body of* CLYTÆMNESTRA, *veiled;*
    ORESTES *and* PYLADES *standing by.*

*Ægisthus.* Zeus, I behold a thing—that hath not fallen,
    But by the jealousy of Heaven !—Nay,
    If there is yet a Nemesis, I unsay it !
    Loosen all coverings from before my face,
    That of me too my kindred may obtain
    The meed of mourning.
*Electra.*              Take them off yourself.
    To see this corpse, and speak with amity,
    Is not my work, but yours.
*Ægisthus.*            Well, you say true,
    And I will do your bidding ; in mean while,
    If she is in the house, call Clytæmnestra.

*He raises the veil.*

*Orestes.* Seek her no further ; she is at your side.
*Ægisthus.* O what is this ?
*Orestes.* Who is it, whom you fear ?
  Who is it, whom you do not recognize ?
*Ægisthus.* Who are the men into whose very toils
  I have fallen, unhappy ?
*Orestes.* Did you never dream
  They were alive, whom you miscall as dead ?
*Ægisthus.* O me, I understand you ! It must be
  No other than Orestes speaks to me.
*Orestes.* Excellent seer ! and yet so long deceived !
*Ægisthus.* I am lost, miserably ! But suffer me
  To speak a little—
*Electra.* Brother, in Heaven's name let him
  No further parley, and prolong discourse.
  Once overtaken by calamity,
  What profit should a man who is to die
  Draw from delay ? Nay, kill him on the spot,
  And cast him forth, slain, to such buriers
  As it is fitting he should meet withal,
  Out of our eye-sight ! This alone can be
  An expiation for my wrongs of old.
*Orestes.* Go thou within, with speed. The contest now
  Lies not in words, but for thy life-blood.
*Ægisthus.* Nay,
  Why do you drag me to the house ? What need
  Of darkness, if the deed is honourable ?
  Why are you backward to despatch me here ?
*Orestes.* Prescribe not thou ! Pass, where thou slew'st my
    father,
  And perish there.
*Ægisthus.* Is it fated that this roof
  Must witness all the ills of Pelops' race,
  That are, or shall be ?
*Orestes.* Thine, at any rate.
  I am soothsayer good enough to tell thee that !
*Ægisthus.* The craft you boast was not inherited, then !
*Orestes.* Thou prat'st, and prat'st ; and the way lengthens
    out ;
  Move on.

*Ægisthus.*　　　Lead forward.
*Orestes.*　　　　　　　　Thou must foot it first.
*Ægisthus.*  Lest I escape thee?
*Orestes.*　　　　　　　Rather, that thy soul
　　May not pass easily; this bitterness
　　I must reserve for thee.　And well it were
　　If this quick justice could be dealt on all—
　　Whoever will transgress the bounds of right,
　　To strike him dead.[18]　　　　　　*[Kills* ÆGISTHUS.
　　　　　　　　So should not villainy thrive.


CHORUS.

　　　O Atreus' seed!
　　How hardly, after many labours past,
　　Art thou come forth to liberty at last,
　　　　Through this new trial perfected indeed!
　　　　　　　　　　　　　*[Exeunt omnes.*

# OEDIPUS TYRANNUS

*swollen foot*

---

## PERSONS REPRESENTED

ŒDIPUS, *King of Thebes.*
PRIEST *of Zeus.*
CREON, *brother to Jocasta the Queen.*
TIRESIAS, *a Prophet, with the title of King.* *blind prophet*
*A Messenger from Corinth.*
*An old Shepherd.*
*A Second Messenger, servant of Œdipus' household.*
JOCASTA *the Queen, wife to Œdipus, formerly married to Laius, the last King.*
ANTIGONE, }
ISMENE, } *daughters to Œdipus and Jocasta.*
*The* CHORUS *is composed of Senators of Thebes.*
*Inhabitants of Thebes, Attendants.*
*A Boy leading Tiresias.*

---

*Scene, before the Royal Palace at Thebes.   Enter* ŒDIPUS;
  *to him the Priest of Zeus, and Inhabitants of Thebes.*

ŒDIPUS.  Children, you modern brood of Cadmus old,
　　　　　What mean you, sitting in your sessions here,
　　　　　High-coronalled with votive olive-boughs,[1]
　　　　　While the whole city teems with incense-smoke,
　　　　　And pæan hymns, and sounds of woe the while?
　　　　　Deeming unmeet, my children, this to learn
　　　　　From others, by the mouth of messengers,
　　　　　I have myself come hither, Œdipus,
　　　　　Known far and wide by name.   Do thou, old man,
　　　　　Since 'tis thy privilege to speak for these,
　　　　　Say in what case ye stand; if of alarm,
　　　　　Or satisfaction with my readiness[2]
　　　　　To afford all aid; hard-hearted must I be,
　　　　　Did I not pity such petitioners.
*Priest.*  Great Œdipus, my country's governor,

Thou seest our generations, who besiege
Thy altars here ; some not yet strong enough
To flutter far ; some priests, with weight of years
Heavy, myself of Zeus ; and these, the flower [3]
Of our young manhood ; all the other folk
Sit, with like branches, in the market-place,
By the Ismenian hearth oracular
And the twin shrines of Pallas.    Lo, the city
Labours—thyself art witness—over-deep
Already, powerless to uprear her head
Out of the abysses of a surge of blood ;
Stricken in the budding harvest of her soil,
Stricken in her pastured herds, and barren travail
Of women ; and He, the God with spear of fire,
Leaps on the city, a cruel pestilence,
And harries it ; whereby the Cadmean home
Is all dispeopled, and with groan and wail
The blackness of the Grave made opulent.
Not that we count thee as the peer of Heaven,
I, nor these children, seat us at thy hearth ;
But as of men found foremost in affairs,
Chances of life and shifts of Providence ;
Whose coming to our Cadmean town released
The toll we paid, of a hard Sorceress,
And that, without instruction or advice
Of our imparting ; but of Heaven it came
Thou art named, and known, our life's establisher.
Thee therefore, Œdipus, the mightiest head
Among us all, all we thy supplicants
Implore to find some way to succour us,
Whether thou knowest it through some voice from
        heaven,
Or, haply of some man ; for I perceive
In men experienced that their counsels best
Find correspondence in things actual. [4]
Haste thee, most absolute sir, be the state's builder !
Haste thee, look to it ; doth not our country now
Call thee deliverer, for thy zeal of yore ?
Never let us remember of thy rule
That we stood once erectly, and then fell ;
But build this city in stability !
With a fair augury didst thou shape for us

Our fortune then; like be thy prowess now!
If thou wilt rule this land (which thou art lord of),
It were a fairer lordship filled with folk
Than empty; towers and ships are nothingness,
Void of our fellow men to inhabit them.

*Œdipus.* Ah my poor children, what you come to seek
Is known already—not unknown to me.
You are all sick, I know it; and in your sickness
There is not one of you so sick as I.
For in your case his own particular pain
Comes to each singly; but my heart at once
Groans for the city, and for myself, and you.
Not therefore as one taking rest in sleep
Do you uprouse me; rather deem of me
As one that wept often, and often came
By many ways through labyrinths of care;
And the one remedy that I could find
By careful seeking—I supplied it.   Creon,
Menœceus' son, the brother of my queen,
I sent to Pytho, to Apollo's house,
To ask him by what act or word of mine
I might redeem this city; and the hours
Already measured even with today
Make me solicitous how he has sped;
For he is longer absent than the time
Sufficient, which is strange.   When he shall come,
I were a wretch did I not then do all
As the God shews.

*Priest.*                         In happy time thou speak'st;
As these, who tell me Creon is at hand.

*Œdipus.* Ah King Apollo, might he but bring grace,
Radiant in fortune, as he is in face!

*Priest.* I think he comes with cheer; he would not, else,
Thus be approaching us with crown on brow,
All berries of the bay.

*Œdipus.*                         We shall know soon;
He is within hearing.

*Enter* CREON, *attended.*

                         My good lord and cousin,
Son of Menœceus,
What answer of the God have you brought home?

*Creon.* Favourable; I mean, even what sounds ominously,
    If it have issue in the way forthright,
    May all end well.

*Œdipus.*                How runs the oracle?
    I am not confident, nor prone to fear
    At what you say, so far.

*Creon.*              If you desire
    To hear while these stand near us, I am ready
    To speak at once—or to go in with you.

*Œdipus.* Speak before all! My heavy load of care
    More for their sake than for my own I bear.

*Creon.* What the God told me, that will I declare.
    Phœbus our Lord gives us express command
    To drive pollution, bred within this land,
    Out of the country, and not cherish it
    Beyond the power of healing.

*Œdipus.*             By what purge?
    What is the tenor of your tragedy?

*Creon.* Exile, or recompense of death for death;
    Since 'tis this blood makes winter to the city.

*Œdipus.* Whose fate is this he signifies?

*Creon.*              My liege,
    We had a leader, once, over this land,
    Called Laius—ere you held the helm of state.

*Œdipus.* So I did hear; I never saw the man.

*Creon.* The man is dead; and now, we are clearly bidden
    To bring to account certain his murderers.

*Œdipus.* And where on earth are they? Where shall be
        found
    This dim-seen track-mark of an ancient crime?

*Creon.* "Within this land," it ran. That which is sought,
    That may be caught. What is unheeded scapes us.

*Œdipus.* Was it at home, afield, or anywhere
    Abroad, that Laius met this violent end?

*Creon.* He went professedly on pilgrimage;
    But since he started, came back home no more.

*Œdipus.* Nor any messenger nor way-fellow
    Looked on, from whom one might have learnt his story
    And used it?

*Creon.*            No, they perished, all but one;
    He fled, affrighted; and of what he saw
    Had but one thing to say for certain.

*Œdipus.*                                   Well
     And what was that? one thing might be the means
     Of our discovering many, could we gain
     Some narrow ground for hope.

*Creon.*                          Robbers, he said,
     Met them, and slew him; by no single strength,
     But multitude of hands.

*Œdipus.*                     How could your robber
     Have dared so far—except there were some practice
     With gold from hence?

*Creon.*                   Why, it seemed probable.
     But, Laius dead, no man stood up to help
     Amid our ills.

*Œdipus.*            What ill was in the way,
     Which, when a sovereignty had lapsed like this,
     Kept you from searching of it out?

*Creon.*                          The Sphinx
     With her enigma forced us to dismiss
     Things out of sight, and look to our own steps.

*Œdipus.* Well, I will have it all to light again.
     Right well did Phœbus, yea and well may you
     Insist on this observance toward the dead;
     So shall you see me, as of right, with you,
     Venging this country and the God together.
     Why, 'tis not for my neighbours' sake, but mine,
     I shall dispel this plague-spot; for the man,
     Whoever it may be, who murdered him,
     Lightly might hanker to serve me the same.
     I benefit myself in aiding him.
     Up then, my children, straightway, from the floor;
     Take up your votive branches; let some other
     Gather the tribes of Cadmus hitherward;
     Say, I will make clean work. Please Heaven, our
          state
     Shall soon appear happy, or desperate.

*Priest.* Come children, let us rise; it was for this,
     Which he himself proclaims, that we came hither.
     Now may the sender of these oracles,
     In saving and in plague-staying, Phœbus, come!

                    [*Exeunt* CREON, PRIEST *and* THEBANS.
                              ŒDIPUS *retires.*

*Enter* Theban Senators, *as Chorus.*

Chorus.

### I. 1.

O Prophecy of Jove, whose words are sweet,
With what doom art thou sent
To glorious Thebes, from Pytho's gilded seat?
I am distraught with fearful wonderment,
I thrill with terror, and wait reverently—
Yeà, Io Pæan, Delian lord, on thee!
What matter thou wilt compass—either strange,
Or once again recurrent as the seasons change,
Offspring of golden Hope, immortal Oracle,
Tell me, O tell!

### I. 2.

Athena first I greet with invocation,
Daughter of Jove, divine!
Next Artemis thy sister, of this nation
Keeper, high seated in the encircling shrine,
Filled with her praises, of our market-place,
And Phœbus, shooting arrows far through space;
Appear ye Three, the averters of my fate!
If e'er before, when mischief rose upon the state,
Ye quenched the flames of evil, putting them away,
Come—come to-day!

### II. 1.

Woe, for unnumbered are the ills we bear!
Sickness pervades our hosts;
Nor is there any spear of guardian care,
Wherewith a man might save us, found in all our coasts.
For all the fair soil's produce now no longer springs;
Nor women from the labour and loud cries
Of their child-births arise;
And you may see, flying like a bird with wings,
One after one, outspeeding the resistless brand,
Pass—to the Evening Land.

### II. 2.

In countless hosts our city perisheth.
Her children on the plain
Lie all unpitied—pitiless [5]—breeding death.
Our wives meanwhile, and white-haired mothers in their train,

This way and that, suppliant, along the altar-side
Sit, and bemoan their doleful maladies;
Like flame their pæans rise,
With wailing and lament accompanied;
For whose dear sake O Goddess, O Jove's golden child,
Send Help with favour mild!

### III. 1.

And Ares the Destroyer, him who thus—
Not now in harness of brass shields, as wont—
Ringed round with clamour, meets us front to front
And fevers us,
O banish from our country!   Drive him back,
With winds upon his track,
On to the chamber vast of Amphitrite,
Or that lone anchorage, the Thracian main;
For now, if night leave bounds to our annoy,
Day levels all again;
Wherefore, O father, Zeus, thou that dost wield the might
Of fire-fraught light,
Him with thy bolt destroy!

### ✓ III. 2.

Next, from the bendings of thy golden string
I would see showered thy artillery
Invincible, marshalled to succour me,
Lycean King!
Next, those flame-bearing beams, arrows most bright,
Which Artemis by night
Through Lycian highlands speeds her scattering;
Thou too, the Evian, with thy Mænad band,
Thou golden-braided patron of this land
Whose visage glows with wine,
O save us from the god whom no gods honour!   Hear,
Bacchus!   Draw near,
And light thy torch of pine!

*Enter ŒDIPUS, attended.*

*Œdipus.* You are at prayers; but for your prayers' intent
You may gain help, and of your ills relief,
If you will minister to the pestilence,
And hearken and receive my words, which I—

A stranger to this tale, and to the deed
A stranger—shall pronounce; for of myself
I could not follow up the traces far,
Not having any key.   But, made since then
A fellow-townsman to the townsmen here,
To all you Cadmeans I thus proclaim;
Whichever of you knows the man, by whom
Laius the son of Labdacus was slain,
Even if he is afraid, seeing he himself
Suppressed the facts that made against himself,
I bid that man shew the whole truth to me;
For he shall suffer no disparagement,
Except to quit the land, unscathed.   Again,
If any knows another—say some stranger
To have been guilty, let him not keep silence;
For I will pay him the reward, and favour
Shall be his due beside it.   But again,
If you will hold your peace, and any man
From self or friend in terror shall repel
This word of mine, then—you must hear me say
What I shall do.   Whoe'er he be, I order
That of this land, whose power and throne are mine,
None entertain him, none accost him, none
Cause him to share in prayers or sacrifice
Offered to Heaven, or pour him lustral wave,
But all men from their houses banish him;
Since it is he contaminates us all,
Even as the Pythian oracle divine
Revealed but now to me.   Such is my succour
Of him that's dead, and of the Deity.
And on the guilty head I imprecate
That whether by himself he has lain covert,
Or joined with others, without happiness,
Evil, in evil, he may pine and die.
And for myself I pray, if with my knowledge
He should become an inmate of my dwelling,
That I may suffer all that I invoked
On these just now.   Moreover all these things
I charge you to accomplish, in behalf
Of me, and of the God, and of this land,
So ruined, barren and forsaken of Heaven
For even though the matter were not now

By Heaven enjoined you, 'twas unnatural
For you to suffer it to pass uncleansed,
A man most noble having been slain, a king too!
Rather, you should have searched it out; but now,
Since I am vested with the government
Which he held once, and have his marriage-bed,
And the same wife; and since our progeny—
If his had not miscarried—had sprung from us
With common ties of common motherhood—
Only that Fate came heavy upon his head—
On these accounts I, as for my own father,
Will fight this fight, and follow out every clue,
Seeking to seize the author of his murder—
The scion of Labdacus and Polydore
And earlier Cadmus and Agenor old;
And such as disobey—the Gods I ask
Neither to raise them harvest from the ground
Nor children from the womb, but that they perish
By this fate present, and yet worse than this;
While you, the other Cadmeans, who approve,
May succouring Justice and all Gods in heaven
Accompany for good for evermore!

1 *Senator.* Even as thou didst adjure me, so, my king,
I will reply. I neither murdered him,
Nor can point out the murderer. For the quest—
To tell us who on earth has done this deed
Belonged to Phœbus, by whose word it came.

*Œdipus.* Your words are just; but to constrain the Gods
To what they will not, passes all men's power.

1 *Senator.* I would say something which appears to me
The second chance to this.

*Œdipus.* And your third, also—
If such you have—by all means tell it.

1 *Senator.* Sir,
Tiresias above all men, I am sure,
Ranks as a seer next Phœbus, king with king;
Of him we might enquire and learn the truth
With all assurance.

*Œdipus.* That is what I did;
And with no slackness; for by Creon's advice
I sent, twice over; and for some time, now,
'Tis strange he is not here.

1 *Senator.*                          Then all the rest
   Are but stale words and dumb.
*Œdipus.*                          What sort of words
   I am weighing every utterance.
1 *Senator.*                          He was said
   To have been killed by footpads.
*Œdipus.*                          So I heard;
   But he who saw it is himself unseen.
1 *Senator.* Well, if his bosom holds a grain of fear,
   Curses like yours he never will abide!
*Œdipus.* Whom the doing awes not, speaking cannot scare.
1 *Senator.* Then there is one to expose him: here they
      come,
   Bringing the godlike seer, the only man
   Who has in him the tongue that cannot lie.

*Enter* TIRESIAS, *led by a boy.*

*Œdipus.* Tiresias, thou who searchest everything,
   Communicable or nameless, both in heaven
   And on the earth—thou canst not see the city,
   But knowest no less what pestilence visits it,
   Wherefrom our only saviour and defence
   We find, sir king, in thee.   For Phœbus—if
   Thou dost not know it from the messengers—
   To us, who sent to ask him, sent word back,
   That from this sickness no release should come,
   Till we had found and slain the men who slew
   Laius, or driven them, banished, from the land.
   Wherefore do thou—not sparing augury,
   Either through birds, or any other way
   Thou hast of divination—save thyself,
   And save the city, and me; save the whole mass
   By this dead corpse infected; for in thee
   Stands our existence; and for men, to help
   With might and main is of all tasks the highest.
*Tiresias.* Alas!   How terrible it is to know,[6]
   Where no good comes of knowing!   Of these matters
   I was full well aware, but let them slip me;
   Else I had not come hither.
*Œdipus.*                          But what is it?
   How out of heart thou hast come!

*Tiresias.*                                        Let me go home ;
  So shalt thou bear thy load most easily—
  If thou wilt take my counsel—and I mine.

*Œdipus.* Thou hast not spoken loyally, nor friendly
  Toward the State that bred thee, cheating her
  Of this response !

*Tiresias.*                          Because I do not see
  Thy words, not even thine, going to the mark ;
  So, not to be in the same plight—

1 *Senator.*                                  For Heaven's sake,
  If thou hast knowledge, do not turn away,
  When all of us implore thee suppliant !

*Tiresias.*                                        Ye
  Are all unknowing ; my say, in any sort,
  I will not say, lest I display thy sorrow.

*Œdipus.* What, you do know, and will not speak ?   Your
   mind
  Is to betray us, and destroy the city ?

*Tiresias.* I will not bring remorse upon myself
  And upon you.   Why do you search these matters ?
  Vain, vain !   I will not tell you.

*Œdipus.*                                  Worst of traitors !
  For you would rouse a very stone to wrath—
  Will you not speak out ever, but stand thus
  Relentless and persistent ?

*Tiresias.*                          My offence
  You censure ; but your own, at home, you see not,
  And yet blame me !

*Œdipus.*                          Who would not take offence,
  Hearing the words in which you flout the city ?

*Tiresias.* Well, it will come ; keep silence as I may.

*Œdipus.* And what will come should I not hear from you ?

*Tiresias.* I will declare no further.   Storm at this,
  If't please you, to the wildest height of anger !

*Œdipus.* At least I will not, being so far in anger,
  Spare anything of what is clear to me :
  Know, I suspect you joined to hatch the deed ;
  Yea, did it—all but slaying with your own hands ;
  And if you were not blind, I should aver
  The act was your work only !

*Tiresias.*                                  Was it so ?
  I charge you to abide by your decree

As you proclaimed it; nor from this day forth
Speak word to these, or me; being of this land
Yourself the abominable contaminator!

*Œdipus.* So shamelessly set you this story on foot,
And think, perhaps, you shall go free?

*Tiresias.*                I am
Free! for I have in me the strength of truth.

*Œdipus.* Who prompted you? for from your art it was not!

*Tiresias.* Yourself! You made me speak, against my will.

*Œdipus.* Speak! What? Repeat, that I may learn it better!

*Tiresias.* Did you not understand me at first hearing,
Or are you tempting me, when you say "Speak!"

*Œdipus.* Not so to say for certain; speak again.

*Tiresias.* I say that you are Laius' murderer—
He whom you seek.

*Œdipus.*             Not without chastisement
Shall you, twice over, utter wounds!

*Tiresias.*              Then shall I
Say something more, that may incense you further?

*Œdipus.* Say what you please; it will be said in vain.

*Tiresias.* I say you know not in what worst of shame
You live together with those nearest you,
And see not in what evil plight you stand.

*Œdipus.* Do you expect to go on revelling
In utterances like this?

*Tiresias.*            Yes, if the truth
Has any force at all.

*Œdipus.*          Why so it has,
Except for you; it is not so with you;
Blind as you are in eyes, and ears, and mind!

*Tiresias.* Fool, you reproach me as not one of these
Shall not reproach you, soon!

*Œdipus.*          You cannot hurt me,
Nor any other who beholds the light,
Your life being all one night.[7]

*Tiresias.*          Nor is it fated
You by my hand should fall; Apollo is
Sufficient; he will bring it all to pass.

*Œdipus.* Are these inventions Creon's work, or yours?

*Tiresias.* Your bane is no-ways Creon, but your own self.

*Œdipus.* O riches, and dominion, and the craft
That excels craft, and makes life enviable,

How vast the grudge that is nursed up for you,
When for this sovereignty, which the state
Committed to my hands, unsought-for, free,
Creon, the trusty, the familiar friend,
With secret mines covets to oust me from it,
And has suborned a sorcerer like this,
An engine-botching crafty cogging knave,
Who has no eyes to see with, but for gain,
And was born blind in the art! Why, tell me now,
How stand your claims to prescience? How came it,
When the oracular monster was alive,
You said no word to set this people free?
And yet it was not for the first that came
To solve her riddle; sooth was needed then,
Which you could not afford; neither from birds,
Nor any inspiration; till I came,
The unlettered Œdipus, and ended her,
By sleight of wit, untaught of augury—
I whom you now seek to cast out, in hope
To stand upon the steps of Creon's throne!
You and the framer of this plot methinks
Shall rue your purge for guilt! Dotard you seem,
Else by experience you had come to know
What thoughts these are you think!

1 *Senator.*  As we conceive,
His words appear (and, Œdipus, your own,)
To have been said in anger; now not such
Our need, but rather to consider this—
How best to interpret the God's oracle.

*Tiresias.* King as you are, we must be peers at least
In argument; I am your equal, there;
For I am Loxias' servant, and not yours;
So never need be writ of Creon's train.
And since you have reproached me with my blind-
ness,
I say—you have your sight, and do not see
What evils are about you, nor with whom,
Nor in what home you are dwelling. Do you know
From whom you are? Yea, you are ignorant
That to your own you are an enemy,
Whether on earth, alive, or under it.
Soon from this land shall drive you, stalking grim,

Your mother's and your father's two-edged curse,
With eyes then dark, though they look proudly now.
What place on earth shall not be harbour, then,
For your lamenting? What Cithæron-peak
Shall not be resonant soon, when you discern
What hymen-song was that, which wafted you
On a fair voyage, to foul anchorage
Under yon roof? and multitudes besides
Of ills you know not of shall level you
Down to your self—down to your children! Go,
Trample on Creon, and on this mouth of mine;
But know, there is not one of all mankind
That shall be bruised more utterly than you.

*Œdipus.* Must I endure to hear all this from him?
Hence, to perdition! quickly hence! begone
Back from these walls, and turn you home again.

*Tiresias.* But that you called me, I had not come hither.

*Œdipus.* I did not know that you would utter folly;
Else I had scarce sent for you, to my house.

*Tiresias.* Yea, such is what we seem, foolish to you,
And to your fathers, who begat you, wise.

*Œdipus.* What fathers? Stop! Who was it gave me being?

*Tiresias.* This day shall give you birth and death in one.

*Œdipus.* How all too full of riddles and obscure
Is your discourse!

*Tiresias.*            Were you not excellent
At solving riddles?

*Œdipus.*            Ay, cast in my teeth
Matters in which you must allow my greatness!

*Tiresias.* And yet this very fortune was your ruin!

*Œdipus.* Well, if I saved this city, I care not.

*Tiresias.*                    Well,
I am going; and you, boy, take me home.

*Œdipus.*                   Ay, let him.
Your turbulence impedes us, while you stay;
When you are gone, you can annoy no more.

                            [*Retires.*[8]

*Tiresias.* I go, having said that I came to say;
Not that I fear your frown; for you possess
No power to kill me; but I say to you—
The man you have been seeking, threatening him,
And loud proclaiming him for Laius' murder,

That man is here; believed a foreigner
Here sojourning; but shall be recognized
For Theban born hereafter; yet not pleased
In the event; for blind instead of seeing,
And poor for wealthy, to a foreign land,
A staff to point his footsteps, he shall go.
Also to his own sons he shall be found
Related as a brother, though their sire,
And of the woman from whose womb he came
Both son and spouse; one that has raised up seed
To his own father, and has murdered him.
Now get you in, and ponder what I say;
And if you can detect me in a lie,
Then come and say that I am no true seer.

*[Exeunt* Tiresias *and Boy.*

CHORUS.

I. 1.

Who is he, who was said
By the Delphian soothsaying rock
To have wrought with hands blood-red
Nameless unspeakable deeds?
Time it were that he fled
Faster than storm-swift steeds!
For upon him springs with a shock,
Armed in thunder and fire,
The Child of Jove, at the head
   Of the Destinies dread,
That follow, and will not tire.

I. 2.

For a word but now blazed clear
From Parnassus' snow-covered mound,
To hunt down the Unknown!
He, through the forest drear,
By rocks, by cavernous ways,
Stalks, like a bull that strays,
Heartsore, footsore, alone;
Flying from Earth's central seat,
Flying the oracular sound
   That with swift wings' beat
For ever circles him round.

## II. 1.

Of a truth dark thoughts, yea dark and fell,
  The augur wise doth arouse in me,
    Who neither assent, nor yet gainsay;
And what to affirm, I cannot tell;
  But I flutter in hope, unapt to see
    Things of to-morrow, or to-day.

Why in Polybus' son they should find a foe,
  Or he in the heirs of Labdacus,
    I know no cause, or of old, or late,
In test whereof I am now to go
  Against the repute of Œdipus,
    To avenge a Labdakid's unknown fate.

## II. 2.

True, Zeus indeed, and Apollo, are wise,
  And knowers of what concerns mankind;
    But that word of a seer, a man like me,
Weighs more than mine, for a man to prize,
  Is all unsure.   Yea, one man's mind
    May surpass another's in subtlety;

But never will I, till I see the rest,
  Assent to those who accuse him now.
    I saw how the air-borne Maiden came
Against him,[9] and proved him wise, by the test,
  And good to the state; and for this, I trow,
    He shall not, ever, be put to shame.

*Enter* CREON.

*Creon.* I am come hither, fellow citizens,
  Having been told that Œdipus the king
  Lays grievous accusations to my charge,
  Which I will not endure.   For if he fancies
  He in our present troubles has endured
  Aught at my hands, either in word or deed,
  Tending to harm him, I have no desire
  My life should be prolonged, bearing this blame.
  The injury that such a word may do
  Is no mere trifle, but more vast than any,
  If I am to be called a criminal
  Here in the town, and by my friends, and you.

1 *Senator.* Nay, the reproach, it may be, rather came
    Through stress of anger, than advisedly.

*Creon.* But it was plainly said,[10] by my advice
    The prophet gave false answers.

1 *Senator.*                    It was said ;
    But how advised I know not.

*Creon.*                   Was this charge
    Of a set mind, and with set countenance
    Imputed against me ?

1 *Senator.*               I do not know.
    I have no eyes for what my masters do.
    But here he comes, himself, forth of the palace.

*Enter* ŒDIPUS.

*Œdipus.* Fellow, how cam'st thou hither ?    Dost thou boast
    So great a front of daring, as to come
    Under my roof, the assassin clear of me,
    And manifest pirate of my royalty ?
    Tell me, by heaven, did you detect in me
    The bearing of a craven, or a fool,[11]
    That you laid plans to do it ; or suppose
    I should not recognize your work in this,
    Creeping on slily, and defend myself ?
    Is it not folly, this attempt of yours,
    Without a following, without friends, to hunt
    After a throne, a thing which is achieved
    By aid of followers and much revenue ?

*Creon.* Do me this favour ; hear me say as much
    As you have said ; and then, yourself decide.

*Œdipus.* You are quick to talk, but I am slow to learn
    Of you ; for I have found you contrary
    And dangerous to me.

*Creon.*               Now, this same thing
    First hear, how I shall state it.

*Œdipus.*              This same thing
    Do not tell me—that you are not a villain !

*Creon.* If you suppose your arrogance weighs aught
    Apart from reason, you are much astray.

*Œdipus.* If you suppose you can escape the pain
    Due for a kinsman's wrong, you are astray !

*Creon.* You speak with justice ; I agree !    But tell me,
    How is it that you say I injured you ?

*Œdipus.* Did you persuade me that I ought to send
　　To fetch that canting soothsayer, or no?

*Creon.* Why yes, and now, I am of the same mind, still.

*Œdipus.* How long is it since Laius—

*Creon.* 　　　　　　　　　　What? I know not.

*Œdipus.* Died—disappeared, murdered by violence?

*Creon.* Long seasons might be numbered, long gone by.

*Œdipus.* Well, did this seer then practise in the craft?

*Creon.* Yes, just as wise, and just as much revered.

*Œdipus.* And did he at that time say one word of me?

*Creon.* Well, nowhere in my presence, anyhow.

*Œdipus.* But did not you hold inquest for the dead?

*Creon.* We did, of course; and got no evidence.

*Œdipus.* Well then, how came it that this wiseacre
　　Did not say these things then?

*Creon.* 　　　　　　　　　　I do not know.
　　In matters where I have no cognizance
　　I hold my tongue.

*Œdipus.* 　　　　　This much, at least, you know,
　　And if you are wise, will say!

*Creon.* 　　　　　　　　　And what is that?
　　For if I know it, I shall not refuse.

*Œdipus.* Why, that unless he had conspired with you
　　He never would have said that Laius' murder
　　Was of my doing!

*Creon.* 　　　　　If he says so, you know.
　　Only I claim to know that first from you,
　　Which you put now to me.[12]

*Œdipus.* 　　　　　　　　Learn anything!
　　For I shall not be found a murderer.

*Creon.* Well then; you have my sister to your wife?

*Œdipus.* There's no denying that question.

*Creon.* 　　　　　　　　　　And with her
　　Rule equal, and in common hold the land?

*Œdipus.* All she may wish for she obtains of me.

*Creon.* And make I not a third, equal with you?

*Œdipus.* Ay, there appears your friendship's falsity.

*Creon.* Not if you reason with yourself, as I.
　　And note this first; if you can think that any
　　Would rather choose a sovereignty, with fears,
　　Than the same power, with undisturbed repose?
　　Neither am I, by nature, covetous

To be a king, rather than play the king,
Nor any man who has sagacity.
Now I have all things, without fear, from you;
Reigned I myself, I must do much I hated.
How were a throne, then, pleasanter for me
Than painless empire and authority?
I am not yet so blinded as to wish
For honour, other than is joined with gain.
Now am I hail-fellow-well-met with all;
Now every man gives me good-morrow; now
The waiters on your favour fawn on me;
For all their prospering depends thereby.
Then how should I exchange this lot for yours?
A mind well balanced cannot turn to crime.
I neither am in love with this design,
Nor, in a comrade, would I suffer it.
For proof of which, first, go to Pytho; ask
For the oracles, if I declared them truly;
Next, if you can detect me in the act
Of any conjuration with the seer,
Then, by a double vote, not one alone,
Mine and your own, take me, and take my life;
But do not, on a dubious argument,
Charge me beside the facts. For just it is not,
To hold bad men for good, good men for bad,
To no good end; nay, 'twere all one to me
To throw away a friend, a worthy one,
And one's own life, which most of all one values.
Ah well; in time, you will see these things plainly;
For time alone shews a man's honesty,
But in one day you may discern his guilt.

1 *Senator.* His words sound fair—to one who fears to
   fall;
   For swift in counsel is unsafe, my liege.

*Œdipus.* When he who plots against me in the dark
   Comes swiftly on, I must be swift in turn.
   If I stay quiet, his ends will have been gained,
   And mine all missed.

*Creon.*                   What is it that you want?
   To expel me from the country?

*Œdipus.*                              Not at all.
   Your death I purpose, not your banishment.

*Creon.* Not without shewing, first, what a thing is jealousy!

*Œdipus.* You talk like one who will not yield, nor heed.

*Creon.* Because I see you mean injuriously.

*Œdipus.* Not to myself!

*Creon.*                    No more you ought to me!

*Œdipus.* You are a traitor!

*Creon.*                    What if you are no judge?

*Œdipus.* I must be ruler.

*Creon.*                    Not if you rule badly.

*Œdipus.* City, my city!

*Creon.*                    The city is mine too,
  And not yours only.

*1 Senator.*                    Good my lords, have done,
  Here is Jocasta; in good time, I see her
  Come to you from the palace; with her aid
  'Twere meet to appease your present difference.

### *Enter* JOCASTA.

*Jocasta.* Unhappy men, what was it made you raise
  This senseless broil of words? Are you not both
  Ashamed of stirring private grievances,
  The land being thus afflicted? Get you in—
  And, Creon, do you go home; push not mere nothing[13]
  On to some terrible calamity!

*Creon.* Sister, your husband Œdipus thinks fit
  To treat me villainously; choosing for me
  Of two bad things, one; to expatriate me,
  Or seize and kill me.

*Œdipus.*                    I admit it, wife;
  For I have found him out in an offence
  Against my person, joined with treachery.

*Creon.* So may I never thrive, but perish, banned
  Of Heaven, if I have done a thing to you
  Of what you charge against me!

*Jocasta.*                    Œdipus!
  O in Heaven's name believe it! Above all
  Revere this oath in heaven; secondly
  Myself, and these, who stand before you here.

*1 Senator.* Hear her, my king! With wisdom and goodwill
  I pray you hear!

*Œdipus.*                    What would you have me grant?

1 *Senator.*  Respect his word; no bauble, heretofore;
    And by this oath made weighty.

*Œdipus.*                    Do you know
    For what you ask?

1 *Senator.*         I do.

*Œdipus.*                Say what you mean, then!

1 *Senator.*  That you expel not, ever, with disgrace,
    The friend, who has abjured it, on a charge
    Void of clear proof.

*Œdipus.*             Now, understand it well;
    Seek this, you seek my death or exile!

1 *Senator.*               Nay,
    By the Sun-god, first of all Gods in heaven!
    So may I perish, to the uttermost,
    Cut off from Heaven, without the help of men,
    If I have such a thought! But the land's waste
    Will break my heart with grief—and that this woe,
    Your strife, is added to its former woe.

*Œdipus.*  Well, let him go, though I get slain outright,
    Or thrust by force, dishonoured, from the land;
    Your voice, not his, makes me compassionate,
    Pleading for pity; he, where'er he be,
    Shall have my hatred.

*Creon.*             You display your spleen
    In yielding; but, when your wrath passes bound,
    Are formidable! Tempers such as yours
    Most grievous are to their own selves to bear,
    Not without justice.

*Œdipus.*            Leave me; get you gone!

*Creon.*  I go; you know me not; these know me honest.
                                 *[Exit.*

1 *Senator.*  Lady, what hinders you from taking him
    Into the house?

*Jocasta.*             I would know how this happened.

1 *Senator.*  A blind surmise arose, out of mere babble;
    But even what is unjust inflicts a sting.

*Jocasta.*  On part of both?

1 *Senator.*         Yes truly.

*Jocasta.*                And what was said?

1 *Senator.*  Enough it seems, enough it seems to me,
    Under the former trouble of the land,
    To leave this where it lies.

*Œdipus.*                               Do you perceive
How far you are carried—a well-meaning man!
Slurring my anger thus, and blunting it?

1 *Senator.* I said it, O my king, not once alone—
But be assured, I should have shewn myself
Robbed of my wits, useless for work of wit,
Renouncing thee! who didst impel the sails
Of my dear land, baffled mid straits, right onward,
And it may be, wilt waft her safely now!

*Jocasta.* For Heaven's sake tell me too, my lord, what
                               was it
Caused you so deep an anger?

*Œdipus.*                               I will tell you;
For I respect you, lady, more than these;
'Twas Creon—at plots which he has laid for me.

*Jocasta.* If you will charge the quarrel in plain terms,
Why speak!

*Œdipus.*                 He says that I am Laius' slayer.

*Jocasta.* Of his own knowledge, or on hearsay?

*Œdipus.*                                         Nay,
But by citation of a knavish seer;
As for himself, he keeps his words blame-free.

*Jocasta.* Now set you free from thought of that you talk of;
Listen and learn, nothing in human life
Turns on the soothsayer's art.   Tokens of this
I'll show you in few words.   To Laius once
There came an oracle, I do not say
From Phœbus' self, but from his ministers,
That so it should befall, that he should die
By a son's hands, whom he should have by me.
And him—the story goes—robbers abroad
Have murdered, at a place where three roads meet;
While from our son's birth not three days went by
Before, with ancles pinned, he cast him out,
By hands of others, on a pathless moor.
And so Apollo did not bring about
That he should be his father's murderer;
Nor yet that Laius should endure the stroke
At his son's hands, of which he was afraid.
This is what came of soothsayers' oracles;
Whereof take thou no heed.   That which we lack,
If a God seek, himself will soon reveal.

*Œdipus.* What perturbation and perplexity
　　Take hold upon me, woman, hearing you!

*Jocasta.* What stress of trouble is on you, that you say
　　　　so?

*Œdipus.* I thought I heard you say Laius was slain
　　Where three roads meet!

*Jocasta.* 　　　　　　　　Yes, so the rumour ran,
　　And so runs still.

*Œdipus.* 　　　　　　And where might be the spot
　　Where this befell?

*Jocasta.* 　　　　　　　Phocis the land is named;
　　There are two separate roads converge in one
　　From Daulia and Delphi.

*Œdipus.* 　　　　　　　　And what time
　　Has passed since then?

*Jocasta.* 　　　　　　　　It was but just before
　　You were installed as ruler of the land,
　　The tidings reached the city.

*Œdipus.* 　　　　　　　　God of Heaven!
　　What would'st thou do unto me!

*Jocasta.* 　　　　　　　　　　Œdipus,
　　What is it on your mind?

*Œdipus.* 　　　　　　　Ask me not yet.
　　But Laius—say, what was he like? what prime
　　Of youth had he attained to?

*Jocasta.* 　　　　　　　He was tall;
　　The first white flowers had blossomed in his hair;
　　His figure was not much unlike your own.

*Œdipus.* Me miserable! It seems I have but now
　　Proffered myself to a tremendous curse
　　Not knowing!

*Jocasta.* 　　　　How say you? I tremble, O my lord,
　　To gaze upon you!

*Œdipus.* 　　　　　　I am sore afraid
　　The prophet was not blind; but you will make
　　More certain, if you answer one thing more.

*Jocasta.* Indeed I tremble; but the thing you ask
　　I'll answer, when I know it.

*Œdipus.* 　　　　　　　Was he going
　　Poorly attended, or with many spears
　　About him, like a prince?

*Jocasta.* 　　　　　　　But five in all;

One was a herald; and one carriage held
Laius himself.

*Œdipus.*                    O, it is plain already!
Woman, who was it told this tale to you?

*Jocasta.* A servant, who alone came safe away.

*Œdipus.* Is he perchance now present, in the house?

*Jocasta.* Why no; for after he was come from thence,
And saw you governing, and Laius dead,
He came and touched my hand, and begged of me
To send him to the fields and sheep-meadows,
So he might be as far as possible
From eyesight of the townsmen; and I sent him;
For he was worthy, for a slave, to obtain
Even greater favours.

*Œdipus.*                    Could we have him back
Quickly?

*Jocasta.*          We could.    But why this order?

*Œdipus.*                                    Wife,
I fear me I have spoken far too much;
Wherefore I wish to see him.

*Jocasta.*                          He shall come!
But I am worthy, in my turn, to know
What weighs so heavily upon you, Sir?

*Œdipus.* And you shall know; since I have passed so far
The bounds of apprehension.   For to whom
Could I impart, passing through such a need,
Greater in place—if that were all—than you?
—I am the son of Polybus of Corinth,
And of a Dorian mother, Merope.
And I was counted most preëminent
Among the townsmen there; up to the time
A circumstance befell me, of this fashion—
Worthy of wonder, though of my concern
Unworthy.    At the board a drunken fellow
Over his cups called me a changeling;
And I, being indignant—all that day
Hardly refrained—but on the morrow went
And taxed my parents with it to their face;
Who took the scandal grievously, of him
Who launched the story.   Well, with what they said
I was content; and yet the thing still galled me;
For it spread far.   So without cognizance

Of sire or mother I set out to go
To Pytho.   Phœbus sent me of my quest
Bootless away; but other terrible
And strange and lamentable things revealed,
Saying I should wed my mother, and produce
A race intolerable for men to see,
And be my natural father's murderer.
When I heard that, measuring where Corinth stands
Even thereafter by the stars alone,
Where I might never think to see fulfilled
The scandals of ill prophecies of me,
I fled, an exile.  As I journeyed on,
I found myself upon the self-same spot
Where, you say, this king perished.  In your ears,
Wife, I will tell the whole.   When in my travels
I was come near this place where three roads meet,
There met me a herald, and a man that rode
In a colt-carriage, as you tell of him,
And from the track the leader, by main force,
And the old man himself, would thrust me.   I,
Being enraged, strike him who jostled me—
The driver—and the old man, when he saw it,
Watching as I was passing, from the car [14]
With his goad's fork smote me upon the head.
He paid, though! duly I say not; but in brief,
Smitten by the staff in this right hand of mine,
Out of the middle of the carriage straight
He rolls down headlong; and I slay them all!
But if there be a semblance to connect
This nameless man with Laius, who is now
More miserable than I am? [15]  Who on earth
Could have been born with more of hate from
    heaven?
Whom never citizen or stranger may
Receive into their dwellings, or accost,
But must thrust out of doors; and 'tis no other
Laid all these curses on myself, than I!
Yea, with embraces of the arms whereby
He perished, I pollute my victim's bed!
Am I not vile?  Am I not all unclean?
If I must fly, and flying, never can
See my own folk, or on my native land

Set foot, or else must with my mother wed,
And slay my father Polybus, who begat
And bred me?[15] Would he not speak truly of me
Who judged these things sent by some barbarous
     Power?
Never, you sacred majesties of Heaven,
Never may I behold that day; but pass
Out of men's sight, ere I shall see myself
Touched by the stain of such a destiny!

1 *Senator.* My liege, these things affect us grievously;
Still, till you hear his story who was by,
Do not lose hope!

*Œdipus.*                    Yea, so much hope is left,
Merely to wait for him, the herdsman.

*Jocasta.*                                   Well,
Suppose him here, what do you want of him?

*Œdipus.* I'll tell you; if he should be found to say
Just what you said, I shall be clear from harm.

*Jocasta.* What did you hear me say, that did not tally?

*Œdipus.* You were just telling me that he made mention
Of "robbers"—"men"—as Laius' murderers.
Now if he shall affirm their number still,
I did not slay him. One cannot be the same
As many. But if he shall speak of one—
One only,[16] it is evident this deed
Already will have been brought home to me.

*Jocasta.* But be assured, that was the word, quite plainly!
And now he cannot blot it out again.
Not I alone, but the whole city heard it.
Then, even if he shift from his first tale,
Not so, my lord, will he at all explain
The death of Laius, as it should have been,[17]
Whom Loxias declared my son must slay!
And after all, the poor thing never killed him,
But died itself before! so that henceforth
I do not mean to look to left or right
For fear of soothsaying!

*Œdipus.*                    You are well advised.
Still, send and fetch the labourer; do not miss it.

*Jocasta.* I will send quickly. Now let us go within.
I would do nothing that displeases you.
                    [*Exeunt* ŒDIPUS *and* JOCASTA.

## Chorus.

### I. 1.

Let it be mine to keep
The holy purity of word and deed
    Foreguided all by mandates from on high
    Born in the ethereal region of the sky,
Their only sire Olympus ; them nor seed
Of mortal man brought forth, nor Lethe cold
      Shall ever lay to sleep ;
In them Deity is great, and grows not old.

### I. 2.

      Pride is the germ of kings ;
Pride, when puffed up, vainly, with many things
    Unseasonable, unfitting, mounts the wall,[18]
    Only to hurry to that fatal fall,
Where feet are vain to serve her.   But the task
Propitious to the city GOD I ask
      Never to take away !
GOD I will never cease to hold my stay.

### II. 1.

    But if any man proceed
    Insolently in word or deed,
    Without fear of right, or care
    For the seats where Virtues are,
    Him, for his ill-omened pride,
    Let an evil death betide !
If honestly his gear he will not gain,
    Nor keep himself from deeds unholy
Nor from inviolable things abstain,
    Blinded by folly.
In such a course, what mortal from his heart
      Dart upon dart
    Can hope to avert of indignation ?
Yea, and if acts like these are held in estimation,
    Why dance we here our part ?

### II. 2.

    Never to the inviolate hearth
    At the navel of the earth,

Nor to Abæ's fane, in prayer,
Nor the Olympian, will I fare,
If it shall not so befall
Manifestly unto all.
But O our king—if thou art named aright—
Zeus, that art Lord of all things ever,
Be this not hid from Thee, nor from Thy might
Which endeth never.
For now already men invalidate
The dooms of Fate
Uttered for Laius, fading slowly;
Apollo's name and rites are nowhere now kept holy;
Worship is out of date.

*Enter* JOCASTA, *attended.*

*Jocasta.* Lords of the land, it came into my heart
To approach the temples of the Deities,
Taking in hand these garlands, and this incense;
For Œdipus lets his mind float too light
Upon the eddies of all kinds of grief;
Nor will he, like a man of soberness,
Measure the new by knowledge of the old,
But is at mercy of whoever speaks,
If he but speak the language of despair.
I can do nothing by exhorting him.
Wherefore, Lycean Phœbus, unto thee—
For thou art very near us—I am come.
Bringing these offerings,[19] a petitioner
That thou afford us fair deliverance;
Since now we are all frighted, seeing him—
The vessel's pilot, as 'twere—panic-stricken.

*Enter a Messenger.*

*Messenger.* Sirs, might I learn of you, where is the palace
Of Œdipus the King? or rather, where
He is himself, if you know, tell me.
*1 Senator.*                                  Stranger,
This is his dwelling, and he is within;
This lady is his children's mother, too.
*Messenger.* A blessing ever be on hers and her,
Who is, in such a perfect sort, his wife!

*Jocasta.* The like be with you too, as you deserve,
　　　　Sir, for your compliment.　But say what end
　　　　You come for, and what news you wish to tell.
*Messenger.* Good to the house, and to your husband, lady.
*Jocasta.* Of what sort?　and from whom come you?
*Messenger.*　　　　　　　　　　　　　　From Corinth.
　　　　In that which I am now about to say
　　　　May you find pleasure!　and why not?　And yet
　　　　Perhaps you may be sorry.
*Jocasta.*　　　　　　　　　　　　But what is it?
　　　　How can it carry such ambiguous force?
*Messenger.* The dwellers in the land of Isthmia,
　　　　As was there said, intend to appoint him king.
*Jocasta.* What!　Is not Polybus, the old prince, still reigning?
*Messenger.* No, truly; he is Death's subject, in the grave.
*Jocasta.* How say you, father?　Is Polybus no more?
*Messenger.* I stake my life upon it, if I lie!
*Jocasta.* Run, girl, and tell your master instantly.

　　　　　　　　　　　　　　　[*Exit an attendant.*

　　　　O prophecies of Gods, where are you now!
　　　　Œdipus fled, long since, from this man's presence,
　　　　Fearing to kill him; and now he has died
　　　　A natural death, not by his means at all!

### *Enter* ŒDIPUS.

*Œdipus.* O my most dear Jocasta, wife of mine,
　　　　Why did you fetch me hither from the house?
*Jocasta.* Hear this man speak!　Listen and mark, to what
　　　　The dark responses of the God are come!
*Œdipus.* And who is this?　What says he?
*Jocasta.*　　　　　　　　　　　　　　He's from Corinth,
　　　　To tell us that your father Polybus
　　　　Lives no more, but is dead!
*Œdipus.*　　　　　　　　　　What say you, sir?
　　　　Tell your own tale yourself.
*Messenger.*　　　　　　　　　　　If first of all
　　　　I must deliver this for certainty,
　　　　Know well, that he has gone the way of mortals.
*Œdipus.* Was it by treason, or some chance disease?
*Messenger.* A little shock prostrates an aged frame!
*Œdipus.* Sickness, you mean, was my poor father's end?
*Messenger.* Yes, and old age; his term of life was full

*Œdipus.* Heigh ho! Why, wife! why should a man regard
The oracular hearth of Pytho, or the birds
Cawing above us, by whose canons I
Was to have slain my father? He is dead,
And buried out of sight; and here am I,
Laying no finger to the instrument,
(Unless, indeed, he pined for want of me,
And so, I killed him!) Well, Polybus is gone;
And with him all those oracles of ours
Bundled to Hades, for old songs, together!

*Jocasta.* Did I not say so all along?

*Œdipus.*                                        You did;
But I was led astray by fear.

*Jocasta.*                                        Well, now
Let none of these predictions any more
Weigh on your mind!

*Œdipus.*                                And how can I help dreading
My mother's bed?

*Jocasta.*                        But why should men be fearful,
O'er whom Fortune is mistress, and foreknowledge
Of nothing sure? Best take life easily,
As a man may. For that maternal wedding,
Have you no fear; for many men ere now
Have dreamed as much; but he who by such dreams
Sets nothing, has the easiest life of it.

*Œdipus.* All these things would have been well said of
                you,
Were not my mother living still; but now,
She being alive, there is all need of dread;
Though you say well.

*Jocasta.*                        And yet your father's burial
Lets in much daylight!

*Œdipus.*                        I acknowledge, much.
Still, her who lives I fear.

*Messenger.*                        But at what woman
Are you dismayed?

*Œdipus.*                        At Merope, old man,
The wife of Polybus.

*Messenger.*                        And what of her
Causes you terror?

*Œdipus.*                        A dark oracle,
Stranger, from heaven.

*Messenger.*                    May it be put in words?
　　Or is it wrong another man should know it?

*Œdipus.* No, not at all.  Why, Loxias declared
　　That I should one day marry my own mother,
　　And with my own hands shed my father's blood.
　　Wherefore from Corinth I have kept away
　　Far, for long years; and prospered; none the less
　　It is most sweet to see one's parents' face.

*Messenger.* And in this apprehension you became
　　An emigrant from Corinth?

*Œdipus.*                    And, old man,
　　Desiring not to be a parricide.

*Messenger.* Why should I not deliver you, my liege—
　　Since my intent in coming here was good—
　　Out of this fear?

*Œdipus.*                    Indeed you would obtain
　　Good guerdon from me.

*Messenger.*                    And indeed for this
　　Chiefest I came, that upon your return
　　I might in some sort benefit.

*Œdipus.*                    But I
　　Will never go, to meet my parents there!

*Messenger.* O son, 'tis plain you know not what you do!

*Œdipus.* How so, old man? in Heaven's name tell me!

*Messenger.*                                        If
　　On this account you shun the journey home!

*Œdipus.* Of course I fear lest Phœbus turn out true.

*Messenger.* Lest through your parents you incur foul stain?

*Œdipus.* Yes, father, yes; that is what always scares me.

*Messenger.* Now do you know you tremble, really, at
　　nothing?

*Œdipus.* How can that be, if I was born their child?

*Messenger.* Because Polybus was nought akin to you!

*Œdipus.* What, did not Polybus beget me?

*Messenger.*                                        No,
　　No more than I did; just so much as I!

*Œdipus.* How, my own sire no more than—nobody?

*Messenger.* But neither he begat you, nor did I.

*Œdipus.* Then from what motive did he call me son?

*Messenger.* Look here; he had you as a gift from me.

*Œdipus.* And loved me then, so much, at second hand?

*Messenger.* Yes, his long childlessness prevailed on him.

*Œdipus.* And did you find or purchase me, to give him?

*Messenger.* I found you in Cithæron's wooded dells.

*Œdipus.* How came you to be journeying in these parts?

*Messenger.* I tended flocks upon the mountains here.

*Œdipus.* You were a shepherd, and you ranged for hire?

*Messenger.* But at the same time your preserver, son!

*Œdipus.* You found me in distress? What was my trouble?

*Messenger.* Your ancle joints may witness.

*Œdipus.*                                      O, why speak you
Of that old evil?

*Messenger.*                    I untied you, when
You had the soles of both your feet bored through.

*Œdipus.* A shameful sort of swaddling bands were mine.

*Messenger.* Such, that from them you had the name you
bear.

*Œdipus.* Tell me, by heaven! at sire's or mother's hand—

*Messenger.* I know not: he who gave you knows of that
Better than I.

*Œdipus.*                    You got me from another?
You did not find me?

*Messenger.*                    No, another shepherd
Gave you to me.

*Œdipus.*                    Who was he? are you able
To point him out?

*Messenger.*                    They said that he was one
Of those who followed Laius, whom you know.

*Œdipus.* Him who was once the monarch of this land?

*Messenger.* Precisely! This man was his herdsman.

*Œdipus.*                                                        Now
Is this man still alive for me to see?

*Messenger.* You must know best, the people of the place.

*Œdipus.* Is any here among you bystanders,
Who knows the herdsman whom he tells us of,
From seeing him, either in the fields or here?
Speak! it were time that this had been cleared up.

*1 Senator.* I think he is no other than that peasant
Whom you were taking pains to find, before;
But she could say as well as any one—
Jocasta.

*Œdipus.*            Lady, you remember him
Whose coming we were wishing for but now;
Does he mean him? [20]

*Jocasta.*              Why ask who 'twas he spoke of?
Nay, never mind—never remember it—
'Twas idly spoken!

*Œdipus.*           Nay, it cannot be
That having such a clue I should refuse
To solve the mystery of my parentage!

*Jocasta.* For Heaven's sake, if you care for your own life,
Don't seek it! I am sick, and that's enough!

*Œdipus.* Courage! At least, if I be thrice a slave,
Born so three-deep, it cannot injure you!

*Jocasta.* But I beseech you, hearken! Do not do it!

*Œdipus.* I will not hearken—not to know the whole.

*Jocasta.* I mean well; and I tell you for the best!

*Œdipus.* What you call best is an old sore of mine.

*Jocasta.* Wretch, what thou art O might'st thou never know!

*Œdipus.* Will some one go and fetch the herdsman hither?
She is welcome to her gilded lineage!

*Jocasta.*                 O
Woe, woe, unhappy! This is all I have
To say to thee, and no word more, for ever!

                           [*Exit.*

1 *Senator.* Why has the woman vanished, Œdipus,
Driven so wild with grief? I am afraid
Out of her silence will break forth some trouble.

*Œdipus.* Break out what will, I shall not hesitate,
Low though it be, to trace the source of me.
But she, perhaps, being, as a woman, proud,
Of my unfit extraction is ashamed.
—I deem myself the child of Fortune! I
Shall not be shamed of her, who favours me;
Seeing I have her for mother; and for kin
The limitary Moons, that found me small,
That fashioned me for great! Parented thus,
How could I ever in the issue prove
Other—that I should leave my birth unknown?


CHORUS.

1.

If I am a true seer,
My mind from error clear,
Tomorrow's moon shall not pass over us,[21]

Ere, O Cithæron, we
Shall magnify in thee
The land, the lap, the womb of Œdipus;
And we shall hymn thy praises, for good things
Of thy bestowing, done unto our kings.
Yea, Phœbus, if thou wilt, amen, so might it be!


2.

Who bare thee?  Which, O child,
Over the mountain-wild
Sought to by Pan of the immortal Maids?
Or Loxias—was he
The sire who fathered thee?[22]
For dear to him are all the upland glades.
Was it Cyllene's lord acquired a son,
Or Bacchus, dweller on the heights, from one
Of those he liefest loves, Oreads of Helicon?


*Enter Attendants with an Old Man, a Shepherd.*

*Œdipus.* If I may guess, who never met with him,
I think I see that herdsman, Senators,
We have long been seeking; for his ripe old age
Harmoniously accords with this man's measure;
Besides, I recognize the men who bring him
As of my household; but in certainty
You can perhaps exceed me, who beheld
The herdsman formerly.

*1 Senator.*                     Why, to be sure,
I recognize him; for he was a man
Trusty as any Laius ever had
About his pastures.

*Œdipus.*                 You I ask the first,
The Corinthian stranger; do you speak of him?

*Messenger.* Yes, him you see.

*Œdipus.*                 Sirrah, old man, look here;
Answer my questions.  Were you Laius' man?

*Old Man.* Truly his thrall; not bought, but bred at home.

*Œdipus.* Minding what work, or in what character?

*Old Man.* Most of my time I went after the flocks.

*Œdipus.* In what directions, chiefly, were your folds?

*Old Man.* There was Cithæron; and a bit near by.

*Œdipus.* Do you know this man, then? Did you see him there?

*Old Man.* Him? After what? What man do you mean?

*Œdipus.*                          This fellow
Here present; did you ever meet with him?

*Old Man.* Not so to say off-hand, from memory.

*Messenger.* And that's no wonder, sir; but beyond doubt
I will remind him, though he has forgotten,
I am quite sure he knows, once on a time,
When in the bit about Cithæron there—
He with two flocks together, I with one—
I was his neighbour for three whole half years
From spring-tide onward to the Bear-ward's day;
And with the winter to my folds I drove,
And he to Laius' stables. Are these facts,
Or are they not—what I am saying?

*Old Man.*                              Yes,
You speak the truth; but it was long ago.

*Messenger.* Come, say now, don't you mind that you then gave me
A baby boy to bring up for my own?

*Old Man.* What do you mean? Why do you ask it me? [23]

*Messenger.* This is the man, good fellow; who was then
A youngling!

*Old Man.*              Out upon you! Hold your peace!

*Œdipus.* Nay, old man, do not chide him; for your words
Deserve a chiding rather than his own!

*Old Man.* O best of masters, what is my offence?

*Œdipus.* Not telling of that boy he asks about.

*Old Man.* He says he knows not what! He is all astray!

*Œdipus.* You will not speak of grace—you shall perforce!

*Old Man.* Do not for God's sake harm me, an old man!

*Œdipus.* Quick, some one, twist his hands behind him!

*Old Man.*                              Wretch
What have I done? What do you want to know?

*Œdipus.* Did you give him that boy he asks about?

*Old Man.* I gave it him. Would I had died that day!

*Œdipus.* Tell the whole truth, or you will come to it!

*Old Man.* I am undone far more, though, if I speak!

*Œdipus.* The man is trifling with us, I believe.

*Old Man.* No, no; I said I gave it, long ago!

*Œdipus.* Where did you get it? At home, or from some other?

*Old Man.* It was not mine; another gave it me.

*Œdipus.* Which of these citizens? and from what roof?

*Old Man.* Don't, master, for God's sake, don't ask me more!

*Œdipus.* You are a dead man, if I speak again!

*Old Man.* Then—'twas a child—of Laius' household.

*Œdipus.*            What,
    Slave-born? or one of his own family?

*Old Man.* O, I am at the horror, now, to speak!

*Œdipus.* And I to hear. But I must hear—no less.

*Old Man.* Truly it was called his son; but she within,
    Your lady, could best tell you how it was.

*Œdipus.* Did she then give it you?

*Old Man.*           My lord, even so.

*Œdipus.* For what?

*Old Man.*       For me to make away with it.

*Œdipus.* Herself the mother? miserable!

*Old Man.*           In dread
    Of evil prophecies—

*Œdipus.*        What prophecies?

*Old Man.* That he should kill his parents, it was said.

*Œdipus.* How came you then to give it to this old man?

*Old Man.* For pity, O my master! thinking he
    Would carry it away to other soil,
    From whence he came; but he to the worst of harms
    Saved it! for if thou art the man he says,
    Sure thou wast born destined to misery!

*Œdipus.* Woe! woe! It is all plain, indeed! O Light,
    This be the last time I shall gaze on thee,
    Who am revealed to have been born of those
    Of whom I ought not—to have wedded whom
    I ought not—and slain whom I might not slay!

                         [*Exit.*

## CHORUS.

### I. 1.

    O generations of mankind!
       How do I find
         Your lives nought worth at all!
   For who is he—what state
   Is there, more fortunate
   Than only to seem great,
      And then, to fall?

I having thee for pattern, and thy lot—
Thine, O poor Œdipus—I envy not
  Aught in mortality;
    For this is he

### I. 2.

Who, shooting far beyond the rest,
    Won wealth all-blest,
  Slaying, Zeus, thy monster-maid,
Crook-taloned, boding; and
Who did arise and stand
Betwixt death and our land,
   A tower of aid;
Yea for this cause thou hast been named our king,
And honoured in the highest, governing
    The city of Thebæ great
     In royal state.

### II. 1.

And now, who lives more utterly undone?
  Who with sad woes, who with mischances rude
  Stands closer yoked by life's vicissitude?
  O honoured head of Œdipus, for whom
  Within the same wide haven there was room
   To come—child, to the birth—
    Sire, to the nuptial bower,
  How could the furrows of thy parent earth—
How could they suffer thee, O hapless one,
   In silence, to this hour?

### II. 2.

Time found thee out—Time who sees everything—
  Unwittingly guilty; and arraigns thee now
  Consort ill-sorted, unto whom are bred
  Sons of thy getting, in thine own birth-bed.
   O scion of Laius' race,
  Would I had never never seen thy face!
For I lament, even as from lips that sing
  Pouring a dirge;[24] yet verily it was thou
   Gav'st me to rise
And breathe again, and close my watching eyes.[25]

*Enter a second* MESSENGER.

**2 *Messenger*.** O you most honoured ever of this land,
    What deeds have you to hear, what sights to see,
    What sorrow to endure, if you still cherish
    The house of Labdacus with loyalty?
    For Ister I suppose or Phasis' wave
    Never could purge this dwelling from the ills
    It covers—or shall instantly reveal,
    Invited, not inflicted; of all wounds,
    Those that seem wilful are the worst to bear.

**1 *Senator*.** There was no lack, in what we knew before,
    Of lamentable; what have you more to say?

**2 *Messenger*.** The speediest of all tales to hear and tell;
    The illustrious Jocasta is no more.

**1 *Senator*.** Unhappy woman! From what cause?

**2 *Messenger*.**                       Self-slain.
    Of what befell the saddest part is spared;
    For you were not a witness. None the less
    So far as I can tell it you shall hear
    Her miserable story. When she passed
    So frantically inside the vestibule,
    She went straight onward to the bed-chamber,
    With both her hands tearing her hair; the doors
    She dashed to as she entered, crying out
    On Laius, long since dead, calling to mind
    His fore-begotten offspring, by whose hands
    He, she said, died, and left to his own seed
    Its mother's most unnatural bearing-bed.
    Nor did she not bewail [26] that nuptial-couch
    Where she brought forth, unhappy, brood on
        brood,
    Spouse to her spouse, and children to her child.
    And then—I know no further how she perished;
    For Œdipus brake in, crying aloud;
    For whom it was impossible to watch
    The ending of her misery; but on him
    We gazed, as he went raging all about,
    Beseeching us to furnish him a sword
    And say where he could find his wife—no wife,
    Rather the mother-soil both of himself
    And children; and, as he raved thus, some Power

Shews him—at least, none of us present did.
Then, shouting loud, he sprang upon the doors
As following some guide, and burst the bars
Out of their sockets, and alights within.
There we beheld his wife hanging, entwined
In a twined noose.  He seeing her, with a groan
Looses the halter; then, when on the ground
Lay the poor wretch, dreadful it was to see
What followed; snatching from her dress gold
        pins
Wherewith she was adorned, he lifted them,
And smote the nerves of his own eyeballs, saying
Something like this—that they should see no
        more
Evils like those he had endured or wrought;
Darkling, thereafter, let them gaze on forms
He might not see, and fail to recognize
The faces he desired!  Chanting this burden,
Not once, but many times, he raised his hand
And stabbed his eyes; so that from both of them
The blood ran down his face, not drop by drop,
But all at once, in a dark shower of gore.
—These are the ills that from a two-fold source,
Not one alone, but in both wife and spouse,
Mingled together, have burst forth at once.[27]
Their former pristine happiness indeed
Was happiness before; but in this hour
Shame—lamentation—Atè—death—of all
That has a name of evil, nought's away!

1 *Senator.*  And does he stand in any [28] respite now
        Of misery, poor soul?

2 *Messenger.*                    He calls aloud
For some one to undo the bolts, and shew
To all the Cadmeans him, his father's slayer—
His mother's—uttering words unhallowed—words
I may not speak; that he will cast himself
Forth of the land, abide no more at home
Under the curse of his own cursing.  Nay,
But he lacks force, and guidance; for his sickness
Is more than man can bear.  See for yourself;
For these gates open, and you will straight behold
A sight—such as even he that loathes must pity!

*Enter OEDIPUS blind.*

### CHORUS.

O sorrow, lamentable for eyes to see!
Sorest of all past ills encountering me!
What frenzy, O wretch, is this, that came on thee?

What Deity was it that with a leap so great—
Farther than farthest—sprang on thy sad fate?
Woe is me, woe is me for thee—unfortunate!

Fain would I gaze at thee, would ask thee much,
Many things learn of thee, wert thou not such
As I may not even behold, as I shudder to touch.

*Œdipus.* Me miserable! Whither must I go?
    Ah whither flits my voice, borne to and fro?
    Thou Power unseen, how hast thou brought me low!

1 *Senator.* To ills, intolerable to hear or see.

*Œdipus.* Thou horror of thick darkness overspread,
    Thou shadow of unutterable dread
    Not to be stemmed or stayed, fallen on my head—

    Woe's me once more! How crowd upon my heart
    Stings of these wounds, and memories of woe!

1 *Senator.* No marvel if thou bear a double smart
    And writhe, so stricken, with a two-fold throe!

*Œdipus.* Still art thou near me—ready still to tend
    And to endure me, faithful to the end,
    Blind as I am, with kindness, O my friend!

    For strange thou art not; but full well I know
    That voice of thine, all darkling though I be.

1 *Senator.* Rash man, how could'st thou bear to outrage so
    Thine eyes? What Power was it, that wrought on
    thee?

*Œdipus.* Apollo, Apollo fulfils,
    O friends, my measure of ills—
    Fills my measure of woe;
    Author was none, but I,
    None other, of the blow;
    For why was I to see,
        When to descry
No sight on earth could have a charm for me?

*1 Senator.* It was even as thou sayest.

*Œdipus.* What was there left for sight?
    What, that could give delight?
      Or whose address,
O friends, could I still hear with happiness?
    Lead me to exile straight;
    Lead me, O my friends, the worst
Of murderers, of mortals most accurst,
    Yea and to Gods chief object of their hate.

*1 Senator.* Of cunning hapless, as of hapless fate,
    I would that I had never known thy name![29]

*Œdipus.*      May he perish, whoe'er 'twas drew me
    Out of the cruel gyve
    That bound my feet, on the lea!
    He who saved me alive,
    Who rescued me from fate,
    Shewing no kindness to me!
        Sorrow so great,
Had I died then, had spared both mine and me.

*1 Senator.* Fain were I too it had been so.

*Œdipus.*      Not then had I become
    My father's murderer,
Nor wedded her I have my being from:
    Whom now no God will bless,
    Child of incestuousness
In her that bare me, being the spouse of her;
Yea if aught ill worse than all ill be there,
    That Œdipus must bear.

1 *Senator.* I know not how to say thou hast done well;
 For it were better for thee now to die,
 Than to live on in blindness.

*Œdipus.*      Tell me not—
 Give me no counsel now, that what is done
 Has not been done thus best.  I know not how
 With seeing eyes I could have looked upon
 My father—coming to the under-world,
 Or my poor mother, when against them both
 I have sinned sins, worse than a halter's meed.
 Or do you think that children were a sight
 Delectable for me to gaze at, born
 As they were born?  Never with eyes of mine!
 No, nor the city, nor the citadel,
 Nor consecrated shrines of deities,
 From which, to my most utter misery,
 I, of all other men in Thebes the man
 Most bravely nurtured, cut myself away,
 And of my own mouth dictated to all
 To thrust out me, the impious—me, declared
 Abominable of Heaven, and Laius' son.
 Was I, who in myself made evident
 So dark a stain, with unaverted eyes
 To look on these?  That least of all!  Nay rather,
 If there were any way to choke the fount
 Of hearing, through my ears, I would have tried
 To seal up all this miserable frame
 And live blind, deaf to all things; sweet it were
 To dwell in fancy, out of reach of pain.
 —Cithæron! wherefore didst thou harbour me!
 Why not at once have slain me?  Never then
 Had I displayed before the face of men
 Who and from whom I am!  O Polybus,
 And Corinth, and the old paternal roof
 I once called mine, with what thin film of honour,
 Corruption over-skinned, you fostered me,
 Found ill myself, and from ill parents, now!
 O you, the three roads, and the lonely brake,
 The copse, and pass at the divided way,
 Which at my hands drank blood that was my own—
 My father's—do you keep in memory
 What in your sight I did, and how again

I wrought, when I came hither? Wedlock, wedlock,
You gave me being, you raised up seed again
To the same lineage,[30] and exhibited
In one incestuous flesh son—brother—sire,
Bride, wife and mother; and all ghastliest deeds
Wrought among men! But O, ill done, ill worded!
In Heaven's name hide me with all speed away,
Or slay me, or send adrift upon some sea
Where you may look on me no longer! Come,
Touch, if you will, a miserable man;
Pray you, fear nothing; for my misery
No mortal but myself can underbear.[31]

1 *Senator.* Creon is at hand; he is the man you need,
    Who must decide and do; being, after you,
    The sole protector left us, for the land.

*Œdipus.* Ah Heaven, what language shall I hold to him?
    What rightful credit will appear in me?
    For I have been found wholly in the wrong
    In all that passed between us heretofore!

### *Enter* CREON.

*Creon.* Not as a mocker come I, Œdipus,
    Nor to reproach for any former pain.
    But you—even if you reverence no more
    Children of men,—at least so far revere
    The royal Sun-god's all-sustaining fire,
    Not to parade, thus flagrant, such a sore
    As neither earth nor day can tolerate,
    Nor dew from Heaven! Take him in instantly!
    That kindred only should behold and hear
    The griefs of kin, fits best with decency.

*Œdipus.* In Heaven's name, seeing that you transported me
    Beyond all hope, coming, the first of men,
    To me the last of men, grant me one boon!
    'Tis for your good, not for my own, I say it.

*Creon.* What is it that you crave so eagerly?

*Œdipus.* Out of this country cast me with all speed,
    Where I may pass without accost of men.

*Creon.* So had I done, be sure, had I not wished
    To learn our duty, first, at the God's mouth.

*Œdipus.* Surely his oracle was all made plain,

         Me, the profane, the parricide, to slay!

*Creon.* So was it said; but in our present need
       'Tis better to enquire what we must do.

*Œdipus.* Will ye seek answer for a wretch like me?

*Creon.* Even you might trust what the God answers, now.

*Œdipus.* Ay, and I charge thee, and will beg of thee,[32]
       Order thyself such burial as thou wilt,
       For her who lies within; seeing it is meet
       Thou do so, for thine own.   But never more
       Be this my native town burdened with me
       For living inmate; rather suffer me
       To haunt the mountains—where my mountain is,
       Cithæron, which my mother and my sire,
       Living,[33] appointed for my sepulchre,
       That as they meant, my slayers, I may expire.
       Howbeit this much I know, neither disease
       Nor aught beside can kill me; never else
       Had I been rescued from the brink of death,
       But for some dire calamity.  Ah well,
       Let our own fate wag onward as it may;
       And for my sons, Creon, take thou no care
       Upon thee;[34] they are men, so that they never
       Can lack the means to live, where'er they be;
       But my two girls, wretched and pitiable,
       For whose repast was never board of mine
       Ordered apart, without me, but in all
       That I partook they always shared with me,
       Take care of them; and let me, above all else,
       Touch them with hands, and weep away my troubles!
       Pardon, my lord; pardon, illustrious sir;
       If but my hands could feel them, I might seem
       To have them still, as when I still could see.

      Antigone *and* Ismene *are brought in.*

   —What do I say?  In Heaven's name, do I not
       Hear my two darlings, somewhere shedding tears?
       And can it be that Creon, pitying me,
       Sends me my dearest, my two daughters, hither?
       Is it so indeed?

*Creon.* Yes, it is I vouchsafed this boon, aware
       What joy you have and long have had of them.

*Œdipus.* Why then, good luck go with thee, and Providence
Be guardian to thee, better than to me,
In payment for their coming !—Children dear,
Where are you?  Come, come hither to my arms—
To these brotherly arms—procurers that
The eyes—that were your sire's—once bright—should see
Thus ! who am shewn, O children, to have been
Author of you—unseeing—unknowing—in
Her bed, whence I derived my being !  You
I weep for ; for I cannot gaze on you ;
Knowing what is left of bitter in the life
Which at men's hands you needs must henceforth
  live.
For to what gatherings of the citizens
Will you resort, or to what festivals,
Whence you will not, in place of holiday,
Come home in tears?  Or when you shall have
  grown
To years of marriage, who—ah, who will be
The man to abide the hazard of disgrace
Such as must be the bane, both of my sons,⁸⁵
And you as well?  For what reproach is lacking?
Your father slew his father, and became
Father of you—by her who bare him.  So
Will they reproach you ; who will wed you then?
No one, my children ; but you needs must wither,
Barren—unwed.  But thou, Menœceus' son,
Since thou art all the father these have left them,
For we, the two that were their parents, now
Are both undone, do not thou suffer them
To wander, vagabond and husband-less,
Being of thy kin ; nor let them fall so low
As are my fortunes ; but have pity on them,
Seeing them so tender, and so desolate
Of all friends, but for thee.  Give me thy hand,
Good sir, and promise this.—To you, my girls,
If you were old enough to understand,
I should have much to say ; but as it is,
This be your prayer ; in some permitted place
That you may breathe ; and have your lot in life
Happier than his, who did engender you.

*Creon.* Get thee in; thou hast bewailed thee enough, in reason.

*Œdipus.* Though it be bitter, I must do it.

*Creon.* All's good, in good season.

*Œdipus.* Do you know how to make me?

*Creon.* Say on, and I shall know.

*Œdipus.* Banish me from this country.

*Creon.* That must the God bestow.

*Œdipus.* But to Gods, above all men, I am a mark for hate.

*Creon.* And for that same reason you will obtain it straight.

*Œdipus.* Say you so?

*Creon.* Yes truly, and I mean what I say.

*Œdipus.* Lead me hence then, quickly.

*Creon.* Go; but let the children stay.

*Œdipus.* Do not take them from me!

*Creon.* Think not to have all at thy pleasure;
For what thou didst attain to far outwent thy measure.

CREON, *the Children, etc. retire.* ŒDIPUS *is led in.*


### CHORUS.

Dwellers in Thebes, behold this Œdipus,
The man who solved the riddle marvellous,
A prince of men,
Whose lot what citizen
Did not with envy see,
How deep the billows of calamity
    Above him roll.
Watch therefore and regard that supreme day;
And of no mortal say
"That man is happy," till
Vexed by no grievous ill
    He pass Life's goal.

[*Exeunt omnes.*

# TRACHINIAE

## PERSONS REPRESENTED

DEIANIRA, *daughter of Œneus the chieftain of Pleuron in Ætolia,* *and wife to Heracles.*

*A bondwoman attending on Deianira.*

HYLLUS, *eldest son of Heracles by Deianira.*

*A messenger, a Melian of Trachis.*

LICHAS, *a herald in attendance on Heracles.*

IOLE, *daughter of Eurytus king of Œchalia, captive-wife to Heracles,* *Nurse to Deianira.*

*An old man attending on Heracles.*

HERACLES.

*The* CHORUS *is composed of ladies of Trachis, friends of Deianira.*

*Œchalian women, captives to Heracles.*

*Attendants on Heracles.*

---

*Scene, before the house of Ceyx, at Trachis.*
*Enter* DEIANIRA *and Attendant.*

*Deianira.* 'Tis an old well-known proverb of mankind,
  "You cannot tell men's fortunes till they die,
  In any case, if they be good or bad";
  But I, before I to the grave decline,
  Know that unfortunate and hard are mine:
  Who while still dwelling at Pleuron, in the house
  Of my sire Œneus, had the sorest scare[1]
  Of any woman of Ætolia
  About my bridal.   For a river-god
  Was suitor for me—Achelous; who
  In three shapes asked me at my father's hands,
  Courting me now in a bull's form confest,
  Now as a particoloured coiling snake,
  Now with an ox-front on a trunk of a man,
  Where out of tangles of a bosky beard
  Rills of spring-water oozed dispersedly.

On such a suitor's pleasure I, poor maid,
Attending, ever prayed that I might die
Ere I drew near his bed.[2]  Howbeit at last
To my relief the illustrious offspring came
Of Zeus and of Alcmena; who with him
Engaging in the arbitrament of fight
Saved me.   What was the fashion of the fray
I cannot tell; I do not know it; he
Who sat and saw it unalarmed might say.
For I sat still, out of my wits with fear
Lest, after all, beauty should bring me sorrow;
But Zeus, the lord of battles, ended it
Prosperously—if indeed prosperously.
For taken to the bed of Heracles,
Ever I have within me fear on fear,
Foreboding ill for him.   For with each night
A labour comes and goes; each night, in turn,
Hands on the torch of labour.[3]   We had children,
Whom he beheld but as some husbandman
An outlying farm, that he has taken in
Merely to sow and reap it.   Such a life
Still would despatch my husband out and home
In service to some master.   But of late,
After he rose superior o'er these trials,
Now, most of all, have I been full of terror.
For since he smote the might of Iphitus,
We dwell in Trachis here, far from our home,
In a friend's house; and whither he has gone
No man can tell; but gone he is, on me
Casting a load of bitter pangs for him.
And I dare say that he is in some trouble;
For no brief space, but full ten months already,
And five to that, bides he, and sends no tidings.
Ay, and it is some formidable trouble;
Witness the tablet that he left with me
In parting; which I often pray to heaven
He did not give me to my injury.

*Attendant.*  Queen Deianira, many a time before
Did I behold you grieving, bathed in tears,
Mourning that Heracles set forth.   But now,
If a slave's counsels may inform the free,
This much even I may say; how is it you,

Being so rich in sons, send none of them
To seek your husband? Hyllus before all,
As were but fitting, if he cared at all
For news of his sire's welfare? In good time
Here is himself at hand, bounding towards home;
So that, if aught I say seem seasonable,
He, and my words as well, are at your service.


*Enter* HYLLUS.

*Deianira.* O child, my son, even from the lowly born
    Words may fall well. This is a bond-woman,
    But she has spoken a frank word.

*Hyllus.*                        What is it?
    Tell it me, mother, if I may be told.

*Deianira.* That now your sire has been so long from home,
    Not to seek where he is brings shame on you.

*Hyllus.* Nay but I know, if one may trust report.

*Deianira.* And where, my son, hear you that he is stayed?

*Hyllus.* This season past, they say, all the year long
    He wrought in service to a Lydian dame.

*Deianira.* If he brooked that, one might hear anything.

*Hyllus.* He is quit of it, however, as I hear.

*Deianira.* Where, dead or living, is he rumoured now?

*Hyllus.* They say he is assailing, in Eubœa.
    Or means to assail, the city of Eurytus.

*Deianira.* Child, do you know he left behind with me
    Sure oracles concerning that same land?

*Hyllus.* In what strain, mother? I never heard of it.

*Deianira.* That he must either end his days outright,
    Or, when he has performed this task, thenceforth
    Lead his whole future life in happiness.
    Child! when his fate so trembles in the scale
    Will you not run to help? Since we are saved
    In his life's safety, or are lost with him.

*Hyllus.* Yes mother, I will go. Had I but heard
    The tenor of these oracles, long since
    Would I have been beside him; as things were,
    His wonted fortune did not let me fear
    Too much, or quake beforehand, for my sire.
    But now I know, I will leave nought undone
    To find out all the truth.[4]

*Deianira.*                    Speed then, my son.
To know that all is well, even if late
We come to know it, is at least some gain.

        [*Exit* HYLLUS.

*Enter Ladies of Trachis, as Chorus.*

CHORUS.

### I. 1.

O Thou who art born of the shadow of night [5]
When night is slain, and from blaze of thy light
Art laid to repose by night, of thee
I ask, O Sun, to reveal to me,
Thou God of the blazing day-beam, where
O where he tarries, Alcmena's heir?
  Whether in sea-channels hiding,
  Or on either coast abiding,
Thou all-transcendent Eye of Heaven, declare!

### I. 2.

For Deianira, well I know,
With a longing heart, like a bird of woe,
(A bride much fought for—an envied prize)
Never sinks to the slumber of tearless eyes,
But bears in her bosom a mindful fear
For her lord's return in safety here;
  On her widowed bed reclining,
  Wistfully at all times pining,
In the terror of misfortune drawing near.

### II. 1.

For as waves are seen thronging and flowing
  Amid the wide sea,
When the south wind or north wind is blowing
  Unweariably,
Such huge Cretan ocean of troubles
  On troubles upbears [6]
The offspring of Cadmus, and doubles
  His portion of cares.
But him some Power stands near to sain and save
For evermore, from the house of the unseen Grave.

## II. 2.

And therefore it is that I chide thee;
    Things pleasant, say I,
May yet be in store to betide thee,
    Howe'er thou deny.
I say, the good hope that remaineth
    Thou need'st not dispel,
For Zeus, who almightily reigneth,
    Gives sorrows as well.
So ever we move in a circle of joy and care,
That whirl like the whirling ways of the Arctic Bear.

For neither shadowy night nor fated sorrow
    Nor wealth abides, but suddenly each is gone;
    Joy finds us, and bereavement thereupon
        Comes, on the morrow.[7]
Wherefore to this I bid thee too, my queen,
Ever hold fast in hope; for who hath seen
        Zeus of his own
        So unregardful grown?

*Deianira.* You come, having been told, as I suppose,
    Of my distress; but you are ignorant—
    And may you never by experience learn—
    What canker gnaws my heart.  For Girlhood feeds
    In the same place, in pastures such as these,[8]
    Where neither heat of the Sun-god, nor rain,
    Nor any breath of tempest, vexes it;
    But in delights it rears an untasked life,
    Up to the point where we obtain the name
    Of wife instead of maiden, and receive
    Share, in the night-time, of solicitudes,
    Portioned with fears, either for spouse or child.[9]
    Hence might each see, regarding her own case,
    Under what burdens I am labouring.
    Troubles indeed right many do I mourn;
    But one, such as I never felt before,
    I will forthwith disclose.  For when our lord
    Heracles sped from home on his last journey,
    He left indoors an ancient tablet, graven
    With characters, which never theretofore
    At any time, starting for fight on fight,

Would he declare to me ; rather he would march
As to achievement, not as to his death ;
While now, as though his life were done, he told me
What of his goods I was to take for dower,
Told me what portion of his heritage
He would assign his children, share by share,
Setting a date beforehand, in such sort
As, when he had been absent from the land
Full fifteen months, either at that same hour
He must needs die, or, overpassing it,
Live ever afterwards without annoy.
So, he declared, it was decreed of Heaven
The toils of Heracles should have their end ;
Even as Dodona's ancient oak, he said,
By the two Peleads [10] uttered.   And of this
The true fulfilment, as it was to be,
Points to this present hour.   Wherefore, dear friends,
As I sleep quietly I start up for fear,
Dreading that I may have to linger on,
The widow of the foremost man of men.

1 *Lady*.   Keep to good words ; for I perceive a man
Crowned with a wreath, coming to give us joy.


*Enter a* MESSENGER.

*Messenger*.   Queen Deianira, first of messengers
I will release you from expectancy.
For be assured, Alcmena's son is living,
And is victorious, and is bringing home
Trophies, from fight, to the land's deities.
*Deianira*.   What is it that you say, old man ?
*Messenger*.                                   That soon
The husband whom you long for will arrive
Here, at your doors, in triumph.
*Deianira*.                                   And from whom,
Townsman or stranger, have you this to say ?
*Messenger*.   Lichas the herald is proclaiming it
To many, in the summer kine-pasture ;
Hearing whose story I came straight away
To be the first to bring to you the news,
And be rewarded, and win grace with you.
*Deianira*.   If he speeds well, why is himself not here ?

*Messenger.* Madam, he is not quite at liberty.
　　　Why, the whole Melian people in a ring
　　　Stand by and question him ; he cannot stir ;
　　　For every one, wishing to ascertain
　　　His heart's desire, will not relinquish it
　　　Before he hears his fill ; so Lichas tarries
　　　Unwillingly, among willing company ;
　　　But you will see him straightway face to face.
*Deianira.* Zeus, thou that holdest Œta's mead unmown,
　　　At last, though late, thou hast vouchsafed us joy.
　　　Lift up your voices, women—you indoors
　　　And you without the gates !　So gather we
　　　The glory of the unexpected orb
　　　Of this report, rising before me now !

### CHORUS.

　　　Loud let the household shout
　　In the shrill treble of maidens, brides to be !
　　　—Let the hearth ring out,
　　And clamour of men join in the harmony,
　　Praising Apollo's name, who bears the quiver,
　　　　Strong to deliver !
　　　Her, withal, ye virgins praise—
　　　Pæan—your pæan raise
　　　To the twin sister—her,
　　The Ortygian Artemis, the deerslayer,[11]
　　　Fire-girt on either hand,
　　　And to the Nymphs, her band !
　　—See, I mount, I soar beyond control,
　　Nor will I spurn the flute—O monarch of my **soul**!
　　Lo, I feel the ivy-frenzy, whirling me along—
　　Evoe !　Evoe !　after the Bacchic throng !
　　　　Hail Pæan, Pæan hail !
　　　　—Dear lady, see,
　　　　It is all here for thee
　　Face to face to witness, without veil.

*Enter* LICHAS, *with* IOLE *and* Œchalian Captives.

*Deianira.* I see it, dear ladies ; my eyes' vigilance
　　　Missed not the vision of this company ;
　　　And Herald, I bid thee welcome, though full late [12]
　　　Arrived, if thou bring'st welcome news with thee.

*Lichas.* Well am I come, and am well greeted, lady,
  As I deserve; good fortune cannot fail
  To win a hearty welcome.

*Deianira.*       Most sweet sir,
  First answer my first craving; it is true
  I shall receive back Heracles alive?

*Lichas.* I left him, certainly, alive and strong,
  And flourishing, and sick of no disease.

*Deianira.* Where? In his own land, or in Asia? Tell me.

*Lichas.* There is a promontory in Eubœa,
  Where to Cenæan Zeus he consecrates
  Altars, and tribute of meat-offerings.[13]

*Deianira.* According to some vow or oracle?

*Lichas.* Vows, made when he was spoiling and o'er-
   throwing
  The country of these women—whom you see.

*Deianira.* And they, whence and who are they, in Heaven's
   name?
  Poor things—if I can judge of miseries!

*Lichas.* These, when he sacked the city of Eurytus,
  He chose for the Gods' portion, and his own.

*Deianira.* Was it against that city he was gone
  The unmeasured space of those uncounted days?

*Lichas.* Not so; most of the time he was detained
  Among the Lydians; by his own account
  Not a free man, but sold to slavery.
  Shame at the word, lady, there need not be,
  When Zeus is known to have effected it.
  Well, sold to Omphale, the native queen,
  He served her, as he says, for a full year.
  And under this reproach he was so nettled,
  That with an oath he bound himself, and vowed
  The time should come he would enslave the man—
  Wife, child and all—who caused him this annoy:
  Nor did he vow in vain; but gathering,
  When he was cleansed, an army of allies,
  He marched against the city of Eurytus;
  For Eurytus, he sware, and he alone,
  Was accessory to this injury;
  Who, when he came into his house a guest,
  Being of old familiar there, stormed at him
  With loud abuse and deep malevolence

Of spirit—saying that although he bore
Arrows inevitable, he was surpassed
By sons of his, in trial of the bow ;
And roared, that being a slave, from a free man
He should take chastisement ; and when in wine
Once, at a feast, he cast him out of doors.
Angered at this, when Iphitus in turn
Came to the slope of Tiryns, to track out
Some horses that were ranging, as he stood
Gazing at something, with his wits afield,
He hurled him from the tower-like mountain-top.
And for that deed the King, being incensed,
Zeus, the Olympian father of us all,
Sent him forth to be sold ; intolerant
For that him only of mankind by craft
He slew ; for had he fought him openly,
Zeus surely would have pardoned that he wrought
By violence, with right upon his side ;
For insolence is loathed, even in Heaven.
Well, they, with tongues of overweening spite,
Now are themselves all inmates of the grave,
Their city enslaved ; while these you look upon,
Once happy, but now fallen on joyless days,
Are journeying toward your presence. Thus your lord
Charged me, and I, being his liege-man, perform.
As for himself, when to his father, Zeus,
He has offered up a solemn sacrifice
For the town's fall, you may expect him here.
That is the best good news of my long story.

1 *Lady.* Mistress, now is your happiness assured,
     Half being in hand, and half reported you.

*Deianira.* How can I but rejoice, as is most meet,
     At hearing this good fortune of my lord?
     The one must follow on the other. Still
     There is occasion for the vigilant
     To fear for one who prospers, lest he fall.
     For a strange pity is come upon me, friends,
     Seeing these poor creatures, houseless, fatherless,
     Wanderers here upon a foreign soil,
     Who were before, it may be, gently born,
     But are now leading lives of bondage. Never,
     O God of battles, may I see thy hand

Thus against seed of mine outstretched!   At least,
If aught thou purpose, whilst I live forbear!
Such are my terrors, in beholding them.
—Who and what are you, miserable girl?
Maiden, or childing mother?   You appear
Skill-less of all such matters, outwardly;
Some lady, too.   Lichas, who is the stranger?
Who was her mother?   Who her father?   Say;
Since her I pity, most of all I see,
For that she only has the wit to feel.

*Lichas.*   What do I know?   Why should you ask me?   A slip
Of those from thence, not of the lowest, it may be.

*Deianira.*   What, of their kings?   Offspring of Eurytus?

*Lichas.*   I do not know.   I did not question her
At length.

*Deianira.*          Nor did you ever get her name
From any of her fellow-travellers?

*Lichas.*                              Nay,
I did my work in silence.

*Deianira.*                        Then, poor maid,
Tell us yourself; for not to know your name
Is melancholy!

*Lichas.*              If she at all wag tongue,[14]
She will do something other than before;
For no word has she uttered, less or more;
But she is always shedding tears, in travail
Of heavy woe, poor creature, since she left
Her storm-swept land.[15]   This state of things is bad
For her own self; but it is pardonable.

*Deianira.*   Well, let her be; and let her pass indoors
In peace, as she likes best, and not be given
Fresh pain by me, more than her present troubles;
For what she suffers is sufficient.   Now
Go we all in; that you may speed your errand,
And I provide for what is wanted there.

              [*Exeunt* Lichas, Iole *and Captives.*

*Messenger.*   First, for an instant tarry where you are,
That you may learn, apart from these, what persons
You are conducting in; and may perceive
Things you should know, nothing of which was told
          you.
Of the whole business I am cognizant.

*Deianira.* What is it? Why do you stop me as I go? [16]
*Messenger.* Stand still and hear; for not in vain you heard
  My former tale; nor will you this, I fancy.
*Deianira.* What, shall we call the others back again,
  Or would you tell it to these maids and me?
*Messenger.* To you and these, freely; but let them be.
*Deianira.* Well, they are gone.   Now let the tale be told.
*Messenger.* Lichas says nothing, of all he spake just now,
  Straightforwardly; but either is a knave
  Now, or before was no true messenger.
*Deianira.* What say you?   Tell me plainly your whole
  mind;
  For what you have announced is dark to me.
*Messenger.* I heard this man, with many a witness by,
  Say that our master conquered Eurytus
  And the high ramparts of Œchalia's town,
  For this girl's sake; and that Love only of Gods
  Allured him to the combat; not his toil
  Wrought with the Lydians, or with Omphale,
  Nor fate of Iphitus hurled headlong; Love—
  Which he slurs over, and unsays it now.
  But when he could not work upon her sire
  To give the maid to be his paramour,
  Dressing up some small grievance for a cause,
  He leads an army against her country, where
  This Eurytus, Lichas averred, was monarch,
  And slays the king her father, and sacks the town.
  And now, you see, he is arrived, and sends her
  To this house, lady; not unthinkingly,
  Nor as a slave; never imagine it!
  That were unlikely, fervid with desire
  As he has been.   Therefore I thought it good
  To you, my mistress, to reveal the whole
  Of what I came to know from this man's mouth.
  Many Trachinians, in mid market-place,
  Heard the whole story, equally with me,
  And can convict him.   If my words give pain
  I am sorry; still, what I have said is true.
*Deianira.* O me unhappy!   What has come to me?
  What bane have I received beneath my roof
  From me kept secret?   O me miserable!
  And was she nameless, as he sware who brings her?

*Messenger.* Nay but in birth, as in her face, a prize!
   Eurytus was her father; she was named
   Iole—of whose descent the fellow there
   Let no word fall—"asking no questions," quoth he!
1 *Lady.* Perish ill doers! those at least, who do
   Evil in secret which beseems them not![17]
*Deianira.* Women, what must I do? How by the tale
   Which is now told me am I thunderstricken!
1 *Lady.* Why go and ask the man; for if you choose
   To press for answers, he will soon speak plain.
*Deianira.* Well, so I will. You do not say amiss.
1 *Lady.* And shall we stay? Or what are we to do?
*Deianira.* Stay; for, without my sending, here he comes
   Of his own motion from the house.

*Enter* LICHAS.

*Lichas.*         Say, lady,
   What message must I take to Heracles?
   I am going, as you see.
*Deianira.*       How speedily
   You are starting—after taking long to come—
   Before we can renew our colloquy!
*Lichas.* If you would ask some question, here I am.
*Deianira.* Ah, will you tell the truth in honesty?
*Lichas.* Great Zeus be witness! yes, of what I know.
*Deianira.* Who is the woman, pray, whom you brought
    hither?
*Lichas.* She's an Eubœan; her birth I cannot tell.
*Messenger.* Fellow, look here; to whom do you suppose
   You speak?
*Lichas.*     What business is it of yours to ask me?
*Messenger.* Answer my question frankly, if you know how.
*Lichas.* To the daughter of Œneus, wife of Heracles,
   The potent Deianira—if my eyes
   Do not deceive me—and my mistress.
*Messenger.*         That
   I wanted—to hear that from you. You say
   This is your mistress?
*Lichas.*      So she is.
*Messenger.*        What then?
   What penalty do you expect to pay,
   If you are found out playing false to her?

*Lichas.* How false? What juggle are you planning?

*Messenger.*                                                                     None.
But, in good earnest, you are acting one!

*Lichas.* I am going.   I was foolish all along
To listen to you.

*Messenger.*                    Not before you answer
Just one short question.

*Lichas.*                           Ask it, if you please.
You are loquacious.

*Messenger.*                          The girl-prize, whom you
Conducted hither—I suppose you know her?

*Lichas.* I do.   But wherefore ask?

*Messenger.*                                    Did you not say
She whom you brought, and do not know by sight,
Was Iole, offspring of Eurytus?

*Lichas.* To whom?   Who will attest you, from what quarter,
That he was present, and heard this from me?

*Messenger.* Many of the townsfolk.   In mid market-place
Of the Trachinians, plenty heard you say it.

*Lichas.* O ay,
I said I heard so.   There's a difference
'Twixt saying one's guess, and speaking rigidly.

*Messenger.* Your guess, indeed!   Did you not say, and
            swear it,
You bring her as a wife for Heracles?

*Lichas.* I bring a wife!   For Heaven's sake, my dear lady,
Tell me his name; who is this stranger?

*Messenger.*                                            One
Present, who heard you say that a whole city
Was subjugated for the love of her;
And that desire for her, notoriously,
And not the Lydian princess, was its ruin.

*Lichas.* My mistress—let the man stand back.   To prate
With a man brain-sick is to play the fool.

*Deianira.* Now in Jove's name, who sends his lightnings
            down
On Œta's wooded height, palter not with me!
For you will say your say to no bad wife,
Or unfamiliar with the ways of men,
How that their nature is to take delight
Not in the same things always.   With Desire
Whoever, like a boxer, fist to fist

Rises in conflict, is not well advised;
For it sways even deities at will,
Ay and myself; and why not one beside
Who is as I am? whence, if I find fault
With my own spouse, caught by this malady,
Or with this woman, who shares with him in that
Which is no scandal, and no harm to me,
I must be mad indeed.   It is not so.
Now if by his instruction you speak falsely,
You are a scholar in no worthy school;
While if you are yourself your tutor here,
You will be found injurious, when you want
To be of service.   Tell me all the truth.
For a free man to earn the name of liar
Is a disaster that dishonours him.
Nor can it be that you will not be known;
For many are they you have talked with, who will
    tell me.
And if you are frightened, you do ill to quail;
For it would vex me not to be informed,
But where's the harm of knowing?   Are there not
    wives—
Others besides—full many—whom Heracles
Took, to himself—and never one of them
Bore evil language or reproach from me?
No more shall she; not though he melt quite through
With his affection; since I have felt pity
For her, as I beheld her, most of all;
For that her beauty was her bane, and she,
Poor soul, brought down, without intending it,
On her own country sack and slavery.
Well, let all this go floating down the gale!
Only I charge you—unto others be
Injurious—but at all times true to me.

1 *Lady.* Hearken; she counsels fairly.   By and by
    You will approve her, and find grace with me.

*Lichas.*  For that I find you human, mistress dear,
    Not wilfully disposed, but humanly,
    The whole truth will I tell you, and hide it not.
    For so it is, even as this man reports;
    It was for her that the fell passion passed
    Through Heracles of late; and for her sake

Her death-strewn native land, Œchalia,
Was desolated by the spear.  All this—
For I must say, also, what makes for him—
He never bade conceal—never denied;
But I myself, my mistress, in alarm
Lest I should wound your bosom with the news,
Was guilty there, if guilt you reckon it.
Now that you know the whole, both for his sake
And yours no less, be patient with the woman,
And be determined firmly to abide
By those same words you spoke concerning her;
Since he, the vanquisher of all beside,
Is wholly mastered by his love for her.

*Deianira.* Yes, that is what I purpose, so to act;
Harm beyond need I do not mean to incur,
Fighting at odds with Heaven.  Now let us go
Inside the dwelling; that you may convey
A message back; and, gift for gift, whatever
Is fitting I should add, may take that also.
Hither you came with a fair company,
And pity it were you should go empty hence.

[*Exeunt* Deianira, *attendant*, Lichas,
*and Messenger.*

## Chorus.

### 1.

Great is the might wherewith ever the triumphs of Cypris
   are won.
The loves of the Gods I pass over, and how she beguiled
   Cronos' son,
Or Poseidon, the shaker of Earth, or Hades, the indweller
   of night,
I tell not; I sing what strong-limbed pair went down to the
   fight—
Fight for the prize of a nuptial, to win this woman to wife,
And battled with buffet on buffet, and wrestled out strife
   upon strife.

### 2.

The first was shaped like a high-horned four-legged bull to
   see,
Achelous, the strong River, from far Œniadæ;

And the son of Jove from Theba, the city of Bacchus, came,
With bended bow, and with brandished club, and with
    spears at aim;
And fired by desire they hurtled together, straight to the
    fray;
And Cypris sat by, with her wand held high, sole queen of
    the day.

There was noise of fists crashing and of bulls' horns clashing,
    And a sound of the twanging of bows;
There were limbs twining in medley, there were forehead-
    thrusts deadly,
    And groans that from both sides rose.

      But the tender fair
        On far-seen upland brows
      Sat, expecting there
        Who should be her spouse;
      As a mother I say what I am saying;
        But the visage of the bride
        For whom men contend
        Wistfully abides the end;
      Then, like a heifer straying,
        Sudden is parted from her mother's side.

*Enter* Deianira.

*Deianira.* Friends, while our guest is parleying in the house
With the girl-captives, on the point to go,
I am come forth to you in private, first
Wishing to tell you my devices, next
To be condoled with for my injuries.
For I have taken to my house a maid—
A maid no more, but mated, to my thinking—
Even as a shipman takes a load on board,
A losing bargain for my heart! And now
We two abide beneath one coverlet
To be embraced. This reward Heracles—
Faithful and good as we reputed him—
Sends, in return for my long house-tending.
And him I cannot be indignant with,
Often afflicted by this malady;
But to keep house with her, and to go shares
In the same marriage-bond—what wife could do it?

For I see bloom on her side coming on,
And on mine fading; and of such an eye
Will pick the flower, and eschew the rest.
This, then, is what I fear; lest Heracles
Come to be called my consort, but her mate,
The younger woman.   Still it is not well
A wife who has discretion, as I said,
Should become wroth; rather in what way, friends,
I may find easement, to deliver me,[18]
Lo, I well tell you.   I have long possessed
A keepsake of a monster of old time,
Put by in a brass vessel, which I took
When yet a girl, out of the mortal wound
Of the shag-bosomed Nessus, as he died;
Who used to carry men across the ford
Of the Evenus, a deep stream, for hire,
With his mere hands, plying without oar or sail.
He, when I first with Heracles a bride
Went, at my sire's disposing, carrying me
Upon his back, when he was in mid-passage,
Touched me with wanton hands.   And I cried out;
And straight the son of Jove turned, and his hands
Launched a winged shaft; and it whizzed through
     the breast,
Into his lungs.   And as the brute expired,
He spake these words; "Child of old Œneus,
If you will hear, you shall have this much profit,
Seeing you were my last of passengers,
Out of my ferrying; for if you collect
The gore that stiffens round my deadly wound,
Just where the black envenomed shafts were dipped
In blood of the Lernæan water-snake,
A medicine for the heart of Heracles
It shall be to you; so that he shall love
No woman whom he looks on, more than you."
Mindful of this, my friends—for since his death
It has been carefully locked up at home—
I dipped this tunic, and threw in the whole
Of what he told me just before he died.
This has been done.   Now never may I know—
Never be taught—malign experiments;
Nay, those who try them I detest; but if

Against this girl by charms I may prevail,
And by a philtre used on Heracles—
Why, means have been supplied; unless I seem
Busied in vain; if so, I will not do it.

1 *Lady.* If there is any surety about things
Yet in the doing, you appear to us
To have resolved not ill.

*Deianira.*           Thus much there is;
The likelihood is there; but in the trial
I never yet engaged.

1 *Lady.*           Well, one must learn
By doing the thing; for though you think you know it
You have no certainty, until you try.

*Deianira.* Well, we shall know directly; for I see
Lichas already at the door; and soon
He will be going. Only let me, by you,
Be covered well; for never in the dark
Need you be brought to shame, though you are doing
What is unseemly.

*Enter* LICHAS.

*Lichas.*           What am I to do,
Daughter of Œneus? Tell me; for we are
Already late, through our long tarrying.

*Deianira.* Why indeed, Lichas, to that very end
Have I been busy, while you stayed to talk
To the girl-guests within; that you should bear
This fine-woven garment [19] to that spouse of mine,
A present from my hand. And when you give it,
Say that no mortal is to put it on
Before himself; and that no sunlight beam,
Or holy fane, or flame from altar-hearth
Is to behold it, till he shall stand up
Radiant, and shew himself, before high Heaven,
Conspicuous, on a day of sacrifice.
For so I vowed, if ever I should see him
Come safely home, or hear of it, to deck him
All duly with this tunic, and display him
As a new votary, in new robes, to Heaven.
And there shall be a seal on what you bear,
Which he will see distinctly corresponds
With the impression of my signet-ring.

Now go; and seek, first, to observe the rule
Not to desire, being a mere messenger,
To exceed your bounds; next, that his grace **and**
    mine
May both together be displayed towards **you**.

*Lichas.* If this Hermetic courier-craft of mine
Is trusty, you shall never find me fail
To carry and present your casket safe,
Adding exactly what you bid me say.

*Deianira.* Now, if you please, set forth; for you know well
How matters stand within the house.

*Lichas.*                                   I know
And will report that they have turned out well.

*Deianira.* Ay, and the stranger's welcome—you have seen
What kind reception I bestowed on her?

*Lichas.* Such as to strike delight into my bosom!

*Deianira.* What more, then, should you tell him? For I
    dread
Your saying, too early, how I long for him,
Ere I can gather if he longs for me.

                    [*Exit* LICHAS; DEIANIRA *retires.*

CHORUS.

I. 1.

O ye who dwell where the warm springs well
    From the cliffs where navies ride,
Who by Œta's peaks or the mid-land creeks
    Of Melia's gulf abide,
Or the shores, deep-bayed, of Her, the Maid
    With distaff all of gold,
Where stand the Gates, where the Grecian States [20]
    Their solemn councils hold.

I. 2.

The clarion sweet no note unmeet
    Shall raise among you soon,
But such as suits with the sound of lutes
    Played to a sacred tune,
Now Alcmena's son, the Jove-born one,
    Comes, bringing in his train
The glorious spoil of all his toil
    To his own home again:

## II. 1.

Whom we waited for and thought, a full twelve-month,
     knowing nought.
  "He is far from his land, upon the wave":
She the while, his loving mate, mourning her unhappy fate,
   Weeping ever, and declining towards her grave:
       Till, stung to wrath, Ares at last [21]
   Gave him release, but now, from days of Labours past.

## II. 2.

Let him come! let him come! Never till he reach his home
   Let the chariot of his oars stand still!
From the island altar where, as 'tis said, he is at prayer,
   Let him speed, with all lover-like good will,
       As by the Centaur's oracle,
   Anointed with the balsam of the suasive spell.

*Deianira* (*advancing*). O women how I tremble lest, in all
   I have just been doing, I have gone too far!
1 *Lady*. What is it, Deianira, Œneus' child?
*Deianira*. I do not know.  But I am sick at heart,
   For fear I should be found, soon, to have done,
   Quite contrary to my fair hope, great harm!
1 *Lady*. Not something in your gift to Heracles?
*Deianira*. Yes, yes!  So that I never shall approve,
   In any, a readiness to undertake
   An action, where the issue is not plain!
1 *Lady*. Tell me what scares you—if it may be told.
*Deianira*. A thing has happened such as, if I tell it,
   O women, you will think a miracle
   Beyond belief to hear.  The fleece, you know,
   Wherewith I was anointing even now
   The vestment-garment, of a sheep's white wool,
   'Tis gone! by nothing in the house devoured,
   But wasting, eaten up of its own self,
   And shrivelling on the pavement.  I will tell you
   At greater length, that you may know the whole,
   How it befell.  Of all the Centaur-beast
   Of yore enjoined me, when he felt the smart
   Of the sharp-pointed arrow in his side,
   I let slip nothing, but remembered it,
   Like writing on brass leaves, indelibly;

And this was what he told me, and so I wrought;
I was to keep this drug always put by,
Away from fire, untouched by the warm beam,
Till, newly spread, I could make use of it.
And so I did; but now 'twas time to use it,
I tore the fluff from a sheep's fleece of mine,
And with a wool-tuft smeared my gift, at home,
Indoors, in secret; folded it, and put it
Inside a coffer, safe, out of the sun,
As you perceived. But going indoors just now
I saw a sight quite indescribable—
Incomprehensible! For as it happened,
I had flung the lock, with which I did the spreading,
Out in the sunlight, into its full blaze.
And as it became warmer it dissolved,
And has all shrivelled up upon the ground,
In form most to be likened to the look
Which sawdust takes, when they cut wood; so lies it,
All fallen away. And from the ground, whereon
It lay before, there spring up clots of foam,
As of rich liquor spilt upon the earth
From vines of Bacchus, when the fruit turns blue.
So that I know not where to turn, for trouble;
But see that I have done a perilous deed.
For from what possible motive—on what score
Could the brute, dying, have shewn good will to me,
For whose cause he was dying? It cannot be!
But, seeking to destroy the man that smote him,
He was beguiling me! Whereof too late
I get the knowledge, when it helps no more;
For I, I only, except I be deceived
Wretch! in my mind, shall be his murderess!
For I know well, the shaft that made the wound
Lamed Chiron, though immortal; and it kills
Wild beasts of every kind, if it but graze them; [22]
And this black gory venom, passing on
From the death-wounds of one victim, how can it
Not slay him too? at least, I fancy so.
Yet am I fixed, if Heracles miscarries,
In the same moment [23] I will die with him;
For life ill-famed is unendurable
To one who claims to have been born in honour.

# Trachiniae

1 *Lady.* Fear about perilous deeds is necessary.
    Still, Hope must not be sentenced, ere her time.
*Deianira.* There is not, in designs which are not honest,
    Even hope, to vouch for any spark of cheer.
1 *Lady.* But in their case who trip not wilfully
    . Anger is mild ; [24] and you should find it so.
*Deianira.* Such words no sharer in the offence would use,
    But one who has no heaviness within.
1 *Lady.* Silence from further talk of this were fit,
    Unless you have a word to tell your son,
    Who went to seek his sire ; for he is here.

*Enter* HYLLUS.

*Hyllus.* Mother, of three things one I would were true
    About you ; that you should have ceased to live,
    Or if you lived, should have been known for mother
    Of some one else, or should have somewhere gained
    A better spirit than is in you now.
*Deianira.* O son, what is it you abhor in me?
*Hyllus.* I tell you that you have destroyed this day
    Your husband—him, I say, who is my sire.
*Deianira.* Oh what word have you uttered, O my child?
*Hyllus.* One 'tis impossible should come untrue.
    For who can undo that which he saw doing?
*Deianira.* How say you, boy? Whence did you learn to say
    That I have wrought a deed so execrable?
*Hyllus.* It is myself have witnessed, with these eyes,
    Not from report, my father's heavy chance.
*Deianira.* Where did you meet him and stand by to see?
*Hyllus.* If you must know, I must relate the whole.
    As he was marching, after having taken
    Eurytus' far-famed city, bringing off
    Trophies and first fruits of successful war,
    There is a promontory in Eubœa,
    Ceneum, washed upon both sides by sea,
    Where he was marking, for his father, Zeus,
    Altars and precincts of a sacred grove ;
    There first I saw him, glad of my desire.
    And just as he was going to begin
    A course of sacrifices, from his home
    Came Lichas, his own herald, bringing him
    Your gift, the deadly gown ; which he put on,

As you had given command ; then of his cattle
Slew twelve tall bulls, the firstlings of the spoil ;
(But he was offering, flocks and herds together,
A hundred head in all.)   And at first starting,
Proud of the beauty and the state of it,
In a blithe mood, poor soul, he began praying ;
But when above the sacred mysteries
Flame, fed with blood, and rich with resinous fuel
Was kindling, out upon his flesh there came
Sweat, and the tunic clung, close to his sides,
As moulded by an artist, limb by limb ;
Next came a racking aching of his bones ;
And straight a venom, as of some deadly snake,
Took to its horrid feast. [25]   Then suddenly
He shouted to the unhappy Lichas—him
Who for your fault was not at all to blame—
What machinations made him bring that gown ?
But he, unhappy, nothing knowing, said
It was your gift alone, just as you sent it.
When he heard that, the while a piercing spasm
Seized on his lungs, he caught him by the foot,
Close to the ancle-joint, and hurled him prone
Against a rock, wave-washed on either hand ;
And smashed the scull, and from the hair, with blood,
Dashed the brains out.   Then the whole people cried
Horrorstruck, seeing him in agony,
And him struck dead ; and there was no man dared
To go and face him ; for he was convulsed,
Now falling down, now rearing himself up,
Crying and moaning, while the rocks around,
Both Locrian headlands and Eubœan capes,
Sounded aloud.   But when his vigour failed,
What with oft throwing him upon the ground,
What with his cries and groanings, hapless one,
Cursing the ill-sorted bed, where by your side—
O wretch—he lay, and the alliance made
With Œneus, for the canker to his life
Which he had found it, then, casting a glance
Aside, out of the smoke that compassed him,
Me he beheld among a numerous host
Weeping, and looked toward me, and called my
      name ;

"Come here, boy; do not shun my misery;
Not even if you had to die with me;
Carry me forth, and set me—best of all,
Where never mortal may set eyes on me;
Or from this land, at least, if you have pity,
At once transport me, that I die not here."
We, when he gave these orders, carried him
On board, and hardly brought him here, to shore,
Convulsed and groaning. And immediately
You will behold him, living, or just dead.
Such designs, mother, and such deeds of yours
Against my father are detected; which
May the Erinys and requiting Right
Avenge on you!—if the prayer be not sin; [26]
And sin it is not; since you made it sinless,
When the best man of all on earth, like whom
Another you shall never see, you murdered!

1 *Lady*. Why do you move off mute? Do you not know
Your silence pleads upon the accuser's side?

[*Exit* DEIANIRA.

*Hyllus*. Let her move off! Let fair winds go with her,
Far as she goes, out of my sight, for good!
For why respect the bubble of a name,
Merely, of mother—all unmotherly
As she has been? Let her depart and welcome!
And may those same delights which she confers
Upon my father come to be her own!

[*Exit*.

## CHORUS.

### I. 1.

Look, children, in what sense
The heaven-sent voice, of the ancient prescience,
Bursts on us all at once, which prophesied,
When the full months of the twelfth harvest-tide
Should have run out, they should conclude his line
Of Labours, to the son of Jove divine!
And this it wafts right on, safely to shore;
For how could one who sees the light no more
Yet be the slave
Of labours, in the grave?

## I. 2.

For seeing how Destiny,
Armed with the Centaur's bloody mystery,
Framer of treasons, is anoiling him,
A venom, too, being slaked into each limb
Fathered by Death, born of a serpent's hiss,
How shall he see one sunrise after this?
Round him what Hydra-shape most hideous clings!
What swart-maned monster's murderous guileful stings,
Fevering the vein,
Mingle, to work his bane!

## II. 1.

While she, poor soul, who could perceive
Harm to the house, monstrous, without reprieve,
In this new bridal's hastening speed,
Of these woes some, indeed,
Never inflicted; [27] others, that were planned
  To fatal issues by a foreign mind,
How does she mourn whose was the death-giving hand!
How does she weep soft dews of womanly tears!
But in the impending fate plainly appears
  Mischief huge, and cunningly designed.

## II. 2.

A fountain of tears has broken bound;
A plague—O misery! is diffused around,
Such as before no suffering
On our magnificent king [28]
Came, even from foes, to call for sympathy.
  O thou black lance, foremost of battle-spears,
It was thy point from towering Œchaly
Conducted hitherward a hurrying bride;
But Cypris, who in silence walked beside,
  Causer of this now manifest appears.

1 *Lady.* Am I deceived? or do I hear some voice
    Of mourning through the dwelling, newly raised?
    What do I say?

2 *Lady.* There is a cry not undistinguishable
    Indoors, yea, a sad wailing; the abode
    Has something new to shew us.

1 *Lady*.                Look at her,
How strange toward us, and with gathered brows,
The beldam speeds, to signify some tale.

*Enter* NURSE.

*Nurse*. O maidens dear!
How has that gift we sent to Heracles
Been the beginning of great woes to us!
1 *Lady*. O mother, what new deed have you to tell?
*Nurse*. The latest of all journeyings Deianira
Has taken; a journey without stirring.
1 *Lady*.                 What,
You do not say she is dead?
*Nurse*.                 You have heard all.
1 *Lady*. She has died, unhappy!
*Nurse*.               Yes, I say again.
1 *Lady*. Death-boding wretch! How do you say she died?
*Nurse*. Most desperately, for the way of it.
1 *Lady*. Tell us what sort of death she met with, woman.
*Nurse*. Herself she slew.
1 *Lady*.            What wrath—what frenzy-fit
Could grasp the steel, the harming weapon? How
Could she contrive, singly, and execute
Death—upon death?
*Nurse*.          Through the sword's woeful cleaving.
1 *Lady*. O dolt, did you look on at this rash deed?
*Nurse*. Yes, I looked on; for I was standing by her.
1 *Lady*. Who was it,—how—quick, tell us—
*Nurse*.                 She herself,
Of her own self, set her own hand to do it.
1 *Lady*. What say you?
*Nurse*.          Sooth.
1 *Lady*.            Unto this house is born
How great a Fury—born of this new bride!
*Nurse*. Too great, indeed. But far more vehemently,
Had you been by to witness what she did,
Would you have pitied her.
1 *Lady*.             Could woman's hand
Bear to accomplish this?
*Nurse*.           Yes, ruthlessly.
But you shall hear, that you may bear me out.
After she came into the house, alone,

And saw her son spreading in the vestibule
An easy litter, to return with it
And meet his father, first she hid herself
Where none might see her; knelt before the hearth,
And groaned that she had been left desolate;
And wept at touching any household gear
That she was wont to use, poor thing, before;
And to and fro ranging about the palace,
If any of her servants met her view,
She wept, poor miserable, to gaze on them;
Chiding her own sad destiny, and theirs,
Her household's—for the future hers no more.[29]
When she left this, suddenly I saw her dart
Into the bed-chamber of Heracles;
And I kept watch, close hidden in the shade,
Spying unobserved; and saw the woman fling
Bed-clothes, spread out, upon his bed. This done,
She sprang up into it, and so sat her down
Among the pillows; then, forcing a way
For the warm fountains of her tears, she said—
"O bed and bower that are mine, henceforth
Never again shall I lie down to rest
In your embrace; farewell for evermore!"
Thus much she spake; and with unflinching hand
Undid her dress, which had a golden brooch
To fasten across her bosom; and laid bare
All her left arm and side. I ran at once,
As fast as I was able, and told her son
What she was doing; and within the time
That we were running thither and back again,
We found she had been stricken in the side
With a sharp-pointed weapon, towards the heart.
And the youth saw it, and shrieked; for well **he**
      knew—
Wretch—that his wrath had brought this thing to pass,
Having been told, too late, by those within,
How she had done it, at the Centaur's word,
Not purposely; and he, poor boy, since then
Has not ceased wailing, crying around her body,
Stooping to kiss her! Side by side with her
Has he been lying prostrate, moaning loud,
How with vile blame, falsely, he had smitten her,

Mourning that he would be bereaved for life
Of her and of his father, both at once.
So is it in this house; wherefore if any
Count on two days, or any more, to come,
He is a fool; for a man has no morrow,
Till with good luck he has got through to-day.

### CHORUS.

#### I. 1.

Which shall I mourn for first?
Which of my griefs is worst?
  Woe is me!   'Twere hard to select.

#### I. 2.

One is at hand, within;
Another about to begin:
  And 'tis all one—have or expect.

#### II. 1.

I would that some home-breeze, some favouring gale, might
    blow,
And waft me far from the spot, that I might not die with woe
Suddenly, merely at seeing the son of Jove, the strong,
Now that in anguish past all cure he is borne along
          Home—as they tell;
          Portent unspeakable!

#### II. 2.

Oh near and not far off is the sorrow at which I cry,
Shrill as a nightingale! for without, strange steps draw nigh,
Bringing him—whither now?   Noiseless and slow they
    come;
Tenderly, as a friend, they bear him.   He is dumb!
          What shall be said?
          Is he asleep, or dead?

*Enter* HYLLUS, *an Old Man, and attendants, carrying*
          HERACLES.

*Hyllus.*   Woe's me for thee, father!   Woe's me for thee!
          Alack, what shall I do?
          What shall I turn me to?
          O woe is me!

*Old Man.*　　Hush, child, lest you excite
　　　　　　Fierce anguish in your father's frenzied breast;
　　　　　　He lives, but barely.　Keep your lips compressed;
　　　　　　　Set your teeth tight.

*Hyllus.*　　　What do you say, old man?　Does he live still?

*Old Man.*　See that you do not wake the slumberer,
　　　　　　Nor start nor stir
　　　　　　The dreadful spasm of suffering, O my child!

*Hyllus.*　　　But with an unapproachable weight of ill
　　　　　　My anguished spirit is wild.

*Heracles.*　Zeus!　In what land am I?
　　　　　　Among what folk do I lie
　　　　　　Worn out with ceaseless pain?
　　　　　　—Woe's me!　Again
　　　　　　The loathsome thing gnaws me.　Alas, Alas!

*Old Man.*　Had you no inkling how far better it was
　　　　　　To hold your peace, and not to scatter, now,
　　　　　　The slumber from his eyelids and his brow?

*Hyllus.*　　　Only I cannot help it, when I see
　　　　　　This sight of agony.

*Heracles.*　O altar floor upon Ceneum's heights,
　　　　　　What sort of grace, grace for what sacred rites,
　　　　　　Could grow to thee—Great Zeus!—out of my
　　　　　　　misery?
　　　　　　What ill, what harmful ill, wrought'st thou for me!
　　　　　　Would that I never had set eyes on thee,
　　　　　　Never beheld
　　　　　　This flower of madness blossom all unquelled.

　　　　　　For what magician,
　　　　　　What physician,
　　　　　　Zeus apart,
　　　　　　Can heal this smart?
　　　　　　A miracle to see
　　　　　　Far off, for me!
　　　　　　O let me—let me—let me rest
　　　　　　In my last last sleep, unblest!
　　　　　　Why do you touch me?　Where do you want to
　　　　　　　lay me?

You will slay me—will slay me!
You have unset
What might be slumbering yet.

Alack, it has fastened on me!  It comes, it comes again!
Where are you, O most faithless of Greeks, for whom, on
the main
Oft, and all woodlands through, worn out with labour and
pain,
Cleansing the ways, I went?  And now, in my agony,
Flame or sword not one will afford to deliver me—
Alas!
Or will condescend to approach me, and separate
My head from life, which I hate!

*Old Man.*  O Alcides' son, this is too heavy a spell
For strength of mine to suffice; do you take hold as well.
Yours is a grip, more strong to preserve, than mine can be.[30]

*Hyllus.*  I lay hold.   But it is not possible for me,
At home or abroad, to find out means to keep him living
Freed from the sense of pain.   Such woes are of Heaven's
giving.

*Heracles.*        Son, where art thou?
            On this side, this side now,
            Raise me and hold by me.
Ah, Ah, thou Power!   It throbs, it throbs again,
The miserable, fierce, insurmountable pain,
            Slaying me utterly!
Again, O Pallas, Pallas, this torment vexes me!
O boy, pity your father, and draw your sword, blame-free,
And strike me under the neck, and relieve the aching
smart
Wherewith your impious mother angers me to the heart;
Whom may I yet behold, so perishing, even so,
As me she did destroy!   O friendly Hades!   O
Brother of Jove!   Send rest, send speedy rest in death!
            Stop my sad breath!

1 *Lady.*  I shudder, listening to the griefs, so great,
            Wherewith, O friends, a king so great is harried.
*Heracles.*  How many and how fierce and sore to tell [31]
            The labours I with body and hands have wrought!
            And such an one not even the Spouse of Jove

Set me, or the abhorred Eurystheus, ever,
As this, which Œneus' daughter crafty-faced
Fitted upon my shoulders—the web-toil
Woven of the Furies, which is killing me.
For plastered to my sides, it has gnawed off
The surface of my flesh, and settles in
And battens on the channels of the lungs,
And has already drained all my fresh life-blood,
And through my whole frame I am overthrown,
Worsted by this unthought-for fetterment!
Treatment such as I never yet endured—
No, not from lances in the battle-field,
Or Giants' earthborn army, or Centaurs' might,
Or Grecian or barbarian, or all lands
Which I, cleansing their borders, visited;
But one sole woman—a female, not a male
By sex—weaponless—puts an end to me.
O boy, now shew yourself my true-born son;
Set not the name of mother all too high;
But with your own hands hale out of the house
And render her that bare you into mine,
That I may know whether you grieve to see
This form of mine abused, rather than hers
Righteously punished.   Up, my son, take courage!
Have pity on me, whom any men might pity,
Weeping and moaning like a girl—a thing
No one could say that he had seen me do
Ever before; rather, where hardships led
I followed uncomplaining.  Now, alas,
Falling from thence, I have been proved a woman.
And now come near; stand by your father's side;
See under what mischance I suffer thus;
Here, I will shew you without coverings;
Lo, behold all, a miserable frame!
Mark me, poor wretch, how I am pitiable!
—O woe!  Alas, ah me,
Again, once more, that racking fever pain
Right through my side!  The desperate gnawing
    plague
Will not release me from its harassing;
O Hades, king, receive me!  O Jove's lightning,
    strike me!

Smite me, O king! Dart down thy thunderbolt,
Father, on me! for once again it revels,
It has blossomed—it has burst forth. O hands—
    hands,
O back and breast, O shoulder-blades of mine,
And have you come to this, who formerly
Beat down by force the lion-habitant
Of Nemea, the perilous beast and wild,
Fatal to herdsmen; and the water-snake
Of Lerna; and the twy-form prancing host
Of Centaurs, insolent, unsocial, rude,
Rampant in might; and the Erymanthian boar;
And the infernal triple-headed hound
Of Hades, the resistless monster, whelp
Of the dread Basilisk; and the Dragon-guard
Of golden apples, growing at the world's end?
And countless other toils I tasted of,
And no man set up trophies over me!
Now here I lie, with dislocated bones,
With lacerated flesh, by a dark mischief
Utterly cast away, unhappy! I,
Named of a mother most illustrious,
Reputed son of Zeus, Lord of the stars!
But be ye sure of this; though I be nothing,
Albeit I cannot move, even as I am,
Her who did this, still, I can overcome;
Let her come only, that she may be taught,
And have it to relate to all, how I,
Living and dying, punished wickedness!

1 *Lady.* Alas for Greece! what mourning I foresee
    Will be her portion, if bereft of thee!

*Hyllus.* Since by vouchsafing silence you vouchsafed
    Room, father, to reply—though you are sick,
    Listen to me; I shall demand of you
    What 'tis but fair I meet with. Lend yourself
    To what I say, not so incensed in spirit
    As you are racked with pain; you cannot, else,
    Learn your mistake, in that which you desire
    To make you glad, and in what angers you.

*Heracles.* Say what you wish, and cease; for I, being
    sick,
    Understand nothing of your stale mystery.

H

*Hyllus.* I am come to tell you of my mother; of
    Her state; and how she erred unwittingly.
*Heracles.* O villain, dare you breathe that mother's name,
    Your father's murderess, in my ears again?
*Hyllus.* Her story is such as must not stay untold.
*Heracles.* No truly, seeing how she transgressed before.
*Hyllus.* Nor will you say so of her deeds to-day.
*Heracles.* Speak; but look to it, lest you be found perverse.
*Hyllus.* I speak. She is dead. She is but now just slain.
*Heracles.* By whom? You tell me wonders, boding ill.
*Hyllus.* By her own hand, none other.
*Heracles.*                 Out, alas,
    Ere, as was fit, she could be slain by me!
*Hyllus.* Even your wrath would be turned, if you knew all.
*Heracles.* It is a strange tale. Tell it your own way.
*Hyllus.* The sum is this; she erred, but she meant kindly.
*Heracles.* Did she do kindly, villain, to slay your sire?
*Hyllus.* Nay, meaning, when she saw the bride within,
    To minister a spell to win your love,
    She was deceived.
*Heracles.*              And what Trachinian was there
    So great a sorcerer?
*Hyllus.*              Nessus long ago—
    The Centaur—made her trust with such a charm
    To impassion your desire.
*Heracles.*           O miserable!
    I am lost, alas, I am undone, undone!
    Light is no more for me! Well do I know,
    Woe's me, in what extremity I stand!
    O son, thou hast no more a father! Go
    Call hither all thy stock of brothers; call
    The sad Alcmena, spouse of Jove in vain,
    That ye may hear me with my latest breath
    Tell what I know, taught by those words from
        heaven.
*Hyllus.* Your mother is not here; for some time past
    She has dwelt at Tiryns, hard by the sea shore.
    And of your sons she has taken some with her,
    And rears them there herself; and some, you know,
    Dwell in the city of Thebes; but all of us,
    Father, here present, hear, and will obey,
    If aught there be to do.

*Heracles.* Then hearken thou
The matter: it is time for thee to shew
What sort of man thou art, who art called mine.
It was foreshewn me by my sire of old
That by no creature breathing I should die,
But by some dweller in Hades, who was dead.
And so it is, this Centaur-monster, dead,
As heaven foreshewed it, was the death of me,
Who am alive.  And I will shew thee too,
Fulfilled at the same time, late prophecies
Confirming those of old, which I wrote down,
When I was come into the sacred grove
Of the earth-couching Sellian highland-men,
From my own father's many-tongued oak-tree.
Which at this present pulse and point of time
Said my deliverance should be complete
From my incumbent labours; and I thought
I should do well; but it was nothing else,
Really, but death for me; for to the dead
There comes no labour more.  Therefore, my child,
Now these things come out clear, thou must become
Once more thy sire's ally, and not await
My voice to spur thee on; but of thyself
Yield, and assist me; recognizing it
For best of laws, a father to obey.

*Hyllus.* Father, I shrink from grappling with the drift
Of such discourse; but I will do your pleasure.

*Heracles.* First, place your hand in mine.

*Hyllus.* To what intent
Urge you this pledge upon me, all too far?

*Heracles.* Give it at once, and disobey me not.

*Hyllus.* See, there it is; I will gainsay you nothing.

*Heracles.* Swear by the head of Jove now, who begat me.

*Hyllus.* What to perform?—Am I to say this, too?

*Heracles.* To execute the deed I bid you do.

*Hyllus.* I swear it, and take Jove to witness.

*Heracles.* Pray
You may find punishment, if you transgress!

*Hyllus.* I shall not find it; for I shall perform.
Natheless I pray.

*Heracles.* Now, do you know Jove's peak,
On Œta's top?

*Hyllus.*                          Yes I have often been
    Up there to sacrifice.
*Heracles.*                    To that spot, now,
    In your own arms you, and what friends you choose,
    Must carry up my body; lop much timber
    Of the deep-rooted oak, and fell therewith
    Much wild male-olive, and your burden cast
    Thereon; and take a pine-wood torch, alight,
    And fire it.   And let no sound enter in
    Of weeping; but without one groan or tear,
    As you are mine, perform it.   Else will I
    In anger haunt you, even from beneath,
    Yea, with a curse, for ever.
*Hyllus.*                          Father! Oh
    How have you wrought with me?   What have you
        said?
*Heracles.* What must be done.   Otherwise claim, instead,
    Some other sire—be called my son no more.
*Hyllus.* Woe's me again! what do you call me to,
    Father? to be your slayer and murderer?
*Heracles.* Not so; but the physician of my state
    And only healer of my misery.
*Hyllus.* How can it heal, to set your body on fire?
*Heracles.* Well, if you shrink from this, still, do the rest.
*Hyllus.* The pains will not be grudged of carrying you.
*Heracles.* Nor store of wood to burn, as I have said?
*Hyllus.* Nothing, save touching it with hands of mine;
    All else I will perform; I will not tire.
*Heracles.* Well, that will be enough.   But add the gift
    Of a small favour to your great ones given.
*Hyllus.* Even if very great, it shall be done.
*Heracles.* You know the maid, daughter of Eurytus?
*Hyllus.* You mean, as I conjecture, Iole?
*Heracles.* Right!   This is all I lay upon you, child.
    When I am dead, as you are dutiful,
    Think of your filial oath; obey your sire;
    Make her your wife, and let no other man
    Ever touch her, who has lain by my side,
    Instead of you; but undertake this marriage,
    O boy, yourself.   Do it! for in small things
    To disobey me, and in great obey,
    Spoils all your former bounty.

*Hyllus.*                                    O my heart!
    To be incensed with a sick man is wicked;
    But who could bear to see him minded thus?
*Heracles.* You mutter, as if meaning to do nought
    Of what I say!
*Hyllus.*                    Why, who would take her, ever,
    Who was the sole cause of my mother's death,
    And more than that, of your being—as you are?
    Who that was not infatuate could do it?
    Father, 'twere better that I too were dead,
    Than living, joined with my worst enemies!
*Heracles.* It seems this fellow will not do me right
    Now I am dying. But know, the curse of Heaven
    Awaits you, if you disobey my words.
*Hyllus.* O me! Belike you will be saying, straight,
    You are in pain!
*Heracles.*                    Yes—you are stirring me
    From slumber of my torment.
*Hyllus.*                                    Miserable!
    How utterly at a loss I am!
*Heracles.*                          Because
    You do not choose to mind your father's bidding.
*Hyllus.* But father, am I really to be taught
    Impiety?
*Heracles.*            It is not impiety
    To gratify my heart.
*Hyllus.*                          Do you then bid me
    To do it, and incur no guilt?
*Heracles.*                                    I do.
    I call the Gods to be my witnesses.
*Hyllus.* Then I will do it. I will not refuse,
    If I can shew the Gods it is your work.
    Wicked I never can appear, my sire,
    If I obey you.
*Heracles.*              You are right at last.
    And add to these, my son, the boon of speed,
    So that before some spasm or frenzy-fit
    Falls on me, you may place me on the pyre.
    Come, hasten, lift me. This is rest from woes—
    The hero's life brought to its latest close.
*Hyllus.* Well father, since you order and compel it,
    Nothing impedes our doing all this for you.

*Heracles.*             Come, come along,
                    Ere yet again
                    They wake thy pain,
                        O stubborn heart!
                With bridle strong,
                    Of steel, of stone,
                        Silence each groan;
                    Finish thy part
                    Rejoicingly,
                        Hard though it be.

*Hyllus.*    Raise him, followers; freely, now,
                Pardon what I do, in me;
             Freely, too, in Gods allow
                Folly, for the things you see;
             Who though sires, though fathers named,
             See such sufferings unashamed.[32]
             What is future, no man knows;
             But what is present, full of woes
             Is to us—to them disgrace,
             And, of the whole human race,
             Cruellest to the man who bears
             This extremity of cares.

Nor do thou, maiden, stay in the house, [33]
Who seest great deaths and marvellous,
And sufferings many and strange indeed,
And none of them, save what Zeus decreed.

                                    [*Exeunt omnes.*

# PHILOCTETES

## PERSONS REPRESENTED

ULYSSES, *prince of Ithaca.*

NEOPTOLEMUS, *the young prince of Scyros, son of Achilles.*

PHILOCTETES, *prince of Trachis, son of Pœas.*

*A scout attending on Neoptolemus, afterwards disguised as the master of a trading vessel.*

HERACLES.

*The* CHORUS *is composed of Scyrian sailors, followers of* NEOPTOLEMUS. *Mate of the Scyrian crew; Attendants.*

---

*Scene, a desert place on the coast of Lemnos; in the background a cave.*

*Enter* ULYSSES, NEOPTOLEMUS, *and Attendant.*

*Ulysses.*  This is the shore of Lemnos' sea-girt isle,
Untrod by mortals, uninhabited,
Where once, O scion of the first of Greeks,
Achilles' offspring, Neoptolemus,
Under commission from our generals
I set on shore the Melian, Pœas' son,
His foot all bleeding with an ulcerous wound;
What time it was not possible for us
To set our hands in peace and quietness
To a drink-offering or burnt-sacrifice,
But ever with wild desecrating cries
He kept the whole encampment in distress,
Groaning, lamenting.   But why tell this tale?
It is no time for many words from us,
Lest he should learn of my arrival hither,
And so the whole contrivance be upset
By which I think to take him presently.
Now you must work, and help to accomplish it;

So look around, where in this neighbourhood
There is a grotto with two entrances,
So situate, that at one or other end
There is a sunny seat when it is cold,
While in the summer time a breeze sends sleep,
Blowing through the tunnelled chamber.    And
        perhaps
A little underneath, on the left hand,
You may discover a fresh water-spring,
If it is still in being.   Go up thither
Softly, and report if what I say applies [1]
To this same spot, or no ; so may you hear
The sequel of my story, and I tell it,
And both work on in concert.

*Neoptolemus* (*ascending the rocks*).        King Ulysses,
Your work lies not far off ; for I believe
I see a cave, such as you say.

*Ulysses.*                                    High up,
Or low ?   I cannot mark it.

*Neoptolemus.*                          Here, above ;
And here's a foot-print on the threshold ! [2]

*Ulysses.*                                              See
That he is not asleep inside !

*Neoptolemus.*                      I see
An empty habitation ; tenantless.

*Ulysses.* Nor any household furniture within ?

*Neoptolemus.* Yes, flattened leaves, as of some inmate's bed.

*Ulysses.* And the rest empty, and nothing under-roof ?

*Neoptolemus.* Here is a cup cut out of wood, the work
Of a rude craftsman ; and a pair of flints, too.

*Ulysses.* What you exhibit is his treasure-heap !

*Neoptolemus.* Hilloa ! here are some rags as well, still warm,
Full of some pestilent unwholesomeness.

*Ulysses.* The man lives in these precincts, it is clear,
And cannot be far off.   How could a man,
Lame with an old affliction in his limb,
Walk any distance ?   But he has gone out,
Either in quest of food, or of some herb,
If he knows any anodyne.   Send therefore
Your follower to scout, lest unawares
He fall on me ; for he would like to get me,
Rather than all the Argives, in his power.

*Neoptolemus* (*descending*). He is going, and the track shall be
      secured.                         [*Exit Attendant.*
      Now speak again, and say, what is your pleasure.

*Ulysses.* Son of Achilles, you must shew yourself
      Stout on this errand; not in limbs alone,
      But also in service—if you hear a thing
      Novel, of a kind you have not heard before;
      Since you are here to serve.

*Neoptolemus.*                What are your orders?

*Ulysses.* You are to inveigle, by the words you utter,
      The spirit of Philoctetes. When he asks
      Who and whence are you, say—Achilles' son;
      This is not to be hidden; and you sail homeward,
      Deserting from the Achaians' naval host,
      Hating them with a mighty hatred; who,
      Sending for you with prayers to come from home,
      As their sole means of taking Ilium,
      Thought it not meet to give you, when you came,
      Achilles' armour, which you claimed of them,
      But gave it to Ulysses in your room;
      Saying what you please of evil against me
      The extremest of extreme. For by so doing
      You will not hurt me; but if you refuse
      To do this duty, you will bring down trouble
      On all the Argives. For if this man's arrows
      Are not first captured, 'tis impossible
      That you should vanquish the Dardanian hold.
      Now, how that intercourse there cannot be
      With him on my part, while on yours there can,
      Both safe and solid, learn. You have made voyage
      Not under oath to any, nor compelled,
      Nor of the army that at first set sail;
      But nought of this can be denied of me;
      Hence, if he sees me, shafts in hand, I perish,
      And shall involve you with me in my ruin.
      This is the thing to be devised, then; how
      You shall appropriate the unrivalled weapons.
      Of course [3] I know that it is not your nature
      To say such words, or compass knaveries;
      But, for 'tis sweet to get the gain of winning,
      Dare! In the end, we shall be justified.
      Now, for a day's short fragment, lend yourself

To ruthlessness; and then to after-time
Be called the most religious of mankind!

*Neoptolemus.* The sort of things I chafe to hear prescribed,
Son of Laertes—these I hate to do;
'Tis not my nature to do ought by guile;
Not mine, nor, as they say, his who begat me.
Ready I am to bring the man by force,
And not by fraud.   For he, lame of one foot,
Will not worst us at force, we being so many.
Nevertheless, being sent to work with you,
I am averse to be called recreant;
But I prefer, sir king, rather to fail
In doing well, than to succeed by ill.

*Ulysses.* Son of an excellent father, I myself
Was youthful once, and had a backward tongue,
And an officious hand; but now through trial
I find the words and not the acts of men
Always prevailing.

*Neoptolemus.*                    Why, what else do you bid me
But tell a lie?

*Ulysses.*                    I tell you by deceit
To capture Philoctetes.

*Neoptolemus.*                    Why by guile
To bring him, rather than persuading him?

*Ulysses.* He cannot be persuaded; and by force
You could not take him.

*Neoptolemus.*                    Has he some resource
Of strength so formidable?

*Ulysses.*                    Unerring darts,
Whose points are tipped with death.

*Neoptolemus.*                    And is it not
Within a bold man's part, to cope with him?

*Ulysses.* No, save by guile he take him, as I say.

*Neoptolemus.* Do you not think foul shame to say things false?

*Ulysses.* Not when the falsehood brings me safety.

*Neoptolemus.*                    Why,
With what a face could a man blurt it out? [4]

*Ulysses.* You must not scruple, when you work for gain.

*Neoptolemus.* What do I gain, if he should come to Troy?

*Ulysses.* Nought but these shafts take Troy.

*Neoptolemus.*                    And am not I
The man to storm it, as was prophesied?

*Ulysses.* Not you apart from these, nor these from you.
*Neoptolemus.* Well, I may have to seek them, that being so.
*Ulysses.* You will achieve two prizes, if you do it.
*Neoptolemus.* Which? If I knew them, I might not refuse.
*Ulysses.* To be called wise and valiant, both in one.
*Neoptolemus.* Go to, I'll do it, and let all shame go by.
*Ulysses.* Do you remember what I told you?
*Neoptolemus.* Yes,
    Rely on't; I assented once for all.

*Re-enter Attendant.*

*Ulysses.* Do you remain then, and await him here;
    But I will hence, lest I should be espied,
    And send your scout off to the ship again;
    Then, if I deem that you are wasting time,
    I will send this same fellow back once more,
    Disguised like a sea-captain in costume,
    That he may not be known; from whom, my son,
    Gather, as he speaks in parables, whate'er
    Has relevancy of his words. Meanwhile
    I seek the vessel, and leave this to you;
    May Hermes the Conductor be our guide
    In cunning, and the civic Victory,
    Athana, who preserves me evermore.
                [*Exeunt* ULYSSES *and Attendant.*

*Enter Scyrian Sailors, as Chorus.*

I. 1.

*Chorus.* What, O my master, what should I conceal—
  A stranger on strange soil—and what reveal,
    To ears of one inclined suspiciously?
  Tell me: for his art passes other art,
      And counsel other counsel, in whose hand
      Is Jove's Olympian sceptre of command.
    And now to thee
      Has come, O son, all this time-honoured sway;
  Wherefore declare what serviceable part
    Thou hast for me to play.

*Neoptolemus.* Now, for perhaps it pleases you to pry
    In corners, for the spot where he may lie,

Use your eyes with freedom ; but whenever
    From these halls shall come a traveller grim,
To my side step forward, and endeavour
    To afford me help to cope with him.

### I. 2.

*Chorus.* Master, thou bidd'st me heed, as I did heed,
    To keep an eye on thy most urgent need ;
Now tell me in what sort of habitation,
    And in what quarter, he is wont to dwell ;
    That I should know is not unseasonable,
    Lest he from somewhere unexpectedly
    Should light on me.
What is his beat, or what his usual station ?
    What errand may he now be going about,
    Within doors or without ?

*Neoptolemus.* Thou seest this abode, tunnelled quite through,
    Making a stony resting-place ?
1 *Scyrian.*                   And whither
    Has the poor habitant betaken himself ?

*Neoptolemus.* 'Tis plain to me that in his need of food
    He is gone gleaning through this neighbourhood.
For they say it is his way of living,
    Game to shoot with arrows from his bow,
And with grief of sickness ever grieving
    Still to find no healer for his woe.

### II. 1.

*Chorus.*     Him do I pity !   For that he,
    Meeting no eye of sympathy,
      With not a friend at hand to heed,
    Hapless, alone for evermore,
    Is stricken with a disease full sore,
      Is driven by every passing need.
    How—oh how, thus desolate,
    Bears he up against his fate ?
    Woe for the wiles poor mortals plan !
    Woe for the hapless tribes of man,
Whose troubles overfill their vital span ! [5]

### II. 2.

He, perchance of no less worth
Than the men of elder birth,
Destitute of all things good,
Lies apart, in solitude;
Harbouring with the shaggy bear,
Or the pard with spotted hair;
In disease, in want, forlorn,
Cureless anguish he has borne;
While Echo on the uplands high,
Sounding afar, makes low reply,
With insuppressive voice, to his bitter cry.[6]

*Neoptolemus.* None of these things are marvellous to
me;
For from above, if I know anything,
Those sufferings came upon him, by the hand
Of the hard-hearted Chrysa; and what now
He bears of labours, far from comforters,
Cannot but be by some God's providence,
For that he should not, in assault of Troy,
Draw to the head the unconquered bolts divine,
Before that hour shall come when, we are
told,
It is Troy's fate to be subdued by them.

### III. 1.

*Chorus.* Hush, my son.

*Neoptolemus.* Why?

*Chorus.* A sound rose clear
As of the tramp of a wearied man,
This way, or that; I hear—I hear
A voice articulate, of one [7]
Pacing onward, as best he can;
Yes, the hoarse tone
That marks a soul worn down with pain,
From afar I know;
For loud and plain
That note of woe.

### III. 2.

But, my son—

*Neoptolemus.*          What?

*Chorus.*                    Bethink thee anew;
          For the man is not far, but near,
      Not, as a shepherd swain might do,
          Piping a tune of merry cheer,
      But either, stumbling, he cries perforce
          With far-heard shout,
      Or viewing the strange unwelcomed course
          Of a ship to ground;
          For he sends out
          A scaring sound.

*Enter* PHILOCTETES.

*Philoctetes.* Ho strangers, who are you, who have
          put in
      With galley to this coast—sea without port,
      Shore without shelter?  Of what land or race
      Am I to guess you? for your garments' guise
      Is Grecian—best beloved of all to me;
      And I would hear you speak.   Be not struck dumb
      With terror at the wildness of my looks;
      But pitying an unhappy man—alone—
      Desolate thus and friendless in his wrongs,
      If you are come in friendship, speak to me.
      Give me some answer!  'Twere unnatural
      I should lack this from you, or you from me.

*Neoptolemus.* Sir stranger, know this first, we are of Greece;
      Since this you fain would learn.

*Philoctetes.*                O sound most welcome!
      Ah what a thing it is to be addressed,
      After long years, by such a man as you!
      What need, my son, caused you to put in hither—
      To come this way?  What impulse?  Which of winds
      Most friendly?  Say all this to me, aloud,
      That I may know your name.

*Neoptolemus.*                I am by birth
      Of the isle of Scyros; I am sailing home;
      My name's Neoptolemus, Achilles' son;
      Now you know all.

*Philoctetes.*          O son of sire most dear—
Sprout from a friendly soil—the foster-child
Of ancient Lycomedes, on what errand
Made you this land, from what port voyaging?
*Neoptolemus.* From Ilium, truly, am I steering now.
*Philoctetes.* How say you? for you did not sail, I know,
With us at first, when we set out for Troy.
*Neoptolemus.* Why, were you partner in that enterprise?
*Philoctetes.* O son, do you not know the man you look on?
*Neoptolemus.* How should I know a man I never saw?
*Philoctetes.* Nor did you ever hear my name, nor word
Of the afflictions that were killing me?
*Neoptolemus.* Nothing of what you ask me do I know.
*Philoctetes.* O what a drudge and sport of Gods am I!
Of whose ill plight no whisper ever came
To my own home, or any coast of Greece,
But they who thrust me out unrighteously
Laugh and keep silence, while my sickness ever
Grows on me and increases more and more.
O boy! O son, calling Achilles sire,
I am the man who, may be, thou hast heard
Was master of the arms of Heracles,
The son of Pœas, Philoctetes! whom
The Captains twain and the Cephallenite king
Cast out thus shamefully—deserted—sick
Of a consuming wound—pierced through and
    through
By the destroying viper's venomous fangs;
And in this plight, boy, they exposed me here,
Left me, and went! when from the Chrysean coast
They put in hither with their navy, straight,
Soon as they saw me sleeping on the beach,
Tired with long tossing, in a sheltered cave,
They laughed, they went, they left me! casting me
A few mean rags, a beggar's garniture,
And some poor pittance, too, of nourishment,
Such as, I pray, be theirs! O then, my son,
What sort of waking, think you, from that sleep
Had I when they were gone! How did I weep,
How did I wail, for my calamities!
Seeing the ships which I was leader of
All gone away, and no man in the place

Who should suffice me, or should comfort me
In the disease of which I laboured; yea
Though I sought everywhere, nothing I found
Left to me, save my anguish; and, my son,
Of that no lack indeed!   Hour after hour
Passed by me; and I must needs make shift alone,
Under this scanty shelter.   For my food,
This quiver sought out what supplied my need,
Hitting the doves on wing; then to the mark
Of the shot bolt I had to crawl, with pain,
Dragging a wounded foot.   If upon this
I wanted to get anything to drink,
Or, as in winter when the hoar frost lay,
To break some sticks to burn, this, creeping forth,
I had to manage, in my misery.
Then there would be no fire; but striking hard
With flint on flint I struck out painfully
An obscure spark, which keeps me still alive.
Thus shelter overhead, not without fire,
Furnishes all, save healing of my sore.—
Come now and hear about the isle, my son;
No sailor willingly approaches it;
For anchorage there is not, or a port
Whither a man might sail, and make his mart
By traffic, or find welcome; prudent men
Do not make voyage here.   Some one, perhaps,
Might land against his will; for these things oft
Will happen in the long-drawn life of men;
But such, my son, when they do come, in words
Pity me, and in compassion give me, say
Some morsel of food, or matter of attire;
But that thing no man, when I hint it, will do—
Take me safe home; but this tenth year already
In hunger and distress I pine and perish,
Feeding the gnawing tooth of my disease.
The Atridæ, and Ulysses' violence,[8]
Have done me all this wrong; the like of which,
O boy, may the Olympian Gods give them
One day to suffer, in revenge for me!

1 *Scyrian.*  I feel I pity thee, O Pœas' son,
As much as any of thy visitors.

*Neoptolemus.*  And I myself, in witness to this tale,

Can swear 'tis true ; for I have felt their malice—
The Atridæ—and Ulysses' violence.[8]

*Philoctetes.* Have you a feud, too, with the villain sons
Of Atreus, and are furious, at your griefs ?

*Neoptolemus.* I wish my hand could some day satisfy
The measure of my fury, that Mycenæ
And Sparta, both, might know, how Scyros also
Is mother of stout hearts !

*Philoctetes.*　　　　　Well said, my son !
What do you charge them with ? what is the cause
Of your deep anger ? why have you come hither ?

*Neoptolemus.* O son of Pœas, I will tell you—yet
I hardly shall know how—what injuries
They did me when I came.　After Fate brought
Achilles to his end—

*Philoctetes.*　　　　　O woe is me !
Tell me no more, till I have learnt this first,
If Peleus' son is dead ?

*Neoptolemus.*　　　　　Yes, he is dead ;
Killed by no man, but by a God ; subdued
By Phœbus, as they tell me ; arrow-slain.

*Philoctetes.* Well, noble was the slayer, and the slain.
O son, I know not whether I shall first
Explore your grievance, or lament for him.

*Neoptolemus.* Poor soul, I should have thought your own enough
For you to mourn, without your neighbours' troubles !

*Philoctetes.* You have said right ; therefore begin once more
Your story of the way they injured you.

*Neoptolemus.* There came for me, in a fine painted vessel,
The great Ulysses, and the foster-sire
Of my own father, saying, (either in sooth
Or, perhaps, feigning,) that it was forbidden,
Now that my sire had fallen, that any man
Other than I should storm the towers of Troy.
This tale propounding, in this sort, sir friend,
They did not let me linger very long,
Before I straight embarked ; urged most of all
By yearning for the dead, that I might see him
Before they buried him ; for I never saw him ;
And then the tale, no doubt, made for my honour,
That I should take the Towers, if I went.

Well, after two days' voyage I arrived
At black Sigeum, with a gale astern;
And forthwith in a circle all the host
Hailed me as I stepped on shore; swearing they saw
The dead Achilles come to life again.
All the same, dead he lay; and I, poor fool,
When I had mourned him, after no long space,
Going to the Atridæ, (friends, belike, of mine,)
Claimed my sire's arms and other property.
But they put forth—oh, a most pitiful tale!
"O offspring of Achilles, all the rest
That was your father's you may take, and welcome!
But those arms own another master now,
Laertes' son."   I burst out weeping straight,
And stood up in deep wrath, and spake with anguish;
"You villain, did you dare to give my arms
Without my leave to any man but me?"
Then said Ulysses, who was standing by,
"Yea my son, rightly have they given them,
For, on a time, he owed his life to me."
I, in a rage, straightway belaboured them
With all sorts of abuse, sparing for nought,
If that man was to snatch my arms from me!
Who, being thus driven, although not choleric,
Cut to the heart at what he heard me say,
Retorted thus; "You were not with us!   You
Were absent from your duty! and, since you come
To bluster, you shall never sail off with them
To Scyros!"   After flouts and injuries
Of such a nature, I am steering home;
Spoiled by Ulysses, basest, and base-born,
Of what is mine.   Still, him I do not blame
Like those in power.   For a city all
Follows its leaders; a whole host, the same;
And men who are unruly become bad
By force of teaching.—All my tale is told.
May whosoever is the Atridæ's foe
Be dear to Heaven, as he must be to me.

CHORUS. I.

O Mother, thou who gavest birth
To Zeus himself!   Silvan Earth,

Who fillest all with bread;
Who dost control
The floods that roll
Over Pactolus' golden bed;
On thee we cried, Mother adored,
When on this man was outpoured
All the Atridæ's pride;
What time they gave
Harness and glaive,
His father's—setting him aside:
Immortal Queen, thee we invoked,
Who behind thy lions yoked,
Slayers of the herd, dost ride!
There was won
For Lartius' son
Glory surpassing all beside.

*Philoctetes.* Strangers, you seem to have sailed here to me
With a clear passport, in your injuries
Not dissonant with mine; I recognize
The Atridæ's doings, and Ulysses' hand.
For I am certain he would have a voice
In every evil word and wickedness,
And that thereout he is not like to bring
Anything just to pass. I wonder, though,
Never at this—but that the greater Ajax,
If present, seeing it done, permitted it.

*Neoptolemus.* He was no more, my friend; had he been
living,
I never should have been so plundered.

*Philoctetes.* How?
What did you say? Is he too dead and gone?

*Neoptolemus.* He walks no more on earth.

*Philoctetes.* O woe is me!
But not the son of Tydeus! Not that son
Of Sisyphus, palmed on Laertes! They
Will not have died! Pity they were ever born!

*Neoptolemus.* Not they, you may be certain; they are now
Flourishing right bravely in the Argive host.

*Philoctetes.* And what of him, old, valiant and my friend,
Nestor of Pylos? He was wont to avert
With wise advice the mischiefs of their doing.

*Neoptolemus.* Badly he fares, indeed; since he has lost
     Antilochus, a son of his,[9] by death.

*Philoctetes.* Alas! You tell me two calamities
     In the same breath! of two, who least of any
     I could have wished to hear were dead! Good lack,
     What must we look to, when such men have perished,
     The while Ulysses still survives, when he,
     Instead of them, ought rather to have been
     Reported slain!

*Neoptolemus.*            A clever gamester [10] he.
     But, Philoctetes! even clever plans
     Are sometimes foiled.

*Philoctetes.*            Now tell me in Heaven's name,
     Where did you leave Patroclus all this while,
     Who was your father's darling?

*Neoptolemus.*            He had died, too.
     And, in short compass I may say to you—
     War never slays a bad man in its course,
     But the good always!

*Philoctetes.*            I can bear you out.
     And while we talk of it, I will enquire
     After a man—unworthy indeed, but shrewd
     And apt of speech—what is become of him.

*Neoptolemus.* Who but Ulysses is it whom you mean?

*Philoctetes.* I did not speak of him; but there was one
     Thersites, who was always trying to speak,
     By no means only once—where none would have him;
     Know you if he still lives?

*Neoptolemus.*            I never saw him
     But I did hear that he is yet alive.

*Philoctetes.* He may well be so! Nothing ever died
     That was pernicious; but the Deities
     Foster it well; yea, they delight to turn
     All that is profligate and villainous
     Backward from Hades, while the good and just
     They speed on their way ever. In what light
     Must we regard these things? how praise them?
       when
     Praising things heavenly, I find faults in Heaven!

*Neoptolemus.* I, O thou son of an Œtæan sire,
     Shall take good care henceforward to survey
     Ilium and the Atridæ from afar;

And where the mean are mightier than the brave,
And goodness withers, and the coward bears rule,
I never will approve such company;
But rock-bound Scyros shall suffice for me
Henceforward, and contentment with my home.
Now to my ship I go; farewell to thee,
Thou son of Pœas; may you fare right well!
And may the Powers restore you from disease
According to your wish.   Let us be going;
That whensoever Heaven vouchsafes us means
Of sailing, we may start.

*Philoctetes.*                    Already, son,
Are you afoot?

*Neoptolemus.*                Yes, we must time our voyage
By watching from hard by, not out of sight.

*Philoctetes.* Now for your sire's, your mother's sake, O son,
And any dear one's whom you have at home,
Suppliant I beg, leave me not here alone,
Abandoned to such evils as you see,
And all you have heard I dwell in!  Stow me, say
For ballast!  The discomfort well I know,
Is much, of such a cargo; bear it, though!
To noble natures shame is odious; while
Kindness brings honour.   And to you, my son,
There were foul shame in leaving this undone;
But in the doing the fullest meed of praise,
Should I come living to the Œtæan land.
Come now, the trouble will not last a day
Venture it!  Take me, throw me where you please,
Into the hold, into the bows, the stern,
Wherever I shall plague my mates the least!
Consent, my son, yea by prayer-answering Jove!
Hearken, I beseech you at your knees—although
A hapless wretch, being lame; ah leave me not
Forsaken here, where is no trace of men!
But either take me safe to your own dwelling,
Or to Chalcodon's homesteads, in Eubœa;
And thence to Œta, and Cape Trachis, and
Sperchius'[11] fair stream will not be far to go.
So shall you bring me to my father's arms,
For whom 'tis long that I have been afraid
He has already died; for oftentimes

By those who have come did I send to him, with
　　prayers
That he would send and fetch me safe again;
But either he is dead, or I suppose
My emissaries, as is natural,
Making small count of what was due to me,
Pushed on their voyage home. But now—for you
I come to as conductor, equally,
And messenger yourself—pity me, and save me;
Seeing how on all sides danger lies in wait,
And 'tis by hazard that mortality
Fare well, or fare not well; and to his danger
A man should look, who is untouched by trouble,
And when he lives at ease then most of all
Watch, lest destruction take him unawares.

### Chorus. 2.

Have compassion, O my chief!
He has told of many a grief,
　　Many a painful care;
　　　　Such load of woes
　　　　May none of those
　　Whom I cherish have to bear!
But if, sir king, thou hatest thus
The bitter sons of Atreus,
　　Hear what my sentence is;
　　　　Change the bane
　　　　Into gain,
　　Bane they meant, to gain of his;
To the home he longed for so,
Swiftly embarking, let us go;
　　Our ship is tight and yare;
　　　　Thus would I
　　　　In safety fly
From the revenge the Gods prepare.

*Neoptolemus.* Take care you do not play at being kind
　　Now, but as soon as you are overwhelmed
　　By the proximity of his disease,
　　No longer seem the same, as you now promise.
1 *Scyrian.* No fear of that. It is impossible
　　That you shall ever have this stone to cast,
　　With right, at me.

*Neoptolemus.*                 Well, it were shame indeed
    That I should seem reluctant, more than you,
    In labour for a stranger at his need.
    Come then; if you think fit, let us set sail.
    Let him start quickly; for the ship shall take him,
    And none shall say him nay.  Heaven only guide
    us
    Safe from this land, thither, where we would go!

*Philoctetes.* O day most happy! O most welcome face!
    O sailors dear! How shall I prove indeed
    What debt of gratitude you lay on me!
    Let us be going, my son; first taking leave
    Of the unhomelike home that is within,
    That you may learn what sort of life I lived,
    And what stout heart I kept.  For I suppose
    No other beside me, seeing the sight
    With his eyes, merely, would have borne it all;
    While I was taught by long necessity
    To be resigned to ills.

1 *Scyrian.*                Stay, let us listen;
    Two persons, one a sailor from your ship,
    And one a stranger, are approaching us;
    Hear what they say before you go within.

*Enter Attendant disguised as a trading captain, and Mate.*

*Attendant.* Son of Achilles, this your shipmate, who
    With other two kept guard over your vessel,
    I bade inform me in what place you tarried,
    Since I have crossed you, not intending it,
    But by chance, somehow, having come to moor
    At the same ground.  Sailing as shipmaster
    With a small convoy home from Ilium
    To Peparethus, famed for grape-clusters,
    When I had heard the sailors, one and all,
    Were of the crew that had embarked with you,
    I thought it better not to hold my peace,
    Nor to make sail till I had spoken with you,
    And been rewarded, as is fair.  Perhaps
    You have heard nothing of your own concerns—
    The new designs the Argives have on you?
    Nor mere designs, but deeds, now in the doing,
    No longer loitered over.

*Neoptolemus.*                              Truly, sir,
The merit of your forethought must secure
My gratitude, if I am no churl born.
But tell me what you mean; that I may learn
What last new scheme you know of from the host.

*Attendant.* Old Phœnix and the sons of Theseus
Are gone, with galleys, in pursuit of you.

*Neoptolemus.* To bring me back by parley, or perforce?

*Attendant.* I know not. What I heard I come to tell you.

*Neoptolemus.* Is it for the Atridæ Phœnix and his mates
Are taking this in hand so hastily?

*Attendant.* Be sure 'tis doing, and that without delay.

*Neoptolemus.* How was it Ulysses was not prompt to sail,
As his own post, in this? Did some fear stay him?

*Attendant.* He and the son of Tydeus were just starting
After another, when I put to sea.

*Neoptolemus.* Who could that be, for whom Ulysses' self
Would have embarked?

*Attendant.*                              Well, he said—somebody;
But tell me first, who is this personage?
And do not speak out loud.

*Neoptolemus.*                              This, stranger, is
The famous Philoctetes!

*Attendant.*                              Then don't ask me
Anything more, but with what speed you may
Take yourself off, out of this land, and sail.

*Philoctetes.* What says he, boy? Why does the shipman talk
Aside to you, making his trade of me?

*Neoptolemus.* I do not know as yet; what he would say
He must speak out to you, to these, and me.

*Attendant.* Seed of Achilles, do not tell of me,
For saying what I ought not, to the host;
Many are the friendly acts they do to me,
And I to them, such as a poor man may.

*Neoptolemus.* I am the Atridæ's enemy; and he,
Hating the Atridæ, is my greatest friend.
If, as you say, you came to do me good,
No word you have heard must you conceal from us.

*Attendant.* My son, mind what you are doing.

*Neoptolemus.*                              So I do.

*Attendant.* I shall hold you accountable for this.

*Neoptolemus.* Do, but say on.

*Attendant.*                    I will.   The two you wot of,
The son of Tydeus and Ulysses, sail
To arrest this man ; and they have sworn an oath
To bring him, either by persuading him
With oratory, or else by dint of force.
So all the Achaians heard Ulysses say
Openly ; for he had full confidence,
More than the other, to accomplish it.

*Neoptolemus.* And for what cause did the Atridæ turn
After so long so vehemently to him
Whom all this while they had kept in banishment ?
What remorse touched them, or what Nemesis
And force of Gods who punish wickedness ?

*Attendant.* All this, for you perhaps have heard it not,
I will explain.   There was a high-born seer,
A son of Priam's, Helenus by name,
Whom he we speak of, he we call—the knave—
By all disgraceful and vile epithets,
Ulysses—sallying forth by night, alone,
Captured, and bound ; and brought him, and displayed
Amidst the Achaian ranks, a goodly prize !
Who gave them oracles of all beside,
And that they never would be conquerors
Of Troia's towers, unless they could persuade
And bring this person from the island here
Where he dwells now.   This when Laertes' son
Heard the seer say, he undertook forthwith
To fetch the man to the Achaians' presence ;
He rather thought, taking him willingly ;
But if reluctant, then against his will ;
Which if he failed of doing, he staked his head
To be cut off by any man who pleased !
My son, you have heard all ; my counsel is,
For you and him and any other man
For whom you have regard, to lose no time.

*Philoctetes.* Me miserable !   Did he, the utter pest,
Swear to cajole and fetch me to the host ?
I am as likely to come up to light,
When dead, from Hades, as his father did !

*Attendant.* Of that I know not.   Now to my ship I go.
To the best ends may Heaven attend you both !
                                   [*Exit.*

*Philoctetes.* Is it not monstrous that Laertes' son
    Should ever hope, boy, with soft soothing words
    To take me, and to shew me from his vessel
    To all the mob of Argives? He, than whom [12]
    I easier would hearken to the snake—
    The abhorred snake, which has thus made me lame!
    But there is nothing which he will not say,
    Nothing he dares not do! And now, I know
    That he will come; well, my son, let us go;
    So that a breadth of sea may sunder us
    Far from Ulysses' vessel! Let us hence;
    A timely haste is the right means to afford
    Sleep and refreshment when our toil is past.

*Neoptolemus.* Were it not well, when the head-wind shall cease,
    Then to set sail? for it is adverse now.

*Philoctetes.* Winds are fair always, when you fly from harm.

*Neoptolemus.* Nay but this gale is adverse to them also! [13]

*Philoctetes.* No gale blows adversely to plunderers,
    When robbery and rapine are in hand.

*Neoptolemus.* Well then, if you think fit, let us be off;
    And take, out of your dwelling, anything
    For which you have most use, and most desire.

*Philoctetes.* Some things I need, though from a scanty store.

*Neoptolemus.* What is there, which is not on board my vessel?

*Philoctetes.* A herb I have, with which I always lull
    This ulcer best, and soothe the pain away.

*Neoptolemus.* Well, bring it forth. What would you take
    beside?

*Philoctetes.* If any of my arrows have been dropped
    Unheeded, that I should not leave them here
    For any man to gather.

*Neoptolemus.*              What, are those
    The famous bow and arrows in your hand?

*Philoctetes.* These and no other are they, which I carry.

*Neoptolemus.* May I look at them close, and handle them,
    And do them worship, as a god?

*Philoctetes.*               Both this,
    My son, and anything besides of mine
    Is at your service, which may profit you.

*Neoptolemus.* I have the longing; but no more than thus—
    I would, an if I might; if not, no matter.

*Philoctetes.* Modestly spoken! Yes my son, that may you,

You who alone have given me to behold
This light of day—to see the Œtæan soil—
My aged sire—my friends! who set me up,
From underneath, over my enemies!
They shall be yours to touch and give me back
At pleasure; and to boast that, for your merit,
Alone of mortals you laid hand to them.
'Twas in return for kindness I first got them.

1 *Scyrian.*[14] To see you, and to have you for a friend,
    Pleases me well; for he that knows the way
    To return good for good, must be a friend
    Better than all possessions.

*Neoptolemus.*                 Now go in.

*Philoctetes.* That will I, and take you with me; for my ailment
    Craves to have you for an auxiliary.

            [*Exeunt* PHILOCTETES *and* NEOPTOLEMUS.

### CHORUS.

#### I. 1.

I have heard the tale that was told—
    I did not behold—
What by Cronos' invincible son
    To Ixion was done,
Who approached Jove's bed, whom he bound
    To a wheel whirled round;
But I know of no other, by hearing or seeing, that is,
No mortal, tied to a loathlier fate than his,
Who for no violent deed, or stain of fraud on his name,
But being as good as the good are, perishes here in shame.
    At this, too, I wonder,
       How, listening to the shock
    Of the surges' thunder
       About his lonely rock,
Still, still he endured the continual cares and fears
       Of a life, all tears!

#### I. 2.

Where none but himself to greet—
    No use of his feet—
Nor any neighbour he found,[15]
    Of the region round,

In whose compassionate ears
                To bewail, with tears,
His raw deep-festering sore—who might stay the flood,
From wounds of his raging foot, of the fevered blood,
When a fit came on, with soothing herbs, the growth of the
        soil;
But hither and thither ever, hobbling along with toil,
        He would crawl, where healing
                Might be found, for his journey's pain—
        Like an infant feeling
                For its nurse's arms in vain—
Whensoever the soul-consuming Fury's force
                Had out-spent its course;


## II. 1.

                Raising no seed
Out of the hallowed lap of earth, for food;
                Nor aught beside of good,
Such as the cunning spirit achieves of men;
                But only now and then
What he might hit, with arrows from the string
                Sped on swift wing
                His appetite to feed.
Poor soul, that never in a ten years' space
        Revelled in one full draught of wine outpoured,
But ever had to journey with set face
To any standing pool he had explored!


## II. 2.

                But met withal
Now by a child of warriors, his allies,
        He shall at length arise,
Happy, out of woes, and magnified by them.
        Who with sea-traversing stem,
The tale of many months being complete,
                Conducts his feet
                Back to his fathers' hall,
Where dwell the Meliad Nymphs—and to the banks
        Of Spherchius; where, with fire of Heaven all-
        bright,
The brazen-shielded Hero joins the ranks
        Of all the Gods, high o'er Mount Œta's height.

*Enter* NEOPTOLEMUS *and* PHILOCTETES.

*Neoptolemus.* Move forward, if you will. Why, without reason,
 Are you so silent? Why stand thus aghast?
*Philoctetes.* Eh, eh!
*Neoptolemus.* What is it?
*Philoctetes.*      Nothing serious. On, my son.
*Neoptolemus.* Are you in pain, from your unhealed disease?
*Philoctetes.* No, not at all; I think 'tis better now.
 O Heavens!
*Neoptolemus.*    Why do you groan, and call on Heaven?
*Philoctetes.* To come and save me, and be good to me.
 Eh, eh!
*Neoptolemus.*   What is the matter? Won't you tell me?
 Must you be silent thus? You seem in pain.
*Philoctetes.* I am ruined, my son, and shall not have the power
 To hide my anguish from you. Well a day!
 It goes through me, it goes through me! Woe
  is me!
 I am ruined, my son; I am gnawed, my son. Alack,
 Alack the day! Alack, alack the day!
 For Heaven's sake, if you have a sword, my son,
 Ready to hand, smite me upon the foot,
 Cut it off quickly! Spare not for my life!
 Quick, boy!
*Neoptolemus.*    What is it, thus suddenly begun,
 For which you moan so, and bewail yourself?
*Philoctetes.* You know, my son.
*Neoptolemus.*      What is it?
*Philoctetes.*        You know, boy!
*Neoptolemus.*          What?
 I know not!
*Philoctetes.*    How, you know not? Lack, alack-a-day!
*Neoptolemus.* Truly the stress is dreadful of your sickness.
*Philoctetes.* Yes, dreadful beyond utterance; pity me!
*Neoptolemus.* What must I do?
*Philoctetes.*      Do not betray me, in terror;
 For it is come, after an interval,
 By winding ways; as it was gorged before,
 So now, it seems, the same.[16]

*Neoptolemus.*                                    Alas, poor wretch—
  Wretch that you seem, truly, for all your troubles!
  Would you I should touch you, and take hold of you?

*Philoctetes.* Not that, by any means; but take this bow,
  As you were asking me but now, and keep
  And guard it, till this spasm of my disease,
  Now present, slackens.   For sleep seizes me
  After this agony has run its course;
  It cannot end before; but you must leave me
  To sleep in quiet.   And if in the meanwhile
  Those men arrive, I charge you in Heaven's name,
  That neither freely nor against your will,
  Nor any how, you suffer them to get it;
  Lest you become the slayer of your own self,
  And of me too, who am your supplicant.

*Neoptolemus.* Take heart; so far as foresight can ensure,
  It shall not pass, save to your hands and mine.
  Hand it to me, and luck go with it!

*Philoctetes* (*giving the bow and arrows*).          Here,
  Take it, my son; but adore, first, the Power
  Whose name is Jealousy; so may it prove
  To thee not baneful, as it was to me
  And him who was its owner ere my time.

*Neoptolemus.* Heaven grant it so to us! and grant us, too,
  A favourable and swift passage thither,
  Where God ordains, and whither we are bound.

*Philoctetes.* Ah but I fear, my son, your prayers are vain;
  For here again are welling drops of blood,
  Red from the wound, and I expect some change.
  Alack, fie on it!   Alack again, my foot,
  What evil you will work me!   It grows upon me;
  It comes on close.   O wretched that I am!
  You know the worst; pray do not go away!
  O well-a-day!
  Thou man of Cephallenia, would this pang
  Could grip thy breast, right through thee! Fie, alack!
  Alack once more!   O you two generals,
  Agamemnon and Menelaus, would that you
  Might have this plague to bear, instead of me,
  As long a time as I!   O me, woe's me!
  O Death, kind Death, how is it that always called,
  Thus, every day, thou canst not ever come?

O youth, good youth, good now, take hold of me,
And burn me in that thrice welcome Lemnian flame,
As on a time unto Jove's offspring I,
Earning those weapons, which you carry now,
Thought it no sin to do!   What say you, son?
What do you say?
Why are you silent?   What are you about?

*Neoptolemus.*  Why, I was sighing with grief, at your distress.

*Philoctetes.*  Nay my son, all the same, do not lose courage;
For it comes sharply, and goes away with speed.
Only I entreat, do not abandon me!

*Neoptolemus.*  Fear not, we will remain.

*Philoctetes.*                        Will you remain?

*Neoptolemus.*  Be assured I will.

*Philoctetes.*                    I do not think it meet
To put you on your oath, my son.

*Neoptolemus.*                    Why no;
Since I may not arrive without you!

*Philoctetes.*                        Reach
Your hand, for pledge.

*Neoptolemus.*            I pledge it, to remain.

*Philoctetes.*  Yonder now, yonder—

*Neoptolemus.*                    Whither say you?

*Philoctetes.*                            Above—

*Neoptolemus.*  What do you rave of now?   Why do you stare
At the orb above us?

*Philoctetes.*          Let me, let me go.

*Neoptolemus.*  Let you go—whither?

*Philoctetes.*                    Let me be awhile.

*Neoptolemus.*  Leave hold I will not.

*Philoctetes.*                    You will kill me, if
You touch me!

*Neoptolemus.*          I quit hold then, if indeed
You are more sober now.

*Philoctetes.*              Take me, O Earth,
Dying, as I am! for my infirmity
No longer lets me keep myself upright.

                    [*Throws himself on the ground.*

*Neoptolemus.*  It seems he will be fast asleep, ere long;
For see, his head sinks backward.   How the sweat
Stands over all his frame! and a black vein
Has opened on the surface of his foot,

Discharging blood.   Well, let us leave him, friends,
In quietness, till he has fallen asleep.

*Chorus.*    Sleep, thou that know'st not pain,
        That know'st not care,
    Blest and twice blest again,
        Come, with soft air !
    Keep from his eyes this light,
    Which overspreads our sight
    Now, of the noonday bright ;
        Come, saviour fair !

**1** *Scyrian.* [17]    Look, my son ; where standest thou ?
        How wilt thou proceed ?
    What shall be thy study now ?
        Dost thou see, and heed ?
    Wherefore are we lingering ?
    Time, that orders everything,
    To our very feet doth bring
        Power for all our need.

*Neoptolemus.*    He hears no sound, indeed ; but this is plain,
    For us to have his weapons is no gain,
        Sailing without himself.   Him God bade
            bring ;
        His is the garland ; and to boast in vain,
            And lie, and fail, is a disgraceful thing.

*Chorus.*    God will provide a way ;
        But as for thee,
    Low, low, my son, convey
        Thy words to me ;
    For of all souls that weep,
    Stricken with sickness deep,
    Their sleep, which is not sleep,
        Is quick to see.

**2** *Scyrian.*    Now, so far as thou hast power,
        Stealthily, my son,
    This examine, this explore,
        How it shall be done :
    For—thou knowest whom I would name—
    If your counsels are the same,
    There await you bale and blame
        Your prudence cannot shun.

*Chorus.*   The breeze blows fair, the breeze blows fair, my
        King;
    And without help, and without sight,
    Stretched out he lies, as in the night,
    (Sleep is good in the warm sun-light,)
Powerless of hand and foot and everything!
He sees not, looks not, answers not with speech.[18]
    More than the dead who are beneath at rest;
My son, so far as my poor thoughts can reach,
    The toil that has no risk is best.

*Neoptolemus.*  Peace, I say, and be careful; for the man
    Opens his eyes, and raises up his head.
*Philoctetes.*  O daylight, that receivest me from sleep!
    O sojourn unexpected of these strangers!
    I never could have boasted, O my son,
    That you would bear to abide my sufferings,
    With such compassion tarrying at my side
    To afford help.   Not so complacently
    Did the Atridæ, our brave generals,
    Bear to endure this plague! but, son of mine,
    For noble is your nature and your birth,
    You, though oppressed with noise and noisomeness,
    Made light of all these ills!   And now, my son,
    Since of my torment there does seem to be
    Some respite, some oblivion, raise me up
    With your own hand; set me upon my feet;
    So that, as soon as numbness gives me leave,
    We may proceed on board, and straightway sail.
*Neoptolemus.*  I am right glad to see you beyond hope
    Awake and still alive and without pain;
    For you did seem, being so far gone already,
    To all appearance, a dead man.   But now
    Raise yourself; or if you prefer it, these
    Shall carry you; for they will not grudge the trouble,
    When you and I both choose to have it so.
*Philoctetes.*  I thank you, son; raise me, as you are minded;
    But let these be, lest they be overcome,
    Before they need, with noisomeness.   Enough
    The task for them, to live with me on board.
*Neoptolemus.*  So be it.   But stand upright and take fast hold.
*Philoctetes.*  Fear not.   The old exercise will straighten me.

I

*Neoptolemus.* Alack! What next, in the world, am I to do?

*Philoctetes.* What is it, boy? what were you going to say?

*Neoptolemus.* I do not know what way I ought to turn
    My perplexed speech.

*Philoctetes.*                    But what perplexes you?
    Do not talk thus, my son!

*Neoptolemus.*                    Only already
    I have gone too far to help it.

*Philoctetes.*                    It is not
    The offence of my disease induces you
    Now to refuse to take me in your crew?

*Neoptolemus.* All is offence, when any man forsakes
    His proper self, to do what fits him not,

*Philoctetes.* But you, in aiding a good man, do nothing,
    Say nothing, to bely your parentage.

*Neoptolemus.* I shall be shamed. That is what tortures me.

*Philoctetes.* Never, by what you are doing! What you say
    Causes me fear.

*Neoptolemus.*            O Heavens, what shall I do?
    Must I be proved twice base, both hiding that
    I should not hide, and saying what is most shameful?

*Philoctetes.* If I am not a fool, this fellow seems
    Like to betray me, leave me, and so set sail!

*Neoptolemus.* Leave you? Oh no! Rather what tortures
    me
    Is that I am conveying you, to your sorrow!

*Philoctetes.* What say you, son? I do not understand.

*Neoptolemus.* I will hide nothing from you; 'tis to Troy
    You are to sail, to the Achaians, and
    The Atridæ's fleet.

*Philoctetes.*                    Woe's me! what did you say?

*Neoptolemus.* Do not cry out, before you are informed—

*Philoctetes.* Informed! of what? What would you do to
    me?

*Neoptolemus.* First cure you of this disease, and afterwards,
    Along with you, when I get there, storm Troy!

*Philoctetes.* And do you really mean to do it?

*Neoptolemus.*                                'Tis ruled
    By strong Necessity; pray, be not angry!

*Philoctetes.* I am undone, unhappy! I am betrayed!
    O stranger-guest, what hast thou done to me?—
    Give back my bow at once!

*Neoptolemus.*          That cannot be ;
    For duty and advantage both oblige me
    To obey those in power.

*Philoctetes.*         O thou fire !
    Thou universal horror !    Masterpiece
    Abominable, of monstrous villainy !
    What hast thou done to me ?    How hast thou
       cheated me !
    Art not ashamed, O rogue, to look at me
    Thy supplicant, me thy petitioner ?
    Thou hast robbed me of my life, taking my bow.
    Give it back, I beg thee !    Give it back, I pray !
    By our father's gods, son, do not take my life !
    Woe's me ! he does not even answer me !
    He means to keep it—see, he turns away !
    You bays, you promontories, O you haunts
    Of mountain brutes, O cliffs precipitous,
    To you—for other hearers have I none—
    Present, my old familiars, I appeal ;
    See how Achilles' son is wronging me ! [19]
    Swearing to take me home, to Troy he drags me ;
    And pledging his right hand, he has obtained—
    Relic of Jove-born Heracles—my bow,
    Meaning in the Argives' sight to flourish it ;
    Like some strong prisoner, by force he drags me,
    And knows not he is killing a dead man,
    A vapour's shadow, an unsubstantial shade !
    For in full strength he never had captured me,
    Since even thus he had not, save by guile ;
    But now, unhappy, I have been deceived.
    What must I do ?    Nay, give it back to me ;
    Nay, even yet, be thy true self once more ;
    What say'st thou ?    Thou art dumb !   I am lost,
       unhappy !
    O double-portalled frontal of the rock,
    Back, once again, I come and enter thee,
    Bare, without means of life ; but I shall starve
    Here, in the fields alone ; not killing now
    Winged bird, or silvan quarry, with my bow,
    But I myself, wretched, when I am dead,
    Yielding a meal to things on which I fed.
    Creatures I chased before will now chase me ;

And I shall pay for bloodshed with my blood,
By practice of a seeming innocent!
O may'st thou perish!—not yet, until I know
Whether thou wilt repent, and change thy purpose;
But if thou wilt not, evil be thine end!

*Enter* ULYSSES, *behind.*

1 *Scyrian.* What shall we do? For us to embark, sir king,
    Or yield to this man's prayers, now lies with you.
*Neoptolemus.* A strange compassion has come over me,
    Not now at first, but some time since, for him.
*Philoctetes.* Pity me, O boy, for Heaven's sake! Publish
    not
    Your own shame to the world, in cheating me!
*Neoptolemus.* O what am I to do? Would I had never
    Left Scyros! These things are so hard for me.
*Philoctetes.* You are not vile; but you have come, 'tis plain,
    Primed with disgraceful teaching, from the vile.
    Now take to other leaders, as is meet,
    And give me up my weapons, and set sail.
*Neoptolemus.* O men, what shall we do?
*Ulysses* (*advancing*).               What are you doing?
    You wicked knave! Come back! Give me that bow!
*Philoctetes.* O who is this? Ulysses do I hear?
*Ulysses.* Yes, to be sure, Ulysses; I am here.
*Philoctetes.* O, I am bought and sold! I am undone!
    Then it was he who was my kidnapper,
    Who robbed me of my weapons!
*Ulysses.*                       Doubtless, I;
    None else; that I avow.
*Philoctetes.*             Give back my bow,
    Give it me, boy!
*Ulysses.*            That shall he never do,
    Even if he would. Now, you must march with these,
    Or they shall force you.
*Philoctetes.*             They—by force—take me,
    O vilest and most impudent of men!
*Ulysses.* If you will not go freely.
*Philoctetes.*            O thou soil
    Of Lemnos! O thou all-subduing flame
    Lit by Hephæstus! Is it to be borne,
    That he should force me from your borders?

*Ulysses.* Zeus

It is, if you would know—Zeus, this land's master—
Zeus, who has willed these things.  His servant I.

*Philoctetes.* Caitiff, what words dost thou devise to say?
Alleging Gods, thou makest thy gods liars!

*Ulysses.* Not so, but faithful.  You are bound to go.

*Philoctetes.* No.

*Ulysses.* Yes, I say; you must obey me, here.

*Philoctetes.* Me miserable! my father, it appears,
Gat me no freeman, but a bond-slave!

*Ulysses.* Nay,
Peer of the best, with whom it is your fate
To storm Troy's walls, and to demolish them.

*Philoctetes.* No never, even in extremity,
While this firm steep of earth remains to me.

*Ulysses.* What would you?

*Philoctetes.* Leap head foremost off the rock,
From the top to the bottom, and dash out my brains!

*Ulysses.* Seize him! don't let him do it.

[PHILOCTETES *is seized.*

*Philoctetes.* O you hands,
How are you abused, for lack of your old string,
Made prisoners by this fellow!  Thou, whose thoughts
Are nowise wholesome, nowise generous,
How hast thou supplanted me!  How hast thou
stalked me!
Employing as a cover for thyself
This youth, unknown to me, unmeet for thee,
But meet, indeed, for me; who nothing knew,
Save to perform what was commanded him,
And even now feels manifest remorse
At his own errors, and my sufferings.
But thy base soul, peering through crannies ever,
Well, although simple and without his will,
Instructed him in evil, to be wise.
And now thou think'st to bind and carry me,
Wretch! from this beach, on which thou didst expose me
Friendless, forsaken, homeless, a dead corpse
Among the living.  Ah, perdition on thee!
Not seldom have I prayed that prayer for thee.
But—for the Gods allot me no good fortune—
Thou livest to rejoice, and I to grieve

At this same thing, that amid many ills
I live, unhappy, laughed to scorn by thee,
And the two captains, sons of Atreus,
Of whom, in this, thou art the minister.
Yet thou through trickery and by force constrained
Did'st sail with them; while I, thrice miserable,
Who volunteered, and brought seven ships with me,
Dishonoured am cast out—by them, thou sayest—
They say by thee!   And now, why do you hale me?
Why carry me away?   To what end?   Me,
Who nothing am, and am long dead, to you?
Abhorred of Heaven!   How is it I am not now
Lame, and of evil savour?   If I sail with you,
How will you manage to burn sacrifice
And pour libations any more to Heaven?
It was your pretext, in extruding me.
Perdition overwhelm you!   As it will,
If Gods love justice, for your wrongs to me.
And I am sure they do; for never else
Would you have sailed after a beggar thus;
But some remorse on my account, from Heaven,
Goaded you on.   But O my native land,
And you, regarding Gods! sooner or late,
If you have any pity left for me,
Grant vengeance, vengeance, vengeance on them all!
Miserable indeed I am; but I should feel
Cured of my plague, if I could see their fall!

1 *Scyrian.*   Ulysses, sorely angered is the man;
And sore the word which he has uttered here,
And unsubmissive to adversity.

*Ulysses.*   I might say much in answer, had I time;
Now, I am master of one thing to say:
Where such-an-one is needed, such am I!
Where there is trial who is just, who brave,
You will not find a man more scrupulous.
No doubt, by nature I am covetous
Of success everywhere; but not with you;
Now, willingly, I will give place to you;
Yes, let him go; do not keep hold of him;
Let him stay here.   We have no use for you,
Now we have got these arms; for we have Teucer
Among us, who has learnt this mystery

And I, too, think that I can draw the string
And point the arrow just as well as you.
What need of you, then?   To your heart's content
Pace Lemnos up and down!   But let us go;
And your reward, it may be, shall confer
Honour on me, which was by rights your own.

*Philoctetes.* What shall I do?   Alas, shall you be seen
    Graced with my arms among the Argives?

*Ulysses.*                          Nay,
    Make me no answer; I am going, I say.

*Philoctetes.* Seed of Achilles, will you go away
    Thus?   Shall I never hear your accents more?

*Ulysses.* Go forward.   Though you be magnanimous,
    Regard him not, lest you should spoil our luck

*Philoctetes.* O sirs, shall I be left here desolate
    By you as well?   Will not you pity me?

1 *Scyrian.* Our captain is this youth; all that he tells you,
    That we say also.

*Neoptolemus.*             By Ulysses here
I shall be told that I am pitiful;
Nevertheless, if this man wishes it,
Until the crew have got the ship's gear ready,
And we have offered up our prayers to Heaven,
Tarry; meantime, perhaps he may take thought
More kindly on us.   Now let us twain set forward;
Do you make haste to follow, when we call.

                 [*Exeunt* Ulysses *and* Neoptolemus,

## I. 1.

*Philoctetes.* Thou nook of the rock—thou cave,
        Now sultry, now icy chill,
    Was it fated never to be
    That I might depart from thee?
        Must thou hold to me still
    In dying, and be my grave?
    Say, O thou dolorous lair
    That rang to my despair,
      Where now shall I seek for store?
        How get my daily bread?
        Ye flutterers overhead,
    Fly on, through whistling air!
      I stay you now no more.

*Chorus.* Surely thyself, thyself would have it so,
         O victim of the curse !
Not from without, not from a stronger foe
         Does this mischance arise,
When, having it in thy power to be wise,
Thou turnest from the better lot to what is worse !

### I. 2.

*Philoctetes.* Ah wretched—wretched indeed,
         Toilworn and pitiful I,
     Who henceforth tarrying here,
     Without one comrade near,
         Must live on ever, and die !
Bringing home no game at need,
     None, on wings of the bow,
     By mastering hands laid low ;
         But a tale of cunning design,
         Close hidden, unscanned by me,
         Beguiled me ! O might I see
That trickster doomed to a woe
     As long, as cruel as mine !

*Chorus.* Destiny, destiny brought thee to this end,
         Sent by the powers divine ;
Thou wert defrauded by no hand of mine ;
         Keep thou for others, friend,
     Thy bitter boding curse ; for as for me,
This is my care, that thou repel not amity.

### II. 1.

*Philoctetes.* Somewhere now, seated by the sea
         Upon the foam-white strand,
     He mocks at me—Ah woe is me !
         And tosses in his hand
What no man ever took away—
What gave me meat from day to day.

O bow of mine, from hands of mine
         Ravished—how pityingly,
Surely, thou must thy gaze incline—
         If thou hast sense—toward me,
The friend of Heracles of yore,
Me, that may use thee now no more !

Now thou art handled in my place
  By a right cunning lord,
And viewest his deceits how base,
  And him, the foe abhorred,
By whose unworthy arts arose
For me—O Zeus![20] a thousand woes.

*Chorus.*    He acts a manly part
Who justifies whatever makes for gain,
    And, while so doing, yet refrains to dart
A tongue of malice forth, to inflict pain.
Chosen out of many for the task, that king,
    In following the behest
Of those who sent him, was accomplishing
    Succour for all the rest.


## II. 2.

*Philoctetes.* Come hither you wild feathered brood,
    And tribes of fierce-eyed beasts,
Who on these mountains seek your food,
    Whom this lone island feasts;
No longer from your lairs take flight;
I wield no more those shafts of might.

Alas for my unhappy lot!
    No longer need you fear;
Weak is the watch that guards this spot;
    Now is your time!   Draw near,
Avenge you, glut you, freely dine
On this infected flesh of mine!

My breath of life is well nigh spent;
    Whence shall I get me bread?
What mortal can find nourishment
    Merely by breezes fed,
Of nothing, henceforth, making spoil
In all the foison of the soil?

*Chorus.*    If thou at all hold dear
The friendly stranger, who in all good will
    Draws near to thee, prythee do thou draw near;
Learn, and learn well, 'tis not beyond thy skill

To turn thy back upon this destiny,
So piteous to sustain,
So checkless of the manifold misery
That follows in its train.

### III.

*Philoctetes.* Again, again
Thou dost remind me of mine ancient pain,
O best of all who have been here as yet!
Ah, why would'st thou undo me?
Oh what hast thou done to me?

1 *Scyrian.* Why say'st thou this?
*Philoctetes.* Because thy hopes are set
On carrying me to that same Trojan land
Which I detest!

1 *Scyrian.* Yea, for I think that best,
*Philoctetes.* Begone at once! Leave me behind!
1 *Scyrian.* Welcome, right welcome to me is this command,
Which I right gladly obey.
Away, away,
Let us aboard, each to his place assigned.

*Philoctetes.* For God's sake, I adjure you, leave me not!
Nay I beseech you!

1 *Scyrian.* Soft!
*Philoctetes.* O strangers, stay,
In Heaven's name!

1 *Scyrian.* What
Criest thou?
*Philoctetes.* Alas, destiny, destiny!
O foot, my foot, what shall I do with thee
In all my after life? O woe is me!
O strangers, come, come back, come back again!

1 *Scyrian.* What, to do something different
From that thou didst set forth as thine intent?
*Philoctetes.* Let it not give offence
That reeling under a tempestuous pain
I cry aloud, words without sense!

### IV.

1 *Scyrian.* Come, poor sufferer, as we counsel thee.
*Philoctetes.* Never, never, know it for certainty!

Not though he, whose hand
Wields the lightning brand,
With its meteor rays
Should set me all ablaze!
Down with Troy—with all
Those beneath its wall—
All who had the heart
To banish far apart
This limb—this foot of mine!
But O my friends, incline
One boon to accord, I pray!

1 *Scyrian.* What would'st thou really say?

*Philoctetes.* Reach me, if you have it, here
A sword, an axe, or spear.

1 *Scyrian.* So you may do—what violent deed, I wonder?

*Philoctetes.* Cut flesh from bone—hew joint from joint asunder!
Death—death is my desire.

1 *Scyrian.* How so?

*Philoctetes.*       Seeking my sire.

1 *Scyrian.* Where, on earth?

*Philoctetes.*            In the Grave.
For now no more, I know,
Lives he beneath the sun.—
O city, O native city,
Might I but see thee, I, the man they pity,
Who left thy sacred wave,
And went as aider to the Danaan foe!
—My days are done.     [*Retires.*

1 *Scyrian.* By this you would have seen me, some time since,
Marching to join my ship, but that I marked
Ulysses coming, and Achilles' son
Drawing nigh toward us.

*Enter* ULYSSES *and* NEOPTOLEMUS.

*Ulysses.*            Will you not declare
Upon what errand you are creeping back,
Hastening so eagerly?

*Neoptolemus.*         Yes, to undo
The wrong I did before.

*Ulysses.*         Monstrous! What wrong?

*Neoptolemus.* That at your word and the whole host's—

*Ulysses.* You did
A deed—of what kind, unbecoming you?
*Neoptolemus.* Catching a man by shameful frauds and tricks—
*Ulysses.* What man?  O Heavens! have you some new
design—
*Neoptolemus.* No, nothing new; to Pœas' offspring, though—
*Ulysses.* What will you do?  Truly I am afraid—
*Neoptolemus.* From whom I had these weapons, back once
more—
*Ulysses.* O Zeus, what will you say?  You do not mean,
Surely, to yield them?
*Neoptolemus.* Yes, for shamefully
And against justice I gat hold of them.
*Ulysses.* 'Fore Heaven, do you say this to outrage me?
*Neoptolemus.* If to speak truth is outrage?
*Ulysses.* What is this,
Achilles' son?  What have you said?
*Neoptolemus.* Desire you
I should repeat the same words twice and thrice?
*Ulysses.* I should have wished to hear them not at all!
*Neoptolemus.* Be well assured, you have heard me out.
*Ulysses.* There is—
There is a man to stop your doing so.
*Neoptolemus.* What!
Who is there who will stop my doing it?
*Ulysses.* The whole Achaian people, I for one.
*Neoptolemus.* Wise as you are, you utter nothing wise.
*Ulysses.* You neither say nor seek to do things wise.
*Neoptolemus.* If acts are just, they are better than if wise.
*Ulysses.* How just—what by my counsels you obtained,
That to surrender back?
*Neoptolemus.* The sin I sinned
To my own shame, I will essay to mend.
*Ulysses.* And in so doing not fear the Achaian host?
*Neoptolemus.* Being in the right, I quail not at **your**
menace.
It is no force of yours which I obey,
Thus acting.
*Ulysses.* Not the Trojans, then, but you
Will I assail in fight!
*Neoptolemus.* Come what come may!
*Ulysses.* See you this right hand feeling for the hilt?

*Neoptolemus.* Ay? You will find me playing at that same
　　　game,
　　And ready, too!

*Ulysses.* 　　　　　　Nay, I will let you be.
　　Rather I will depart and tell the tale
　　To the whole army, which shall punish you. [*Retires.*

*Neoptolemus.* You are discreet; and if you prove as wise
　　Always, perhaps you will escape scot-free.
　　Thou son of Pœas, Philoctetes! Ho!
　　Come out, and leave this rock-built tenement!

*Philoctetes* (*within*). What new alarm is thundering at my
　　　cave?
　　What would you, sirs? Why do you call me forth?

(*Entering*). Ha, 'tis ill done! Are you not come to add
　　Some heavy suffering to my sufferings?

*Neoptolemus.* 　　　　　　　　Nay,
　　Fear nothing; hear the words I am come to say.

*Philoctetes.* I am afraid; I trusted you before,
　　And through fair words fared foully.

*Neoptolemus.* 　　　　　　　　Is it not
　　Within the bounds, that one may turn again?

*Philoctetes.* Just such you were when you purloined my
　　　weapons,
　　In language honest, secretly my bane.

*Neoptolemus.* But not so now. Still, I would hear from you
　　Whether you are minded to persist in staying,
　　Or to set sail with us.

*Philoctetes.* 　　　　　Stop, say no more;
　　For all that you can say will be in vain.

*Neoptolemus.* So resolved are you?

*Philoctetes.* 　　　　　　As I say, and more so.

*Neoptolemus.* I wish you would have hearkened to my
　　　words;
　　But if I am not speaking seasonably,
　　I have done.

*Philoctetes.* 　　　Yes, all you say will be in vain;
　　For you shall never find me favourable,
　　Who have by guile robbed me of my livelihood,
　　And after, come to give advice to me—
　　Offspring most vile, of a most worthy sire!
　　Destruction seize you all! the Atridæ first,
　　Next Lartius' son, and you!

*Neoptolemus.*                               Curse us no further;
But come and take your weapons from my hand.
*Philoctetes.* What? Am I being beguiled a second time?
*Neoptolemus.* The holy majesty of Jove most high
Bear witness—no!
*Philoctetes.*                               O sayer of sweetest things—
If you speak truth!
*Neoptolemus* (*giving the bow and arrows*). The deed **shall**
testify.
Stretch out your hand, and repossess your weapons.
*Ulysses* (*advancing*). In the Atridæ's name, and the whole
host's,
That I forbid! Be the Gods witnesses!
*Philoctetes.* Whose voice—was it Ulysses'—that I heard,
My son?
*Ulysses.*                               Doubt it not! and you see me ready
To pack you off, by force, to Troia's shores,
Whether Achilles' son consents, or no.
*Philoctetes.* At your cost be it, unless this dart go wrong!
*Neoptolemus.* Nay, by no means! For Heaven's sake do **not**
shoot!
*Philoctetes.* Let go my hand, dear boy, for Heaven's sake!
*Neoptolemus.*                                                              **No,**
I will not.                               [*Exit* ULYSSES.
*Philoctetes.*                 Oh, why did you frustrate me
In slaying an adversary and enemy
With my own shafts?
*Neoptolemus.*                               Because 'twere honourable
Neither for you nor me.
*Philoctetes.*                               Of this, at least,
Be certain; that the army's foremost men,
The falsehood-mongers of the Achaian host,
Are brave in words, but cowards at the steel!
*Neoptolemus.* So be it. You have your bow, and need **not**,
now,
Feel indignation or despite at me.
*Philoctetes.* Yes, you have shewn the nature, O my child,
From which you sprang; no son of Sisyphus,
But of Achilles, who was praised the most
Among the living, when he was alive,
And is, among the dead.
*Neoptolemus.*                               It pleases me

That you should praise my father, and myself;
Still, hear what I would have you do for me;
There is necessity for men to endure
The fortunes given from Heaven; but whosoe'er
Lies under voluntary miseries,
As you do, it is right that none on such
Should bestow pardon, or should pity them.
But you are savage, and reject advice,
If a man warn you kindly; deeming him,
For very hate, an adversary and foe.
Yet I will speak, yea, and by Zeus I swear it;
And know this well, and write it on your heart;
I tell you, you are sick of this disease
By Heaven's decree, for coming near the guard
Who watches over the hypæthral close
Of Chrysa—the concealed snake-sentinel;
And you shall never find a cure, be certain,
Of your sore malady, while the same sun
Rises on this side and on that goes down,
Till of your own will you shall come to Troy,
And meet Asclepius' sons, who are in our ranks,
And so be lightened of your plague, and then
With these your arrows, and with me to aid,
Conquer the city's towers before them all!
How do I know all this? Why, I will tell you;
There is a man of Troy prisoner to us,
Helenus, a seer of seers; and he says plainly
That these things so must be; and furthermore
That it is doomed, by the next harvest-time,
All Troy should fall; else, if he lie in this,
He is willing to pay forfeit by his death.
Now you know all, choose to agree with us!
For honourable is the accruing gain,
If you, being singled out for the Greeks' champion,
Should come to healing hands, and therewithal,
Win glory in the highest, by taking Troy,
That city of many woes!

*Philoctetes.*                    Detested life!
Why dost thou hold me above ground, yet seeing, —
O why not let me go, down to the grave?
Alas, what shall I do? How can I be
Deaf to his words, my friendly counsellor?

Am I to yield, then? How, an if I do,
Shall I go forth—wretch—in the face of day?
With whom shall I consort? How, O you eyes,
The witnesses of all things done to me,
Will you endure my having fellowship
With Atreus' offspring, who destroyed me? How
With the pernicious son of Lartius?
For it is not the pain of what is past
That galls me; but I fancy I foresee
What at their hands I needs must yet endure.
For those who have begotten evil deeds
Of their own minds, are by their own minds trained
In all things else to evil. And in this
I am surprised at you; for it was right
That you should never go to Troy, yourself,
Nay, should keep me away; and, for the men
Who wronged you, spoiling you of your father's
    treasure,
Who judged the hapless Ajax not so worthy
Of your sire's weapons, as Ulysses [21]—what!
Will you join league with them, and force me to it?
Not so my son! but as you sware to me,
Carry me home; stay you in Scyros; leave
Wretches like them to perish wretchedly!
So will you gain a twofold gratitude,
From me and from my father, and not come,
Through helping villains, to resemble them.

*Neoptolemus.* All that you say is fair; still, I desire
    That trusting to the Gods, and to my story,
    You would consent to sail, and leave this land,
    Under my friendly convoy.

*Philoctetes.*                     What, to Troy?
    To the detested son of Atreus?
    With this unlucky foot?

*Neoptolemus.*                  Rather, to those
    Who shall relieve you and this ulcerous limb
    From torment, and redeem you from disease.

*Philoctetes.* O sayer of strange things, what words are
    these?

*Neoptolemus.* What will end well, I know, for both of us.

*Philoctetes.* And in saying this have you no dread of Heaven?

*Neoptolemus.* What dread should a man have, of profiting?

*Philoctetes.* Profit to me, or the Atridæ?
*Neoptolemus.*                               Why
          To you; being friendly, and my advice the same.
*Philoctetes.* Friendly, and want to give me to my foes?
*Neoptolemus.* O sir, learn to be prudent, in your troubles.
*Philoctetes.* I know that you will ruin me, by this tale.
*Neoptolemus.* I shall not; but I say, you grow no wiser.
*Philoctetes.* Do I not know the Atridæ cast me out?
*Neoptolemus.* But how if they will bring you safely back?
*Philoctetes.* To behold Troy?  Never, with my good will!
*Neoptolemus.* Then what is to be done, if I in talk
          Fail to persuade you to do aught I say?
          'Twere easiest I should cease from words, and you
          Live on, as now, without deliverance.
*Philoctetes.* Leave me to suffer that which I must suffer.
          But what you promised, giving me your hand,
          To send me home—this, my son, do, I pray you;
          And do not linger, or take further thought
          On Troy; Troy has made sorrow enough for me.
*Neoptolemus.* If you will, let us be going.
*Philoctetes.*                               O well said, at length
*Neoptolemus.* Lean on me as you are walking.
*Philoctetes.*                               Yea, with all my strength.
*Neoptolemus.* But how shall I avoid the Greeks' anger?
*Philoctetes.*                                         Never care!
*Neoptolemus.* What if they lay waste my country?
*Philoctetes.*                               Shall not I be there?
*Neoptolemus.* What assistance will you bring us?
*Philoctetes.*                               With Heracles' bow—
*Neoptolemus.* How say you?
*Philoctetes.*               I will repel them.
*Neoptolemus.*                               Kiss the soil, here, and go.


                    *Enter* HERACLES, *above.*

*Heracles.* Nay, not yet; first hear my precepts,
          Child of Pœas!  It is thy privilege
          Thou should'st list to Alcides' accents,
          Thou should'st see him!  I come, forsaking
          Seats ethereal, for thy benefit,
          Merely to tell thee Jove's high counsel,
          Merely to hinder

That mad course thou followest.  Do thou
Give good heed to the words I say.—

And first I will inform thee of my fortunes,
How after all my labours past and done
I have attained to immortality,
As thou may'st witness.   And thyself, be sure,
Must go through this experience, and so make,
By these thy labours, thy life glorious.
Go with this man to Troy; there first of all
Thou shalt be healed of pitiful disease,
And chosen first in prowess of the host,
Shalt deprive Paris with my shafts of life,
The causer of these ills; and shalt take Troy,
And to thy halls send booty, by the host
Awarded thee for prize, to thy sire's dwelling,
Pœas, in Œta's upland, thine own land.
And of what spoils that host shall give thee,
    bring,
For my bow's work, a tribute to my pyre.²²
—You too, son of Achilles, I exhort;
For neither have you power to capture Troy
Without his aid, nor he apart from you;
But like two lions ranging side by side
Each be the other's guard.
[*To Philoctetes.*]          —Lo, I will send
Asclepius to Troy, to cure your sickness;
For needs must Ilium a second time
Fall by my arrows.   But remember well,
When you lay waste the land, to have respect
For what is due to Heaven; for all things else
Stand in the counsels of our father Jove
Second to this.   The praise of piety ²³
Cleaves to a mortal in his hour of death,
Nor perishes, whether he die or live.

*Philoctetes.* O thou whose accents, long desired, I hear,
    Whose face, though late, I see, unto thy precepts
    I will not be rebellious.

*Neoptolemus.*                    No, nor I.

*Heracles.* No longer, then, delay to accomplish them;
    Time and the wind astern urge on to sail.

                                    [*Disappears.*

*Philoctetes.* One greeting to the country, ere I go.

Farewell to the old familiar cave,
To the roaring bass [24] of the breaking wave
    And the Naiads of the dale !
Where many a time my hair was wet,
Deep in the inmost nook beset,
    Lashed by a southern gale !

Where often the voice of my lament
Amid the storm was backward sent,
    Echoed from Hermes' brow ;
O springs, with your liquid Lycian freight,
Never expecting a joy so great,
    I leave you—I leave you now !

Farewell to the sea-girt Lemnian land !
Give us good convoy from the strand,
    Where friendly counsels lead,
And the prevailing word of Doom,
And the all-mastering Power, by whom
    These issues were decreed.

CHORUS.

All together on our way
Let us to the Sea Nymphs pray
To prosper our return this day.

                     *[Exeunt omnes.*

# OEDIPUS COLONEUS

---

## PERSONS REPRESENTED

OEDIPUS.

ANTIGONE, } *his daughters.*
ISMENE,

THESEUS, *king of Athens.*

CREON.

POLYNICES, *son to Œdipus.*

*A Stranger, an inhabitant of Colonus.*

*A Messenger, an Athenian attending on Theseus.*

The CHORUS *is composed of citizens of Colonus.*

*Guards attending on Theseus and Creon.*

*An attendant following Ismene.*

---

*Scene, Colonus, before the Sacred Grove of the Erinyes.*

*Enter* OEDIPUS *and* ANTIGONE.

*Œdipus.* Antigone, child of a blind old man,
  What lands are these, or what the folk whose gates
  We have attained?  Who shall receive to-day
  With stinted alms the wanderer Œdipus ?—
  Asking but little ; than that little still
  Obtaining less ; and yet enough for me.
  For my afflictions and the weight of years
  And something, too, of my own dignity
  Teach me contentment.  If you see, my child,
  Some resting-place, either by sacred grove
  Or secular dwelling, stay me and set me down,
  That we may find out in what place we are ;
  For strangers from inhabitants to learn
  We are come hither ; and what we hear, to do it.
*Antigone.* Towers are there, O my father, Œdipus,
  Covering a city, I perceive, afar ;

256

This place, as I suppose, is consecrate;
It blooms with laurel, olive and the vine;
Thick-flying nightingales within it warble;
Here stretch thy limbs, upon this rough-hewn stone;
For thou art aged to have come so far.

*Œdipus.* Seat me and guard me still; for I am blind.
*Antigone.* I know—that is an old tale—tell not me.
*Œdipus.* Well, can you teach me whither we are come?
*Antigone.* To Athens, that I know; but not the quarter.
*Œdipus.* So much we heard from every passenger.
*Antigone.* But shall I go and ask what place it is?
*Œdipus.* Why yes, my child; if it seems hospitable.[1]
*Antigone.* O yes, there are some dwellings.—There's no need,
    I think: for here's a man, I see, close to us.
*Œdipus.* What, moving and approaching hitherward?
*Antigone.* Yes, here, I mean, at hand. Say what is needful;
    This is the man.

*Enter a Stranger, an inhabitant of Colonus.*

*Œdipus.*                  Stranger, this maiden tells me
(Whose eyesight serves both for herself and me)
Of your approach, an apt intelligencer
Of things we cannot guess—
*Stranger.*               Ere you ask further
Come from that seat; you trespass on a place
No foot may desecrate.
*Œdipus.*               What is the place?
To what God dedicated?
*Stranger.*            It is kept
From touch or dwelling: the dread Goddesses
Hold it, the daughters of the Earth and Gloom.
*Œdipus.* Who? By what solemn name denominate
Might I invoke them?
*Stranger.*            By the natives here
They would be called the All-seeing Favourers;
Other fit names elsewhere.
*Œdipus.*            May they receive
With mercy me their suppliant; and I
From this land's harbour will go forth no more!
*Stranger.* What does this mean?
*Œdipus.*             'Tis my misfortunes' weird.

*Stranger.* Truly I dare not turn him out, before
    I tell the rest—without authority.

*Œdipus.* Sir, in Heaven's name do not begrudge me—me
    A wanderer—what I crave of you to say!

*Stranger.* Explain, and I will show I grudge you not.

*Œdipus.* What ground is this we have been treading on?

*Stranger.* You shall hear all I know.  First the whole place
      is holy,
    Inhabited by dread Poseidon; next
    The Deity that brought fire abides in it,
    Titan Prometheus; this same spot you press
    They call the Brass-paved Causeway of the land—
    Rampart of Athens; the adjoining farms
    Boast them Colonus mounted on his horse
    For their chief patron, and the people all
    Are called by and in common bear his name.
    These are the facts,[2] sir stranger; honoured not
    So much in story, as cherished on the spot.

*Œdipus.* Did you say any men lived hereabouts?

*Stranger.* Yes truly, and that they bear this Hero's name.

*Œdipus.* Have they a chief, or lies it with the folk
    To hold debate?

*Stranger.*               These parts are in the rule
    Of the king of the City.

*Œdipus.*              Who is he whose might
    And counsel sway them?

*Stranger.*              Theseus is his name,
    Old Ægeus' son.

*Œdipus.*              Would one of you go fetch him?

*Stranger.* What should one tell or move him to come here
    for?

*Œdipus.* Say, to gain much by a small act of kindness.

*Stranger.* And where's the service in a man that's blind?

*Œdipus.* There will be eyes in all that I shall say.

*Stranger.* Come, this you may, sir, and without offence;
    (Since you are worshipful to look upon,
    Saving God's hand;) stay there where I first found
      you,
    While I go tell this to the burghers round,
    (Here, not in the city;) they will soon decide
    If you shall tarry, or depart once more.     [*Exit.*

*Œdipus.* My daughter, has the stranger gone away?

*Antigone.* Yes, he has gone.   You may say anything
　　　Securely, father; none are here but I.
*Œdipus.* Queens, with stern faces!   since of all this land
　　　First in your sanctuary I seated me,
　　　To Phœbus, as to me, turn no deaf ear,
　　　Who, prophesying of those my many woes,
　　　Spake of this respite for me at the last
　　　That when my journey ended, in a land
　　　Where I should find asylum, at the shrine
　　　Of awful Powers, and hospitality,
　　　There I should round the goal of my life-sorrow,
　　　There dwell, a blessing to my hosts—a curse
　　　To those who sent me into banishment;
　　　Giving me rede a sign of this should come,
　　　In earthquake, thunder, or lightning out of heaven.
　　　Now I perceive it is from none but you,
　　　The faithful omen that has guided me
　　　Along my pathway hither to this grove.
　　　Else I should never in my wayfaring
　　　Have met you first so fitly—strangers you
　　　To wine, as I am—or have taken seat
　　　Upon this awful footstone, all unhewn.
　　　Now therefore, Goddesses, bestow on me,
　　　According to Apollo's oracle,
　　　Some passing, some quick finish of my life;
　　　If I appear not still unperfected [3]
　　　In my continual servitude of toils,
　　　The extremest mortals know.   Come, you kind
　　　　　daughters
　　　Of ancient Gloom!   Come, thou that bear'st the
　　　　　name
　　　Of mightiest Pallas, Athens, first of cities,
　　　Have pity upon this miserable ghost
　　　Of what was Œdipus!   He is not now
　　　Such as of old.
*Antigone.*　　　　　　　Hush! there are people coming,
　　　Elders in years, who note you where you sit.
*Œdipus.* I will be silent, and do you conceal me
　　　Apart within the grove, till I may learn
　　　What language these men hold; for in the knowledge
　　　Prudence consists for what we have to do.
　　　　　　　　　　[*Œdipus and* ANTIGONE *retire.*

*Enter Citizens of Colonus, as Chorus.*

*Chorus.*   Look! Who was it? Where abides he?
     In what nook or corner hides he—
Of all men—of all mankind the most presuming?
     Search about.   Spy him, there!
     Seek him out everywhere.
A vagrant—some vagrant the grey-beard must have been,
     None of our countrymen.
Otherwise he never would have dreamt of coming
To the untrodden thicket of the Virgins here,
Of the mighty Powers, whom to name we fear,
     Whose abode we pass unprying,
     Without babble or loud crying,
     Keeping mouth closely pent
     Save on what is innocent.
     Now, 'tis said, void of dread,
Some one has intruded on the sacred space;
     I the bound searching round
Cannot yet alight upon his hiding place.

*Œdipus* (*advancing, with Antigone*). I am the man; for by
     the sound I see you,
     As is the saying.
*1 Citizen.*          Hilloa! hoa! who is this,
     Dreadful to see, dreadful to hear?
*Œdipus.*          I pray you,
     Do not regard me as a trespasser—
*1 Citizen.* Averting Jove! who may this old man be?
*Œdipus.* One of a sort far other than the first
     To be deemed happy, O you guardians
     Over this land; I am myself the proof;
     I should not otherwise be groping thus,
     Led by another's eyesight, or, being great,
     On slender moorings come to anchorage.

*Chorus.*   Eh thine eyes! thy blind eyes!
     Wert thou thus, as I surmise, [4]
For sad life—for long life—equipped from life's beginning?
     None the more, if so be,
     Shalt thou score, spite of me,
On curses fresh curses, by sinning—yea, by sinning.

But that thou trespass not
On the grassy coverts of this hallowed spot,
Where the bowl of water by the herbage quaffed
Flows with mingled runnels of a sweetened draught—
    Beware, beware sirrah stranger!
    Get thee hence! Avoid thy danger!
    (His long start costs me dear;)
    Thou tired vagabond, dost hear?
    Though thou bring word or thing
Hither for debate, avoid the sacred glen!
    Passing where all may fare
Speak with freedom; but refrain thee, until then!

*Œdipus.* Daughter, what course is to be thought of, now?
*Antigone.* My father, what the citizens observe
    That should we also; yield in what we must,
    And hearken. [5]
*Œdipus.*              Well, give me a hand.
*Antigone.*                              You have it.
*Œdipus.* Sirs, let me meet no wrong, if I remove
    Trusting in you.
  *Citizen.*            Never against thy will
    Out of these sanctuaries, ancient sir,
    Shall any drag thee.
*Œdipus.*                  Am I to proceed?
1 *Citizen.* Yes, further yet.
*Œdipus.*                    Still further?
1 *Citizen.*                            Damsel, lead,
    And bring him further on; for you perceive.
*Antigone.* Follow, my father, follow in my train,
    With feet all darkling.
1 *Citizen.*                  Man of woes, endure,
    Being as thou art, a stranger on strange soil,
    To abhor whate'er the City has held in hate,
    And what She loves, to honour.
*Œdipus.*                          Come, my child,
    Lead me where, stepping without sacrilege,
    Something we may impart, something receive;
    And let us not contend with fate.
1 *Citizen.*                          Halt there!
    No further bend thy steps, over that ramp
    Of rock in front.

*Œdipus.*                    What, thus?

1 *Citizen.*                        Yes, as you have it.

*Œdipus.* May I be seated? [6]

1 *Citizen.*                    Yes, if you bend sideways,
And sit down low, just on the edge of the stone.

*Antigone.* Father, this is my office; gently take
One step with my step, and commit—

*Œdipus.*                        Eh me!

*Antigone.* Thine aged frame to loving hand of mine.

*Œdipus (seated).* Ah, my misfortune!

1 *Citizen.*                    Man of woes, declare
(Now that thou art at ease) what was thy birth,
What toil-worn wanderer thou art, what country
We are to know for thine.

*Œdipus.*                    Ah strangers,
I am an outcast; but forbear, forbear—

1 *Citizen.* Why do you put this matter from you, sir?

*Œdipus.* Forbear, I say, to ask me what I am,
Nor seek nor question further.

1 *Citizen.*                        Wherefore so?

*Œdipus.* Awful my birth.

1 *Citizen.*                Tell it.

*Œdipus.*                        O child—ah me,
What must I answer?

1 *Citizen.*                    Of what seed thou art
Of the father's side, sir, say.

*Œdipus.*        -                Woe's me, my child,
What will become of me?

*Antigone.*                Speak, for you tread
The very verge.

*Œdipus.*            I will; I have no refuge.

1 *Citizen.* Ye are both long about it; make more speed!

*Œdipus.* Know ye of one from Laius—

1 *Citizen.*                        Ha, how? how?

*Œdipus.* And of the race of Labdacus—

1 *Citizen.*                        O Jove!

*Œdipus.* Miserable Œdipus?

1 *Citizen.*                And art thou he?

*Œdipus.* Have ye no fear at what I say—

*Citizens.*                        Oh! oh!

*Œdipus.* Unhappy!

*Citizens.*        Out, O out!

*Œdipus.*                          Now, daughter,
    What must we look for next?
*Citizens.*                          Off, off,
    Out of the place!
*Œdipus.*                    And what you promised me,
    What will you make of that?

*Chorus.*  No retribution hath Fortune in store
    For the man who requites what he suffered before;
    Treason, by treason withstood, and surpassed,
    Pays a man trouble, not favour, at last.
    Now back with you, back!   You have sailing orders.
    Get out of this place!   Go forth from our borders!
    Bring to our gates no more evil fates!
*Antigone.*  Pious strangers,
    Although you brook not
  The old man's presence, my father, here,
    To what he did
    (Though not with purpose)
  Listening, lending an open ear,
  Me, not the less, poor maid, I entreat,
  Pity, O strangers, who fall at your feet—
  Fall at your feet, for my father's sake only
    With eyes unblasted facing your face,
    Even as though born one of your race,
  So mercy may light on the helpless and lonely!
  On you, as on Heaven, we depend; reject not
  The prayer of the poor, for grace we expect not.
  By all you hold dear as your own heart's blood!
  By your brood!  By your bed!  By your need!  **By**
    your God!
  You will find no man, searching with heed,
  But he must follow, if God lead.

1 *Citizen.*  Daughter of Œdipus, both him and you,
    Trust us, we pity alike, in your distress;
    But, reverencing Heaven, we have no power
    To go beyond what has been told you now.
*Œdipus.*  What is the use of reputation, then,
    Or what of good report, flowing all to nothing,
    If it be said of Athens, that she is
    The most religious and the only state
    Able to guard the stranger in distress,

And that she only can suffice his need,
While you—to me—what have you done with it?
Who from these steps dislodged me, and then, in fear
Of my name, merely, are expelling me;
For of my person it is not, or my deeds;
The things I did were rather done to me—
If I must speak of that my parentage,
For which, as well I know, you are scared at me.
And after all, where was my villainy?
I but requited evil done to me;
So that, although I did it knowingly,
Not even then should I be proved a villain.
But as it is, I went the way I went
Unwittingly; and suffered at the hands
Of those who knew that they were injuring me.
Wherefore in Heaven's name I beseech you, sirs,
Even as you raised me from my seat, now save me,
And do not, in your reverence for Gods,
Make nought of the Gods' dues; rather consider
How that they mark the virtuous among men,
And mark the wicked too; and that escape
Was never yet, of any man profane.
In whose obedience tarnish not the fame
Of Athens the august, lending your hand
To any act of profanation.   No!
As you received the suppliant, on your promise,
So rescue and preserve me; and survey
These brows, of ill aspect, not without honour.
For holy and righteous am I, who come hither,
And I bring profit to these citizens;
And when that lord arrives, who is your leader,
If you will hearken, I will tell you all;
In the mean time see that you deal not falsely.

1 *Citizen.* We needs must feel a certain awe, old man,
  At that which you suggest; for it is couched
  In words of no light weight.   Sufficeth us
  That the land's rulers should decide the case.

*Œdipus.* And where is he who rules this country, sirs?

1 *Citizen.* He keeps his father's hold, here; but a post,
  The same who sent me hither, is gone to fetch him.

*Œdipus.* Do you suppose he will give heed, or take,
  For a blind man, the trouble to draw near.

*1 Citizen.* Ay truly, when he hears your name.

*Œdipus.* But who
Is there to tell him that?

*1 Citizen.* 'Tis a long way;
But travellers' gossip often gets abroad,
Which when he hears, he will come, never fear.
For far and wide, old man, has your name travelled;
So that, although he sleep, and tarry long,
Hearing of you, he will make haste and come.

*Œdipus.* I wish he may, for his own city's good
And mine. For who does not befriend himself
By doing good?

*Antigone.* O Jove, what shall I say?
What shall I think, my father?

*Œdipus.* But what is it,
Antigone, my child?

*Antigone.* I see a woman
Coming toward us, mounted on a horse
Of Ætnean breed; and a Thessalian bonnet
Is on her head, tied close about her face,
To screen it from the sun. What shall I say?
Is it—or not? or do my thoughts mislead?
Yes! No! I know not what to say. Alack,
It is no other. Yes, and she looks joyful
At spying me, as she draws near, and shews
It is no other than Ismene's self!

*Œdipus.* How say you, child?

*Antigone.* Why, that I see your child,
My sister; you can tell her by the voice.

*Enter* ISMENE *and attendant.*

*Ismene.* Father—and sister! the two names to me
That are most dear! How hardly have I found you,
And hardly can regard you now, for grief!

*Œdipus.* O child, are you come hither?

*Ismene.* O my father,
Hapless to look on!

*Œdipus.* Are you here, my child?

*Ismene.* After much trouble, yes.

*Œdipus.* Touch me, my girl.

*Ismene.* I touch you, both of you.

*Œdipus.*                    Offspring of mine—
     Sisters—
*Ismene.*          Alas, what miseries—
*Œdipus.*                  Hers and mine?
*Ismene.* Yes, and my own, wretch that I am!
*Œdipus.*                   My child,
     Why did you come?
*Ismene.*        Father, in care for you.
*Œdipus.* You wanted me?
*Ismene.*         Yes, and to bring you news
     In person, with my one true servant here.
*Œdipus.* And the young men your brothers, where have they
     Bestowed their labour?
*Ismene.*          They are—where they are;
     It is a heavy time with them, just now.
*Œdipus.* O how exactly fitted are that pair,
     In character and training, for the ways
     Followed in Egypt! For the husbands there
     Sit within walls and weave, while out of doors
     Their partners fare, winning their daily food.
     Even so, my children, they who fittingly
     Should bear this burden which you bear, like maidens
     Keep house at home, while in their stead you two
     Are toiling to relieve my miseries.
     One, from the time she left her nursery
     And grew to her full strength, in my train ever
     Wanders in wretchedness, an old man's leader,
     Through the wild forest often journeying
     Foodless and footsore, toiling painfully
     Often—in rain and the sun's sultriness,
     Holding the comforts of her life at home
     As nothing, to the tending of her sire.
     While you, my child, sallied out once before
     Bringing your father all the oracles
     That were delivered as concerning me,
     Without the Cadmeans' knowledge, and became
     My faithful watcher, when they banished me;
     And now again—what story are you come
     To tell your father? what dispatch, Ismene,
     Transported you from home? for you are come
     Not empty, at least; of that I am assured;
     Nor without bringing me some cause for fear.

*Ismene.* What sufferings, my father, I endured,
  Seeking your lodging and abiding-place,
  I will pass over; for I do not care
  To feel the pain twice over, in the travail,
  And after, in the telling.  But the ills
  Now compassing your two unhappy sons—
  These I have come to shew.  For formerly
  They were both eager that the sovereignty
  Should pass to Creon, and the city, so,
  Not be defiled; professing to regard
  The inveterate perdition of the race,
  Such as had fastened on your woeful house;
  But now some God, and an infatuate mind,
  Has caused an evil struggle to arise
  Between that pair, thrice miserable, to seize
  Upon the government and royal power.
  And now the lad, the younger of the twain,
  Is robbing Polynices of the throne,
  Who is his elder, and has driven him forth
  Out of his native land.  He, taking flight
  (As is the general rumour in our ears)
  To Argos in the Vale, is gaining there
  New comrades and connexions to his side,
  Swearing that Argos either shall forthwith
  Humble the glory[7] of the Cadmeans' land,
  Or else, exalt it to the height of heaven.
  Dear father, this is not a wordy tale;
  'Tis dreadful fact; and at what point the Gods
  Mean to take pity upon your woes, I know not.
*Œdipus.* And did you hope already that the Gods
  Would have some care for my deliverance?
*Ismene.* Yes, father, after this new oracle.
*Œdipus.* What is it?  What has been revealed, my child?
*Ismene.* That you shall be by the inhabitants
  Sought to hereafter, for their safety's sake,
  Whether in life or death.
*Œdipus.*                    But who could profit
  By such as I?
*Ismene.*              On you, 'tis said, their power
  Comes to depend.
*Œdipus.*              What, now my life is finished,
  Do I begin to live?

*Ismene.*       'Tis the Gods, now,
 Uplift you, who destroyed you formerly.

*Œdipus.* To fall when young, and be set up when old,
 Is poor exchange !

*Ismene.*      And on this errand know
 That Creon will be here, and that ere long.

*Œdipus.* With what intent, my daughter ?  Construe me.

*Ismene.* To lodge you in the parts near Cadmean soil,
 So they may have you in their power, but you
 Never set foot within its boundaries.

*Œdipus.* How are they helped by my lying at their doors ?

*Ismene.* Your being buried inauspiciously
 Brings them disaster.

*Œdipus.*      Even without a God
 One might conclude so far.

*Ismene.*       Therefore they seek
 To attach you, near their land, where you may be
 No longer your own master.

*Œdipus.*      Do they mean
 To shroud me in the dust of Thebes ?

*Ismene.*       Nay, father,
 Taint of a kinsman's blood forbids it you.

*Œdipus.* Then they shall never get me in their power.

*Ismene.* That will go hard with men of Thebes one day.

*Œdipus.* How should that be, my child ?

*Ismene.*       Through wrath of yours,
 When they approach your grave.

*Œdipus.*      Child—what you say—
 Whence did you hear it all ?

*Ismene.*      From envoys sent
 To inquire at Delphi's shrine.

*Œdipus.*      Was Phœbus he
 Who hath said these things of me ?

*Ismene.*      So they report
 Who came to Thebes.

*Œdipus.*      Did either of my sons
 Hear it ?

*Ismene.*    Yes, both alike, and well they know it.

*Œdipus.* And did the varlets, when they heard it, still
 Prefer their kingship to regard for me ?

*Ismene.* I grieve to hear the question ; all the same,
 Such is my news.

*Œdipus.*                    Then may the Gods not quench
The fated strife betwixt them, and the end
May it be for me to give them, of that battle
On which they are set, levelling their spear-points now!
So neither shall that one of them abide
Who holds the sceptre now, and throne, nor he
Who has departed ever more return:
Who verily, when I who fathered them
Was thrust out of the land so shamefully,
Stayed not nor screened me; but between them I
Was sent adrift, sentenced to banishment.
"A favour," you may say, "the city then
Granted me, as of course, at my desire";
Nay truly! for upon that selfsame day
When my brain boiled, and to be stoned and die
Seemed sweetest, there was no one that stood up
To help me to my craving; but long after,
When all the trouble was no longer green,
And I perceived my passion had outstripped
The chastisement of my offences past,
Then was it that this happened; then the city
Violently drave me from the land, at last;
While they, their father's offspring, in whose power
It lay to help their father, would not do it,
But I have had to wander, out and on,
Thanks to the little word they would not say,
In beggary and exile.   And from these,
Being maidens, all that nature lends to them,
Both sustenance and safety by the way,
Ay and familiar comfort, I receive;
While they preferred to their own father thrones
And sceptred rule and territorial sway.
But me for an ally they shall not gain;
Nor ever from their Cadmean monarchy
Shall benefit flow to them; this I know,
Hearing the oracle she brings me now,
And minding, too, that ancient prophecy
Of mine, by Phœbus brought to pass on me.
So now let them send Creon after me,
And every lusty catch-poll in their town;
For, gentlemen, if in the train of these,
The awful Powers who guard your village-ground,

You shall decide to summon up your force
In my behalf, then will you, for this city,
Procure a mighty saviour, and entail
Troubles on those, who are my enemies.

1 *Citizen.* First, you have won our pity, Œdipus,
Both for yourself and for your daughters; next,
Seeing that beside this pleading you propose
Yourself, to be a saviour for our land,
I am disposed to give you some good counsel.

*Œdipus.* Stand my friend, most kind sir; and I will do
All that you bid me.

1 *Citizen.*                    Come and institute
Rites of purgation to the deities
Whose ground you trespassed on, when you came
        hither.

*Œdipus.* After what fashion, sirs? instruct me.

1 *Citizen.*                                First
Bring holy water from a running stream;
But let your hands be pure.

*Œdipus.*                    And afterward,
When I have drawn the limpid wave?

1 *Citizen.*                                There stand
Bowls, of an artist's carving; garland thou
Their rims, and the two ear-handles.

*Œdipus.*                                With twigs,
Or bits of wool, or how?

1 *Citizen.*                    With a lock of wool,
New-shorn, ta'en from a yeanling ewe.[8]

*Œdipus.*                                So be it.
And after, how am I to make an end?

1 *Citizen.* Turn to the region where the dawn begins,
And pour libations.

*Œdipus.*                    From the vessels, there,
Of which you spake, am I to pour them?

1 *Citizen.*                                Yes,
From each of three, one; and the last bowl drain.

*Œdipus.* This last—how must I fill it, for the rite?
Tell me this too.

1 *Citizen.*                    With honey and water; add
No drop of wine.

*Œdipus.*                    And when the bosky soil
Has taken these?

*1 Citizen.*             Strew thrice nine olive-boughs
    On either hand; and offer up this prayer.

*Œdipus.* Ay, that is of most moment.   Let me hear it.

*1 Citizen.* That as we call them Favourers, they would deign
    With favouring breasts to accept the supplicant,
    And save him; pray yourself, or in your stead
    Some other, speaking in an undertone,
    Not so as to be heard.   Then come away
    And do not look behind you.   This performed,
    I will stand by you gladly; otherwise,
    O stranger, I should have my fears for you.

*Œdipus.* Girls, do you hear these people of the place?

*Antigone.* We hear them well.   Tell us what we must do.

*Œdipus.* I cannot go; for neither have I strength
    Nor eyesight for the work—two hindrances;
    One of you two go and discharge this duty;
    For I suppose one spirit will suffice
    For tens of thousands, with good will, to do it.
    Make haste and set about it, anyhow;
    But do not leave me by myself alone;
    For in my frame there is not strength enough
    To creep unaided, or without a guide.

*Ismene.* Well, I will go and do it.   But the place—
    I want to know where I must look for it.

*1 Citizen.* Lady, beyond this thicket.   Anything
    That you may need, there is one dwelling there
    Who will inform you.

*Ismene.*             I will betake me to it.
    Guard you our father here, Antigone.
    We may not take account of labour, even
    If we do labour, in a parent's cause.       *[Exit.*

I. I.

*1 Citizen.* Stranger! 'Tis cruel to awake again
    The long since deadened pain;
    And yet I fain would learn—

*Œdipus.*             What is it, friend?

*1 Citizen.* The story of all that self-disclosed [9] distress—
    Pitiful, remediless—
    Wherewith it was thy fortune to contend.

*Œdipus.* Nay do not, for your hospitality,
    Open my ruthless wounds!

1 *Citizen*.                    I long to know,
     And to know right, that which is noised of thee
     So widely, and so unremittingly.

*Œdipus*. Woe's me!

1 *Citizen*.            Bear with me, I pray thee.

*Œdipus*.                     Woe, ah woe!

1 *Citizen*. Hearken to my request;
     For I too hearken in all, at thy behest.

### I. 2.

*Œdipus*. Guilt overwhelmed me, friends—whelmed me, in
        sooth,
     (God be my witness!) undesigned, unsought; [10]
     Nought was of purpose in the ills I wrought.

1 *Citizen*. To what effect?

*Œdipus*.            The city bound the chain
     Of an unhappy nuptial-bond on me,
     That knew not what I did.

1 *Citizen*.           Didst thou in truth,
     As I hear said,
     Share an ill-omened-bed
     With her—who was thy mother?

*Œdipus*.               O, I die,
     Stranger, to hear it uttered! And these twain—

1 *Citizen*. How say'st thou?

*Œdipus*.          Young
     Daughters of mine, twin curses!

1 *Citizen*.               God!

*Œdipus*.                   Are sprung
     From the same mother's travail-pangs, as I.

### II. 1.

1 *Citizen*. Are these thy off-spring?

*Œdipus*.              Yes,
     And their sire's sisters also.

1 *Citizen*.           Alas!

*Œdipus*.                 Alas,
     Wave upon wave of evils, numberless!

1 *Citizen*. Thou didst endure—

*Œdipus*.           I endured misery;
     Yea, it abides with me.

1 *Citizen*. Thou didst commit—

*Œdipus.* Nay, I committed nothing!

1 *Citizen.* How was that?

*Œdipus.* I but received a boon, wretch that I was!
Such, that my service never merited at
The city's hands, to have the gift of it.[11]

## II. 2.

1 *Citizen.* How then, unhappy one? Wert thou the
cause—

*Œdipus.* What next? What wouldst thou know?

1 *Citizen.* Of thine own father's murder?

*Œdipus.* O my heart!
Thou hast struck me a second blow,
Smart upon smart!

1 *Citizen.* Didst thou kill—

*Œdipus.* Yea, I killed him. But the deed
Had something in it—

1 *Citizen.* What is there to plead?

*Œdipus.* Appealing to the laws.

1 *Citizen.* How could that be?

*Œdipus.* I will declare to thee;
Those whom I slew would have been slayers of me;[12]
Whence legally stainless, and in innocence,
I stumbled on the offence.

1 *Citizen.* Here is our master Theseus, Ægeus' son,
Come, at thy word, to do thine errand here.

*Enter* THESEUS.

*Theseus.* Many aforetime having brought to me
The bloody story of thine eyes put out,
O son of Laius, I was ware of thee;
And now, from rumour as I came along,
I am the more assured; for by thy garb
And thine afflicted presence we perceive
That thou art really he; and pitying thee,
Thou forlorn Œdipus, I would enquire
With what petition to the city or me
Thou and thy hapless follower wait on us?
Instruct me; for calamitous indeed
Must be the case disclosed by thee, wherefrom
I should start backward; who remember well
How in my youth I was a wanderer,

Even as thy self; and strove with perils no less
In my own person, on a foreign soil,
Than any on earth; wherefore no foreigner,
Such as now thou art, would I turn aside
From helping to deliver; knowing well
That I am human, and have no more share
In what to-morrow will afford, than thou.

*Œdipus.* Theseus, thy nobleness—without much talking—
Hath so vouchsafed, that little is required
For me to say. For thou hast named for me
Both who I am, and from what father sprung,
And from what country coming; wherefore now
Nothing is left me, but to speak the thing
Which I have need of, and my say is said.

*Theseus.* That very thing now tell, that I may know it.

*Œdipus.* I come, meaning to give this sorry body
A gift to thee; not goodly to the eyesight;
But better is the gain to come of it
Than beauty.

*Theseus.* But what gain do you suppose
Your coming brings?

*Œdipus.* In due time you will know;
Not just at present.

*Theseus.* At what period
Will the advantage of your gift be shewn?

*Œdipus.* When I am dead, and you have buried me.

*Theseus.* O, you are claiming life's last offices;
But all that lies between—either you forget,
Or prize at nothing.

*Œdipus.* Yes, because in them
I have all the rest summed up.

*Theseus.* Tiny indeed
Is this request you proffer!

*Œdipus.* No; look to it;
The coming struggle is not—is not light.

*Theseus.* Do you speak of your own offspring and of me?[13]

*Œdipus.* King, they would fain convey me thither.

*Theseus.* Well,
If you are not unwilling—to stay banished
Were hardly for your honour.

*Œdipus.* When I wished it,
They were the hindrance!

*Theseus.*                       O insensate one,
Wrath is not fitting in adversity!

*Œdipus.* When you have heard me, censure; but as yet
Spare me.

*Theseus.*          Say on; for inconsiderately
It fits me not to speak.

*Œdipus.*                  Theseus, I have suffered
Wrongs upon wrongs, most cruel.

*Theseus.*                       Do you mean
The old misfortune of your birth?

*Œdipus.*                         O no;
There is no Greek who does not babble of that!

*Theseus.* What is this sickness then, of which you ail,
Sorer than human?

*Œdipus.*             Thus it stands with me;
By my own offspring was I hunted forth
Out of my country; and I never more
Can, as a parricide, again return.

*Theseus.* Then why should they desire to send for you,
To make you live remote?

*Œdipus.*                 The divine lips
Leave them no choice.

*Theseus.*              What sort of detriment
Are they afraid of, from the oracles?

*Œdipus.* It is their destiny to be overthrown
Here, in this land.

*Theseus.*           And how shall come about
The bitter feeling between them and me?

*Œdipus.* Dear son of Ægeus, to the Gods alone
Belongs it never to be old or die,
But all things else melt with all-powerful Time.
Earth's might decays, the body's might decays,
And belief dies, and disbelief grows greenly;
And varying ever is the passing breath
Either 'twixt friend and friend, or city and city.
For to some now, and by and by to some,
Their friendship's pleasantness is turned to gall,
Ay, and again to friendship. So in Thebes,
Though all be now smooth weather there toward you,
Yet, as he goes, the multitudinous Time
Gives birth to multitudinous nights and days,
Wherein, at a mere word, shall Theban steel

Sever your now harmonious hand-claspings !
Then shall my sleeping and invisible clay,
Cold in the ground, drink their warm life-blood—if
Jove be still Jove, and Jove-born Phœbus true.
But since it is unpleasing to declare
The words that sleep unuttered, suffer me
To stay as I began, making but good
The pledge you gave ; and you shall never say
(So but the Gods do not prove false to me)
That you received, into this land of yours,
In Œdipus, a thankless habitant.

1 *Citizen.*  The man, my Liege, has constantly averred
He will perform these and like offices
Unto our land.

*Theseus.*          Who is there would reject
The tender of goodwill from such as he,
To whom, indeed, the hearth of comradeship
With us is ever open ?  and besides,
He, coming as a suppliant to the Gods,
Pays no small tribute to the land, and me.
Mindful whereof, I never will repel
The favour that he proffers ; nay, I will
Replant him [14] in our country.   And if here
'Tis pleasant to the stranger to abide,
I shall enjoin you to take care of him ;
Or if it pleases him to go with me—
Why, Œdipus, I leave to you the word,
Which you will choose.   Your pleasure shall be mine.

*Œdipus.*  O Zeus, shower blessings on such men as this !
*Theseus.*  Which is your fancy ?  To go home with me ?
*Œdipus.*  If it were lawful.   But the spot is here—
*Theseus.*  For you to do—what ? for I shall not hinder.
*Œdipus.*  For me to vanquish those who have banished me—
*Theseus.*  You magnify the advantage of your presence.
*Œdipus.*  If what you say abides, and you perform.
*Theseus.*  Be easy about me ; I shall not fail you.
*Œdipus.*  I will not swear you, like some caitiff !
*Theseus.*                                        Nay,
     You would gain nothing more than my word gives
          you.
*Œdipus.*  How will you do it ?
*Theseus.*                        What fear you specially ?

*Œdipus.* There will come those—
*Theseus.*                    These will take care for them!
*Œdipus.* Mind how you leave me—
*Theseus.*                    Teach not me my duty!
*Œdipus.* Needs must, who fears.
*Theseus.*                    My spirit is not afraid.
*Œdipus.* You do not know the threats—
*Theseus.*                    I know that none
Shall drag you from this place in spite of me.
As for their threatenings—many are the threats
In anger spoken often, but in vain ;
For when the reason has come home again,
The threats are vanished.   And for them, I know,
Though they take heart to talk portentously
Of carrying you away, yet it may happen
The sea between us will be found full wide,
And hardly navigable.   I bid you, rather,
Be of good cheer, apart from my resolve,
Since Phœbus sent you hither ; and, at least,
Even in my absence, I am well assured
My name will guard you from all injury.        [*Exit.*

### CHORUS.

#### I. 1.

Stranger, thou art come to rest
Where the pasturing folds are best
Of this land of goodly steeds,
In Colonus' glistening meads,
Where the clear-voiced nightingale
Oftenest in green valley-glades
Loves to hide her and bewail ;
Under wine-dark ivy shades,
Or the leafy ways, untrod,
Pierced by sun or tempest never,
Myriad-fruited, of a God ;
Where in Bacchanalian trim
Dionysus ranges ever
With the Nymphs who fostered him ;

#### I. 2.

And with bloom each morning there
Sky-bedewed, in clusters fair

Without ceasing flourishes
The narcissus, from of old
Crown of mighty Goddesses,
And the crocus, rayed with gold;
Nor do sleepless fountains fail,
Wandering down Cephissus' streams;
But with moisture pure return,
Quickening day by day the plains
In the bosom of the vale;
These nor choirs of Muses spurn,
Nor the Queen with golden reins,
Aphrodita, light-esteems.

### II. 1.

Also there is a plant, self-sown,
Untrained, ungrafted—never known,
That I have heard, in Asian soil,
Or Pelops' mighty Dorian isle,
Which, terror of the spears of foes,
In this our land most largely grows—
Grey nurse of boyhood, the Olive-Leaf;
Plant neither youth nor veteran chief
Shall e'er destroy with violent hand;
For that the face of Jove above it,
An ever watching guardian, and
The azure-eyed Athana, love it.

### II. 2.

And further, more than all, we boast
The great God's bounty, prized the most
Of honours by our Mother-state—
Fair sea, fleet steed, and fruitful strain.
O Cronos' son, Poseidon, King,
Thou givest her this praise to sing!
Thou didst for these highways create
The bit, the courser to refrain;
And thy good oar-blades, fashioned meet
For hands of rowers, with bounding motion
Follow the Nereids' hundred feet,
In marvellous dance, along the Ocean.

*Antigone.*  O highest extolled of lands, it is for thee
    To illustrate, now, these glorious words of praise!

*Œdipus.* What is there new, my daughter?
*Antigone.*                                        Here comes Creon
    To meet us, father, and not escort-less.
*Œdipus.* Now let the bourn of safety stand revealed,
    Friendliest of seniors, on your part, for me!
**1** *Citizen.* Courage, it is at hand.   If we are old,
    The vigour of our country has not aged.

*Enter* CREON, *attended.*

*Creon.* Gentle inhabitants of this your land,
    I read it in your eyes, you have conceived
    Some sudden apprehension at my coming;
    But spare reproach, and have no fear of me.
    For with no forceful aim am I come hither,
    Being an old man, and knowing I am arrived
    Before a city of no meaner power
    Than any in Hellas; rather, I am sent—
    Old as I am—for to persuade this man
    To come along with me to Theban soil,
    Not upon one man's errand, but enjoined
    By all the folk, since it has fallen to me,
    By kinship, to bewail most grievously
    Of our whole city his calamities.
    Now therefore, O thou luckless Œdipus,
    Listen to me, and turn thy footsteps home.
    All the whole Cadmean people call for thee,
    And rightly; and among them I the most;
    Who, if I be not basest of mankind,
    As much the most, old sir, grieve at thy troubles,
    Beholding thee in misery, far from home,
    And yet a wanderer always, tramping on,
    Indigent, leaning on one handmaiden,
    Who I—God help me! never had surmised
    Could fall to such a depth of ignominy
    As this unhappy one has fallen to,
    Thee and thy blindness tending evermore
    In habit of a beggar—at her age—
    Maiden as yet, but any passer's prey!
    What, is it shocking, the reproach I cast
    On you, and on myself, (wretch that I am!)
    And the whole house?   Then by our fathers' **Gods,**
    Since what is blazed abroad can not stay hidden,

Hearken to me, and hide it, Œdipus;
Consent to seek your city and father's roof;
Not without salutation to this town,
For she deserves it well; yet it were just
More worship should be paid to her at home,
Who was your foster-mother formerly.

*Œdipus.* Thou aweless villain, ready to adduce
Specious invention of just argument
From every case, why this attempt on me?
Why do you seek to take me, a second time,
In such a snare as must torment me most
If I were in your power? For formerly,
When I was sick of my domestic ills,
When to avoid the land had charms for me,
You would not grant the favour I desired;
But when I was now sated of my frenzy,
And it was pleasant to wag on at home,
Straightway you thrust me forth! you cast me out!
Never a jot you cared for all this kinship!
And now once more, when you perceive this city
And all her sons in friendship at my side,
You try, with your soft cruel words, to part us!
And yet what charm lies in befriending men
Against their will? since if a man to you
Refused a favour, when you begged for it,
And would give nothing, and then afterwards,
When you were satisfied of your desire,
And all the grace was graceless, proffered it,
Would not the pleasure so received be vain?
Such are the offers which you make to me,
Good in pretence, but evil in the trial.
Yea, these shall hear how I will prove you base;
You are come to take me, yet not take me home,
But plant me in your confines, that your city
May come off free from harm, of this land's doing:
You shall not have it! This, though, you shall
　　　have;
My spirit for evil haunting evermore
About your land; and this my sons shall have,
As much of my domain as may suffice
For them to die in! Can I not discern
Better than you what is the case of Thebes?

Far better; having better oracles,
Phœbus, and Zeus himself, who is his sire.
But treacherous is the tongue you have brought
    hither,
And of sharp edges; and in using it
You shall take more to hurt you, than to heal.
But—for I know I make no way with you—
Go! and let us live here.  Give us content,
We are well enough provided, as we are.

*Creon.*  Do you think my game is lost, as to your matters,
    In this discussion, rather—or your own?

*Œdipus.*  All that I care for is that you should fail
    Either to persuade me, or these by-standers.

*Creon.*  O wretched man, have you no growth of sense,
    At last, to boast of?   Do you hug reproach
    To your old age?

*Œdipus.*           You are adroit in tongue;
    But righteous know I none, who speaks fair speeches
    Whate'er his cause.

*Creon.*           To say what's seasonable,
    And to say much, are different.

*Œdipus.*              You, no question,
    Say—O how little—and that seasonable!

*Creon.*  Not in the judgment of a mind like yours!

*Œdipus.*  Depart; for I will speak for these as well;
    Do not come cruising, keeping watch on me,
    Where I must dwell.

*Creon.*           These I attest, not you;
    But for the answer you will make your friends,[15]
    If I once catch you—

*Œdipus.*           Who can capture me
    Against the will of my defenders?

*Creon.*              Yea,
    Capture apart, you will be vexed anon.

*Œdipus.*  What sort of act is there behind this menace?

*Creon.*  Of your two daughters one I have just seized
    And sent; and her I will take presently.

*Œdipus.*  O sorrow!

*Creon.*  You will have more occasion to sing sorrow,
    Immediately, for this!

*Œdipus.*           You have seized my daughter?

*Creon* (*pointing to Antigone*).  Yes, and will seize her, soon!

*Œdipus.*                                    Ho, gentlemen!
    What will you do? Will you prove false to me?
    Will you not hunt the villain off your soil?
1 *Citizen.* Withdraw sir, straightway; for you deal not rightly
    In this; nor yet in what you did before.
*Creon* (*to the attendants*).    Now is your time; carry the
    girl away;
    By force, if she will not consent to go.
*Antigone.* Unhappy, whither shall I fly? What help
    Of God or man shall I lay hold on?
1 *Citizen.*                                    Sir,
    What are you doing?
*Creon.*                      I will not touch the man;
    Only this maiden, who belongs to me.
*Œdipus.* You lords of Athens!
1 *Citizen.*                      Sir, you do not rightly!
*Creon,* I do.
1 *Citizen.*      How rightly?
*Creon.*                      I carry off what is mine.
                     [*Seizes* ANTIGONE.

*Œdipus.* Help, Athens!

*Chorus.*      What d'ye mean, sirrah stranger?
    Will you not leave hold?
    You will come, presently,
    To a trial of force!
*Creon.*                      Keep off!
*Chorus.*    Not from you, till you desist.

*Creon.* I tell you, you will have to fight my city,
    If you do me a harm.
*Œdipus.*                      Did I not say so?
1 *Citizen* (*to the attendant*). Take your hands off that maiden
    instantly!
*Creon.* Keep your commands for those you rule!
1 *Citizen.*                                    I tell you,
    Let go!
*Creon* (*to the attendants*). And I tell you, to go your ways.

*Chorus.*      Come on, here, come!
    Come on, neighbours all!
    The town is being spoiled—
    Our town, by force of arms!
    Come on, here, to me!

*Antigone.* I am dragged away, unhappy! O sirs—sirs!

*Œdipus.* Where are you, daughter?

*Antigone.*                 Here, borne along perforce.

*Œdipus.* Reach out your hands, my child!

*Antigone.*                 I am not able.

*Creon.* Will you not take her on?

             [*Exeunt attendants with* ANTIGONE.

*Œdipus.*                 Wretch that I am!

*Creon.* At least you shall not any longer make
    Of these two crutches an excuse to roam;
    But since you choose to gain a victory
    At the expense of your own land, and friends,
    By whose commands, although myself am royal,
    I do these things, why take it! for in time
    You will find out, I know, that neither now
    Are you doing well to your own self, nor yet
    Did so before, crossing your friends, to indulge
    The frenzy, which is your perpetual bane.

1 *Citizen.* Hold there, sir stranger!

*Creon.*                 Touch me not, I say.

1 *Citizen.* If they are lost, I will hold fast to you!

*Creon.* You shall soon spare a weightier pledge to Thebes;[16]
    For I will lay my hands not on them only.

1 *Citizen.* What will you turn to?

*Creon.*              I will seize him too,
    And carry him off!

1 *Citizen.*             You speak a perilous word.

*Creon.* I swear it shall be done forthwith.

1 *Citizen.*                 Unless
    The ruler of this country hinder you![17]

*Œdipus.* O shameless voice! Would'st thou lay hands
    on me?

*Creon.* Silence, I say!

*Œdipus.*             Nay, may these Goddesses
    Leave me but breath enough to lay this curse
    On thee, thou monster! who hast torn away
    No other than an eye—by force—from me,
    Lost—like the eyes I lost before! For this,
    May the all-seeing among Gods, the Sun,
    Give to thyself, and to thy family,
    Even such a life in thy old age as mine!

*Creon.* You natives of this country, mark you this?

*Œdipus.* They mark us both, and understand that I,
    Wronged by thy deeds, with words defend myself.
*Creon.* I will not check my fury; though alone,
    And slow with age, I will arrest him here.

*Œdipus.* Unhappy that I am!

*Chorus.*
    How swollen is the pride
    You are come with hither,
    If you think, sir stranger,
    To accomplish this!

*Creon.*                I think it.
*Chorus.*     Not, so long as Athens stands!

*Creon.* In his own right a weak man overcomes
    A strong one.
*Œdipus.*       Hear ye what he mutters?
1 *Citizen.*                       What
    He never will perform, [Zeus be my witness!] [18]
*Creon.* That Zeus may know; you cannot.
1 *Citizen.*              Is not this
    Violence?
*Creon.*     Yea, violence! but ye must bear it!
                         *[Attacks* ŒDIPUS.

*Chorus.*
    Help, people all!
    Help, lords of the land!
    Come on quickly, come!
    They pass here, indeed,
    Beyond all the bounds!

*Enter* THESEUS, *attended.*

*Theseus.* What cry was that? What is it? In what panic
    fear
    Did you stay me sacrificing at the altar here
    To the Sea-God your patron? Speak, tell me the
    need
    At which I have hurried hither, with less ease than
    speed.
*Œdipus.* O dearest friend—for your accost I know—
    I have but now been miserably abused
    At this man's hands!
*Theseus.*     How? Who misused you? Speak!

*Œdipus.* Creon here, whom you see, has torn away
    The one poor pair of children left to me!
*Theseus.* How say you?
*Œdipus.*              You have heard how I am wronged.
*Theseus.* Some servant go as quick as possible
    To the altars by, and make the people all—
    Horsemen and footmen—from the sacrifice
    Hurry, with loosened reins, to the chief points
    Where pathways meet by which the packmen come,
    Lest the girls pass, and I become a mock
    To this my guest, worsted by violence.
    Go, as I bid you, quickly;       *[Exit Guard.*
                As for him,
    Were I as far in anger as he merits,
    I had not suffered him to pass unscathed
    Out of my hands; but now, with the same law
    Shall he be suited, which he brought with him—
    That, and no other—Sir! you shall not stir
    Out of this country more, till you have brought
    And set those maidens here, for all to see;
    Since you have wrought unworthily of me,
    And of your lineage, and of your own land,
    Who, entering on a state that cares for right,
    And decides nothing without precedent,
    Must set at nought our country's officers,
    And in this onslaught hale away by force
    And make a prize of anything you please;
    Deeming my city to be void of men,
    Or manned with slaves, and my own self worth
        nothing!
    And yet it was not Thebes taught you this baseness;
    Thebes is not used to nourish lawless men,
    Nor would approve you, if she heard of you
    Despoiling me, yea and the Gods, by force
    Dragging away poor creatures—suppliants.
    I, if I did intrude upon your land,
    Even if I had a cause more just than any,
    Never, without the country's ruler's leave,
    Whoever he might be, should have been found
    Haling and leading captive; but I know
    How guest to host ought to comport himself.
    But you disgrace a state, that deserved better—

Your own—by your own act; and your full years
Leave you at once devoid of sense, and old.
So said I once before, and I now tell you;
Except you want to be compelled to stay
Against your will, an alien, in this land,
Have the girls brought back hither instantly !
You hear me say it, and what I say, I mean.

1 *Citizen*. Do you see the pass you have arrived at, Sir ?
How you seem honest by your parentage,
And are found doing deeds iniquitous ?

*Creon*. Not for that I account this city void
Of counsel or of manhood, as thou sayest,
O son of Ægeus, have I done this thing ;
But apprehending no enthusiasm
About my kindred could have fallen on these,
That they, against my will, should cherish them ;
And I felt certain they would not receive
A man polluted, and a parricide,
Nor one with whom was found the consciousness
Of an incestuous wedlock ; such a Hill
Of Ares, rich in counsel, I well knew
To be established in this land of theirs,
That suffers not such vagabonds to dwell
Within their city's bounds ; and in that trust
I undertook to make this capture mine.
And even this I should not have essayed,
But for the bitter curse by him denounced
On me, and on my race ; for which, being wronged,
This, in return, I judged it right to do.
For of resentment there is no old age,
Other than death.    No fret can reach the dead.
Now, you will do just what you please ; for me—
Me friendlessness makes insignificant,
Although my words are just ; yet when assailed,
Old as I am, I will attempt revenge.

*Œdipus*. O front of impudence ! Which thinkest thou
Now to defile—My grey hairs, or thine own ?
Who hast spit forth out of thy mouth at me
Murders and marriages and accidents,
Which to my grief, not of free will, I suffered ;
Such was the will of Heaven, that had some cause
For wrath, it may be, with our house, of old.

Since for myself, I know you cannot find
Any reproach of wrongfulness in me,
That could have doomed me to commit these wrongs
Against myself and mine; for, answer me,
If to my father by an oracle
The revelation came that he should die
By his son's hands, how can you justly tax
Me with the fact, whom neither father yet
Then had begot, or mother had conceived,
Me, who as yet had not begun to be?
And if thereafter proving—as I proved—
Hapless, I did lay hands upon my sire
And slay him, nowise knowing what I did,
Nor yet to whom I did it, how, I ask,
Can you with reason blame the unconscious deed!
And for my mother—are you not ashamed,
O miserable! at forcing me to name
Her marriage, your own sister's—as I will—
I will not now be silent, you being grown
To such a monster of outspokenness!
She bare—ah yes, unknowingly she bare
Me—who not knew! Woe worth the while to me!
And having given me birth, she brought me forth
Children—her own reproach! But of set purpose,
For one thing, well I know, you spit this venom
On her, and me; whereas I wedded her
Unwitting, and unwillingly speak of it.
But not for this my marriage, nor for that—
That parricide, which you continually
Throw in my teeth, bitterly upbraiding it,
Do I consent to be called infamous.
For answer me a question; but this one;
If any person here upon the spot
Drew near to kill you—you the just one—whether
Would you enquire if he that sought your life
Were your own father, or requite him straight?
You would requite the offender, I conceive,
If you love life; not look about for law.
Just such was the misfortune I incurred,
Led by the hand of Heaven; for which, I fancy,
Not even my father's spirit, were he alive,
Could say one word against me. And yet you—

(For just you are not, but think well to utter
All things, both lawful and unlawful,) you
Slander me with these sayings before them all!
Yea, you make free to fawn on Theseus' name,
And upon Athens—how decorously
She hath been ordered; and so lauding her,
You miss out this, that if there be a land
That knows what reverence to the Gods is due,
'Tis she herein excels, whence to remove
Me, the old suppliant, you assail my person,
And seize my daughters, and make off with them.
Wherefore these maiden Powers I invoke
With supplications, and with prayers adjure
To come, as aiders and auxiliaries;
So you may learn what sort of men they are,
By whom this city is defended.

1 *Citizen.*                         Sir,
The stranger is a good man; and his woes
Are horrible, and worthy of relief.

*Theseus.* Enough of words; they speed, who have done the
        wrong,[19]
While we, of the injured party, stand here still.

*Creon.* What is it you bid a poor weak man to do?

*Theseus.* To shew the way, and to take me along,
That, if you have these maidens, whom we seek,
Inside our bounds, yourself may find them for me;
But if your guards are making off with them,
We need not toil; for there are others there,
No laggards, whom they never shall evade,
Crossing our frontiers, to give thanks to Heaven.
Lead forward! Know, sir captor, you are caught!
Fortune has trapped you, hunter! So it is,
Nothing abides of what is got by guile.
And you shall have no help; I am sure you have
        come
Not single, nor unfurnished, to the point
Of violence, such as you have here essayed,
But there was some one whom you trusted in.
I must look to it; I must not let this city
Be feebler than a single mortal's arm.
Do you take my sense? Or does my speaking seem
As idle, now, as when you framed this project?

*Creon.* Being here, you may say on, I shall not cavil;
    But once at home, I shall know my part, too.
*Theseus.* Ay, threaten us, and so—march! You, Œdipus,
    Abide securely here; and credit me,
    Till I have given your children to your arms,
    Except I shall die first, I will not leave it.
*Œdipus.* God speed you, Theseus, for your nobleness,
    And for your duteous providence towards me.
                [*Exeunt* THESEUS, CREON *and Guards.*

CHORUS.

I. 1.

I wish that I could be
Where foes are gathering fast,
Soon to be hurled together, brand on brand,
With clamour of battle! along either strand—
Pythian, or that where by the torches' light
Sit Queens, dispensing many a holy rite
To worshipping mortals on whose lips hath passed,
In mystic ritual, the golden key
Borne by their ministering Eumolpidæ;
Soon, methinks, there
Shall Theseus, the awakener of the fight,
And that unconquered virgin pair,
Amid the fields hard by,
Join voices in one loud effectual rescue-cry!

I. 2.

Or haply pass they now
Out from the Œatid meads,
Nigh to that snow-clad mountain's western brow,
Flying on fleet steeds
Or swift contending chariots? He shall fail!
The battle spirit of our Athenian race
Is terrible; terrible in pride of place
Are Theseus' children; lo where brightly shines
Curb beyond curb, and all along the lines
Of bridle-piece on bridle-piece of mail
Come charging on
Horsemen on horses, warriors who revere
Athana, her to whom the horse is dear,
And him, the Sea-God, the land's guardian,[20] Rhea's own son!

### II. 1.

Are they at work? Do they linger yet?
  How I court the thought I shall greet,[21] ere long,
Those maids much injured—the maids who met
  From kindred hands injurious wrong.
Zeus works—he is working a thing to-day;
  Prophet am I of a well-won field;
O would that I were as a storm-winged dove,
Swift and sure, on a cloud above
To soar to Heaven, and so survey
  The arms that triumph, the arms that yield!

### II. 2.

Hail, great Master of Gods in heaven,
  All-seeing Zeus! With conquering might
To the chiefs of our land by Thee be it given
  To obtain this prize—to achieve this fight!
So Pallas Athana, thy awful maid,
  Grant it! Phœbus, too, I invoke,
The Hunter-God—come, visit us here,
With the chaser of dappled swift-footed deer,
Thy sister—come, bring aid upon aid
  To this our country and these our folk!

1 *Citizen.* You will not say, sir wanderer, to your seer,
  He is no sayer of sooth; for I perceive
  Those girls conducted hither back again.
*Œdipus.* Where? where? How say you?—What was that
  you said?

*Enter* Theseus, Antigone, Ismene *and Guards.*

*Antigone.* O father, father, might some Deity
  Give you to look upon this best of men,
  Who brings us back to you!
*Œdipus.*                         Child, are you there,
  You and your sister?
*Antigone.*                     Yes; for Theseus' hands
  And his good followers', here, redeemed us.
*Œdipus.*                                     Come,
  My girl—Come to your father, both of you,
  And let me clasp your form—as I despaired
  Ever should be!

*Antigone.*                Have what you ask—the leave,
    Not without longing.

*Œdipus.*                Where—where are you?

*Antigone.*                                Here,
    Both of us, coming close.

*Œdipus.*                My darling sprays!

*Antigone.* O ay, dear to the stem!

*Œdipus.*                Props of my frame!

*Antigone.* Poor hapless props, of a poor frame indeed!

*Œdipus.* I have my darlings! Now I could even die
    Not all unhappy, these being by my side.
    Daughters, support me—one on either hand—
    Growing to the plant, from which you took your
        growth,
    So shall you end [22] this wretched groping—lonely
    Until you came; then tell me, in fewest words,
    All that has happened; tender maids like you
    Need not to make long speeches.

*Antigone.*                    Father dear,
    This is the man who rescued us; to him
    You must give ear; his is the deed; my part
    Will be full brief. [23]

*Œdipus.*                O Sir, be not amazed,
    If seeing my children here, out of all hope,
    Makes me prolong discourse to weariness.
    For well I know, this kindness, joy to me,
    No other than yourself has shewn towards them.
    For you, and no man else, delivered them;
    And may the Gods bestow as I desire
    On you, and on this land; since among you
    Alone of men did I find piety,
    And gentle dealing, and all truthfulness.
    I know it, and these thanks are my return;
    For what I have, I have, only through you.
    And now, O king, stretch out your hand to me,
    For me to touch, and kiss, if kiss I may,
    That forehead. Yet—what am I babbling! How
    Can I desire that you should touch a man—
    Wretch that I am! to whom what taint of ills
    Cleaves not? I cannot; nor will suffer you;
    Only the man who has experienced it
    Can sympathize with misery such as mine.

There, where you stand, I greet you; and henceforth
Be duly mindful of me, as to-day.

*Theseus.* That in the pleasure these your children bring
You set wide bounds to your discourse of it,
That you preferred their converse in my room,
I have not felt amazement; no annoy
Possesses me, for this; I do not care
To have my life made glorious with fine speeches,
Rather than by my actions. And I shew it;
Seeing I have failed in nought of what I sware,
Old man, to you; for here they are with me,
Alive, unharmed of what was threatened them.
And now, what need to make a bootless boast
Of how the field was won? things which yourself
Will come to know from these, having them with
    you;
But on a matter I have met withal
In coming here just now, advise with me;
Since, though it seems a trifle, it is strange;
And it behoves us to make light of nothing.

*Œdipus.* What is it, son of Ægeus? Tell me; I
Know nothing of the things you hint.

*Theseus.*                         They say
A man, who is no countryman of yours,
And yet akin, has come and seated him
Before our altar of Poseidon here,
Where I was offering, when you summoned me.

*Œdipus.* What countryman? What is it that he seeks
In taking sanctuary?

*Theseus.*                I do not know;
Save only that with you, as I am told,
He asks for a few words, an easy boon.

*Œdipus.* But of what kind? This is no sanctuary
Taken for a trifling matter.

*Theseus.*             As they say,
The object of his journey is to come
To speech of you; then to depart, in safety,
The way he came.

*Œdipus.*           Who can it be, that seats him
As suppliant thus?

*Theseus.*           Think if you have some kinsman
In Argos, who might seek this boon of you.

*Œdipus.* O best of friends, stop, say no more!

*Theseus.*                           What ails you?

*Œdipus.* Do not request me—

*Theseus.*                 To what purport, say?

*Œdipus.* I know full well who is the suppliant,
    When I hear this.

*Theseus.*             Who can it be, with whom
    I am to have a quarrel?

*Œdipus.*                 O king, my son;
    My abhorred son, whose words of all men's else
    Most grievously could I endure to hear.

*Theseus.* But why? Can you not listen, and still not do
    What you mislike? How is the hearing pain?

*Œdipus.* Most alien to a father's ears, sir king,
    Has that voice grown; do not put stress on me
    To yield in this.

*Theseus.*             Look if the sanctuary
    Does not compel it; whether a regard
    Must not be paid towards the God.

*Antigone.*                       My father,
    Hearken to me, young though I am who speak.
    Suffer this friend to gratify the God
    And his own heart, in that which he desires;
    And grant it us, to let our brother come.
    Take heart! You cannot be seduced, perforce,
    From your resolve, by words that grate on you;
    But where's the harm of hearing? By discourse
    Are deeds, maliciously designed, bewrayed.
    You gave him being; then, if he did to you
    The wickedest and worst of injuries,
    Not even so, dear father, were it right
    For you to do him evil in return.
    O let him come! Others have bad sons too,
    And keen resentments; but, on being advised,
    They are charmed in spirit by the spells of friends.
    Look to the past, not to the present; all
    That you endured through mother and through sire;
    If you regard it, you will find, I know,
    That harmful passion ends in further harm.
    You have reminders of it far from slight,
    Maimed of your sightless eyes. Let us prevail!
    It is not right that they whose prayers are just

Should play the beggar ; nor that you yourself,
Who are being kindly treated, should not know
How to requite the kindness you receive.

*Œdipus.* Child, I am conquered, by your words and his ;
Your pleasure is my pain ; be it as you please ;
Only, if he you speak of shall come hither—
Sir host—never let any one get power
Over my life !

*Theseus.* Twice to be told such things
I do not need ; once is enough, old man ;
Nor would I boast ; yet be sure, safe you are,
If any of the Gods takes care of me.

[*Exit* THESEUS, *attended.*

CHORUS.

I.

Whoso thinks average years a paltry thing,
        Choosing prolonged old age,
He, to my mind, will be found treasuring
        A foolish heritage.
For when a man hath given him to fulfil [24]
        What length of days he will,
Then many things are dealt him, in long days,
        That border hard on pain,
And things that please are hidden from the gaze ;
    And when the doom of Hades is made plain,
Whereto belongs no bridal, and no quire,
        Nor any sound of lyre,
            Death, at the end,
        Waits, an impartial friend.

II.

Never to have been born is much the best ;
        And the next best, by far,
To return thence, by the way speediest,
        Where our beginnings are.
While Youth is here, [25] with folly in his train,
        (So full of cares our lot,)
Whose feet can fare beyond the reach of pain ?
        What pains beset them not ?

Murders, seditions, battles, envy, strife;
>Yea and old age, in hateful friendlessness,
This is our portion at the close of life,
>>Strengthless—companionless;
>>>Wherewith abide
>>Ills passing all beside.

Such are the aged; such am I;
>>But he, this man of woes,
Is beaten down on every hand,
>Like to some wintry Northern strand,
>>Vext by the Ocean's blows;
Such waves of ill, so fell and high,
>>Smite him, without repose;
Some from the settings of the Day,
>>Some from his rising light,
Some on the midmost noontide ray,
>>Some from the Alps of Night.[26]

*Antigone.* And here we have the stranger, I suppose—
>Nay, father, unattended—coming up
>This way; his eyes are wet with streaming tears.
*Œdipus.* Who is the man?
*Antigone.*         The same whom all along
>We guessed at, Polynices. He is here.

### *Enter* POLYNICES.

*Polynices.* Alack, what shall I do, girls? Must I first
>Mourn my own ills, or this my aged sire's,
>Beholding him? Whom I have met withal
>Outcast with you, here, on a foreign soil,
>Clad in a garb, whose horrid grime antique
>Has grown to suit with his antiquity,
>Marring his frame, while on the breeze his hair
>Streams from his eye-abated front uncombed,
>And, as it seems, akin to these, he bears
>The scrip, for his poor belly's provender!
>The which I recreant all too late perceive,
>And do confess I am proved the worst of men
>By your condition. Ask what I have done
>Of none but me. But seeing how Clemency,
>Even by the side of Zeus, sharing his throne,
>Rules, in all acts, so let her find a place,

Father, with you ; for remedies, indeed,
Still may remain, of what has been amiss,
But aggravations none.—Why are you silent?
Father, say something ! Do not turn away !
Will you return me not an answer back ?
Insult me with a dumb dismissal? Tell
Not even why you are enraged with me ?
O offspring of this man, sisters of mine,
Try you to move our father's countenance,
Inexorable, unapproachable,
Not to dismiss me, the God's worshipper,
Thus in disgrace, answering me never a word !

*Antigone.* Unhappy brother, what you come to seek
Tell us yourself; for out of many words,
Stirring delight, or breathing pity, or pain,
Come, to the voiceless, powers of utterance.

*Polynices.* I will speak out; for you direct me well;
First calling to my aid the God himself,
Up from whose shrine the sovereign of this land
Raised me, and sent me hither, promising me
Audience and answer and safe conduct hence.
The which I shall expect to meet with, sirs,
From you, from these my sisters, and my sire.
Next, I would tell you, father, why I came.
I have been driven out of my native land,
Because I claimed, being of an elder birth,
To seat me upon your imperial throne ;
For which Eteocles, though my junior born,
Not overthrowing me in argument,
Nor coming to the test of arms or act,
But tampering with the people, exiled me.
Whereof the cause, above all else, I say,
Is your Erinys ; and from soothsayers,
Moreover, so I hear. For when I came
To Argos of the Dorians, I obtained
The daughter of Adrastus to my wife,
And made confederates along with me
As many of the land of Apia
As are deemed first, and have been best approved
In war ; meaning to gather against Thebes
My host of the Seven Lances in their train,
And either die upon the field, or else

Banish the authors of my banishment.
So be it! Then, why am I come hither now?
Father, with expiatory prayers to you,
Both for myself and my allies, who now
In seven arrays under seven pennons stand
All round the plain of Thebes. Among them comes
Amphiaraus the strong spearman, first
In war, first in the acts of augury;
The second is Ætolian, Œneus' son,
Tydeus; a third Eteoclus, Argive-born;
Talaus his father sends Hippomedon
Fourth; and the fifth, Capaneus, vaunts himself
That he will set the castle of Thebes on fire
And burn it to the ground; the sixth springs forward,
Parthenopæus the Arcadian, named
As being born of mother theretofore
Long time untamed, the trusty progeny
Of Atalanta; and your own son I—
(Or if disowned, then by ill destiny
Begotten, but at least called yours), I lead
The undaunted host of Argos against Thebes.
And all together for these children's sake,
Father, beseech you, and by your own life,
Praying you relax your heavy wrath at me,
Now marching to avenge me of that brother
Who thrust me forth, spoiled of my father-land.
For if there is a truth in oracles,
They say success is to the side you choose.
Wherefore I implore you, by the water-springs—
Yea by the Gods of Thebes, hearken and yield;
For I am poor and exiled; so are you;
And under the same lot both you and I
Cringe to a stranger for a lodging. He
Meanwhile, at home, a monarch, well a day!
Lives delicately, and derides us both;
But with short effort, after small delay,
If you cooperate with my design,
Him will I shatter! and so take you home,
And in your own house place you, and myself,
And cast him out by force. With your goodwill
I may indulge this boast; but, without you,
I must lack strength even to come off with life.

1 *Citizen.* Now for his sake who sent him, Œdipus,
    Say what is meet, and send the man away.
*Œdipus.* Sirs, wardens of this country—were not he
    Theseus, who sped him on his way to me,
    Deeming it fitting I should answer him,
    He never should have heard my voice at all!
    But now, being so far graced, he shall depart
    With that within his ears shall sober him
    All his life long. O most desertless villain,
    Who, when you held the sceptre and the throne
    Which now your brother has achieved in Thebes,
    Yourself expelled me—your own father—me
    Made homeless—drove to wear this livery,
    Which you shed tears to see, now you have come
    To walk in the same evil straits with me!
    This is no stuff to weep for; rather is it
    For me to bear, mindful, howe'er I live,
    That you are my destroyer. For you made me
    Familiar with this woe; you exiled me;
    And by your act made vagabond, I beg
    My daily bread from others. Had I not
    Fathered these girls, to be my cherishers,
    I had been dead, for aught you did for me;
    But now these keep me, these my cherishers,
    These men, not women, for their ministering;
    And ye are sprung from others' loins, not mine,
    Wherefore Heaven frowns upon thee—yea, not yet
    As it soon shall frown, if these cohorts move
    Toward Theba's hold; for it may never be
    That thou shalt storm that city;[27] rather, first,
    Thou, and thy brother as well, blood-stained, shalt
      fall.
    Such curses upon you I denounced before,
    And summon, now, to come and fight for me,
    And make you learn true filial reverence,
    And cease your scorn, although the sire be blind,
    Who fathered sons like you! These did not so.
    Therefore thy supplication and thy throne
    Fall 'neath its sway, if Justice as of old
    Sits equal in the ancient rule of Jove.
    Hence! I disown thee, reptile! of base souls
    Basest! and take with thee this doom of mine,

Never to win thy native land in fight,
Nor to return to Argos in the Vale,
But by a kindred hand thyself to fall,
Him having slain, who was thy banisher.
This is my curse! And to the abyss I call,
Hated, of Hades, where my father is,
To be thy place of exile; and I call
These Powers, and Ares, who in both of you
Hath sown this monstrous hate. Hear me, and go;
And as you go, tell all the Cadmeans,
Ay, and your trusty allies, what recompense
Is to his own sons dealt, by Œdipus.

1 *Citizen.* I am sorry, Polynices, for the errand
On which you came; now get you back with speed.

*Polynices.* Woe for my journey, woe for my mischance,
Woe for my comrades! To an end like this
Did we set out from Argos on our way!
Such as it is impossible to tell
To any of my fellows, or to turn
Their footsteps backward; only this is left,
Silent, to meet my fate. O misery!
Sisters of mine, his daughters! You have heard
The hard words of our father, cursing me;
I charge you in Heaven's name, if that father's
     curse
Shall be fulfilled, and a return for you
Be granted home, do not you look on me
With contumely, but lay me in my tomb,
And grant me funeral rites. Then on that praise
Which from your labour for your father's sake
You now derive, shall rise a second praise,
As ample, through your ministering to me.

*Antigone.* Polynices, I entreat you, yield to me!

*Polynices.* Tell me in what, dearest Antigone!

*Antigone.* March back at once to Argos! Do not ruin
Yourself—and Thebes!

*Polynices.*                    That is impossible;
How could I lead the selfsame army forth,
If I had faltered once?

*Antigone.*                    But why again
Must you get angry, boy? Where is your profit
In overthrowing your country?

*Polynices.*                               To be banished
        Is a dishonour; and for me, the elder,
        To be so flouted by my brother.
*Antigone.*                                  Then
        Do you not see that you are carrying out [28]
        His prophecies forthright, who spells you death,
        Each from the other's hand?
*Polynices.*                        He wishes it.
        No, no retreat is left us.
*Antigone.*                            Woe for me!
        But who that heard the things he prophesied
        Will dare to follow?
*Polynices.*                    Nay, we will tell no tales.
        It is the merit of a general
        To impart good news, and to conceal the bad.
*Antigone.* Is this the course you have resolved on, boy?
*Polynices.* Ay—stay me not.   Now to this course of mine
        Must I give heed, luckless and evil made
        By him, my father, and his cleaving curse.
        But as for you, God speed you, as you do
        My hest in death—since you will have nought further
        To do for me in life.   Unhand me now.
        Farewell.   You will behold my face no more.
*Antigone.* O woe is me!
*Polynices.*            Do not lament for me.
*Antigone.* Who but must mourn thee, brother, rushing thus
        On death foreseen?
*Polynices.*            If needs must, die I will.
*Antigone.* Not so, but hear me!
*Polynices.*                Ask not what may not be.
*Antigone.* Unhappy that I am, if I lose thee!
*Polynices.* This is in Destiny's hands, or thus to be,
        Or not to be.   For you—the Gods I pray
        You never meet with ill; for you deserve,
        All will confess, not to be miserable.        [*Exit.*

CHORUS.

I. 1.

Here are new griefs, new and calamitous,
From sources new, made manifest to us,
        Of the blind stranger's making;
        Except, indeed, his fate is overtaking:

For of no doom from Heaven can I declare 'tis vain.
    The end Time sees, yea, sees alway;
      Time, that o'erthrows to-day,
  Time, that with morning's light uprears again.
                              *[Thunder.*

1 *Citizen.* Heavens! how it thundered!
*Œdipus.* Children, my children! will some bystander
  Fetch the most excellent Theseus hither?
*Antigone.*                      Father,
  What is the end for which you summon him?
*Œdipus.* This thunder, winged by Jove, must carry me
  Straightway to Hades.   Send at once, I say.
                              *[Thunder.*

### CHORUS.

### I. 2.

Hark with what might the unutterable roar
Of Jove's own bolt comes crashing down once more!
    The very hair on my head
    Stands up for dread;
My spirit quails.—There flames lightning from Heaven
    again!
    What will the issue be?
I tremble at it: for surely not in vain
Is it sent forth—never innocuously.    *[Loud thunder.*

1 *Citizen.* You mighty Heavens! Thou Jove!
*Œdipus.* Daughter, the appointed ending of my life
  Has found me, and may not be averted more.
*Antigone.* How do you know it? By what conjecture
  comes
  This certainty?
*Œdipus.*             I feel it. With all speed
  Let some one go and fetch this country's king.
                             *[Thunder.*

### CHORUS.

### II. 1.

Hark again, hark,
    The echoing clap resounds on either hand.
Have mercy, O God, have mercy, if aught of dark
  Thou art now bringing to our mother-land!

May he bring luck who meets me!
Nor, now the man who greets me
Is fraught with doom, let it be mine to share
A fruitless boon—King, Jove, to thee I make my
prayer!

*Œdipus.* Is the man nigh, my children? Will he come
While I still live, and reason rules my mind?

*Antigone.* What is the trust, which in your mind you crave
To breathe in Theseus' ears? [29]

*Œdipus.*                                    To pay to him,
For good he did me, a complete return,
Such as I promised in receiving it.

### CHORUS.

#### II. 2.

Hither, my son,
Quick, quick—howbeit thine offerings are placed
High in the hollow of his altar-stone
To the sea's lord, Poseidon, come with haste!
Thee and thy city and friends
The stranger-guest pretends
To pay with profit, for his profiting,
In righteous measure.   Hasten and come forth, our
king!

*Enter* THESEUS, *attended.*

*Theseus.* What is this general din, sounding anew,
Loud from yourselves, and from the stranger plain?
Is it that bolt from Jove, or shower of hail,
Has burst upon you?   Anything, while Heaven
Is raising such a storm, is credible.

*Œdipus.* King, thou art here at need; yea, and some God
Has given thee good speed of this thy way.

*Theseus.* What is the new event which has arisen,
O son of Laius?

*Œdipus.*                          End of life to me.
And I am anxious not to die forsworn,
In what I promised to this city and thee.

*Theseus.* But under what death-symptom do you labour?

*Œdipus.* The Gods are their own heralds, telling me,
Belying nought of tokens fixed before.

*Theseus.* How do you say that this is shewn you, sir?
*Œdipus.* The frequent thunderings continuous,
    And frequent-flashing arrows, from the hand
    Invincible—
*Theseus.*                You move me; for I see
    You are a mighty soothsayer, and your words
    Do not come false. Say, then, what we must do.
*Œdipus.* I will inform thee, son of Ægeus,
    Of what shall be in store for this thy city,
    Beyond the harm of time. Of my own self,
    Without a hand to guide me, presently
    I will explore a spot wherein, in death,
    I am to rest. Never to any man
    Say where 'tis hidden, or whereabouts it lies;
    So may it ever bring thee vigour, more
    Than many bucklers, or the hireling spear
    Of neighbours. But the place—a mystery
    Not to be put in language, thou thyself
    Shalt learn when thou goest thither, but alone;
    For not to any of these citizens,
    Nor to my daughters, though I love them well,
    Will I declare it. Keep it to thyself;
    And, when thou art coming to the end of life,
    Disclose it but to one, thy foremost; he
    To him who shall come after shewing it,
    For ever. So shalt thou inhabit still
    This city, unwasted by the earth-sprung seed;
    While swarms of towns, however men may live
    Good neighbours, lightly try to injure you.
    For the Gods mark it well, though they are slow,
    When any turn to folly, and forsake
    Their service; such experience, Ægeus' son,
    Do thou eschew; nay, what I preach, thou knowest.
    Now—to the place! The message from on high
    Urges me forth; let us not linger now.
    Here, follow me, my daughters! in my turn,
    Look, I am acting as a guide to you,
    As you were mine, your father's. Come along!—
    Nay, do not touch me; let me for myself
    Search out the hallowed grave where, in this soil,
    It is my fate to lie. Here, this way, come;
    This way! for Hermes the Conductor and

The Nether Queen are this way leading me.
O Light—my Dark—once thou wast mine to see;
And now not ever shall my limbs again
Feel thee!   Already I creep upon my way
To hide my last of life in Hades.   Thou,
Dearest of friends—thy land—thy followers—all,
May you live happy; and in your happiness
Fortunate ever, think of me, your dead!

[*Exeunt* ŒDIPUS, THESEUS, ANTIGONE,
ISMENE, *and attendants.*

### CHORUS.

#### 1.

If sound of my prayers may rise unto Her who is hid from
   sight,
If worship of mine may approach thee, the King of the
   shadows of night,
              Aïdoneus, Aïdoneus—
              I entreat that this stranger
May pass right well, without sound of grief, by a painless
   doom,
To the hiding-place of the dead beneath, and the Stygian
   home.
—Though many are the sorrows that visit thee, many thy
   labours in vain,
It may be, a Power that is righteous intends to uplift thee
   again.

#### 2.

Hail, Queens of the realms of Earth!   All hail, the uncon-
   quered frame
Of the Hound, that crouched, we were told, at the Gate
   whither all men came,[20]
              And growled from its caverns,
              (So the story went ever,)
As Hades' champion and guard—whose steps, I pray, may
   be led
Far off, when the stranger comes to the nether fields of the
   dead!
—O Thou that art born of Earth, the begotten of the Deep,
Thee I invoke, the giver of unending sleep.

*Enter a Messenger.*

**Messenger.** Sirs, to cut short, as far as possible,
What I would say—Œdipus is no more ;
But for what there befell, there are no words
To tell it in brief space ; nor was it brief,
All that was done.

**1 Citizen.**                     Is the poor wanderer gone ?

**Messenger.** Yes, he is quit of his life-trouble.

**1 Citizen.**                                             How ?
Was't by some heaven-sent end—poor soul—and
    calm ?

**Messenger.** Truly the event is meet to wonder at.
First, in what fashion he set forth from hence,
You must have seen, being present, even as I ;
None of his company conducting him,
But he himself shewing to us all the way.
Next, having reached the threshold of that chasm
Whose root is in the Brazen Stairs below,
There, upon one of the diverging paths,
Nigh to the hollowed basin where are kept
The tokens of the sure-abiding bond
'Twixt Perithous and Theseus, he stood still ;
Thence halfway to the stone from Thoricus,
Betwixt the hollow pear-tree and marble tomb,
He sate him down ; then doffed his grimy robe ;
And then, crying to his daughters, bade them bring
Waters to wash, and pour, out of some stream ;
Which twain, proceeding to the opposing slope
Of verdurous Demeter, with small delay
Brought to their father that he sent them for ;
And him they washed, and decked in such attire
As is in use ; and when, now, nought remained
Unsatisfied of all that he desired,
Sounded from Hades thunder, and the maids,
As they heard, shivered ; and at their father's knees
Fell down, and wept, beating their breasts, and raised
Wailings prolonged, unceasing. He the while,
Soon as he heard their bitter note of woe,
Folding his arms about them, said ; " For you,
My girls, this day there is no father more ;
For all things now are ended that were mine ;

And now no longer need you bear for me
The burden of your hard tendance, hard indeed—
I know it, my children; but one single word
Cancels the evil of all cares like this;
Love, which ye had from no one more than me;
Of whom bereft, you for the time to come
Must live your life." So they all wept aloud,
Clinging to each other; but when they were come
To end of lamentation, and the cry
Rose up no longer, silence reigned awhile.
Then suddenly some voice shouted his name;
So that the hair of all stood up for fear;
For a God called him—called him many times,
From many sides at once: "Ho, Œdipus,
Thou Œdipus, why are we tarrying?
It is full long that thou art stayed for; come!"
He, when he felt Heaven summoned him, bespake
That the land's king, Theseus, should come to him;
And, when he came, said to him, "O dear friend,
Pledge me, in the ancient fashion, your right hand
To these my children, (and you, girls, give him yours,)
And swear—never to yield them willingly,
But as you purpose now to accomplish all
In kindness, ever, that is good for them."
He, of his gentleness, agreed; and sware,
(But not condoling,) to his guest, to do it.
And straightway as he sware it, Œdipus,
Touching with sightless hands his daughters, said:
"Now, children, you must leave this place; bear up
In spirit, as befits your nobleness;
Look not upon the sights you may not see,
List not the voices which you must not hear,
But with all speed depart; let but the king,
Theseus, be present, and behold the end."
While he thus spake, we hearkened, all of us;
Then followed we the maidens, grieving sore,
With streaming tears. When we had gone apart,
After short space we turned, and saw far off—
The man, indeed, nowhere still visible—
Only the king's self, holding up his hand
Over his face, so as to shade his eyes,
As if some sight of terror had appeared,

Awful, intolerable to gaze upon;
Then, in a moment, without interval,
We saw him kneel, worshipping Earth, and Heaven
The abode of Gods, both in one act, together.
But he—what death he died, save Theseus' self
There lives not any mortal who can tell.
For neither any fire-fraught thunderbolt
Rapt him, from Heaven, nor whirlwind from the sea
Stirred up to meet the moment; but some guide
Sent from above, or depth of the earth beneath
Opening to take him, friendly, without pain.[31]
For not as of one mourned, or with disease
Grown pitiable, was his departure; but
If any ever was so, wonderful.
—If what I say seems folly, I can spare
The assent of those to whom I seem a fool.

1 *Citizen.* And where now are his daughters, and those
friends
Who did attend them?
*Messenger.*                      They, at least, not far;
For sounds of wailing unmistakeable
Declare them to be moving up this way.


*Enter* ANTIGONE *and* ISMENE.

### I. 1.

*Antigone.* Alas, it is for us, it is for us to rue,
Not once alone, but evermore anew,
Unhappy that we are, the fatal strains
Of our sire's blood implanted in our veins.
For whom, erewhile,
We ceaselessly endured a world of toil,
And have to tell, at last, of most unmeasured ill,
Beheld and suffered, still.
1 *Citizen.* But what has happened?
*Antigone.*                      You can guess it, friends.
1 *Citizen.* He is gone?
*Antigone.*           Yes, as one would most wish for him.
—What wonder?   In whose way
Nor war nor ocean lay,
But viewless regions rapt him home,
Sudden, by some mysterious doom,

While on our sight
The gloom of night,
Deathful and desolate, is come.
For how shall we sustain
Life's heavy load of toil,
Wandering o'er the billowy main,
Or on some foreign soil?

*Ismene.* I know not.   O that with my sire's last breath
I by some sudden death
Might perish! for the life that is to be
Seems worse than death to me.

*Chorus.* O children, worthiest pair, what heaven may send
Bear—to the end,
And let your grief be mild; the way by which you came
You have no cause to blame.

I. 2.

*Antigone.* Even the ills of life, it may be, we regret.
For what indeed was no-wise charmful, yet
Became, to me, a life not without charms
The while I had my father in my arms.
O father dear,
Wrapped evermore in nether darkness drear,
O not for thine old age mightest thou ever be
Unloved by her and me!

1 *Citizen.* He fared—?
*Antigone.*                      He fared even as he wished to do.
1 *Citizen.* How was it?
*Antigone.*                      Upon that foreign soil he chose
Died he!   For ever laid
Low, in the kindly shade,
He left behind no tearless grief,
No measured mourning, dull and brief,
These eyes are wet
With weeping yet,
Nor know I how to find relief.
Oh not for thy desire
In a strange land to die,
Need'st thou have perished, O my sire, [32]
Thus, with no loved ones by!

*Ismene.* O wretched that I am!   What future fate
Me must await

And thee, my sister, lingering here alone,
And our dear father gone!

*Chorus.* But now he is at last thus happily
From life set free,
Cease this lamenting, friends! From evils, in some shape,
No mortal can escape.

## II. 1.

*Antigone.* Back let us haste, dear sister!
*Ismene.* What to do?
*Antigone.* A longing is upon me—
*Ismene.* What?
*Antigone.* To view
The earth-bound home—
*Ismene.* Of whom?
*Antigone.* Our father—woe is me!
*Ismene.* But is it not forbid? Do you not see?
*Antigone.* Why should it make you chide?
*Ismene.* This too, that—
*Antigone.* Well, what next?
*Ismene.* Without a tomb,
Lonely, he died!
*Antigone.* Take me to him, and slay me by his side!
*Ismene.* Alas, unhappy, whither should I flee,
To live, once more, a life of misery,
In the old loneliness and poverty!

## II. 2.

1 *Citizen.* Dear friends, fear nought!
*Antigone.* Where should I shelter me?
1 *Citizen.* Truly there was a shelter, long ago—
*Antigone.* How?
1 *Citizen.* For your fortunes, that they should be free
From evil destiny.
*Antigone.* Nay, that I know.
1 *Citizen.* What is it, then, that doubles your concern?
*Antigone.* 'Tis that I know no way for our return
To our own home.
1 *Citizen.* Care not to seek it!
*Antigone.* I am overcome
With weariness.

1 *Citizen.*                    Time was, you were so.
*Antigone.*                                          Yea,
    Sorely before, but now surpassingly.
1 *Citizen.* Truly it was yours to stem a stormy sea!
*Antigone.* Whither, O Jove, shall we direct our way?
    Towards what point of hope—alas the day!
    Doth God impel me, and forbid my stay?


### III.

*Enter* THESEUS, *attended.*

*Theseus.* Children, cease to lament; for griefs, where
    Grace from the Nether Gods awaits us,
    Blessing all fortunes,
      Sorrow is causeless; nay, were sin.
*Antigone.* O son of Ægeus, we are thy suppliants.
*Theseus.* For what boon, my children?
*Antigone.*                               We too
    Fain would look on our father's tomb.
*Theseus.* Nay, the approach to it is forbidden us.
*Antigone.* King, how say you, master of Athens?
*Theseus.* He, my children, gave me commandment
    That no mortal's foot should trespass
    Near those precincts,
    Or give name to the ark of refuge
    Where he dwells; which things, he told me,
    Duly observing,
    I might evermore keep these confines
    Free from annoyance;
    And so Heaven o'erheard me swear it,
      And the omniscient Oath of Jove.
*Antigone.* Well, if such be the way he willed it,
    Let that fully suffice.   Now send us
    Back to our ancient Thebes; it may be
    We may ward off ruin, impendent
    O'er our brethren.
*Theseus.* I will do it at once, and all things
    Such as I purpose, for your service,
    And his pleasure, our dead, this moment
    Rapt far from us; I may not tire.

*Chorus.* Cease, no longer upraise your wailing;
    All these promises shall not fail.            [*Exeunt.*

# THE LOST DRAMAS.

FROM the old Greek Lexicons of Photius, Suidas, Hesychius and their brethren, from the grammatical writings of Phrynichus, Eustathius and others, and from allusions scattered over the field of later Greek literature, we derive the names of about 100 lost dramas of Sophocles. Quotations from these have also survived to us, and extracts, to the amount of about nine hundred lines in all. The total of 963 so-called fragments, as accumulated in Dindorf's *Poetæ Scenici Græci*, to which more have since been added, is made up by including hundreds of notices of single Sophoclean words, taken from the Lexicographers and grammatical writers, and also several allusions and passing notices. Omitting these, and a few of the shorter passages, either hopelessly corrupt, apparently spurious, or of no poetical importance, it has been attempted in the following selection to include everything that can fairly be considered capable of translation of these remains of Sophocles.

Of the sources from which extracts have been derived, the most important is the *Ecloga*, or Scrapbook, of Stobæus, or John of Stobi, a village in Macedonia. He appears to have been a cultivated gentleman of the fourth or fifth century A.D., who devoted his leisure to the compilation of a large work, in several books, of Elegant Extracts from Classical Authors, arranged according to their subject-matter. The work was intended for the use of his son, whom he was educating. The third book, commonly called the *Florilegium* of Stobæus, consists of scraps of poetry, chiefly of a moralizing tendency, of which a large portion are drawn from the plays of Sophocles. Plutarch, especially in his *Moralia*, stands next in importance of these sources; and Athenæus, in the *Deipnosophistæ*, third. Of the remainder a great part are furnished by Scholiasts, that is, by the writers on the margins of old manuscripts of notes, by way of illustration to passages on which they were commenting.

No records have come down to us whereby the order of composition, among the lost dramas, can be ascertained. The attempt to group them in tetralogies has proved a failure; nor are there, except in a few cases only, any means of discovering which of the titles preserved was that of a Satyric play.

The arguments can in some cases be recovered from the mythographical writings of Apollodorus, Parthenius, and others, among Greek writers, and of Hyginus and his imitators among the Latins.

In the cases of plots drawn from the Epic poets, they are furnished us by Proclus. I follow an arrangement based upon that of Welcker (*Die Griechischen Tragoedien mit Rücksicht auf den Epischen Cyclus*,

Bonn, 1839), whose reference numbers I have appended to the names of
the play; those of Dindorf, *Poetæ Scenici Græci*, Oxf. 1851, are pre-
fixed to the several fragments.

I take first a group of dramas on subjects belonging to Attic
tradition.

## I. ATTIC LEGENDS.

### *Triptolemus, Orithyia, Tereus, Creusa* or *Ion, Ægeus, Phædra.*

The loss of the *Triptolemus* (48) is much to be regretted. It has
been argued from a passage in Pliny (*Hist. Nat.* XVIII. 12. 1) that this
was one of the earliest plays by Sophocles; perhaps the very drama by
which his reputation was established, when, on the bringing to Athens
of the remains of Theseus, a special appointment of arbitrators was
made, on the nomination of Cimon and the generals, to decide the prize
between himself and Æschylus. If this were so, the interest of the subject-matter of the play may probably have
contributed to the victory of Sophocles over his great rival. Triptolemus
was an Attic hero, the founder of Eleusis, the place where the most sacred
rites of Athenian religion were celebrated. The interest of the plot may
have centred in the conspiracy of Cepheus against his life. But its
principal attractions must have lain in the entry of the hero, fresh from
his tour of the habitable world, riding in his flaming car, impelled by

### 538

#### Two dragons coiled about the axle tree

—in his account of strange races and distant lands, which he had visited,
sowing the corn, the gift of Demeter; and in the procession to Eleusis
with which the drama probably concluded. For a fine representation
of the Dragon-car and its rider see the remarkable contemporary vase
(British Museum, E. 137, *Monumenti Inediti*, Vol. ix., Pl. xliii.) signed
by Hiero. Earlier vases omit the snakes, and it seems probable that
Sophocles may have invented them. From Dionysius of Halicarnassus
(*Antiq.* I. 12) we learn how the Goddess came to Triptolemus and
despatched him on his beneficent errand. From her address, describing the route he was to take, we have

### 535

#### And on the tables of your memory
#### Set my words down.

### 527

#### And all that lies behind you to the right,
#### And all Œnotria, and the Tyrrhene gulf,
#### And the Ligurian land, shall welcome you.

### 537

#### Then must you turn

Elsewhere Triptolemus himself is speaking. We have allusions to
"Italy, blest with white wheat" (529), preserved in a translation by

Pliny, to Illyria (541), and to "the borders (or confines) of Carthage" (536). "Charnabon, who now rules over the Getæ" (528), we understand from Hyginus (*Poet. Astr.* 2. 14) to have given him an inhospitable reception, and slain one of his dragons, which was replaced by Demeter. There is also in Strabo (xv. p. 687) a fragment of an unnamed drama, probably belonging to this place.

### 782

Whence I beheld, haunted by Bacchanals,
Renownéd Nysa; her the hornéd God,
Iacchus, deems his foster-mother dear;
There no bird utters clamour

and one in which there is a plagiarism from Æsch. *Pers.* 181

### 761

Meseemed it the two Continents approached

The purpose of his journey, the dissemination of corn-culture, accounts for allusions to "pickled fish," "millet-seed," and "beer"; and to "the cup which has no foot, and cannot be set on table" (531, 534, 533, 541); and to the same place, probably, we may refer

### 539

—and there, too, came,
Eldest of Gods, joyous Festivity.

An interesting passage referring to the Eleusinian procession may perhaps be added from Plutarch (*Mor.* pp. 98. A, 102. B) as restored by Hermann;

### 724, 743

March, all you folk, masters of handicrafts,
Who venerate the grim-eyed Queen of Toil,
Daughter of Jove, with baskets on your heads;
Who weld the lifeless matter with strong hands
Upon the anvil, docile to your blows
Under the heavy hammer:

And this, of the final blessedness of the initiated (*Mor.* p. 21. F)

### 719

Thrice happy they who to the grave depart
With eyes on these ends fixed; they only, there,
Have life; to the others all things there are evil.

There seems no sufficient foundation for the opinion that this was a Satyric Drama. See Hygin. *Fab.* 147; Mythogr. Vat. II. 99; Apollod. I. 5. 2.

In the *Orithyia* (47) the ravished maiden is carried by Boreas north-
wards (Strabo, VII. p. 295)

### 655

Far over all the main, to the ends of earth,
And to night's sources, and the expanse of heaven,
The ancient garden of Phœbus

And this, perhaps, from Cicero's letters (*ad Att.* VI. 16) is taken
from a description of the ravisher

### 753

Not upon small fifes is he blowing, now,
But in fierce blasts, without a cheek-strap

See also Longinus *de Subl.* III. 2.

In the *Tereus* (68) Sophocles handled the tragical story of Procne and
Philomela, a favourite one with him, since he alludes to it in many
passages of the extant plays. (Compare Hygin. 45.) From the opening
of the drama, from a speech of Procne, with which may be compared
that of Deianira which opens the *Trachiniæ*, Stobæus has preserved for
us, among several others, the beautiful passage, the most affecting
perhaps in all the remains of our poet, which describes the lot of woman
in a half-civilized community

### 517

Now, by myself, I am nothing; yea, full oft
I have regarded woman's fortunes thus,
That we are nothing; who in our fathers' house
Live, I suppose, the happiest life, while young,
Of all mankind; for ever pleasantly
Does Folly nurture all. Then, when we come
To full discretion and maturity,
We are thrust out and marketed abroad,
Far from our parents and ancestral gods,
Some to strange husbands, some to barbarous,
One to a rude, one to a wrangling home;
And these, after the yoking of a night,
We are bound to like, and deem it well with us.

This, perhaps, Procne says to her sister

### 522

       —Much
I envy thee thy life: and most of all,
That thou hast never had experience
Of a strange land.

One strophe of a Choric Ode, made up of two fragments, has come down to us ;

### 518, 519

We, one race of mankind, by father, by mother,
    All came forth to the light of the selfsame day ;
No one man is born more great than another ;
      But some are fed with a bitter bread,
      And some with health, and some with wealth,
      And some bend under the forceful span
      Of slavery's yoke ; for the life of man
      Is changed and changed, in every breeze,
By the ingenious woes of our calamities.

And this is the conclusion of the corresponding antistrophe ;

### 718

        —But where is the grace
Of the many things that are loveliest,
If an ill-designing thought in the breast
Fosters the wealth that renders fair our race ?

To this same Chorus we may with probability assign two other scraps of lyric verse, of which the second is quoted by Stobæus as from "the same place" as the end of the first strophe given above :

### 692

'Tis never well, among mankind,
Great wealth with wonder to survey ;
For a man sees life decay
From him, with as brief a day
As the poplar's slender rind.

### 685

Might a man live, and give each hour
Its fill of pleasure ; but the morn
Creeps ever darkling on.

An invocation to the Sun, probably by Tereus, may have opened the Prologue

### 523

        Sun, thou radiance
Foremost in honour with the sons of Thrace,
Lovers of horses

To the scene where Procne learns her sister's fate, probably from a servant, Welcker assigns three fragments, the last quoted by Athenæus (1. p. 33. c) from an uncertain drama ;

### 513

Courage, speak truly, and thou shalt never stumble.

### 512

The whole barbarian race is money-loving.

### 696

O tongue, that has been silent all this while,
How wilt thou bear to tell thy story through?
Sure nought is heavier than the exigence
Under whose stress thou must perforce reveal
The secret of our princes

And to the Chorus, expostulating with her,

### 521

Terrible, Procne, truly ; all the same,
Being mortals, we must bear with tolerance
What Heaven ordains

### 520

Do not shout yet, before you see him dead.

She is then seen

### 525

Hastening along, and in a coloured robe

After her catastrophe a messenger sums up, in a manner little reconcilable with the sentiment usually attaching to the Sophoclean Chorus, to whom I cannot agree in assigning this passage

### 514

He was a fool ; but, in resisting him
With all their might, they were worse fools than he.
One in distress who, being enraged, applies
A remedy too strong for the disease—
He is no skilful leech of maladies.

The Chorus concludes thus :

### 515

Mortal born must think no thought
That becomes not mortal ; this

Knowing well, that there is none
Can assign, save God alone,
Of things future, what must be.

The plot of the *Creusa* or *Ion* (70) was probably similar to that of the well-known drama of Euripides. The Chorus, consisting of handmaids of Creusa, might sing

## 324

I would not offer up my vows
For wealth at home, or wedded spouse,
Beyond the usual measure ;
For slippery are the ways

From speeches, probably, of Ion, we have

## 325

And do not wonder that I hold so close,
O king, to profit ; for even those of men
Who reach old age cling fast to profiting ;
And beside riches, to mankind all else
Is second-rate ; true, there are some esteem
A man in health ; yet to me, no man poor
Appears to be in health, but always ailing.

## 326

The noblest life is that of righteousness ;
The best, freedom from sickness : pleasantest,
When every day one gets what one desires.

He is sent away while the mystery is being declared

## 327

Off, off my son ! this is not for your hearing.

A pretty fragment, quoted as from the *Ion*, is

## 298

'Tis only in Jove's gardens that we reap
The blessings of true happiness.

From other parts of the play four fragments survive :

## 296 (Nauck)

—it is a brave man's part
To bear all nobly.

321

This is most grievous, when, having the power
To order matters rightly, a man's own self
Brings and applies the mischief to himself.

322

But he who boldly goes to meet the ill,
His tongue is honest, and his wits secure.

323

Truly, to tell lies is not honourable;
But when the truth entails tremendous ruin,
To speak dishonourably is pardonable.

To this play, possibly belongs also

777

Eat laurel, chew it, bite it with your teeth:

that is, by way of preparation for giving an oracle.

Theseus, the hero-founder of Athens, was a favourite personage with
Sophocles. The treatment of his character in the Œdipus Coloneus is
well known; there is also a play on his early adventures, the *Ægeus*
(71), from which we have the description, by Ægeus, his father, of
the division of his grandfather Pandion's kingdom, preserved by Strabo
(IX. p. 392)

19

My father set apart for me to pass
Away to the seaside, apportioning me
The best part of this land; to Lycus, second,
He gave the opposite garden of Eubœa;
For Nisus he chose out the level ground
Of the Scironian coast; the land's south portion
Pallas has got, this hard-set giant-breeder.

The fifty tall sons of Pallas were the rivals of Ægeus, and were overcome by Theseus, aided by the treachery of Leos the crier. Sophocles
must have had a difficult task, to avoid wounding the susceptibilities of
those among his audience who belonged to the tribes which supposed
themselves to be named after Ægeus, Pallas, and Leos.
A beautiful simile has been preserved by a Scholiast on Od. II. 106;

24

For as among the leaves of aspen tall,
Though nothing else be shaken, yet its head
Some zephyr stirs, and lightly lifts its wing:

The following, from Pollux, 10. 160, points to the manner in which Theseus was made known to his father (Plut. *Vit. Thes.*), namely, by his drawing his sword "as if he designed to carve with it."

## 21

With a curved blade
He struck and clave down through the ribs and chine.

Ægeus addressing Theseus, after the recognition, says

## 23

How did you only 'scape the highwayman.
As you went forth?

A minor character is thus announced:

## 22

I do not hear—I see—a countryman.

To the Legend of Theseus belongs also the *Phædra* (72), of which Stobæus quotes several fragments, whence the course of the action is to some extent traceable. This reads like a passage from the opening of the drama:

## 607

Not on men only, nor on women, Love
Makes onslaught: but disturbs even the souls
Of Gods above us, and invades the sea.
To keep him off not even almighty Jove
Has power, but yields, and submits willingly.

To the same scene, probably, must be assigned the following fine fragment of an uncertain drama, of which, indeed, the Sophoclean authorship has been doubted; but the reader shall judge whether it is not worthy of him;

## 678

My children, of a surety Cypris is
Not Cypris only, but bears many a name.
Death is her name, and Might imperishable,
And maniac Frenzy, and unallayed Desire,
And Lamentation loud. All is in her;
Impulse, and Quietude, and Energy;
For in the bosoms of all souls that breathe
This Goddess is instilled. Who is not prey
For her? She penetrates the watery tribe
Of fishes; she is in the four legged-breed

Of the dry land; in birds her wing bears sway,
In brutes, in mortals, in the Gods on high.
Which of the Gods does she not, wrestling, **throw**
Thrice over? If it be not blasphemy,
And I blaspheme not, saying what is most true,
She reigns in Jove's own bosom; without spear,
Without a sword, Cypris cuts short all counsels,
Both human and divine.

For a graphic illustration of these last two passages see the beautiful vase from Nola (British Museum, E. 325) representing Eros hovering over a hare; and compare *Antig.* 782.

We may ascribe to the Nurse.

### 612

Sons are the anchors of a mother's life.

And to the ensuing dialogue with the Chorus.

### 609

Pardon me, and pray keep silence. What is shame
To woman, help a woman to conceal.

### 611

Women, no mortal can escape disgrace,
On whom God pleases to send misery;
Stricken from Heaven, we needs must bear our
plagues.

Hippolytus says, later in the action,

### 605

For it is not right
A man of nobleness should please himself,
When he can take no pleasure righteously.

From a dispute, probably between him and Theseus, comes

### 606

For never can a city be secure
In which all justice and sobriety
Are trodden under, and a babbler wields
A rascal goad, and ministers the state.

From the description of Hippolytus, we have his hound

### 619

He fawning low, laying his ears flat back

And from the scene after the catastrophe

### 608

So then, no greater evil could there be
Than a bad wife; nought better, than one chaste.
But from his own experience each man judges.

### 610

Count, among mortals, every happy man,
You will not find one, who is really so.

There remain two passages from the *Eclogæ Physicæ* of Stobæus, of which it does not appear that both are taken from this play. The first probably is not; it is from a dialogue of some one with Theseus, and we cannot with confidence ascribe it to Sophocles:

### 603

And so you lived!   You did not die,
When you went under the earth!
*Theseus.*                                        Nay, Destiny
Does not compel us ere our time.

The other is part of a Chorus:

### 604

The looms adamantine
    Of Destiny weave
All sorts of devices
    Men's souls to deceive;
They cannot be measured,
    They cannot be fled;
[They wait by his threshold,
    They wait by his bed.]

The *Theseus* may possibly have been the same play as the foregoing; but if it is to be identified with any other, the *Ægeus* fits better with the single fragment of it, from a speech by Theseus himself, which tells how he

### 233

—going along the way by the sea-side
Cleansed it of savage monsters.

## II. MISCELLANEOUS LEGENDS.

*Niobe, Tyro, Meleager, Iolaus* or *Iobates, Polyidus, Thamyras,
Hipponous, The Camicians.*

The *Niobe* (46) was doubtless a remarkable play. The slaughter of
the children appears to have been treated as happening at two distinct
periods and places, that of the boys occurring first, at Thebes. We
have in Plutarch (*Mor.* p. 760 D), an allusion to the shout of one of
them, calling to his friend for help (393). Of the scene in which the
maidens and their nurse lamented their death survive two pathetic
passages; the first sister says

### 399

I was the darling of the first of these.

And the nurse, recalling her cares,

### 400

With rags of thin-worn kirtles keeping them
Or warm, or cool; and taking up in turn,
After the night, toil upon toil by day.

The situation of the desolate mother so strongly impressed the poet,
that he recurs to it once and again in his surviving plays. Her apo-
strophe to Earth, as she feels herself turning into stone

### 395

I come; why dost thou call me?

was quoted, with some affectation, by Zeno the Stoic, on the occasion of
the fall which caused his death.

The story of Tyro, of her unwitting union with Poseidon, and of her
eventual deliverance by her twin sons, Pelias and Neleus, from the
tyranny of her step-mother Sidero, became the subject of two dramas
to our poet; or more probably of a single drama, the *Tyro* (49) which
was twice edited. See Apollod. *Bibl.* I. 9. The second edition
opened thus

### 578

What bird is this which cometh forth abroad?

From the early part of the play, in which Tyro is lamenting her case,
we have one passage of some beauty, preserved by Ælian, *N. A.* 11, 18.

### 587

But I go mourning for my tresses lost,
Like a she-colt, caught by the husbandman,
Which in the stables to a ruthless hand
Yields from her neck an auburn harvesting;

Then, ranging in the water-meadows, sees,
Pictured beneath the surface of the stream,
The image of her shadow, with the hair
Shamefully cropped, dishevelled all, and torn;
Oh even a pitiless heart might pity her,
Such is her frenzy, shuddering for shame,
Moaning and mourning for her ravished mane.

Another puns upon the name of Sidero

### 593

But she is warlike—she is one who plainly
Has used cold steel—she has it in her name!

Another, from Athenæus, [XI. p. 475 A, mentions snakes as the inmates of her prison

### 580

—That serpents should be there, in presence,
Upon the table, with the meat and drink!

We are told that the mask of the character was disfigured to show traces of blows. The hideousness of such a make-up, here and in the last scene of the Œdipus, was no doubt palliated, to Greek eyes, by its appearing as a reversion to the archaic. The actors, before masks were invented, stained their faces with the lees of wine.

### 584

Despondency produces sickness too.

### 582

Do not bespatter with a shower of words
Your present fortune; it is one full meet
To be bewailed in silence.

According to Schneidewin, we should place here, and not in the *Tereus*, 520 quoted above, p. 492. But there is no death of a male victim here, in the catastrophe.

From the scene of the recognition, which was brought about by a reference to the boat in which the children were exposed, we have

### 581

         —A soul in trouble
Sees many things when it is laid to sleep.

### 586

Age and delay teach all things

### 583

Yet in the multitude of many men
Neither is a man found worthy, who is well-born,
Nor son of the exceeding worthless, base;
But nothing, in a mortal, is assured.

The *Meleager* (75) is a play rather conjectured to exist, from allusions to the story, than actually quoted. The following couplet may be from the prologue

### 357

On Œneus' fields a boar of monstrous size
The archer-goddess, Leto's daughter, sent.

*Iolaus* (67), *Iobates* (79), *Iphicles* (82) or *Iocles*; all these names have been found or conjectured. The first would be a play on the story of the Heracleids, the second on that of Bellerophon. The following fragment is ascribed to the second;

### 280

Not even old age has learnt to love the tomb.

And this is from either *Iolaus* or *Iocles*.

### 282

Go with good cheer, and may you speed
As well as I well wish you!

The story of *Polyidus*, or *The Seers*, (78) is as follows; Glaucus, the son of Minos and Crete, while yet a child, in chasing a butterfly, fell into a honey-pot, and was lost. His father consulted the Curetes, the priests of Jove; who reminded him of a remarkable three-coloured cow he had in his possession, white, red, and black, and promised that the man who should best say what the three colours of the cow's hide were like, should be able to restore him his son, in life. The puzzle was solved by Polyidus, a seer, who compared the cow's colours to those observed in succession in a mulberry-bush

### 698

First you will see it blooming white, in flower,
Next reddened, in the rounded mulberry,
Next an old age as black as Egypt meets you

Whereupon the task is allotted to him, of which, some one says to him

### 463

You never will attain
To the summit without labour

to find the lost boy : and this he undertakes with the help of divination. At the sacred rite, he says,

### 465

Were present fleece of sheep, and from the vine
Drink offerings, and raisins well preserved ;
Fruits of all sorts, mingled with barley-cakes,
And olive-oil, and that most intricate
Wax-moulded fabric of the tawny bee.

And, from the last mentioned

### 467

He who came forth was the dead corpse, my bane.

The hardest part of his task yet remained, namely,

### 359 (Nauck)

To open the closed portal of the soul.

This he effected with the help of a herb, of which he saw the same use made by a serpent, whose companion he had himself killed in protecting the body. This queer fairy-tale was the subject of plays both by Sophocles and Euripides. There is no authority for considering them satyric dramas. See Apollod. *Bibl.* III. 3 ; Hygin. 136.

The special interest of the *Thamyras* (80) arises from it having been one of the plays in which, according to Athenæus, Sophocles himself acted ; he sustained, we are told, the part of a harp-player in a solo, perhaps that of Thamyras himself ; and from this circumstance was depicted, in the Pœcile, with a harp in his hand. The hero, elected king of Thrace for his skill as a musician—of the land that lies under the shadow of that

### 229

Thracian watch-tower, of Athoan Jove

is said to have contended with the Muses in song ; he was worsted, and forfeited to them both his eyesight, and his art. See *Il.* B. 599. In magnifying the more perfect music Thamyras had imported from Greece, some one speaks contemptuously of the old fashioned Thracian instruments

### 227

Gone is the twanging melody of the shell,
The lyre, the pipes, in which we joyed till now

I follow Nauck's emendation so far, but the fragment is too imperfect
for us to be sure of its full meaning.    Another tells us of

### 228

The jointed lyres, the psalteries,
The dulcet zither's carven frame
Known to the Greeks

A triangular harp or zither is also mentioned.   When defeated,
Thamyras is introduced taking vengeance on his instruments

### 232

Breaking the gold-bound horn—
Breaking the harmony of the string-strained lyre.

To these may be added, from Plutarch, *Moral.* p. 1093 D, a
fragment unintelligible as it stands, describing a poetical frenzy

### 747

—by a mordant monster muse-inspired
Do I burst forth ; and to the rock I come—
—from the lyre, and from the strains
Which Thamyras sings with art preeminent

In the *Hipponous* (81), it is told us, contrary to his usual habit,
Sophocles allowed the Chorus to speak, as in a Parabasis, out of
character.  Some one addresses the unfortunate Periboea

### 284

Wherefore hide nothing ; for all things are disclosed
By the all-beholding and all-hearing time.

She says

### 285

I come from the Olenian pasture-land.

### 281 (Nauck)

For saving medicines are not everywhere
To be discovered, but by forethought only.

For the story see Apollod. *Bibl.* 1. 8.

The scene of the *Camicians*, or *Minos* (83), is laid at Camicus,
afterwards Agrigentum, where Dædalus found refuge after his escape
from Crete.  Minos pursues him, and pleads against him before Cocalus
the king of the country.  He describes how Dædalus came to him for
refuge after the slaughter of Perdix, and relates his ingratitude.

Dædalus defends himself, and tells how he escaped from Crete; on wings, to wit, that

### 303

Lift me, and bear my frame right faithfully.

The catastrophe must have been the scalding to death of Minos in his bath by the daughters of Cocalus. Hygin. 40, 44. Other passages are—this, of the shells through which the clue of the labyrinth was suspended.

### 299

—Of this sea-snail, my daughter,
If we can find one—

### 302

To those who move not, fortune is no friend

### 304

He who when young cares nought for song
Is lost to all the time that's past,
And dead to all that follows.

This last is by some given to Euripides.

### III. Story of Athamas

*Athamas, Phrixus, Ino.*

There is a series of plays upon the story of Athamas and his family, preliminary to the Argonautic Cycle. Of the two bearing the name of Athamas only one line has survived. The first play (51) we must suppose to have embodied the story of Nephele; and Athamas, in the catastrophe,

### 5

Being childless—wifeless—and without a home

stands crowned with the sacrificial wreath before the altar of Zeus Laphystius—a celebrated situation with the ancients, which gave its name to the play—about to be slain by the Achæans in requital for the supposed death of Phrixus. The subject may have been suggested by the remarkable passage Herod. VII. 197, which gives one version of the final event. The second *Athamas*, unless it were merely a new edition of the first, dealt probably with the story of Ino, and may in that case be identified with it (52). A wonderful story told in Hygin. 4, is more probably the plot of the *Ino* of Euripides.

The *Phrixus* (50) has also perished, but with the exception of one spirited line—

### 646

Hound-like they howled, as it were whimpering

(Blomfield's emendation).    There is also a second—

### 647

Goal of our journey, precincts of this land

whence we may conclude that the subject was the fate of Nephele's children in Colchis.

## IV.  THE ARGONAUTS.

*The Lemnian Women, Phineus, Tympanistæ, Women of Colchis, Scythians, Rootgatherers.*

This series of plays belongs to the story of Jason and the Argonauts. Their adventures in Lemnos are the subject of the *Lemnian Women* (53); in which one strange line seems to refer to an image of a cow, set up in the island

### 348

—Athos shadows o'er
The broad back of the Cow of Lemnos' isle.

The *Phineus* (54), a play twice edited, yields nothing but some allusions to a "dried Egyptian mummy," (636) and to the "water of the Scythian Bosphorus," (637) and the comparison of an eye to a tavern-door, (635) which savours of comedy.    The *Tympanistæ*, which may possibly be the second edition of the *Phineus*, affords Stobæus a pretty bit.    We may suppose that Idothea, the second wife of Phineus, is coaxing the Argonauts to remain ;

### 563

Heigh-ho ! what greater joy could you receive
Than to reach land, and then, under some roof,
In slumberous mood, listen to the pouring hail !

Aristophanes, *Plut.* 635, quotes from this play

### 634

Find a kind healer in Asclepius.

In the *Women of Colchis* (55) we have the exploits of Jason, and the loves of him and Medea.    She says

### 313

—Do you promise, with an oath,
To return kindness ?

She tells him the story of Prometheus (315).

From a scene with a messenger, who relates how Jason has fared, we have

### 319 *a*

The flame-blast started forth
Upon its track unfraught with radiance

where I follow Professor Postgate's excellent emendation ; and

### 319 *b*

You would have been surprised to see
The golden blast of flame, shining from far.

A passage of which part is lost tells how " with limbs of brass they breathe out from their lungs—and their nostrils blaze "—(320). Æetes then says—

### 314

Did not the offspring of the earth forth-spring ?
*Mess.*  Ay truly, bristling fierce, with a plumed crest,
In arms of brass, forth from their mother's womb
Dauntless they sprang !

No special place can be assigned to the saw

### 311

'Tis well one who is mortal should so think
As fits mankind.

In the *Scythians* (56) the fortunes of Medea are further pursued. An interlude in tetrameters speaks of her and Absyrtus ; whose fate, as may be conjectured from the name of the play, constituted its principal subject.

### 491

For they sprang not from one wedlock ; but the later-
born, the lad,
Was the offspring of a Nereid ; and the girl Idyia had,
Long before, old Ocean's daughter

From the *Rootgatherers*, or *Pelias* (57), there is a single line which probably stood thus originally (Welcker's reading)

### 433

'Twas no white milk that fed her infancy !

We have also two fine anapæstic fragments. The first is an incantation, found in a Scholiast on Apollonius Rhodius;

### 480

Sun our Master, and Holy Flame,
Spear of Hecate, the way-side Dame,
Borne by her, through Olympus riding,
Or in sacred cross-ways of Earth abiding,
Crowned with oak-wreaths, and coils enwoven
Of savage serpents

The other depicts, as by a flash of lurid lightning, the terrible enchantress in the wood: its preservation is due to Macrobius;

### 479

She turned her eyes from the deed
Backward—she cropped the weed—
She squeezed forth the juice milk-white,
She caught it in coffers bright,

. . . .

And the boxes' covers hide
The pieces of root inside,
Which she, with clamour and crying,
Naked, was chopping, plying
Her sickle's brazen blade.

### V. STORY OF TELEPHUS.

*Aleadæ, Mysians, Telephus.*

There are two dramas, possibly three, on the story of Telephus. The *Aleadæ* (76) has survived in a large number of comparatively uninteresting fragments, from which Welcker has conjectured with much ingenuity that the plot was something as follows. Aleus, king of Tegea, having caused to be exposed Telephus, the son of Auge his daughter by Hercules, on account of an oracle, which declared that the son of Auge should be the death of his own sons, the infant Telephus has been suckled by a hind upon the mountains, and returns to Tegea to claim the honours of his descent at the hands of his uncles Hippothous and Nereus. He relates the story of his miraculous foster nurse; how

### 110

—a wild antlered hind came slowly down
From the precipitous hills

. . . .

Lifting her nostrils and her antler-tynes
Softly she stole

and a long debate ensues, to which the following may be ascribed :
Telephus says

### 98

Then indeed all the affairs of life grow rotten,
When men are minded to cure wrong with wrong.

### 99

It is not easy to withstand the just.

### 100

To feign is base, and is not gentlemanly.

### 101

Yea, and a righteous tongue has mighty strength.

On the other side of the question we have

### 102

Be silent, boy ; silence has many beauties.

### 103

Why make you
Matter of this for many speeches more ?
Excess of words is grievous everywhere.

### 104

Search not out all things ; it is good that much
Should be unknown.

Telephus complains that the cause is going against him, in words
which have by no means lost force, with many centuries of practical
application ;

### 109

Riches gain friends, gain honours, too, for men,
Yea, gain a seat most pleasant, in the chairs
Of topmost sovereignty.   Moreover none
Grow hostile toward riches ; and even those
Who have so grown renounce their enmity.
For riches have a formidable way
Of creeping into spots inviolable
And hard to reach ; and into places where
A poor man could not, even if he came thither,
Obtain what he desires.   An ugly body

And of bad fame riches make wise of speech
And comely to behold.   To them alone
Belongs the power of good and evil cheer,
And to conceal misfortunes.

He seems finally to abandon the attempt to establish his descent by proof.

### 107

Pause there.   It is sufficient to be called
This father's son—if I am really so.
And if I am not, so much the worse for me.
Repute is stronger than reality.

He relies on his apparent worth and prowess,

### 108

Are bastards equal to legitimate?
All excellence has a legitimate birth.

He threatens violence at last—

### 106

No man, I think ; but look, whether it be not
Better to beat one's foe, even impiously,
Than to be told I am myself a slave.

After this would follow the slaughter of the Aleadæ ; the Chorus would naturally take their part, and lament the catastrophe ;

### 105

Nor know I what to say, to cure it ;
When the good give place
To those who are base,
What city could well endure it?

How the play ended, we are not told ; but possibly by the appearance of Hercules, and the announcement on his part, of his paternal relation to Telephus.

In *The Mysians* or *Telephus* (77) the fortunes of Telephus are further pursued.   He seems to have been sent to Mysia by his father, in order that he might find his mother Auge, who had been adopted by Teuthras. The plot must have turned upon the narrow escape Telephus there had of being wedded to his own mother ; but all ends happily, with a recognition between the mother and son (Hygin. 100).   On landing, he is answered by some passer-by—

### 360

Sir, Asia the whole continent is called ;
The Mysians' state, though, is named Mysia.

He replies;

### 358

How sweet it is to the unfortunate,
Even for a little period, to forget
The ills that stand about them !

Here is an anticipation of Milton ;

### 361

And many a Phrygian dulcimer, and crash
Harmonious, of the Lydian psaltery,
Sounds to it, in linked measures, long drawn out.

Asiatic properties are introduced ;

### 362

Armlets, tiaras, and an ermine robe.

And the Chorus, towards the conclusion, say

### 359

No man from toil has perfect rest ;
He who has least, is happiest.

## VI. Story of Perseus.

### *Acrisius, Danae, Andromeda, Larissæans.*

Argos furnished three cycles of legend previous to the Trojan war,
from which Sophocles took subjects. In the *Acrisius* (59), with which
the *Danae* may perhaps be identified, but not, I think, the *Larissæans*,
we have the discovery and condemnation of the princess. To the early
part of the play must belong

### 58

Some one calls : listen ! Or do I bark in vain
To him who is in fear everything rustles.

### 59

No falsehood lingers on into old age.

### 60

A runaway slave, who has had fetters clapped
Upon his limbs, in all things, obviously,
Speaks what will please his master.

(Nauck's reading.)    From the latter part we have

### 62, 61

Brief speech becomes those who think soberly,
In presence of their mothers and their sires :
Specially a maiden, and of Argive race,
Whose glory is in silence, and few words.

One fragment is quoted as from the *Danae* ; Acrisius says

### 176

Your trouble I know not ; but one thing I know,
If this boy lives, I perish.

### 63

Lady, cheer up ; most of our ills, blowing loudly
In dreams by night, grow milder when 'tis day.

This is probably from a dialogue between **Danae** and **Acrisius** ;

### 64, 65

—No man loves life like him that's growing old.
—Yet life, my child, is the best boon of all.
—Yet the same persons cannot die twice over.

### 66

Nor can the living aid the man that's dead,
Seeing that himself must die.

The *Andromeda* (60) survives in the question to Perseus

### 129

On steeds, or wherries, are you voyaging ?

A bold trope is

### 130

Nowise to dread fresh-reeking letters.

There is also an interesting passage on sacrifices ;

### 132

                     For the State
She, as a bloody passover, was slain ;
For savages have the custom, from of old,
To pay to Cronos human sacrifice.

(Scaliger's emendation.)

In the *Larissæans* (61) the story of Acrisius is concluded. Besides one forcible line

### 67

How all men strive to shun a tyrant's face !

there are two passages from a speech of Perseus, or of a messenger, describing the catastrophe at the court of Teutamidas ;

### 68

And many a contest for all comers he
Proclaims ; setting forth cauldrons for a prize
Of beaten brass, and hollow drinking-cups
Of solid silver, or of parcel-gilt,
To the number of twice sixty.

### 69

And to me, who threw third, a man'of Dotis
Came close, named Elatus, in the disk-throwing.

### VII. WARS OF ARGOS AND THEBES.

*Epigoni, Eriphyle, Alcmæon, Amphiaraus.*

Of dramas on subjects from the wars of Argos and Thebes there are, besides the three plays on the story of Œdipus which have come down to us, first the *Epigoni* (41), which however it is difficult to distinguish from the *Eriphyle*, and the *Alcmæon* (42). One of them must have been a drama on the slaughter of his mother by Alcmæon, in requital of her betrayal of his father Amphiaraus. To the opening of this play Welcker assigns the following singular fragment quoted by John of Damascus ; the Sophoclean authorship of which is however doubtful.

### 779

Now that the office of the God, my sons,
Has all been duly done, let us begone
Unto the school, the Muses' nursery.
We must be gaining something every day,
As long as we can better what we know.
Boys, without fee, know how to do amiss,
Learning it of themselves right easily ;
While good, not even if they go to school
Know they by heart, but hardly compass it.
This, then, let us regard, and let us toil,
O children, that we may not seem to be

The sons of untaught men, yea, of a sire
Who dwells in foreign regions.

To fit this passage into some known subject of tragedy, we must
find a pious father long absent from home, and a group of sons, of an
age to be addressed by a tutor, or by one of their own number, as
above. This agrees with the situation of Alcmæon, Amphilochus, and
the other sons of Amphiaraus. The fate of the father is described

### 781

The soil of Thebes
Split, and received him, with his arms, his team,
Chariot and all.

From an address to Eriphyle comes

### 195

O thou unscrupulous, and worse! O woman!
No other of all evils mortals own
Is there, or ever can be, worse than—woman!

Other fragments cannot so easily be placed;

### 194

For in the case of those whom envy follows,
Dishonour is more apt to conquer them
In shameful actions, than in honourable.

From the *Eriphyle* are quoted:

### 202

But virtue's treasures are alone secure.

### 203

For brave men's breasts grow not effeminate.

### 204

But when it is not lawful
To speak with freedom what is for the best,
And the worse counsel in a state prevails,
There errors lead astray the common weal.

### 205

How can I, a mortal, fight with Providence?
When the pinch comes, hope is of no avail.

(Nauck's reading.)

### 206

Keep to good words, now you attain old age.

### 207

—Away!
Sleep is physician of that malady.

### 209

O tongue, among what people thou hast honour
Where words are of more force than actions!

The following are ascribed to the *Alcmæon*;

### 95

I would that I might see you aiming well,
Hitting your mark in honest sentiments.

And from a dialogue between Alcmæon and Adrastus, given by
Plutarch, without author or play :

—You are her brother,
Who slew her spouse!
—And you the murderer
Of your own mother, who bare you!

There is also a Satyric drama on the story of *Amphiaraus.* The
fragments are

### 116

He who is, to this prophet-company,
As crab to pinna

### 122

Dogskin, and hide of a dun cow that lowed

It is not clear what incident in the story of Amphiaraus could have
been made a subject for burlesque, or how such a play could well have
been associated with a trilogy on the subject of the Theban war.

## VIII. LEGENDS OF THE HOUSE OF ATREUS.

### *Œnomaus, Atreus* or *The Mycenæans, Thyestes.*

In the *Œnomaus* (62) the winning of Hippodamia by Peleus, and
the death of Myrtilus the charioteer, constituted the action. From the
threats of the cruel Œnomaus we get three words

### 420

Having afforded, in his scalp cut off,
A napkin, Scythian-fashion!

The fierce Hippodamia declares her love for Pelops,—in the best lines of all those preserved to us by Athenæus

### 421

A touch of love so winning in his face
Has he—a certain lightning of the eyes,
First he himself is kindled, then me too
He inflames all through; measuring his glance by
    mine,
Even as the craftsman's ruler is laid straight,
While he marks out the line.

From the scene in which the plot is laid comes

### 419

But when an oath is added, then the soul
Is made more careful; for it has two things
To guard against; both the reproach of friends,
And sin against the gods.

Pelops must have listened to the warning reminding him of the frustrated anticipations of mother after mother, that

### 418

          —she would have borne a son
Swifter than he; she one, swifter than he.

And this being in vain—

### 422

        —I see you, with a scraper,
Clipping from a bay horse his staring coat.

Two fragments besides contain some poetry:

### 423

Were I an eagle soaring high,
    So might I fly
Over the barren silvery main,
Far as the swell of the ocean plain—

### 424

The breezes blow—but the hen marks them not,
Save when the time is come for her to lay.

We are told that Æschines the orator sustained, when on the boards, the part of Œnomaus in this play.

Of *Atreus* or *The Mycenæans* (63) we have only, from the quarrel of Atreus and Thyestes—

### 144

No, by his cowardice I swear,
On which he battens, being himself a woman,
With men for foes !

And from the uncertain fragments

### 764

The boys whom I begat he has destroyed.

And perhaps, referring to the portent of the sun's turning backward.

### 771

But every man respects
Him who turns back the circle of the sun.

*Thyestes in Sicyon* (64, 65) is another drama which appears to have been twice edited. At least it is not easy, from the story in Hyginus, 88, to which we must refer, to collect the material for two separate dramas. The fragments are uninteresting, except this description of the fabulous vine of Eubœa, preserved by a Scholiast on the *Phœnissæ* of Euripides :

### 239

—For there is a land, Eubœa,
By the sea-side ; there grows ephemeral
The vine of Bacchus ; first in morning bright
The place luxuriates with fair-petalled flowers ;
Next, mid-day fills up the interior mass
Of the unripe fruit ; then comes the afternoon,
And the branch takes a darker hue ; at even
All the fair-flourishing vintage is cut down,
And ferments into wine.

From Stobæus come a handful of the moralizing extracts in which he revels ;

### 234

Not Ares, even, withstands necessity.

### 235

Let us be going with speed. It cannot be
Blame should e'er fasten on a righteous haste.

### 236

It has annoyances, I know: but still,
We must endeavour to endure, as best
We may, the hard necessities of life.
We needs must gain some healing, from such methods.

### 237

For even in words there is a pleasure, when
They cause oblivion of our present ills.

### 238

—Though an old man: but sense, and skill to adorn
At need, are wont to accompany old age.

A sophistical fragment, more in the manner of Euripides, I derive
from Nauck's edition, fr. 227 :

For none is wise save him to whom God pays
    honour ;
But he who looks towards heaven, even though it
    bid him
Overstep right, must set himself to obey ;
For nought is shameful, when prescribed by heaven

### IX.  STORIES FROM THE CYPRIA.

*Alexander, Ulysses Furens, Lovers of Achilles, Scyrian Women, Demand
of Helen, Iphigeneia, Muster of the Achæans, Shepherds,
Troilus, Palamedes.*

In a well-known passage of Athenæus (VII. 3, p. 277) the fondness
of Sophocles is noted for subjects drawn from the Trojan cycle of the
Epic poets ; and, as is further remarked by the author of the Life of
Sophocles, especially from Homer's Odyssey.  About 40 plays in all
belong to these classes.   The ten above-mentioned belong to the Cypria,
or story previous to the Iliad.   The *Alexander* (1) seems to have been a
play on the recognition of Paris, frs. 90, 91.   From the *Ulysses Furens*
(2), a play on the subject of the feigned madness of Ulysses, as detected
by Palamedes, we have, probably spoken by Agamemnon,

### 411

Now you know all ; I have spoken as I was bidden ;
For, in the style of the Argive tongue, a tale
Is brief, even to conciseness.

The adventures of Achilles in Scyros occupied two plays, one Satyric, from which comes a celebrated simile, which fortunately attracted the attention of Stobæus

### 162

This love-disease is a well-pleasing pain;
I might compare it, not amiss, to boys
Who, when the frost appears, under clear skies,
Grasp in their hands a solid icicle;
Who find, at first, charms in its novelty;
But, in the end, neither will the thawing lump
Permit itself to be let go, nor yet
The prize remain, with comfort, in their hold.
So lovers often are, by this same Desire,
Driven to be busy at once, and to refrain.

Peleus says of Thetis

### 163

What labour had I not to undergo?
A lion—and a serpent—water—fire!

A dog is addressed

### 166

You, Boar-catcher!   You whelp of Pelion!

Nestor, or Ulysses perhaps;

### 167

To him, whose tongue flows down with honey

Achilles himself:

### 168

He, in invulnerable panoply,
The work of Vulcan, there

### 169

—from his eyes
Darts javelins

The *Scyrian Women* (3) no doubt followed the Epic story, introducing Thetis, Ulysses, Lycomedes, Deidamia, and perhaps Diomedes. Ulysses chides Achilles thus

### 497

Thou that dost quench thy race's brilliant light,
Born of a father of all Greeks the first,
Fawn'st thou?

Lycomedes, probably, bewails the conditions of old age ;

500

There is no burden like a life prolonged ;
To extreme old age all ills are natural,
Mind gone, work useless, vain imaginings.

The reply must, it seems, be assigned to Diomedes ;

501

If we could cure ills by bewailing them,
Or raise, by weeping, a dead man to life,
Then gold would be less precious than our sorrow ;
But as it is, old man, these remedies
Are ineffectual to restore to light
One hidden in the grave ; else, my own sire
Would have been brought up to the day again,
So far as tears could do it.

Either Lycomedes or Thetis pleads

498

For that war loves to prey upon the young.

And either the same, or Achilles himself, urges—in true sea-faring
style ;

499

In good sooth, sailors are unfortunates,
Whom neither God nor Genius could reward
With as much money as were meed for them ;
A losing folk are they, who either save,
Or gain, or lose, ever, by hazarding
Upon slight chances far-sought merchandize.

The subject of the *Demand of Helen* (7) seems to have been the ex-
pedition of Ulysses and Menelaus to Troy for that purpose, previous to
the sailing of the fleet. We have first, a touch of Helen herself, who
hears her husband's voice, his presence being as yet unknown to her ;

186

Somehow the very accent on his tongue
Wafts me the fragrance of Laconian speech.

Menelaus says, almost certainly in this play, according to Plutarch

713

But my fate ever in a frequent round
Turns, of a God, and changes character.

Even as the moon's appearance in one shape
Cannot continue for two nights the same,
But from the invisible comes forth at first,
Beauteous in its new form, then rounding it;
And soon as ever it appears most brave,
Again dissolves and comes to nothingness.

From this play, too, Plutarch probably took a graceful snatch
of chorus, in which there rises before us a momentary vision of the
banks of the Eurotas, and the girls running races in the meadow—

### 791
—And her, the maid
Whose yet untrailing Spartan skirts flap free
Round her bared limbs—the young Hermione.

A line ascribed to Euripides under this title, who however does not
seem to have written such a play, is by Welcker claimed for Sophocles:
Helen is speaking; Hermione is supposed not to be present;

But I was not a traitress, O my child.

Ulysses, addressing the Trojans, is cheapening what he would obtain
(Hermann's emendation)

### 187
And if we carry a woman off, who paints,
Vexing her faded cheek with pencilling
Deeply worked in

Helen, perhaps at this insult, loses patience:

### 185
'Twere best for me to drink bull's blood at once,
And not to go on being abused by them!

This play appears to be the same that is called in the argument
of the Ajax *The Rape of Helen* (20). Another, the *Marriage of Helen*,
of which nothing intelligible survives, was apparently a Satyric Drama.

In the *Iphigeneia* (4) we have Ulysses again, expostulating with
Clytæmnestra (Porson's emendation)

### 289
A mind of genuine wisdom is a thing
A man should cling to, as polypuses fix
Their body to a rock

And a proverb

> A vinegar jar is a bad honey-pot.

Of the next fragment only the first line appears rightly to belong to
Sophocles.  The Chorus say

### 288

> For easy leisure brings forth nothing good,
> Nor any God assists the indolent.

A lyric passage, referred to a play called *Clytæmnestra*, not elsewhere
noticed, is by Welcker assigned to this play, and supposed to be
descriptive of Clytæmnestra's despair.

### 310

> Some Antæus, as it were,
>     See ye not, involving her,
> And breathing terror, as of Hecate,
>     The Antæan Goddess

But the passage is corrupt, and the meaning cannot be ascertained
with certainty.

The *Achæorum Syllogus* or *Muster of the Achæans* (5) has usually,
but I think erroneously, been identified with the *Syndeipni* or *Feasters*.
The only reason for this identification is, that Athenæus, in one place,
gives as his authority for a quotation "Sophocles in the Achæans'
Syndeipnon."—*Syndeipnon*, the "Dinner party," is several times given
as an alternative name for *Syndeipni*.  Postponing for the present
the discussion of this passage, and of the fragments ascribed to the
*Syndeipni*, it may be proved, from the passage in Plutarch numbered (152)
below, and by a passage quoted by Welcker from a Herculanean MS.,
that Sophocles did write a drama on the story, preserved by Aristotle
(*Rhet.* II. 26) of the muster of the Greeks at Tenedos, and the indignation of Achilles, when not invited, or invited too late, to their banquet.
To this subject all the fragments quoted as from the *Achæorum Syllogus*
seem perfectly appropriate ; while those quoted as from the *Syndeipni*,
or *Syndeipnon*, admit more easily, as will be hereafter shown, of a different concatenation.  The circumstance that a proverb arose out of the
story of the Anger of Achilles, in which the word "deipnon," for dinner,
occurred, may perhaps account for the two plays having been confounded together.

Ulysses, probably, addresses Agamemnon ;

### 150

> Take you the writing tablets ;
> Read, on your throne, if any is absent, who
> Joined in the oath.

Achilles, perhaps in conversation with an embassy, is meditating a desertion of the fleet ;

### 151

The crews already with their punting-poles
Direct the keel along the favouring way
Of our night-voyage.

Ulysses intervenes ;

### 152

           You are not angered
About the banquet ; but you see already
The abodes of Troy—and tremble !

And again,

I know what 'tis you flee from ; not the slight ;
But—Hector is at hand ! ah ! 'tis unsafe
To tarry !

I follow Welcker in not ascribing to this play the spirited fragment (**153**), for which, and for the extant passages ascribed to the *Syndeipni*, see post, pp. 351, 359.

The *Pœmenes* or *Shepherds* (6) is known to have been a drama on the landing of the Greeks in Troia, and the self-devotion of Protesilaus. A graceful element in the plot has been preserved to us by an accident. Two Byzantine writers, frs. 127, 459, mention a particular Persian word as having been used by Sophocles, one ascribing it to this play, the other to an "Andromache," elsewhere unmentioned. Hence Welcker has plausibly conjectured that Andromache was a personage in this drama : and it is easy to see that her presence, as the loving wife of the devoted (and here victorious) Trojan hero, would heighten the tragic interest attaching to the fate of the defeated champion of the Greeks, celebrated as he was, above all others, for the love of his absent wife Laodamia. By way of prologue some one describes the Grecian host landing ;

### 445

For in the early dawn, ere I beheld
Any of the stall-men bringing fresh plucked fodder
To the she-goats, I saw an army march
To the rock by the sea shore

From the same speech perhaps, comes a piece of local colour, one of several traces of which, in single words, have survived :

### 446

—there 'tis the native tunny-fish
Passes the winter, in the Hellespont
Hard by ; in summer the Bosporian folk
Have it in season ; 'tis their frequent food.

The Chorus of shepherds, relating their peaceful mode of life, now interrupted by war, say, of their flocks

### 447

—since for their sakes we slave
Who are their masters; and them, though dumb,
We must give heed.

To them also may belong two snatches of pastoral ditty

### 962

The dams that are with their young,
And the she-goats, would display
Their new-born at their breast.

### 466 (Nauck)

Where neither dun ewe's rustic shepherd

Here also we must place a fragment sometimes ascribed to the *Peleus*, the first letter only of the reference being preserved;

### 438

With wicker baskets wars upon the race
Of purple-fish.

The slaughter of Cycnus by Achilles was introduced, in order, apparently, to restore the balance of victory to the Greeks; the principal tragic interest must however have remained with the fall of Protesilaus, since Cycnus is represented as bragging of his style of fighting in a manner the reverse of elegant (938). It seems indeed to have resembled the Parisian *savate*. To the same speech may belong

### 448

And strike into his jaws a chill
After his noonday fever

Other fragments are (Nauck's reading)

### 449

—there is no wound I know of
That can be healed by speech

### 450

'Tis pleasant to essay one's hand in fight
Till it grows numb with striking

This is Hector's; the Chorus, after the fall of Cycnus, sing

### 451
From each wall
To their fall
Shake the topstones which Poseidon laid.

The *Troilus* (8) has almost entirely perished. Some one says of Peleus, by way of prelude to an unfavourable mention of his son,

### 548
—So it was,
He joined himself in an unspeakable match,
Embracing Thetis, goddess multiform.

After the death of the young prince, the old eunuch, his attendant says—

### 551
—I have lost
The manly boy, my master!

And the Chorus, perhaps

### 560
We pass on to the wells and watering places

to wash the corpse.

The only important quotation from the *Palamedes* (9) has commonly been assigned to the *Nauplius*, though without authority, and assumed to be a continuation of the remarkable fragment (379). But the statement of Eustathius to the contrary is too clear to be thus set aside.

### 380
Did he not through God's favour put away
Scarcity from them, and find out for them
Pastimes most clever, when they sat down tired
With threshing the sea surge—draughtsmen and dice,
A pleasant solace in their idleness?

Welcker suggests that this is taken from a speech by Palamedes, speaking of himself in the third person.

## X. STORIES FROM THE ILIAD.
### *The Captives, The Phrygians.*

It is singular that the Iliad should have afforded Sophocles so few of his plots. The extant plays show that he was familiar with the poem, especially with the first book, and with the more famous passages. It is

possible that he felt the acquaintance of his spectators with its scenes
and language to be in excess of the degree most conducive to interest in
dramas founded upon classic legend.   There are only two, which can
with any likelihood be said to have been drawn from the Iliad.

In regard to the *Captives* (23) I find myself obliged to differ from
Welcker, who has allowed his imagination full scope in the delineation
of a plot, of which the Death of Astyanax, and the distribution of
the Trojan women among the conquerors of Troy, are the main features.
He has overlooked the mention of "Mynes and Epistrophus," fr. 57,
from which, comparing *Il.* ii. 692, I conclude, with Bergk, that the
subject of the drama was the story of Chryseis and Briseis.   This is
confirmed by the fragment

37

Cilla and Chrysa I inhabit, here

(Meinecke's emendation) which belongs, no doubt, to a speech of
Apollo, probably a prologue.   Compare *Il.* i. 37.   Chryses is, no doubt,
the subject of the next scrap—

43

But the old man put on clogs bound round with linen.

And Calchas, perhaps, of the next ;

32

A purger of the army, and well skilled
In his concoctions

33

The shield, like a half-mould, is full of hollows.

We may perhaps ascribe this line to a speech of Achilles vaunting
his deeds, and the next,

34

There has been taken from thee, as it were,
A reed out of thy lyre

to one of Patroclus, condoling with him for the loss of Briseis.   Other
fragments are

35

A scorpion watches behind every stone.

39

If I, being small, have conquered what is—little !

49

From one poor cup a second time I poured

The *Phrygians* (10) seems clearly to have been a play on the Ransom of Hector. Priam says

### 649

> For O my son, Ares delights to slay
> The noble and the good; but the tongue-valiant,
> Avoiding mischief, are beyond annoy;
> For Ares makes no booty of the base.

### XI.  STORIES FROM THE LITTLE ILIAD AND TAKING OF TROY.

*The Æthiopians, Philoctetes in Troia, Dolopians, Lacænæ,*
*Laocoon, Locrian Ajax, Polyxena.*

The Little Iliad and Taking of Troy afforded subjects for many plays: the *Ajax* and *Philoctetes* among them. The *Æthiopians* (11) no doubt had Memnon for its hero. A play under his name, probably identical with this, is mentioned in the argument of the *Ajax*.

### 26

> Wherefore all this I say to please thee, not
> To force thee; thou the while, as do the wise,
> Praise what is honest, stick to what brings profit.

### 27

> Black-a-vised wasp-waists, with a four-winged body
> In prison bands.

These, we are told, are ants: it is, perhaps, a simile for the Myrmidons.

The *Philoctetes in Troia* (14) was no doubt an earlier play than the *Philoctetes* in Lemnos which has come down to us. The fragments seem to show that it did not form part of one trilogy with the other.

### 626

> Death is the last physician of disease.

### 627

> —that you may not be overcome
> With the bad smell of me.

### 631

> —the voiceless inarticulate
> Music of oxen

The *Dolopians* (15) is identified by Welcker with the *Phænix:* he supposes it to have been a drama on the subject of the fetching of Neoptolemus from Scyros. From the second we have

### 643

the thorny artichoke
Fills all the glebe

Part of a description, apparently, of Scyros; and from the first (Toup's emendation)

### 184

He might be like a hare, that in his form
Has a poor runaway roof to cover him.

The *Lacænæ* (16) is easily identified as a play on the fetching of the Palladium from Troy. The scene is before the house of Paris. Either Diomed or Ulysses describes the adventure;

### 336

—and we entered on
A tunnel, narrow, and not free from mire.

Either Helen or one of her Laconian attendants exclaims

### 339

By the Laconian Twins!
Yea by Eurotas also! By the Gods
In Argos, and at Sparta!

Apparently Paris discovers them, and is persuaded by some one to avoid a conflict;

### 337

For Heaven will never—if a man may say it—
Approve in Phrygians, that they should begin
Like insolence with Argives: in this battle
Contend not thou with force!

(Madvig's and Nauck's readings.) The next is from a Chorus

### 339

So shall ye make to cease from daily woes and
parching misery

To this play Welcker refers the spirited passage quoted by Herodian as a specimen of that figure in rhetoric, well known to parliamentary speakers, by which a personal insult is conveyed under cover of a refusal to say or believe anything so monstrous. Ulysses says of Diomed, with whom we must suppose him to have quarrelled, or feigned a quarrel,

### 153

> But I will say—nothing injurious to you!
> Not—that you have been driven forth fugitive
> From your ancestral country; not—that Tydeus
> Sojourns in Argos, as a foreigner,
> Because he killed a blood-relation; not—
> How before Thebæ he cut off the head,
> And gnawed it, of the son of Astacus,
> Cannibal-fashion!

Of the *Laocoon* (17) we have the curious information from Servius that Sophocles gave names to his serpents; Porcis and Chariboea, apparently. It seems likely that their metamorphosis into human shape formed part of the action, or narration. From the scene preluding the sacrifice to Poseidon, we have

### 340

> And a street altar glows with smoky flame
> Through drops of myrrh, barbarian, of sweet smell.

Reflecting on the supposed departure of the enemy, some one says

### 343

> For of toil past there is no reckoning more.

Compare, from the uncertain fragments,

### 672

> Labours are sweet, when labour is o'erpast.

From the sacrificial hymn we have

### 341

> Thou, Poseidon, who art lord
> O'er the cliffs, or glassy wave
> Of the wind-beset Ægean,
> On the lofty crags abiding
> Of all harbours

And from the concluding scene, the speech of a messenger, found in Dionysius of Halicarnassus;

### 342

> Now at the gates Æneas, goddess-born,
> Bearing his father on his shoulders, stands;

Whose silken gown is stained with blood, that flows
Down from the wounds inflicted on his frame
By thunderbolts.    He gathers in a ring
All the full muster of his house-servants,
And Phrygians in a swarm beyond belief
Follow him, willing to be emigrants.

Of the *Ajax Locrus* (21), we have

11

If thou didst harm, then thou must suffer harm ;
......and the Golden Eye of Righteousness
Sees and rewards the unrighteous.

The bold imagery of the second line caused it to be frequently
quoted.   Other relics are

12

Kings become wise in wise men's company.

13

Man is a shadow and a breath, no more.

16

A panther-skin, a Libyan buff-jerkin
Stripped from a spotted whelp.

This last was the sign hung up at the door of Antenor, the Trojan
traitor, to save him from violence during the sack.   Its mention seems
to show that the storm of Troy, including, no doubt, the violent
removal of Cassandra by the hero of the drama from the sanctuary
of Athena entered into the action.   This seems to negative its
identification with the play quoted by Cicero (See *Teucer*, post, p. 534).

The *Polyxena* (24) opens in a spirited manner with the apparition of
Achilles

469

Leaving the borders of the ooze—profound—
Obscure—where sounds no pæan—barren streams
Of Acheron, echoing shrill cries, I come !

Compare the Prologue to the *Hecuba* of Euripides.   Again

471

Out of the gloom, out of the shadowy cloud

And these appear to belong to a dialogue between Agamemnon and
Menelaus

473

An endless coat of ills investing thee

### 468

Do thou, abiding here, in Ida's land,
Gather Olympus' flocks, and sacrifice.

### 470

There is no leader of a multitude
Who can show favour, and suffice, to all;
Since not even Zeus, whose sway is more than mine,
Could befriend all, whether he sent rain or sun,
But, if he came to judgment of mankind,
Would be condemned; how then should I, being
    mortal,
And of a mortal mother, be more knowing
Than Zeus, in goodness?

## XII. THE RETURNS FROM TROY.

*Nauplius, Teucer, Eurysaces, Peleus, Women of Phthia, Chryses,
Aletes, Erigone, Tyndareus.*

There must have been about twelve plays in all, the *Electra*
included, founded on incidents in the Returns of the Heroes from Troy,
and their sequel. The *Nauplius* (25) introduces the old sea-rover, the
father of the pilot Palamedes, lamenting the cruel fate of his gifted son,
and preparing for the returning armament his terrible revenge (Hygin.
116). From the early part of the play may come

### 375

O Jove, who easest grief!
O offerings of the third goblet, due
To saviour Jove!

The lines descriptive of the inventions of Palamedes are of great
interest, and we may well rejoice that Achilles Tatius has preserved
them;

### 396

But this man found out how to build a wall
About the Argive host; discovered weights,
Measures, and numbers; he first fashioned these,
From one to ten, and then again from tens
Invented fifties, up to thousands, he
Alone showed to the army how to give
Signals by beacon, how to set a watch
Over their sleep, and how to mark the hours

Until the morning, and made manifest
What had not been expounded; he traced out
The spaces and the orbits of the stars,
Each in his rank, and the celestial signs,
And, for the shepherds of their ships at sea,
The Dog's chill setting, and the Great Bear's round.

Nauplius proceeds, in another fragment of this play, to speak of
the invention of games

### 381

And chequer-boards, ruled with five lines each way,
And castings of the dice

The existence of this passage renders it less likely that the fragment on
the Palamedes above given can be referred to this play. He concludes
with an adjuration

### 383

And I invoke the all enshrouding Night

From the scene in which the wreck of the fleet was described must
come

### 382

Hung downward, like a chaffinch in the snare

And from the conclusion of the play

### 377

To him who is unfortunate, one night
Is equal to ten thousand; one in luck
Should die, before the second.

Cicero (*Tusc. Disp.* III. 29) tries his hand at a translation of a
passage in Sophocles, telling how Oileus, who had been consoling
Telamon for the death of Ajax the Greater, himself refused consolation,
when informed of the death of his own son, Ajax the Less. Stobæus
has preserved the original, under the name of " Œdipus," which must
be a mistake for "Oileus." This however, as in some other cases, must
not be taken as the name of the play, or of the speaker. There is no
reason to suppose Sophocles wrote an "Oileus." In the *Ajax Locrus*,
above quoted, it is difficult to suppose that Cicero's quotation could
find place. Welcker refers it, accordingly, to the *Teucer* (26). Telamon,
perhaps, is speaking.

### 14

Ay, and the greatest and most wise in mind
You will discover to be just like him—
Giver of good advice to one in trouble;

But when some Power alters the scale—strikes down
Life's balance—for a man till then in fortune,
His many excellent speeches are quite vanished.

Previous to this there must have been a description by Teucer of
the catastrophe of the last play, and of the death of Ajax the Less;

### 507

—and from Heaven
Came lightning, and through lightning thunder brake.

From the lament of Oileus we have

### 508

Alas, my child, how empty a delight
I had of thee, hearing thee glorified
As living! But the Fury in the dark
Was mocking at me, and I did not know
That I had been deluded in my joy!

Finally Telamon drives Teucer forth, as hinted in the *Ajax* of our
poet. A couplet has been preserved, without name of play or author,
by Trypho (*Rhet. Gr.* VIII. 738), which is probably taken from his
speech in deprecation of his father's wrath. The use of the third person
may be compared with that suggested in the *Palamedes*, above, and the
tone with that of Teucer's defence of his brother, in the *Ajax*.

But Teucer stayed the Phrygians, in mid leap
Over the trenches, with his archery.

Whether there was, besides the *Teucer*, a *Eurysaces* (27) by Sophocles appears questionable. Only one word is preserved to us under
this title.

It is not easy to understand why Welcker should consider the *Peleus*
(28) to be the same play with the *Women of Phthia*. Aristotle (*Poet.*
c. 18) mentions the two plays, as belonging to the class which he calls
"ethical." The *Peleus* deals with the return of Neoptolemus from
Troy, and the restoration of his grandfather to the throne of Epirus,
from which he had been ousted by Acastus, his elder son by a mortal
wife, whom he had married before Thetis. A female attendant pro-
logizes.

### 434

Sole housekeeper, I tend in his old age
And foster Peleus, son of Æacus,
Over again; for he who is growing old
Becomes a child once more.

This may be from the scene of the recognition of Neoptolemus by Peleus

### 442

O Zeus, do not deceive me ; slay me not
Without a spear

The rest are hardly to be assigned :

### 439

And rubbing with dry unguent through the folds

### 436

'Tis better not to be, than to live ill.

Of the *Women of Phthia* nothing can be clearly ascertained. It may have been another version of the story of the sorrowful old age of Peleus, who was said by Callimachus to have died in exile at Cos. There are three fragments

### 622

You are a young man ; you have much to learn
And much to hear, and long to stay at school ;
Try to be learning, ever, some new knowledge
That is of use.

### 623

—I'll be your tutor,
The aged, of the aged.

### 624

—The sentence of the parricide
Would have been called down on him.

The story of the *Chryses* (30) carries us again to the family of Pelops. According to Hyginus, 101, this Chryses was grandson of the Chryses in the Iliad, and son of Chryseis by Agamemnon. Orestes and Iphigenia take refuge with him, after their escape from Tauris, and are on the point of being delivered up to Thoas, when discovery is made by old Chryses of their relationship, which saves them. No fragment of interest has survived, except a line addressed to Hestia, as the "prow" or eminent object (?) of libations—an untranslateable metaphor.

Welcker identifies the *Aletes* (31) with the *Erigone*, and denies that any *Tyndareus* existed, separated from them. But he allows that there may have been two plays on the return of Orestes and Iphigenia to Greece, in one of which the scene may have been laid at Delphi, the plot embracing the recognition of Iphigenia by Electra, while the second dealt with the arrival at Argos, and the deposition and death of Aletes, the usurping son of Clytæmnestra and Ægisthus. But of the former of these nothing is extant, while of the scraps assigned to the

*Erigone* nothing shows clearly whether Erigone of Argos, the sister of Aletes, is meant, or rather the more celebrated heroine of the Attic Swing Festival, the daughter of Icarius. This line is from the *Erigone*:

### 215

What I suspect, I wish to see for plain.

And there is one passage under the name of the *Tyndareus*, on the familiar Sophoclean topic:

### 572

'Tis never seemly to felicitate
The fortunes of a man, as prosperous,
Before his life shall have been lived by him
Completely through, and he have ceased to live
For in a brief and scanty period
The assignment of an evil Deity
Destroys an all-pervading happiness,
When as things shift, and Heaven will have it so.

Stobæus gives us no less than seven fragments from the *Aletes*, the majority evidently drawn from a single scene, that of the "claim of title" set up by Orestes against Aletes. To the latter speaker belong—

### 91

If you are noble, as you call yourself,
Show us whose son you are, and whence you came;
No tale can throw a stain on generous breeding.

Orestes may reply

### 92

Well didst thou speak, not at all grievously.
For a fair ancestry, coming to proof,
Would obtain good repute, rather than blame.

### 88

An upright man, and of just sentiments,
Discerns far more than a philosopher.

Aletes breaks off with

### 89

Much wisdom often waits on brevity.

### 90

For he who loves to be for ever talking
Does not perceive he plagues his company.

This may possibly have been from a speech by an attendant, or by Tyndareus—

### 94

'Tis dreadful that the wicked—men who spring
From evil ancestors—should prosper well,
While those who are both good themselves, and born
From noble parents, are unfortunate.
Unmeet it was Deities should order so
These lines for mortals ; meet it was, the pious
Should from the Gods have some clear benefit,
While those who are unrighteous underwent
Contrariwise to them, clear punishment,
In quittance for their sins : so, nobody
Of evil nature would be prosperous.

The last may be from the conclusion of the play :

### 93

Oh who would ever count men's happiness
As great, or little, or as that which none
Anywhere honour ?   For of all they have
Nothing abides the same !

### XIII.  STORIES FROM THE ODYSSEY

*Nausicaa, The Phæacians, Syndeipni.*

Of plays from the Odyssey, we must lament the total loss of the *Nausicaa* (33).  This is the play in which, according to the well-known story, Sophocles acted the part of an attendant maiden, and distinguished himself as a ball-player.  The princess calls her followers, with Homeric simplicity,

### 391

To wash our gowns and linen-petticoats !

We may assign to Ulysses, watching the game, the unplaced fragment

### 872

—and the missile rolls
    Before my feet

Where the missile (or javelin) is, we are told, "a ball."  Envious Time, or the Caliph Omar, has robbed us of the rest of what may have been a very charming play.

The *Phæacians* (34) survives to us only in the punning lines on the name of Ulysses, of which the following perhaps is as good a rendering as they deserve

### 408

Rightly am I named *Odysseus*, after ills ;
For many *odious* to me I have *used* ill.

And in a passage from the narrative of Ulysses.

### 407

To the Sirens, Phorcus' daughters, next I came,
Who chant the lays of Death.

From some further surviving indications it seems to have been a Satyric play.

We now come to the *Syndeipni* or *Feasters* (35), otherwise called *Syndeipnon*, or *The Dinner Party*. This I conclude, following Welcker, to have been a drama of importance, a tragedy, on the story of Ulysses and the Suitors of Penelope, as related in the 20th and following books of the Odyssey. It will be noticed that the addition of this play to the number of those on subjects taken from the Odyssey only makes up the total of this class to three ; a number which hardly justifies the remark above quoted, from the Life of Sophocles, as to the fondness of the poet for such subjects. But if for the Odyssey, strictly so called, we substitute the adventures of Ulysses, generally speaking, many others would have to be added. The confusion of this drama with the *Achæorum Syllogus* has arisen from the quotation by Athenæus (I. 17 D.), as from " Sophocles in the *Achæans' Syndeipnon*," of a well-known comical passage, founded on a Homeric incident, and partly taken from the *Osteologi* of Æschylus, which appears to have been a Satyric drama on the fate of Melanthius and the maidservants. But lower down, (I. 17 F.) Athenæus classes Sophocles with Æschylus and Homer as introducing "the suitors" in this connexion. The suitors of Penelope were naturally of Achæan race ; but it is not necessary to hazard any further supposition, in this respect, than that Athenæus made a slip in quoting the title of the play. Ulysses is prologizing, apparently ; he relates the events of his first encounter with Irus and the Suitors, and describes, with mock heroic irony, their maltreatment of him ;

### 147

But in his wrath he hurled the unsavoury vase,
Nor missed me ; and about my pate the vessel,
Breathing no scent of myrrh, brake, and my senses
Were routed by no friendly fragrance !

Of this passage part of the first line, and all the second, are found, as above noted, in a fragment of Æschylus. It does not seem likely that Sophocles would have transferred the incident to a different story.

The topic reappears in an allusion made by Cicero, writing to his brother Quintus, who was at the time with Cæsar's army in Gaul. "Of your Sophoclean *Dinner Party* I do not think much; though I perceived you acted the play in fun." (Cic. *ad Qu.* 2. 16.) There had probably been some horse-play at the mess-table. Quintus Cicero was himself an amateur translator, and had turned four dramas into Latin, as the fruits of his winter-quarters' leisure; one of which, the *Erigone*, he sent to his brother; but it was lost on the way.

We find traces, next, of a spirited banquet scene; the Chorus sing

### 146

Hateful and slothful is forgetfulness
Of the Pierian maids;
But remembrance of song
Is most blest unto mortals,
Upholding the brief
Isthmus of life.

Ulysses taunts Eurymachus, perhaps;

### 148

It is not right thus to be carrying round
A greasy chin—or that an o'ergrown boy,
Noble by birth, should be esteemed the son
Not of his father, but—his appetite!

And Antinous, perhaps, from an unnamed play

### 706

—you shine in raiment
That apes the woman!

Eurymachus may have replied

### 727

But you are kicking, like a well-fed colt;
Your belly and jaws are full!

From the scene of the trial with the bow we have

### 149

Bring ye—let some one mingle and fill up
A mighty bowl.   He, like a labouring steer,
Never will work, till after a good meal

where again we have a Homeric incident reproduced ; and from the speech of some suitor, after Ulysses is made known, we get

155

You stick at nothing !  How the old Sisyphus
Is big and manifest in you everywhere,
And he, who was your mother's father.

A fragment of an uncertain drama must belong to the same scene

963

—for the bow
Is marvellous slippery

a scrap which appears almost conclusive as to the fact, that Sophocles did write a drama on this subject ; and thus renders it improbable and unnecessary to ascribe these passages to the *Achæorum Syllogus*. Welcker adds, from the *Uncertain Fragments*, as taken from the final scene of this play.

869

In what a guise our executioner
Is gone !

819

Be silent ! hush !  What is that noise indoors ?

693

A hive of dead men buzzes, and I hear
A stir

## XIV.  THE LATER LIFE OF ULYSSES.

*Euryalus, Ulysses slain by a prickle.*

Of the later life of Ulysses several stories are told, two of which, at least, were the subjects of Sophoclean Dramas.  The plot of the *Euryalus* (37) we know from Parthenius, 3, but no fragments have survived.  It is not worth repeating.  The *Foot-bath*, or *Ulysses slain by a prickle* (36), probably opened with the return of Ulysses from his second wandering, and the recognition of him by Euryclea, in washing his feet, transferred from his first return, as told in the Odyssey.  Then followed the landing of Telegonus, the son of Ulysses by Circe, and his encounter with his father, who is brought in wounded to death by the prickle of a sea-fish, with which the lance of Telegonus was pointed. There are several references to the oracle of Dodona, with which the singular prophecy of Tiresias in the Odyssey was somehow worked up.

401

Neither to Pytho nor Dodona's fields
Shall any man persuade me now to go.

Zeus dwelling in Dodona, at home with men.

The sooth-saying holy Dodonæan maids—

⸺and cause to cease the Power
Praised in Dodona—

403

⸺Wearing what sort of gift
Upon his gleaming shoulders?

404

Bearing a winnowing fan upon his shoulders

402

If any man shall now come forth; if not,
Say so.

Cicero tells us of a play by Pacuvius on the same subject, in which he finds matter for comparison unfavourable to Sophocles, from the Stoic point of view. Sophocles, it seems, made Ulysses lament too much over his wound, to suit the Roman taste.

With the death of the favourite character of our poet—Ulysses was introduced by him in more than a dozen plays—ends the series of fragments which can on authority or with any reasonable ground be assigned to particular tragedies.

XV. SATYRIC PLAYS.

*Cedalion, Pandora, Hybris, Dionysiacus, Inachus, Hercules at Tænarus, Cophi.*

There remain a few fragments ascribed to Satyric plays, on miscellaneous subjects. The *Cedalion* was a drama on the story of Orion (Erat. *Catasterism.* XXXII.). Cedalion was the slave of Vulcan, given by him to the blind giant to be his guide. He rode upon Orion's shoulders. The fragments are

305

Indeed my limbs have somewhat given way
Through panic!

A striking simile follows :

### 307

I gain no notion from your words, no more
Than a white paling from a whitened stone !

### 308

Whate'er may be forthcoming, the universe
Is a dream-shadow.

Abuse of slaves :

### 309

      Food for the scourge—the goad—
Eaters of others bread !

The connexion of the first of the two following fragments with the story of *Pandora* is evident enough :

### 432

And first, begin to knead clay with your hands

The second implies a drinking scene :

### 429

And as he quaffs a brazen horn held high,
She, with her delicate arm, will coax the man
When he is full.

*Hybris* was, in one story, the name of the mother of Pan.   We have of it

### 595

Lethe, that is destitute of all,
Dumb—voiceless.

From a play called *Dionysiacus*, or more probably, from "a Dionysiac play," i.e. a Satyric drama, we get

### 182

      How did I come to find
A flower of grief so painless ?

which refers, we are told, to the discovery of wine.

The *Inachus* was a Satyric play, of which the scenery and subject recalled the Golden Age ;

### 267

      Happy they, who then
Shared the immortal strain, divine

Arms are laid by as useless

### 269

And all are full of weaver-spiders.

### 278

Rough hoarseness rises from the tortoise-lyre.

### 272

—together with
Winter's returning shade

Mankind play games; the cottabus especially

### 257

The splash of wine—the amorous, foreign game—
Sounded in every home.

An anapæstic ode addresses Inachus, and describes the river named
after him

### 256

O Inachus our ancestor!
Son of Oceanus, father of waters!
Who in lands of Argos art preeminent,
     On Hera's hills,
And 'mongst Pelasgians in Etruria—

   .    .    .    .    .    .    .

### 265

For he flows from Pindus' height,
From Lacmus, from Perrhæbia,
To Acarnania, to the Amphilochi,
And mingles with the streams of Achelous.

   .    .    .    .    .    .    .

Thence to Argos, dividing his wave,
He is come—to the Lyrcian folk.

Two lines of dialogue

### 255

          —I assent;
But know that, as the proverb runs, a man
Might become known from very small beginnings.

Iris is introduced by Hermes

### 261

What woman is here? A round Arcadian hat

Inachus is dried up : Io says

268

—and my father-river, Inachus,
Is in the same condition as the dead.

According to Toup, (*Emend. in Suid.* II. 464) Inachus, a rough old man crowned with reeds, Io, in heifer-form, Argus, all over eyes, Iris, Hermes, and similar figures may have been introduced, making up an entertainment not very unlike a popular burlesque on the modern stage.

The *Hercules at Tænarus* seems to have been a favourite play, on the subject of the descent of Hercules to Hades. Hercules says

218.

I gathered wood enough for cooking dinner
So that I might not lack it half way through.

219.

—they cherish in the land a snake,
The fountain's guardian.

The story, how snakes came to be the guardians of fountains, was told by Sophocles in another satyric drama, the *Cophi*, or *Dumb Men*, of which only the plot is preserved (Ælian, *N. A.* 6). Prometheus, who had given fire to mankind, was betrayed by his ungrateful beneficiaries ; and in order to reward their treachery, Zeus gave them the drink of perpetual youth. With their usual stupidity, Mankind put it on an ass's back, and drove it before them : now the ass, being thirsty, came to a fountain, which was guarded by a serpent ; and was easily persuaded by that crafty animal to barter the draught of youth for a draught of water. Thus the race of snakes obtained their peculiarity of an annual renewal of youth, while men and donkeys remain subject to thirst, and are, moreover, sometimes bitten by snakes, which produces a worse fever of thirst than any.

## XVI. UNKNOWN DRAMAS.

The melancholy task remains of putting together such fragments as cannot even be attributed, by any probable conjecture, to one or other of the lost plays. Of these the largest harvest is afforded by Stobæus ; but the value of his selection is lessened through his extravagant fondness for abstract remarks, which appear trite when detached from their context, on the general fitness or unfitness of things. Such are

656

But stroke of God no mortal can evade.

N

657

Time, that uncovers all, brings all to light.

658

Much hidden wisdom is disclosed at last
  By Time, to those who seek—
Time, and the strong extremity of life.

659

But when Heaven hides things heavenly, though
  thou search
All nature through, thou canst not find them out.

660

One wise man perishes
At hands of many fools.

661

For a good man will succour the distressed.

662

But a good will is as a mighty god.

663

Yet the unprosperous are not deaf alone,
But seeing they see not what is manifest.

664

—There are no comely names
To fit uncomely deeds.

664

To take delight
In shameful pleasures is not ever right.

666

—Fortune does not side
With the despondent.

667

Why, modesty is no help in misery;
For silence fights upon the accuser's side

### 668

Why praise you this? For every man in wine
Is passion's captive, and devoid of sense;
And pouring out much babble, to no purpose,
Unwillingly has to hear the selfsame language
Which of free will he used.

### 669

But when a man is taken in a fraud
He must be dumb, however plausible.
The case is grievous, when a man of merit
Is conscious of some matter

More interest attaches to the following;

### 670

So women, too, forswear the bitter pangs
Of child-bearing; but, when they cease from pain,
Become entangled in the selfsame toils,
O'ermastered by the presence of desire.

### 671

For that no oath sits heavy upon a knave.

### 673

Utter no secret! Bolts and bars are nothing.
That you may apprehend it easily,
No secret, on the tongue, does not slip off it.

### 674

For where the children overbear their sires
That is no city of sagacious men;

        —It is good to follow
The customs of the country.

### 675

High place demands many high qualities:
But of small efforts no great glory ensues.

### 676

Opinions have more power than violence.

### 677

Though body is enslaved, yet mind is free.

### 679

But where's the household, among all mankind,
Ever was rich, though swol'n with luxury,
Apart from a good woman's housewifery?

### 680

     —for in a fatherless house
The woman has the spirit of a man.

Instead of Dindorf's (681), I read, with Brunck (859, Nauck),

Poverty, blended with impiety,
Utterly ruins and upsets a life.

### 682

O mortal race of men, and miserable,
How are we nothing, except shadow-like,
Drifting about, mere cumberers of the earth!

### 683

For 'tis not given, save to Gods, to live
With no misfortunes.

### 684

God! surely there is no defence for men
From our innate and heaven-sent miseries.

This last is by some ascribed to Euripides

### 686

But a wise gamester ought to take the dice
Even as they fall, and pay down quietly,
Rather than grumble at his luck.

### 687

For hope is she who feeds the multitude

### 688

The wise admit no dotage, in whose breast
Reason subsists, nurtured by God's own day;
For forethought is great benefit to men.

The second line, here, is hardly Sophoclean.

### 689

For whoso in misfortunes longs for life
Is either cowardly, or insensible.

### 690

—Now he is dead, I long to die with him.
—Your day of fate will find you—never hasten.

Later investigations have added, from the same source,

### 839 (Nauck)

How want of knowledge is a parlous ill

### 840 (Nauck)

—and folly
Is most of all akin to wickedness.

### 849 (Nauck)

The rightly happy must remain at home.

### 866 (Nauck)

Whatever mortal quails too much at death,
He is a fool; this is in Destiny's keeping;
And when his hour is come to die, though fleeing
Even to the courts of Jove, he cannot 'scape it.

### 868 a (Nauck)

But time obscures and brings to oblivion all.

Two lines come from the supplement of John of Damascus, (see also (736) quoted above).

### 691

Truth ever has most strength of what men say.

### 780

The gratitude of an unmindful man
Passes away.

Out of Photius, derived by him from Helladius Chrestomathius, comes

### 694

A woman's vows I write upon the wave.

Athenæus affords a few good passages : among them are 420, 696, 698, quoted above.   Also

### 697

To get drunk—

Solace of care !

### 699

Courage ! you have in me a mighty bar
To shut this terror out.

### 700

And a chorus of mute fish, wagging their tails,
Applauded their own mistress.

### 701

To be compelled to drink
Is just as bad as being compelled to thirst.

### 702

For though you offer to a thirsty man
All the wise saws in the world, you could not more
Delight him, than by giving him to drink !

### 703

—Thou accurst of Heaven,
Who with thy wine-jugs art so riotous !

### 704

And deep in my heart a daughter of Fear
Keeps revel, with no joyous cheer.

From the Etymologicon Magnum we have a characteristic passage ;

### 705

But never yet the insolence of youth
Grew into soberness ; but in the young
Blossoms and fades, blossoms and fades again.

Clement of Alexandria, from whose *Pædagogus* we derive 706 quoted above, gives us also, in his Miscellany (*Stromata*) four passages ascribed to Sophocles, one of them religious, monotheistic, if not Christian, in tone, and one an offensive fragment, written by no means in pure Greek.   These I omit.   The two others are also found, in part, in Plutarch, and may therefore be considered genuine.

## 707

And such, I know, is God; unto the wise
A giver, ever, of dark oracles:
But unto fools a sorry schoolmaster,
And of brief speech.

## 709

Before what Deity thou must appear . . .
Who knows not favour or benevolence,
But takes delight in right, and in right only.

Plutarch is a rich mine of Sophoclean fragments. Unluckily he never names the play from which he is quoting; but several have been assigned above, on probable grounds, to particular dramas. Others are—

## 710

Ye Gods, what passion, or what love-desires
Laid hold upon him!

## 711

Whoso has dealings with an emperor,
Becomes his slave, though he approach him free.

## 712

Matter for many bits, and rudders too!

## 714

Swift the conviction of adversity
To make its way

## 715

Of all work, if a man begin it well,
'Tis like that the end also will be good

## 716

Straits of the infernal regions, and back-swirl
Of the abyss

## 717

—Profit is sweet, even if it spring from falsehood.
—The words of falsehood do not bring forth fruit.

I add the former of these two lines from Nauck's edition (749).

718

Men may be honoured, though unpropertied.
A beggar, if his mind is honourable,
Is none the worse

720

For Ares, blind, O women, and seeing nought,
With a swine's snout routs up all miseries.

723

What can be taught, I learn ; what can be found
I seek ; the rest I did require of heaven.

725

Mourn you a mortal, now he is no more,
All ignorant if the future brings him gain ?

726

Not honour, no, unhappy one !   Disgrace
Rather, and maddening of your mind, were there !

728

Not harps—not lyres—with dirges will agree.

From the next line, ascribed to "Admetus in Sophocles," it has
been conjectured that our poet wrote an *Alcestis*, which has entirely
perished ;

730

But my own house-cock summoned him to the mill

This is said of Apollo : we cannot be far wrong in adding, with
Welcker, from a Scholiast on Pindar,

758

O Land of Pheræ, hail ! O kindred fount,
Water of Hyperea ! Stream most dear
Unto the Gods !

which must belong to the same play ; but whether it was really an
*Alcestis*, or rather a play on the fortunes of Apollo in Admetus's
service, I am inclined to doubt.

From Plutarch also come

732

Search all mankind—most of the hearts you search
Will be found base.

### 733

Purge bitter bile with bitter medicine.

### 734

I blame you not; you speak ill, but act kindly.

### 735

Talk about running carries not so far
As to the course's end.

### 737

A tardy onset, in the words of eld,
Hardly can penetrate a listening ear;
Each, afar off, can see, but near, is blind.

### 738

Lovers of horses, drawers of bows of horn,
Wrestlers, with shields clanging like bells

### 739

There was a first occurrence, once for all,
Of everything that had not yet occurred.

### 741

Men who have lost such friends as these are merry;
Men who have such, pray to be free from them.

### 742

—For arms, in poverty,
Shine brightly, and excel; but, as time passes,
A house enwrapped in sloth nods to its fall.

### 744

Persuasion hath an awful countenance.

### 745

The goose domesticated, and the dove,
Our house and hearth-mate

### 746

For excellently even a different speech
Works union twixt us two.

### 748

Blown high, like the hoar down of thistle-seed

### 749

This is God's gift; what the Gods give, my child,
No man need ever shun.

### 783

Dragged it down, as a leaden weight the net.

### 879

Fair-fruited Cytherea

And (not in Dindorf)

### 755 (Nauck)

Fair words proceed not from a deed unfair.

From various sources, chiefly the notes of Scholiasts, we have

### 750

—Let him not give counsel,
Who has not endured like me!

### 754

I shut my eyes, and open them, and stand up,
Not so much watched as watcher.

### 755

For though I have to choose one of the three
I will untie (the knot)

That is, we are told, one way of suicide, either steel or halter, or
leaping from a rock.

### 756

Buying and selling—you propounded them
Like some Sidonian—some Phœnician pedlar!

### 757

'Tis the same corner of the soul of man
Where pain and pleasure both have being; at least,
Happening on either fortune, he sheds tears.

### 759

—for Zeus already
On the supremest seat of Gods

### 762

An old man's wrath, like hatchet of soft iron
Whets on the hand, but gets blunt instantly.

### 763

For ever fairly fall the dice of Jove.

### 764

First I proclaim, let no ill words be uttered.

The line usually coupled with this Welcker attributes to the *Atreus*.
(See above, p. 517.)

### 766

—The sceptre-perching eagle,
Watch-dog of Jove—

### 768

So that Jove's forehead might grow smooth with joy.

### 769

For I was not his bastard brother,
But owned the same father as he, none other;
Zeus, and no mortal, was author of me.

### 770

I hate a searcher into mysteries.

### 772

—May the Sun pity me,
Whom the wise name progenitor of Gods,
And Sire of all things!

### 773

The friends of the unlucky are far away!

### 778

That city of seven gates thou call'st Thebes, where
only
Do mortal mothers bring forth deities.

### 784

—A chatterbox
Of supreme cleverness, Laertes's son.

### 813

But bloody vengeance from above will dart

### 822

I set aside the want of willingness.

### 823

For what is hidden purposely indoors
Ought never to be heard by those outside.

### 858

When a man sings in the Bœotian mood

### 862

    —for thy advice
Is mere old age.

### 865

    —for effeminate men,
Practised in speaking

### 884

'Tis better to incur some bane
Than pocket a disgraceful gain.

### 886

Thou, like a Lydian loadstone, didst draw hither
The steel from far.

### 902

You fawn, and bite ; you are a treacherous hound !

### 943

Thy Virgin Daughter's solemn mysteries.

I add, lastly, from Nauck's edition, five more passages from among
the scanty gleanings which escaped previous researches.

### 682 (Nauck)

I offered to the Gods, upon the shore,
Lambs a year old.

### 738 (Nauck)

For that which Nature gives a man—
Pluck out that you never can.

### 804 (Nauck)

Hastening at the shuttle-songs
Which wake the sleeper up.

### 810 (Nauck)

Would you were wise in deeds, as well as words !

### 818 (Nauck)

It were much better that we should proceed
With our hired horse, picked men, than with all arms.

Grace, vivacity and dramatic force are visible even in these comminuted splinters of poetic work. But very little of these characteristics can be reproduced by the translator, who labours, here, under insuperable difficulties.

# NOTES

---

## ANTIGONE.

ALL the early plays of Sophocles have perished. But the *Antigone* is probably the earliest of those which have survived, and in any case it should never be printed after the *Œdipus Coloneus*, as if it were intended as a sequel, to complete the Tale of Thebes. For well-sustained energy, for vivid delineation of character, for varied pace, and for lucidity of expression, it shews the art of the master already at its best, and ranks with the greatest dramas of all literature. Of points not sufficiently brought out by commentators I would note the passion of the speech with which Antigone bursts upon the stage; the picturesque grouping, emotional, not chronological, of the incidents of recent war celebrated in the first chorus; the earliest known employment of a humorous element in tragic dialogue, in the scenes with the Sentinel; the lighting up, as it were, of the forensic dialogue with passion, in the scenes between Creon and the sisters, and between Creon and Hæmon; and the "power in small things," for which Shakspeare is praised by Coleridge, here shewn in the brief part of Eurydice. Of the more conspicuous merits of the piece nothing need here be added to the praises of all, I think, who have written of it.

**Page 1. 1.** This line, which cannot be bettered, is from Donaldson's version of the play.

2. I follow the interpretation given by Boeckh, reading ὅτι, not ὅ τι. The broken question is in keeping with the swift excitement of the speech; Jebb's explanation involves an awkward inversion, and a punctuation incompatible with effective delivery.

3. I follow Porson's correction, ἄτης ἔχον.

**Page 2. 4.** I omit χρησθείς, which I cannot construe, but do not follow Dindorf in omitting the line.

5. If Kennedy's interpretation is to be followed, read—

> This is the matter which has been proclaimed
> By your *good* Creon, as they say—and mine—
> Mine too, I do confess !

But the more usual rendering is preferable.

6. This line Dindorf omits, unnecessarily.

**Page 4. 7.** "The man who came from Argos" is of course Adrastus. See *O.C.* 1302.

**Page 5. 8.** I follow the reading ἀντιπάλῳ δράκοντος.

9. I cannot reconcile myself to the absence of the name of the thunder-stricken enemy. The accusative participle ὁρμῶντ', left standing by itself, is surely questionable Greek; and to link it with ὅς τοτε, in the next stanza, deprives the whole passage of its poetic emphasis.

378

I believe that the proper name, Καπανῆ', lurks behind that superfluous second genitive, καναχῆς. This it seems occurred (among other suggestions) to Mr. Blaydes. If with this reading the comma is transferred from ὑπερόπτας to χρυσοῦ, the passage, to my ear, gains both in sound and sense.

10. The form of the participle τανταλωθεὶς involves a mythological allusion, which ought to be preserved in translation.

**Page 7.** 11. Sixteen lines from this place were quoted by Demosthenes in his great speech on the Embassy, and followed by an effective contrast between the conduct here prescribed for the statesman and that displayed by Æschines in the negotiation with Philip. But we are not to take for serious the insinuation that Æschines, as an actor of the "third parts" in drama, had really played Creon in the Antigone.

**Page 8.** 12. Read κ' εἰ not καὶ, and make one sentence of this and the next line.

13. Read ταχώς, not βράδυς.

14. Read δεδραγμένος, not πεφαργμένος.

**Page 9.** 15. Read μὴ εἰδέναι, not πᾶς τὸ μή.

**Page 11.** 16. Read λάλημα, not ἄλημα.

**Page 14.** 17. I follow the reading τοίουσδ' ἐν ἀνθρώποισιν ὤρισεν, recommended by Jebb. The line can by no means be omitted, as by Dindorf.

**Page 16.** 18. The force of ἑλών has been generally overlooked. Antigone is trying to save Ismene.

**Page 18.** 19. The interpretation "But not without my having spoken" (to warn you) appears incompatible with the context. Ismene is sympathetic throughout.

20. I do not follow Dindorf, but the traditional arrangement, which gives this line to Antigone. That Sophocles was no bondman to the rule of alternate dialogue may be gathered from other passages besides this.

**Page 19.** 21. I do not adopt Dindorf's reading ὁ τέτατο, but I adopt the conjecture κόπις, since no sense can be made of ἁμᾷ κόνις. For the sentiment, compare Llywarch Hen, as translated in Guest's *Orig. Celt.* vol. II. p. 292:

> Unprenn agouit arnav
> Odieine ys odit ;
> Ac auynno duv derffit.

> One tree with the tendril on it
> Is escaping, it may be ;
> But what God shall have willed, let it come !

22. I follow Jebb's reading ὁ πάντ' ἀγρεύων, and in the next line θεῶν ἄκματοι μῆνες.

**Page 20.** 23. Read πάμπολύ γ', not πάμπολις.

**Page 21.** 24. I follow those who read συμμάχου δορὸς, but suppose it to mean simply "spearmen fighting in concert," not "forces allied with our own," which has no point in this context.

**Page 23.** 25. Compare Shakspeare *A.Y.L.I.* I. i. 56 :

> Come, come, elder brother, you are too young in this.

Other similarities of expression may be traced, as of Prospero's "fellowly drops" with the φιλάδελφα δάκρυα of l. 527, of Sonnet III. 5 with l. 569, of *J.C.* I. ii. 153 with l. 737, and of *Hamlet*, I. v. 77 with l. 1071.

Page 24. 26. It is sometimes allowable to cut a new facet, in resetting a diamond. I have made the whole of this passage an address to Eros; in the original the form of sentence is varied, but this was not consistent with my metre, which is, I need hardly say, with some others in this play, of Mr. Swinburne's invention, taken from his *Atalanta in Caledon*, which appeared when I was engaged upon it.

27. I read, with the MSS., τῶν μεγάλων πάρεδρος ἐν ἀρχαῖς θεσμῶν.

Page 26. 28. Omissions of lines in some of Dindorf's texts have been rather rashly made. I do not follow him in the places noted under this reference.

29. Either this line or the next must go. I have supplied a few words to fill the gap.

Page 27. 30. Read ταλαίφρων ἄγομαι τάνδ' ἑτοίμαν ὁδόν.

Page 28. 31. Τίνος νόμου δὴ is emphatic; "there is law," she would say, "as well as justice, on my side." The omission of this passage cannot, I think, be justified. I do not say it is not a blemish, according to our views of art; but the language is Sophoclean. I do not suppose the poet to say, with the lady in Herodotus, "and other children, if I lost those I had," but "and a child by another husband, if I lost this one," that is, the husband she has been speaking of.

Page 29. 32. The son of Dryas was named Lycurgus, the fierce stepdame Eidothea, and the imprisoned mother Cleopatra.

33. Read with Jebb πελάγει.

Page 32. 34. Τροχούς, the MS. reading, is followed by Potter and Donaldson. "Many *courses* of the sun" would imply days; but hours seem wanted here. The epithet ἀμιλλητῆρας suits wheels better than courses.

Page 33. 35. I take Até as the object after πάρα, not as the instrument after πατάξαι. Like Nemesis, Thanatos, etc., Até tends, in Sophocles, towards personification.

Page 35. 36. Read ὦναξ, not Ναξίαις.

Page 37. 37. Κρεμαστήν has always been translated as if it were equivalent to κρεμαμένην, actually "hanging." But this makes Hæmon's behaviour ridiculous; the first thing he would do was to take down the body, and the subsequent description shews that this was what, in fact, he had done.

38. Ἤρεισε πλευραῖς μέσσον must mean, I think, "pressed to his ribs, in the middle of them"; that is to say, where they meet. A man could hardly commit suicide by leaning *sideways* on his sword.

Page 39. 39. I follow the interpretation of Professor Lewis Campbell. Dindorf omits half a line.

**Page 40.** 40. I follow the reading favoured by Jebb, ὀξυθήκτῳ βωμία περὶ ξίφει.

**Page 41.** 41. I read ἐρῶμεν. The plural gives a force to the preposition in συγκατευξάμην, which is otherwise sacrificed.

## AJAX.

THE *Ajax* appears first of the extant plays in the most ancient lists, and is probably second only in date to the *Antigone*, which was transferred from its proper place, in order to countenance the erroneous idea that it formed a trilogy with the two plays named after Œdipus. Jebb conjectures, from the large number of manuscripts, that the *Ajax* was an especial favourite for use in schools. Ajax having become, in later ages, the eponymous hero of an Attic tribe, the subject had a particular interest for Athenians, and the name of Athens appears, in one of the Choruses, as if it had a particular interest for the followers of Ajax. The play shews an advance upon the *Antigone*, in respect of the free handling of the humorous element in dialogue. The propriety of the conduct of the play, in giving so large a scope to the contest over the burial of the hero, has been well maintained by Jebb; it is this which enables the final victory to shift to the side which enlists the sympathies of the audience.

**Page 44.** 1. I omit the comma after βαλοῦσα. The modern parenthesis should not be lightly resorted to, to explain difficulties in Sophocles.

2. This rendering seems better, on the whole, than to suppose, with Dale, that the sense is interrupted.

**Page 47.** 3. Read ἀμάρτοις.

**Page 48.** 4. It appears to me better to adopt the emendation ἠρεμίας, with Dindorf, than to understand τυχῆς after ἡμερίας. It ought to have been ἡμερίου (βάρους).

**Page 51.** 5. Properly "to women silence adds a charm." But a proverbial expression is wanted, and the English proverb appears legitimate in the context.

6. Read εὕερον, not εὕκερων.

**Page 58.** 7. The two lines in this speech which Dindorf omits do not appear capable of defence.

8. Compare Shakspeare, *Cor.* III. i. 195:

> He's a disease that must be cut away.

Shakspeare seems to have borrowed the metaphor from a passage in Plutarch's life of his hero, where however the application is different.

**Page 59.** 9. I have in this fine chorus taken the liberty of adapting a translation by Praed, which I printed in the collected edition of his *Poetical Works*, vol. ii. p. 349. In many places Praed does not give the true meaning of the original; and the last strophe, in particular, has been re-written.

10. Read μίμνων λειμώνι᾽ ἔπαυλα ... εὐνῶμαι.

11. There is a metaphor here from the wrestler who "draws a by," and has to be fought with after the first antagonist is overthrown; but such an allusion cannot be pointedly translated without destroying the proportions of the lyric.

**Page 61. 12.** When Sophocles says the tempest blast puts the sea to rest, he means no more than that a time will come when even the tempest will leave even the sea to rest. Compare *O.T.* 1223. This is touched up by Calverley:

> Stern tempest-blasts at last sing lullaby
> To groaning seas,

which is perhaps as pretty an instance as could be quoted of ornamental rendering. But Nemesis is at hand, if the diction of Sophocles is meddled with. What has Ajax, and what has the tempest of his frenzy, to do with cradle-songs? To embroider a metaphor on a Sophoclean simile is by no means safe.

**Page 63. 13.** I take τοῖς κυρίοις as dative of τὰ κύρια "the authorities." See *O.C.* 915.

**Page 64. 14.** The "breaking out" or "forth" has proved a puzzle to commentators. I think it must be a metaphor from the game surrounded by hunters, the Scottish Tinchel.

**Page 65. 15.** I do not follow Dindorf in omitting this line.

**16.** I follow Hermann in retaining these two lines. The next two Dindorf is no doubt right in rejecting.

**Page 68. 17.** A word has dropped out. A translator may be allowed to supply the gap, without asking whether Ἀχιλλείων will fit the gap.

**Page 69. 18.** Compare Shakspeare, *A.W.E.W.* v. iii. 60:

> Our rash faults
> Make trivial price of serious things we have,
> Not knowing them, until we know their grave.

**19.** This speech—than which there is nothing more affecting in the seven plays—is terribly spoilt, if the quibble is used by Tecmessa, that "the death of Ajax is *more* bitter for me, than sweet for his enemies." Read accordingly ἤ, "in that," or "even as," not ἤ, "than," which requires that μᾶλλον should be supplied. No instance has been produced of ἤ used for μᾶλλον ἤ, without some word preceding it indicating choice or comparison. The reading ἤ must have been present to Eustathius (see his comment on *Odyssey*, v. 34), for he quotes the passage as a case of simple comparison between opposites, on the pattern of "Honey is as sweet, as wormwood is bitter," not of antithesis *a fortiori.* Compare *Tr.* 1020, and Jebb's comment.

**20.** Read ἠμπόληκας, not ἠμπόληκα σε.

**Page 72. 21.** The rhyme is in the original, and was clearly intentional.

**Page 80. 22.** The pointed repetition of ἐσθλὸς, in three places, ll. 1345, 1352, 1399, has been generally overlooked. There is an extraordinary vigour in these concluding scenes, as if Sophocles had anticipated the cavils at his plot—that it lingers, or stands still altogether, after Ajax is dead—and had determined that the play should, if not as a whole, yet in each of its parts, offer defiance to the cavillers.

**Page 81. 23.** I find myself obliged to differ from many authorities, who render κομίζειν "to bring," *i.e.* to bring to the funeral of Ajax. Having just absolutely rejected the presence of Ulysses himself, how can Teucer be willing that he should bring others? Rather, he promises him the exact return of his own courtesy, "whatever dead comrade you want to bury, I shall not make a grievance of it, any more than you have done on the present occasion." For κομίζειν as used by Sophocles in the technical sense of "bearing to the grave," see line 1048, and *Electra*, 1114.

**Page 82. 24.** A line here rejected by Dindorf and others, Jebb included, I have not seen my way to drop. It requires, however, that a syllable should be supposed to have dropped out in the preceding line, perhaps δή before πω, as suggested by Jebb.

## ELECTRA.

THE view taken formerly of the relation between this play, the *Choephoræ* of Æschylus, and the *Electra* of Euripides, has of late been challenged, without, as I think, sufficient justification. It is now suggested that it was written after that of Euripides, and represents a reversion to the traditional handling of the story. I do not see any trace in this play of allusion to the innovations due to Euripides; on the other hand l. 1288 does undoubtedly seem to reflect on the treatment by Æschylus of the crisis of the plot. The odd device of the marriage of Electra to a peasant was, I conceive, suggested to Euripides by the stress Sophocles lays upon the hopelessness of marriage in Electra's case and in her sister's, ll. 165, 186, 960. Had the version of Euripides come first, we might expect to find in these passages some such qualification as that no suitable alliance could be anticipated, or no alliance that would produce offspring who would be in a position to raise an army. Apart from this point, of chronological order, any ready-made comparison between the respective merits of the two plays has or ought to have small attraction for an English reader; but it may not be amiss to note that the *Electra* of Euripides can only be brought by its admirers under consideration side by side with that of Sophocles, after its supernatural *dénouement* has been arbitrarily dismissed as of no account. Euripides may be the better for this as a theosophist, but hardly as a dramatic artist. The special merit of this play resides in the beauties contained within it; as a whole it suffers, for modern readers, from the unloveliness of the story.

**Page 84. 1.** I follow Jebb's reading, ἵν᾽ ἕσταμεν.

**Page 85. 2.** This is usually rendered "air coextensive with earth." Literally it is "air that shares equally with earth." The question is, in what is it that air and earth are said to share? Surely in *light*, the first object addressed, and the only subject of the verb, ἦσθον. Earth and air are attested as the domains of light; this is good poetry and good sense; but the statement that earth and air are coextensive is a mere cosmical proposition, of no poetical importance whatever.

**Page 86. 3.** τεκνολέτειρα is "child-destroying," with a mythological allusion to the story of Itys and Philomela.

**4.** I do not follow Dindorf in omitting this and the preceding line, but read αἱ τοὺς εὐνὰς, κ.τ.λ.

**Page 90. 5.** I do not adopt Dindorf's alteration, γᾶ, nor his punctuation of l. 316.

**Page 98. 6.** This line has been differently rendered in four ways, according as the "just opinion" is taken to be that of Clytæmnestra, or of Electra, and according as Electra is held to be exhorted to blame her own party, or her relations, *i.e.* her foes. I follow the interpretation which is supported by the greatest number of authorities. Dindorf's punctuation favours a different view.

**Page 102. 7.** I follow Porson's correction, ἀθλ' ἅπερ.

**Page 103. 8.** See the capital story told by Sir F. Doyle, in his *Reminiscences*, p. 93. His view is now generally adopted by scholars.

**Page 104. 9.** My interpretation of τμητοῖς ἱμᾶσι differs from those usually followed. The significant repetition of the adjective with ὁλκοῖς, l. 861, makes it difficult for me to regard it as a mere otiose epithet, "shapely," or "dainty," or "cut out" as opposed to "twisted." Moreover Sophocles does not appear to use such epithets, as Homer does. If we consult the representations of war or racing chariots given on vases, we find (British Museum, B. 82, 273, etc.; Gerhardt, *Auserlesene Griechische Vasenbilder*, IV. cclii. ccliii.; *Monumenti Inediti*, IV. liv.) that the right and left hand reins were not continuous in early times, but consisted of eight separate straps, of equal length, the right and left hand four respectively being usually braced or knotted together just over the horses' hind-quarters, and divided by a rope or rail, which passed from the front of the chariot to a tall peg fixed either in the yoke or pole. If a charioteer, slipping over the front of the chariot, were caught in one of the forks or clefts of the reins occasioned by these knots, he would hardly be able to extricate himself. It is not the case, as Professor Campbell supposes, that the driver, in Greece, at this period, passed the reins round his body; and I do not think this is implied by Eur. *Hip.* 1221.

It is physically impossible that such a fall could have been backwards, as Paley thought, or that a driver falling backwards could be entangled in the reins. All the vases represent the driver as leaning far forwards. The "giving rein" to the right hand trace-horse, and "pulling in" of the left hand one, would be effected by a simple movement of both hands to the right. It is to be observed that the slipping of individual reins back or forward in the grasp, with four separate straps, unknotted, in each hand, besides a long goad to carry, would be both difficult and unsafe.

**Page 106. 10.** Compare Shakspeare's *Rich. II.* Act V. Sc. v. 103:

Patience is stale, and I am weary of it.

**Page 107. 11.** Schiller, who was intimately acquainted with this play, has made excellent use of this circumstance of horror, in the agony of Thekla—

Ward ihm sanft
Gebettet, unter den Hufen seiner Rosse?
*Wall. Tod*, Act IV. Sc. v.

He is less happy, when he recurs to the *Electra* for assistance in the parting between Max and Wallenstein, and transfers to the old warrior Electra's "I was thy nurse," etc., l. 1147.—

Ich selbst war deine Wärterin, nicht schämt' ich
Der kleinen Dienste mich, ich pflegte deiner
Mit weiblich sorgender Geschäftigkeit.

12. I do not adopt Dindorf's reading νῶ, nor his πότμον in l. 1075.

**Page 113.** 13. I follow Jebb in the interpretation of this difficult passage. If Electra is praised in the strophe for aiming at the "double prize," it would make an anticlimax, that she should be congratulated in the antistrophe on obtaining the single, though higher reward.

**Page 115.** 14. See Shakspeare, *Pericles*, Act III. Sc. i. 56. Interesting as it is to trace resemblances of expression in the works of the greatest poets, it is not to be suggested that Shakspeare, directly or indirectly, borrowed from Sophocles, except only, as in *Aj.* 964, *O.T.* 1415, where the sentiment had become a common place of mediæval and renascence literature.

**Page 119.** 15. I follow Jebb's explanation, and read οὐδ' ἂν ἔσχον ὁρμὰν ἄναυδον.

**Page 121.** 16. If "dearest light" meant "dearest sight," and referred to the old servant's face, then in l. 1224 it must similarly refer to Orestes. But this is precluded by Orestes' answer.

**Page 123.** 17. I adopt Hermann's reading. Mr. Whitelaw's makes the doom fade, not the house. Otherwise, he argues, the deed of Orestes would be spoken of as a new "crime." But why a crime? It is a new stage, anyhow, in the extinction of the house of Pelops, and as such, a new manifestation of the doom.

**Page 127.** 18. I consider Ægisthus to be struck dead with the first word of this line, as he comes within the shadow of the fateful roof. It is quite unnecessary to suppose him walked off the stage, in order that he may be killed inside, in the bath-room, after the play is ended; and the suggestion of Professor Murray, that he is reserved to be tortured before he is killed, appears to me a mere fancy, due to misunderstanding of the words of Orestes, which ought rather to be interpreted with reference to the horror Ægisthus has just expressed, at recognizing the old curse upon the roof-tree.

## ŒDIPUS TYRANNUS.

THIS play may be considered as holding a central position among the dramas of Sophocles still extant, and indeed among the extant remains of Greek tragedy as a whole. Its celebrity has been due, in the first place, to the excellence of the plot; but this is not its only merit; the clash of character in the dialogue, the varied music of the choric odes, the best of poetry and the best of rhetoric, combine with the terrible effect of the catastrophe to produce an impression of mastery, of matured excellence, unequalled in literature for two thousand years after.

The story that precedes the opening of the play has been a good deal misunderstood, with the result that a supposed weak point in the construction, the ignorance of Œdipus as to the facts of his predecessor's death, has been the subject of censure which appears exaggerated. It is supposed that Œdipus on his way from Delphi to Thebes meets Laius on his way from Thebes to Delphi at a point casually indicated as the place where some branch road (from Ambryssus or elsewhere) happens to join it, and after slaying him and his party goes straight to Thebes, to the place from whence Laius started, and where he was the reigning king, is chosen to succeed him, and marries his widow, without any inquiry by the Theban authorities as to the facts which produced a vacancy in the throne, or curiosity on his own part as to the identity of his victim. But this was not the story as known to the Athenian audience, and it is inconsistent with numerous indications in the play. After careful examination of the locality I think I have shewn (*Journal of Hellenic Studies*, vol. xxi. p. 48) that while Laius was proceeding direct to Delphi by the old road which runs due West from Lebadea, (not round by Chæronea and Daulia, along the road now followed by tourists), Œdipus was not on his way to Thebes, but was turning northward, in the course of fleeing "as far as possible from Corinth," at the point where the branch road to Daulia leaves the road followed by Laius ; so that, had he been by a minute further advanced on his way, the catastrophe would never have happened. It is not in the gorge of Zymenó, but in the open land further East, between the exit of the gorge and the well of Korakolithó, that the spot is to be sought where the three roads, from Thebes, Delphi and Daulia, must formerly have met, and where, as Pausanias records, there stood in his time a monument reputed to be the tomb of Laius. The shepherd who survived is supposed to have taken some time to recover from the blow by which Œdipus thought that he had killed him with the rest. Meantime Œdipus turns up at Orchomenus (see Nicolaus Damascenus, p. 15) and is said to have raised a band who pretended to be robbers (see Natalis Comes, *Mythol.* ix. p. 1020, quoting from Philochorus *De Sacrificiis*, and Johan. Antioch. Fr. 8). He finally comes to Thebes, probably from the North, and encounters the Sphinx ; but shortly before his arrival tidings of Laius's death had at last reached the city ; and in consequence of his services to the state he is very naturally elected to fill the vacant place. The shepherd comes home only to find Œdipus installed ; he confirms the previous report, but takes care to add nothing which can point to a possibility of identifying the slayer. It is surely not extraordinary that in times which preceded the organization of an international police no trouble was taken or curiosity displayed as to the circumstances of the death abroad of a king generally hated and despised, whose departure had left his kingdom a prey to the monster.

Page 128. 1. The olive branches carried in the hand are said to have been twined with wool, much as our children weave ribands in their May-day garlands. The effect, however, must have been as if the whole crowd had been crowned with a common garland, and I doubt if the poet was thinking about the wool.

2. I follow Kennedy's punctuation and explanation.

Page 129. 3. I do not adopt Dindorf's correction ἐπ' ἠθέων.

4. In saying "the correspondences of their counsels actually exist" I suppose no more to be meant than this, "the things that actually exist correspond with their counsels." I think Kennedy has proved that ζώσας does not here mean "prospering," nor συμφοράς "results." But I have not seen my way to adopt his explanation of the passage.

Page 133. 5. I take νηλέα in its usual meaning. Sophocles is about to call the dead bodies θανατφόρα—death-breeding, and prepares for the horror by a suitable adjective "pitiless."

# Notes

**Page 137. 6.** For the correct interpretation of this speech I am indebted to the Master of Trinity College, Dr. Butler. All the translators, except Doyle, have gone wrong, myself formerly among the herd. What Tiresias did know, and had put from his mind, was not the truth of the saw he quoted, but the circumstances of the death of Laius. These, we must remember, had been so completely hushed up by the old shepherd, that Œdipus had never even heard them.

**Page 139. 7.** The word τρέφει, as elsewhere in Sophocles (compare l. 294 and *Tr.* 116) seems to have no specific meaning of being nurtured, but to correspond to our idea of belonging to or having to do with a thing.

**Page 141. 8.** It seems clear that Œdipus retires at the conclusion of his own speech; Tiresias, from his blindness, remaining unaware of the fact. If Œdipus heard what Tiresias was next to say, there would be little left for him to discover as the play proceeds: for an intelligent man could not but set this prophecy beside that of the older oracle which he details at line 791, and draw the inevitable conclusion.

**Page 143. 9.** Dindorf omits some words here; but probably the strophe is slightly defective.

**Page 144. 10.** Read τοῦπος δ' ἐφάνθη. Note the triple repetition of γνώμη.

11. This line, which cannot be bettered, is from Doyle's version of the play.

**Page 145. 12.** I follow the MSS. reading ταῦθ' ἅπερ "precisely those things which," and construe μαθεῖν "to know." I do not think Creon is setting up a claim to put questions—(they could not be "the same questions") to Œdipus: I think he is claiming to be the learner—the man to whom all this is new. The other interpretation is of course suggested by the careless retort of Œdipus.

**Page 147. 13.** This seems to me better sense and rhythm than "do not turn the trivial grief into a great one."

**Page 152. 14.** An emendation of Dindorf, ὄχους for ὄχον, is not followed.

**Page 153. 15.** Two lines omitted by Dindorf are restored.

16. I have endeavoured to shew (*Journal of Classical and Sacred Philology*, vol. xx. p. 111) that ἕν' οἰόζωνον means simply "one individual," and that the theory of "separable epithets," that is, the notion that a compound epithet can sometimes be treated as two attributes, not as one adjective qualified by the other, is baseless.

17. Dindorf's emendation σὸν for τὸν is not followed. It makes nonsense of a forcible passage.

**Page 154. 18.** Read ἀκρότατα γεῖσ' ἀναβᾶσ'.

**Page 155. 19.** Read κατεύγμασιν, not κατάργμασιν.

**Page 159. 20.** Read τόνδ' οὗτος λέγει; not τόν θ', and in the next line τί, not τίς.

**Page 160. 21.** In this difficult passage Dindorf's reading, οὐκ ἔτι τὰν ἑτέραν, appears improbable. The oath—if such it be—"by Olympus!" I omit.

**Page 161. 22.** The poet clearly meant to suggest the paternity of Loxias. Of two ingenious emendations, by Jebb and Arndt, I greatly preferred the first; but I notice that in a second edition Jebb withdrew it, feeling that he had not solved the difficulty attending a corresponding emendation of the strophe.

**Page 162. 23.** It appears better Greek, and is certainly more effective dialogue, to make two questions, not one, of this line.

**Page 164. 24.** I have adopted Jebb's justly celebrated emendation, ὥσπερ ἴαλεμον χέων.

**25.** Strange to say commentators are by no means agreed as to the meaning of the last three words of this ode, "through thee ... I closed my eyes." Did they close them in sleep, secure in having Œdipus as guardian? Or did they close them in death, as it were, through despair at his misfortune? In the latter case we must suppose a metaphor within a metaphor—death substituted for extreme trouble, and then slumber for death. I think κατεκοίμησα must denote grateful rest, not such rest as can be put for death, where death is put for the extremity of trouble. This gives an ending to the stanza at once simple, pathetic and congruous.

**Page 165. 26.** An Homeric turn occurring in the original is here represented by a Miltonic inversion, preserving the epic colour.

**Page 166. 27.** It is impossible to follow Dindorf in omitting these lines. I follow Jebb's correction of the MS. reading.

**28.** Read τινι, not τίνι.

**Page 168. 29.** If we adopt the correction ἂν γνῶναι, which makes the Chorus wish, not that they had never known who Œdipus really was, but that they had never known him at all, it adds force so to render the previous line as to express that his skill, which was originally their good fortune, had proved a misfortune in the end.

**Page 170. 30.** Read with Jebb τ' αὑτοῦ. I follow Kennedy's interpretation of αἷμ' ἐμφύλιον.

**31.** Compare Shakspeare, *K. John*, III. i. 64 :

—leave those woes alone, which I alone
Am bound to underbear.

**Page 171. 32.** Read προστρέψομαι, not προτρεψομαι.

**33.** Read ζῶντε, not ζῶντι.

**34.** Read προσθῇ, not προθῇ.

**Page 172. 35.** Read γόνοισιν, not γονεῦσιν.


## TRACHINIÆ.

WHEN it is remembered that Sophocles wrote upwards of one hundred plays, and that it must always have been the best that had the best chance of preservation, it is not without a special interest that we turn to the *Trachiniæ*, of which hard things have been said, to discover what a Sophoclean Drama of only second or third rate excellence may possibly have been like. There is no denying that fault may be found with this play—for a defective unity in the interest, for too great indulgence in narrative, and for occasional weaknesses of expression. The attempt, carried further in the *Philoctetes*, to base tragic emotion upon physical pain, does not commend itself to our modern taste, or to our northern temperament. There is something to remind us of Euripides, not at his best, both in the plan and in the execution of it. But when all is said, we have still the sympathetic excellence of the whole part of Deianira ; we have the noble imagery of the first Ode, the ecstasy of the Dancing Song, and the lovely change of music in the third ; we have the gorgeous rhetoric of the great speech of Heracles ; and those who fail to appreciate in such passages the hand of the master must indeed be partial observers. The usual difficulties of the translator are augmented by the frequent differences, among good scholars, in matters of interpretation ; and these differences are largely due to corruption in the text, or to expressions which rightly or wrongly raise a suspicion of corruption. The play belongs to the later work of the poet.

**Page 174.** 1. Read ὄκνον, with the MSS., not ὄτλον.

**Page 175.** 2. "His bed." Wunder's alteration, τοῦδε for τῆσδε, is rejected by other editors ; but my rendering is within permissible limits, I think, in either case.

3. The key to the interpretation of this passage is I think the word πόνον, which is used in this play almost as a specific name for the "labours" of Heracles. See ll. 170, 875. There is, further, in the word διαδεδεγμένη an allusion to the torch-race, or λαμπαδηφορία.

**Page 176.** 4. I do not follow Dindorf in transposing these couplets, or in omitting either of them.

**Page 177.** 5. I have never been able to persuade myself that αἰόλος, as an epithet of night, here and in l. 132, has wandered so far from its Homeric meaning as to be equivalent to "star-spangled" or "twinkling with stars." "With fleeting shadows" I should render it ; otherwise it is a mere otiose epithet, such as Sophocles does not use ; though Buttmann (*Lexil.* sub. v.) seems to think this a recommendation. On the other hand ἐναριζομένα does seem to have parted with all meaning of "being stripped" or "despoiled."

6. I can make no sense of this passage, in its general relation to the context, if either τρέφει or αὔξει is taken to indicate any fortunate or glorious result for the hero. The brighter side of the picture is introduced by ἀλλὰ in the next line. I follow Hermann's interpretation.

**Page 178.** 7. I follow Mr. Pretor's rendering.

8. I have nowhere seen any emendation of this exquisite passage which I can adopt with satisfaction. The original reading of the best MSS. seems to me to have been too hastily abandoned. I would render αὑτοῦ "where it finds itself." The demonstrative force of τοιοῦσδε is my key to the passage. She points to the cattle-pastures, where the cows are feeding ; they are stationary, not like horses, which range. See ll. 188, 271, 529, and compare the beautiful fragment, *Tereus*, 517.

9. This line, omitted by Dindorf, can by no means be spared.

**Page 179.** 10. Jebb has shewn that the Peleads were the priestesses at Dodona.

**Page 180. 11.** I omit θεὰν, with the MSS.

**12.** I follow the punctuation of the *Poet. Sc. Gr.*, not that of Dindorf's small edition.

**Page 181. 13.** "Meat-offerings," *i.e.* offerings of the fruits of earth, as in the English version of the *O.T.* by King James's translators. The Victorian translators have altered it to "meal offerings," which would not suit this passage.

**Page 183. 14.** I follow the MSS. reading, διοίσει, and adopt Mr. Pretor's interpretation.

**15.** διήνεμον may possibly be a mere epithet, a reminiscence of the Homeric ἠνεμόεσσαν. But Sophocles seems to be fond of charging his epithets with meaning, even when he adapts them from Homer. Compare τμητοῖς ἱμᾶσι, in *El.* 747. The order of the words, and a comparison of πολύφθορος, l. 477, make for this interpretation.—For τύχη, meaning the way in which things happen, see l. 724.

**Page 184. 16.** I have rejected Dindorf's punctuation, here and in l. 444.

**Page 185. 17.** Point is given to this apparently trivial piece of moralizing, if we compare Deianira's language in l. 596, and the assent of the Chorus. See also l. 691.

**Page 190. 18.** I adopt Jebb's emendation, λώφημα.

**Page 191. 19.** Read τόνδε γ' εὐυφῆ, not τανανφῆ, as Dindorf.

**Page 192. 20.** "The Grecian States"—their Assemblies, that is, or Parliaments; ἀγόραι in the Greek.

**Page 193. 21.** I read οἰστρηθείς, not εὖ στρωθείς, or αὖ στρωθείς, as Dindorf. It must be Heracles, not Deianira, who is released, through the madness of Ares, from the "day of Labour."

**Page 194. 22.** Read χῶνπερ, not χ' ὥσπερ.

**23.** ὁρμῇ seems here to have the derivative meaning of an instant of time. The English and Latin word "moment" has undergone the same conversion.

**Page 195. 24.** "Not crabbed" is a tempting equivalent for πέπειρα, but it is perhaps hardly smooth enough for this context.

**Page 196. 25.** By changing ὡς to ὣς, and altering the punctuation, we avoid making Hyllus speak as if with knowledge that the poison was that of the Hydra.

**Page 197. 26.** The modern notion of "sin," it has been urged, was unknown to a pagan Greek. This may be so; and yet, it seems to me, the opposite of sin is fairly well denoted by θέμις.

**Page 198. 27.** προσβάλλω, here and in l. 580, I take in its simple meaning, "contribute," or "throw in": throw, that is, either in addition to something else, or on the top of some receiver. The Scholiast who imagined that it could mean "paid attention to," or "comprehended," seems to me to travel a long way round, and bring nothing home.

**28.** Accepting the theory, that in this corrupt passage Ἡρακλέους is a gloss, representing some periphrasis for the hero, I think ἀγάκλειτον must be an epithet of him, and not of πάθος.

**Page 200. 29.** I adopt Jebb's emendation, τῆς ἐπ' ἄλλοις, and follow his interpretation.

**Page 203. 30.** Read ἐς πλέον, not ἔμλεον.

**31.** This speech has been well translated by Cicero. I follow him, and the MSS., and not Dindorf, in reading καὶ λόγῳ κακά.

**Page 210. 32.** This summing up of the moral of the story, as in the case of Teucer's speech in the *Ajax*, it is impossible to reconcile, unless by toning down the expressions, with the conventional piety sometimes attributed to Sophocles; especially if we refer back to l. 140. The other aspect of the fate of Hercules is well stated at the conclusion of the *Philoctetes*.

**33.** I read ἐπ' οἴκων. The MSS. reading has never, I think, been satisfactorily explained. The "maiden" addressed is the Chorus-leader, certainly not Iole.

It is a striking illustration of the degraded state of family life at Athens, in this Golden Age of its literature, that notwithstanding the tender and sympathetic hand with which the great Artist has delineated the wrongs and character of Deianira, that

queen of marriage, a most perfect wife,

he does not seem to have felt that his audience would require any such rehabilitation in her case, by way of funeral rites or posthumous honour, as he was careful to indicate in the case of Ajax and of Œdipus.

## PHILOCTETES.

THE *Philoctetes* is a work of the old age of Sophocles. The interest turns mainly upon character, and (what is unusual, if not unique, in Greek Drama) upon the play of emotion in a single mind, that of Neoptolemus, a part which notwithstanding this does not give its name to the piece, and was not even played by the leading actor. The extent to which Sophocles had by this time freed himself from convention we never shall fully know, but we may from this form some conjecture. In the soul of the heroic youth, and in his conduct, the whole action of the play may be said to pass. Philoctetes is a great figure; he is a Sophoclean Prometheus; but Neoptolemus is the boy-hero of a romantic story, analogous—in so far as the classical genius can allow of analogy— to an eighteenth century tale. In the descent of Heracles at the close may be traced the influence of Euripides. The episode of the attendant disguised as a sea-captain is not very effective: but the great scene, where Philoctetes first makes the acquaintance of Neoptolemus, is of a picturesque beauty that can hardly be entirely missed, even in a translation.

**Page 212. 1.** I suppose ἔχει πρὸς to mean "have relation to," and the subject of the sentence, ἅ, to be the description just given; which is not clearly distinguished from the locality itself, the object of προσελθών, because Ulysses is pretty sure he has hit the place.

**2.** I adopt Bergk's excellent conjecture, οὔδει for οὐδείς. That there is a στίβος is plain, for it is twice mentioned further on, in ll. 48 and 203.

**Page 213. 3.** Dindorf's emendation, παῖ, seems no improvement.

Page 214. 4. I read λακεῖν, not λαλεῖν.

Page 216. 5. μέτριος, "moderate," that is to say in regard to misfortunes.

Page 217. 6. I follow Jebb's reading of the passage. Sophocles has here coined a striking epithet, for which Shakspeare supplies me with a substitute. Compare Milton's "inexpressive nuptial-song."

7. Read στίβον, not στίβου.

Page 220, 221. 8. The word βία having come to mean "violence," since Homer's time, when βίη only meant "might," Sophocles I think uses it here in Homeric form, but with Attic meaning. Compare his use of Homeric epithets, *El.* 746, *Trach.* 327.

Page 224. 9. I do not follow Dindorf in adopting Hermann's correction, ὃς παρῆν, γόνος.

10. The old English word "gamester," for a wrestler, exactly expresses παλαιστής in this context.

Page 225. 11. In following Pope, who shortens the quantity of Classical proper names, whenever by so doing he can throw back an accent, I believe that I am conforming to the genius of the English language. But inasmuch as a contrary practice is now fashionable, I submit these considerations; first, Sperchius, with the i accented, makes a line unreadable at sight by an English reader; next Spercheios is a combination of letters too exotic for use in English literature; thirdly Spercheius is neither Greek nor English.

Page 230. 12. Read οὖ θᾶσσον, not οὔ.

13. Dindorf's change of οὔκ to οἶδ᾽ seems unnecessary.

Page 231. 14. The ascription to the Chorus-leader of this speech, the authenticity of which, as a part of the speech of Philoctetes, or of Neoptolemus, has been challenged, appears to me fully to meet any difficulty arising from its inconsecutiveness. Dindorf omits three lines unnecessarily.

15. I have followed the interpretation which, since Lessing, has usually been assigned to κακογείτονα. But I do not see how the word can mean "a neighbour to his misfortunes"; and I trust a better solution may hereafter be discovered.

Page 233. 16. Rejecting Dindorf's emendations, I venture to read αὐτὴ for αὕτη, that is to say ἡ αὐτή. The metaphor is of a wild beast that has killed its prey and gorged itself, and comes back through the wilderness to fatten on it again. The speech in the Greek is suggestive of a man gasping with pain; "Here it comes—the same as ever—after an interval—by winding ways—(wild-beast-like, as it were), just as when it was glutted before." He is giving a reason, not why they need not leave him, but why he fears that they will.

Page 236. 17. I adopt Professor Campbell's suggestion for the distribution of the stanzas of this Ode between the personages of the Chorus.

Page 237. 18. I follow the MSS. reading, not Dindorf. Similarly in the next line, ἐμᾷ, not ἀμᾷ.

**Page 239.** 19. This is one of those passages in which the Greek Aorist must be translated by a Present. Another has been pointed out to me by Professor Jackson in *O.T.* 1003. It is, of course, always better to avoid the English Perfect, if possible, in rendering a Greek Aorist. Compare l. 1259.

**Page 245.** 20. Read κάκ' ἐμήσατ' ὦ Ζεῦ.

**Page 252.** 21. Dindorf omits these two lines. But there was plenty of opportunity, during the interlude ll. 676-729, for Neoptolemus to tell Philoctetes the particulars of the death of Ajax.

**Page 254.** 22. I follow Jebb's interpretation.

23. Εὐσέβεια here is the praise of piety, like ἀρετὴ l. 1420. Retaining ἧ γὰρ, we must render συνθνῄσκει "accompanies into the realm of Thanatos." Dindorf omits three lines.

**Page 255.** 24. κτύπος ἄρσην is the same with ἀρσένων κλαγγά, *Trach.* 207; in English the "bass" voice of manhood.

## ŒDIPUS COLONEUS.

THERE does not seem to be much reason for questioning the tradition which has given to this play the interest of having been the last work of its great author. It is even said not to have been acted till four years after his death. Upon this tradition a new light has been thrown by the ingenious speculation of Professor Campbell (*Classical Review*, vol. xx. p. 3), who suggests that the play was written at the time of the short-lived revolution of the Four Hundred, Sophocles being more or less in sympathy with the knights who promoted it; that it was intended to influence the minds of its audience in favour of their proceedings, and to mitigate the natural repugnance of Athenians to their transfer of the assembly to Colonus; that it may have been still in preparation when the counter-revolution took place, and in consequence was not produced, at that time, upon the stage. It is the longest tragedy that has come down to us. It may perhaps be said to be the most Sophoclean; that is to say, it exhibits more than any the qualities which, as noted in the Introduction, are specially characteristic of his work.

Among many things that might be written by way of general note to this drama I confine myself to two points of topography, the problem of the Brazen Threshold, and the geography of the abduction and capture.

In the passage which begins at l. 56, all the MSS. read χαλκόπους ὁδός, the Brass-paved Way; but this has been altered to ὁδός, "threshold," following a Scholiast on l. 1590, who identifies with this spot the "steep-down threshold, rooted deep in earth on steps of brass," to which Œdipus proceeds on leaving the stage. Much confusion and difficulty is caused by the alteration. It becomes necessary, as its first author saw, to suppose that the scene is shifted in the course of the play, from one part to another of the grove; but of this the text gives no indication, and no adequate dramatic reason for it has been suggested. There is no particular significance in the suggestion that Œdipus would in that case meet his death at the exact spot where he first took seat in the grove; for he moves away from it of his own accord (l. 113) on the entrance of the Chorus, and it is a different spot from which they insist on his removal (l. 160) with so much emphasis. Everything points to Œdipus remaining undisturbed at the place where he was authorized to remain (l. 192), until under the divine inspiration he goes forward (l. 1542) to new ground, as yet unvisited and undescribed.

But it is assumed that the quotation from Istros, given by a Scholiast on l. 1059, where he speaks of a route, or of a measurement, as παρὰ τὸν χαλκοῦν προσαγορευόμενον, obliges us to understand ὁδός, not ὁδός. No doubt the substantive implied cannot be ὁδός, but it might be τόπος, χῶρος, πέτρος, or the like. The Scholiast on l. 57 says expressly Ἴστρος μνημονεύει τῆς Χαλκῆς Ὁδοῦ, "Istros is referring to the Brazen Way; and so," he adds, "does Astydamas."

Upon the whole the balance is, I think, in favour of keeping Ὁδός here, and thus making a clear distinction between "The Brass-paved Way" (a proper name) and the chasm described in l. 1590, with its ideal foundations in the brazen steps leading to the infernal world.

Jebb's suggestion that the "Brazen Threshold" was a name both for the chasm in particular, and also for the region in which the chasm and the first resting-place were both situated, appears to me inconsistent with the wording of ll. 55, 56, where "all this place" is a whole, of which the Χαλκόπους Ὁδός, "the spot you press," is indicated as a part only.

That the Brass-paved Way is also called Ἐρεῖσμ' Ἀθηνῶν may remind us of the Boulevards at Paris, the Forbury at Reading, and similar names given to the sites of old fortifications before a town. Although the Scholiast is in error in suggesting that there were "brass mines" at Colonus, it is possible that lumps of metal, of which the "Stone from Thoricus" was a specimen, had been brought from the mines (see Professor Campbell's translation, l. 1595), and used in constructing old defensive works of which the Brass-paved Way was a relic.

For the abduction incident I have in the *Journal of Hellenic Studies*, vol. xxi. p. 45, given the results of examination upon the spot of the possible bearings of the various place-notes which are given in three passages of the play (ll. 897, 1019 and 1044). I suppose Theseus in the first to arrange for occupation of the points "where pairs of pack-men's routes most of all converge," so that the girls should not be carried past them. This I interpret, not of some particular junction of two roads leading to Thebes, but of all the principal spots where country paths meet in the suburbs of Athens, close at hand; such convergences as are referred to l. 1592; they must have been well marked, but not very numerous, at Colonus. This plan fails, as Theseus expects it will in the second passage; but, as he says there, it does not signify, for he has other pursuers, from whose pursuit they will never get clear over the frontier. In the third passage we have the lyric description of two routes by which, after emerging from the suburbs, the pursuit has to be conducted; one is along the Sacred Way, by Eleusis and Œnoe, through the Pass of Dryoscephalæ, to Thebes; the present carriage road, in fact; the other is the well-known Pass of Phyle, a horse-path, the depression of which, to the west of the patch of snow which still lingers in April upon the peak of Parnes, is clearly visible from Colonos. The plain meaning of these passages has been missed, and an absurdity fastened upon Sophocles, in the desire to find some point, at a distance from Athens, where two roads to Thebes may meet, and where the guards could lie in wait (after receiving, we must suppose, a telegraphic message from headquarters), hoping to pounce upon the abductors, when they arrived. There is no such point, there is no such meeting of the roads, and nobody, surely, was ever caught by a device of such simplicity.

Page 257. 1. ἐξοικήσιμος, "suitable for settlement," hence "hospitable in appearance," must here mean inhabited, rather than habitable.

Page 258. 2. I take ταῦτα as resuming ὅσα, l. 53, not χῶρος, etc.

Page 259. 3. τι μειόνως ἔχειν may be either "too insignificant," that is, for grace, or "not having yet suffered enough." I follow the Scholiast.

Page 260. 4. This appears to me all one question; the "conjecture" cannot refer to his being old and poor, which is self-evident; therefore it must refer to his having been born blind. I consider μακραίων not as "an old man," but "one destined for long life," as in *Ant.* 987, *O.T.* 1099. I do not follow Dindorf's reading, or punctuation.

Page 261. 5. Read κἀκούοντας.

Page 262. 6. I follow the MSS., ἢ 'σθω;

Page 267. 7. τιμῆ καθέξον must I think embody a poetical antithesis with βιβῶν πρὸς οὐρανόν. "Shall keep down, or shall exalt to heaven, in honour." The interpretation "shall possess in honour" misses this.

Page 270. 8. I suppose γε to be inserted after οἰὸς, with many good authorities; and I read λαβών, not βαλών, at the end of the line.

Page 271. 9. φανείσας I think must be significant in this context; it is the remarkable revelation of the mystery which excites curiosity.

Page 272. 10. Read ἀέκων instead of ἑκών.

Page 273. 11. I follow Hermann's explanation.

12. I follow the reading recommended by Professor Jebb (Mekler's), which seems to effect a satisfactory solution of a serious difficulty in the argument.

Page 274. 13. I read κἀμοῦ, not ἢ 'μοῦ.

Page 276. 14. I adopt the explanation given by Professor Postgate of ἔμπαλιν, in an interesting note on some passages in this play, which appeared in the *Journal of Class. and Sac. Phil.* x. 87.

Page 281. 15. I follow the MSS., not Dindorf's alteration.

Page 283. 16. Dindorf makes a question of this, apparently without necessity.

17. I follow Professor Jebb and others in giving this v. to the chorus.

Page 284. 18. Half a line has here disappeared, but the sense seems evident.

Page 288. 19. I read ἐξειργασμένοι (Prof. Jebb, from F. A. Schmidt), not ἐξηρπασμένοι.

Page 289. 20. I take γαιάοχον as in *O.T.* 160. Professor Jebb's objections may possibly be met by considerations I have elsewhere urged; see note on *Phil.* 314, etc.

# 396 Sophocles

Page 290. 21. I follow the emendation ἀντάσειν τᾶν κ.τ.λ. recommended by Professor Jebb.

Page 291. 22. I read κἀναπαύσετον, with the MSS.

23. The reading recommended by Professor Jebb (Wex's) appears to me to have for the first time given a tolerable solution of the difficulty involved in this line.

Page 294. 24. I take πλέον as the neuter of πλέος (Ionic word), not of the Attic πλέων. This makes it unnecessary to alter θέλοντος.

25. This is a difficult passage, but there is no necessity for altering it. I consider youth, not the age succeeding to youth, to be contrasted with old age; I supply μόχθων or καμάτων after ἕξω, and πλάνοις after ἔνι. πολύμοχθος is parenthetic.

Page 295. 26. I fail to see any plausibility in the supposed reference, under ῥῖπαι, to the stars. There is good evidence that the ancients used this name for the Rhipæan hills; and the fragment of Alcman, which calls them the "bosom of deep Night," appears tolerably conclusive as to the meaning here. Otherwise, "the blasts of Nigh seems to me to have quite sufficient connotation of a northerly orig for poetical purposes.

Page 298. 27. The attempt to explain the MSS. reading, by supposin Œdipus to quibble here on the different values of words like ἄστυ anc πόλις, is to say the least unsuitable, if not disfiguring, to the context.

Page 300. 28. I follow Professor Jebb in taking ἐκφέρει as 2nd pers. sing., mid., not 3rd pers., act.

Page 302. 29. Antigone can hardly be intended to ask her father why he wants to keep his senses; nor yet, in view of his reply, to ask what he would have Theseus promise him. I take τὸ πιστὸν actively (see l. 1031); then reading with Hermann ἐμφῦσαι, and taking φρενὶ with θέλοις, which I think is justified by the fact of its repetition from the preceding line, a tolerable meaning is obtained for a very difficult line, not, perhaps, anywhere quite satisfactorily explained.

Page 304. 30. I read πολυξένοις, not πολυξέστοις.

Page 307. 31. I read ἀλύπητον, not ἀλάμπετον.

Page 308. 32. I do not follow Dindorf in omitting this line.